Sophia–Maria

The Stuppach Madonna of Matthias Gruenewald, with its "transfigured corporality," has been chosen as a cover illustration because of its ability to suggest an other-worldly dimension to Mary. This accords with the book's central thesis that Sophia, Divine Wisdom, incarnated in Mary.

Sophia–Maria

A Holistic Vision of Creation

Thomas Schipflinger

Translated by
James Morgante

SAMUEL WEISER, INC.

York Beach, Maine

First published in 1998 by
Samuel Weiser, Inc.
Box 612
York Beach, ME 03910-0612

Library of Congress Cataloging-in-Publication Data
Schipflinger, Thomas
    [Sohpia-Maria. English]
    Sophia—Maria : a holistic vision of creation / Thomas Schipflinger.
      p.   cm.
    Includes bibliographical references and index.
    ISBN 1-57863-022-3 (pbk.: alk. paper)
    1. Wisdom (Biblical personification) 2. Wisdom—Religious aspects—
Christianity—History of doctrines. 3. Wisdom—Religious aspects—
Comparative studies. 4. Mary, Blessed Virgin, Saint. I. Title.
BS580.W58S3513   1997
232.91—dc21   97-23006
                                             CIP

MV
Typeset in 11/13 Palatino

Cover art is "Madonna and Child" by Matthias Gruenewald (1455-1528).
Stuppach Parish Church, Wurttemburg, Germany. Bridgeman Art Library,
London. Used by permission.

Printed in the United States of America

05 04 03 02 01 00 99 98
10 9 8 7 6 5 4 3 2 1

The paper used in this publication meets the minimum requirements of the
American National Standard for Permanence of Paper for Printed Library
Materials Z39.48-1984.

Contents

Changing Views of Wisdom, 4
The Historical Milieux of the Wisdom Books, 8
The Personal Conception of Wisdom, 11
Wisdom's Origin, 13
Wisdom as the Torah, 16
Wisdom's Functions and Characteristics, 17
Wisdom's Teaching: A Message of Life and Salvation, 21
Solomon: Archetype of a Wisdom-Seeker, 24
Wisdom's Beneficent Effects, 29
Wisdom Has Appeared on Earth, 33

Illuscrations

Color plates

Foreword

This work repeatedly asserts that Holy Wisdom, the Divine Sophia, appeared in the world as prophesied by the prophet Baruch (Bar. 3,37) and that this appearance took place in Mary. Theologically expressed, Sophia became human in Mary.

Though this idea may seem unusual and novel to Western Theology and Mariology, it is a conception that is deeply rooted in the Russian Church's devotion to Mary. By way of explaining how I arrived at this point of view I would like to relate part of my biography.

While in Russia during the Second World War I had become interested in Russian icons and subsequently came across a book about the Russian Orthodox Church. I was especially captivated by a chapter about Sophia and Russian Sophiology (teachings concerning Sophia) where I read for the first time the names Soloviev, Florenski and Bulgakov—who represented the flowering of modern Russian Sophiology. According to them Mary the Mother of God is most intimately related to the Divine Sophia, or Holy Wisdom, and is actually presented as Wisdom's human form.

In those days the epistle readings on Marian feast days were taken largely from the Wisdom Books of Holy Scripture and this had caused me to ask again and again why readings about Holy Wisdom were used. I had suddenly been struck with an illuminating answer: Mary is Wisdom's human form; Holy Wisdom appeared on earth in Mary! With this realization the peace and joy of certainty overcame me, and with the same sense of firmness I felt the impulse to dedicate my life to Holy Wisdom, to investigate Her secret and to make it known.

A seed had been planted which took root in me. Though there were times of neglect due to the war and theological studies which followed, it continued to grow, protected by a conscious devotion to Mary. It received further nourishment through religious and scientific interests, such as my study of the Chinese philosophy of nature (Confucianism and Taoism) during the years I spent in China (between 1948–1951). When I subsequently returned home to Germany, pastoral responsibilities hardly left any time for the theme of Holy Wisdom, although my interest remained alive. At the beginning of the 1970s however, when illness forced me to rest, I was able to occupy myself with Marian questions, such as Mary's title, "Lady of All Nations." From this point on Wisdom became my foremost concern and held me fast.

An article written by Dr. Reinhold Stecher, Innsbruck's present Bishop, about Holy Wisdom in the Book of Proverbs, inspired me to a more comprehensive study. The memory of my Russian wartime experience was still vivid within me and led to a study of Wisdom from the perspectives of Holy Scripture, theology, and comparative religion, as far as pastoral duties allowed. As my studies and reflections seemed to show signs of progress, I began to consider putting the fruits of my labors into manuscript form.

After retirement I relocated to Munich which allowed me to attend university lectures. They helped me to ground my thinking and stimulated further thought. I was also able to fulfill the wish to study Sanskrit, a language which is very important for the study of comparative religion. While continuing to make new discoveries I now had the time to sort through the material I had gathered and to bring the present volume to completion.

As a way of introducing the book's *leitmotif*—that Mary is Sophia's human form—I would like to quote the remarks of the Russian Sophiologist Paul Florenski about the Novgorod icon of Divine Sophia (see chapter 16):

We have before us the wonderful icon of God's Sophia, the icon of his purest Mother (p. 248) . . .

This icon shows us the unspeakable purity of the virginity of God's Most Holy Mother; above Her is Christ, God's Logos, who so loved this Sophia that He willed to be born of Her flesh (p. 249) . . .

Who is this great, royal, feminine being, neither God nor God's eternal Son, neither angel nor saint? Is She not the true sum total of humanity, in an elevated and complete form, the living Soul of the World, deeply sensed and felt by our forefathers, the devout builders of the Sophia churches and the painters of the Sophia icons (p.253) . . .

The human appearance of this Sophia is Mary. Mary is Sophia's human form. . . . Sophia is the first who was created and also the first who was redeemed, the Center and Heart of all created beings. She is the Guardian Angel of all creation (p. 228 ff.) . . .

The Mother of God is once again Sophia. . . . The saints honored in Mary, God's Mother, the Bearer of Sophia, the visible appearance of Sophia Herself on earth.[1]

In the years following the publication of the original German edition of *Sophia Mary* in 1988, the wish was voiced for the ap-

---

[1] Paul Florenski, *La Colonne et le Fondement de la Vérité*, trans. from Russian by Constantin Andronikov (Lausanne: L'Age d'Homme, 1975), pp. 248–249, 253, 228. Translator's note: Although Florenski does not say so, he is paraphrasing the words of Vladimir Soloviev (see Wladimir Solowjew, "Die Idee der Menschheit Bei Auguste Compte" in: *Deutsche Gesamtausgabe der Werke von Wladimir Solowjew*, vol. VIII, herausgegeben von Szyekarski, Lettenbauer und Mueller, Munich: Erich Wewel Verlag 1980, p. 357); I am indebted to the Soloviev scholar Professor Leonid Sytenko for this clarification.

pearance of an English translation and edition. Fortunately my friend and colleague Robert Powell found a competent translator in James Morgante; and the two of them together found an interested publisher in Samuel Weiser. May the Lord God and His Sophia especially bless this English edition and its pioneers.

Thomas Schipflinger
Lenggries, Germany

Readers interested in learning more about Sophia can contact the Sophia Foundation of North America by writing to the following address:

The Sophia Foundation of North America
P. O. Box 712
Nicasio, CA 94946

Acknowledgments

In his book *Gratefulness: The Heart of Prayer*, David Steindl-Rast writes of the contributions that parents, teachers, and friends make in our lives and how we all need each other. He also speaks of bounteousness growing from gratitude, and says that joy is the expression of true gratitude.[1] My own experience, particularly while writing this book, confirms these sentiments, and I want to acknowledge the many contributions made.

My deepest and most reverential gratitude belong to Sophia-Mary for allowing me to experience Her love and for inspiring me and giving me the strength to research and complete the writing of this volume about Her.

I want to acknowledge the help of all the people who, through God's grace, played a role in this project. There is, first of all, the devout Russian priest in Nevel (Byelorussia) who shared his icons and awakened my interest for Russian Orthodox spirituality. A special thanks goes to Dr. Reinhold Stecher, the Bishop of Innsbruck, for the motivation and encouragement

---

[1] David Steindl-Rast, *Gratefulness: The Heart of Prayer* (New York: Paulist Press, 1984).

stimulated through his article about Sophia,[2] which encouraged me to investigate the subject more thoroughly.

I also want to especially thank Monsignor Dr. Albert Rauch, the director of the Eastern Church Institute, for his expert advice and untiring efforts toward shaping the text and choosing the illustrations (and for including the German edition in the Koinonia Series of the Eastern Church Institute). The English edition was made possible through the dedicated and friendly assistance of Robert Powell, the conscientious efforts of the translator, James Morgante, and the commitment of my English-language publisher, Samuel Weiser. To all I extend my warmest gratitude and ask that God and God's Holy Sophia bless them. It is my hope that this English edition (as well as the German, Spanish, and Russian editions) will promote a deeper understanding and knowledge of Sophia-Mary and devotion to Her.

Lastly, let me request that everyone spread awareness and reverence for Sophia-Mary, for it is knowledge of Her that will make a significant contribution to the ecumenical movement, to peace and unity among nations, and to deliverance from the world's deadly ecological crisis.

---

[2] Reinhold Stecher, *Zeitschrift fur Katholische Theologie*, "Die Persoenliche Weisheit in den Proverbien Kapital 8" (Innsbruck, 1953).

PART 1

SOPHIA
IN HOLY
SCRIPTURE

1

The Wisdom Books of the Old Testament

THE WISDOM BOOKS OF the Old Testament[1] concern the topic of Wisdom (Hebrew: *Chokmah*; Greek: *Sophia*), which is personified in many of the books as a female figure.

Most commentators[2] include five books in this group: Proverbs, Job, Ecclesiastes (also called Kohelet), Eccesiasticus (also called the Wisdom of Jesus the Son of Sirach) and the Wisdom of Solomon (the Book of Wisdom). They have been characterized in the following way:

---

[1] The designation "Old Testament" is used because the point of departure is Christian understanding of the history of revelation and salvation. Jewish tradition designates the Christian Old Testament as the *Tenach* ("Scripture teaching"). It is respectfully acknowledged that some of the texts quoted in the present work are not contained in the *Tenach* (from the Book of Wisdom and the Book of Ecclesiasticus) even though they do belong to the holy books of the Jewish-Alexandrian tradition (*Septuagint*). The Catholic tradition regards them as canonical (they belong to the Bible's fixed inventory).

[2] A. Strobl, "Die Weisheit Israels," in the encyclopedia *Der Christ in der Welt*, Pattloch Aschaffenburg, 1967, pp. 5 and 7. Strobl notes that statements about Wisdom are found in Psalms and the Book of Baruch (3, 9–44) also.

Their common intention is to help humanity find happiness. The theme of the Book of Proverbs is the general search for happiness; the Book of Job depicts the immense difficulty of this search; the Book of Ecclesiastes, the resignation and disappointment that can result; the Book of Eccesiasticus illustrates a successful search; and the Book of Wisdom, the attainment of eternal happiness.[3]

CHANGING VIEWS OF WISDOM

What becomes apparent in the different books is that perspectives about Wisdom gradually changed and were also affected by the historical circumstances present when the individual books were composed.

The *Book of Job* asks why unhappiness exists if humanity is meant to be happy, for in spite of his piety Job's life has become miserable. He implores God to help him understand the meaning of unhappiness and whether the expectation of reward is justified. What he comes to realize is that happiness and recompense for piety are bound up with mysteries which cannot be understood by reason alone. It is only when this is accepted that the Lord who transcends everything can ultimately bring about happiness and well being.

Eventually things do turn out better for Job. The wise attitude that Job expresses at the beginning of his trials: "The Lord gives and the Lord takes away; blessed be the name of the Lord" (Job 1,21) helps him to persevere through much pain and suffering. Trusting surrender, faith, and constancy in trial leads him to happiness.

The *Book of Ecclesiastes* (Greek: *Ecclesiastes*; Hebrew: *Kohelet*) also talks about surrender; yet not surrender born of piety and courage but of disappointment and resignation:

I considered my handiwork, all my labor and toil: it was futility, all of it, and a chasing of the wind . . .

---

[3] A. Strobl, "Die Weisheit Israels," p. 7. Tr: Translation mine.

So I thought, "I too shall suffer the fate of the fool. To what purpose have I been wise? Where is the profit? Even this," I said to myself, "is futile" (Eccles. 2,11,15).

For everything its season, and for every activity under the heavens its time: A time to be born and a time to die . . . a time to weep and a time to laugh . . . a time for war and a time for peace (Eccles. 3,1–8).

To eat and drink and experience pleasure in return for his labors, this does not come from any good in a person: it comes from God (Eccles. 2,24).

Such resigned surrender can lead to an attitude which is accepting of life, taking life as it comes and making the best of it, satisfied with the modest happiness of daily life.

Yet because Ecclesiastes has a tendency toward resignation and even pessimism, the question has been raised as to why it was taken into the Canon of Holy Scripture? It can be answered that the point of view that it expresses does belongs to a universal kind of wisdom that mediates the tensions between hope and despair, ideal and reality, happiness and unhappiness, and success and failure that life brings. Both Ecclesiastes and Job pose questions about the meaning of happiness in a radical way and try to offer solutions that validate existence.

The *Book of Proverbs* contains a summary of the proverbial treasures of the Jewish people and their neighbors gathered over a period of hundreds of years (the Wisdom teachings of the Egyptians and Babylonians in particular were integrated into Judaism). Parts of it are older than Job and Ecclesiastes.

The oldest portion of Proverbs talks about various paths to happiness, and in the portion composed later these paths merge into the way pointed out by Wisdom who appears as a person.

Happiness is initially depicted in worldly terms (riches, honor and personal welfare) but ultimately comes to signify the development of qualities like integrity, fear of the Lord, righteousness, good conduct and willingness to learn. Wisdom is life, but it gradually becomes clear that life signifies more than material riches; it is virtue itself:

> She [Wisdom] is a tree of life to those who grasp her, and those who hold fast to her are safe (Prov. 3,18).

> In my hands are riches and honour, boundless wealth and prosperity. . . . I endow with riches those who love me; I shall fill their treasuries (Prov. 8,18,21).

> Happy the one who listens to me, watching daily at my threshold. . . . For whoever finds me finds life . . . but whoever fails to find me deprives himself (Prov. 8,34–36).

> Wisdom has built her house. . . . Now, having slaughtered a beast, spiced her wine, and spread her table . . . she says . . . "Come, eat the food I have prepared and taste the wine I have spiced" (Prov. 9,1–5).

> Idle hands make for penury; diligent hands make for riches (Prov. 10,4).

> The fruit of humility is fear of God with riches and honor and life (Prov. 22,4).

The *Book of Ecclesiasticus* presupposes "fear of the Lord"—great reverence for God and His Law—as the necessary precondition for happiness:

> The beginning of wisdom is fear of the Lord. . . . Wisdom's garland is fear of the Lord (Ecclus. 1,14,18).

In common with Proverbs, Ecclesiasticus also enumerates many gifts of Wisdom—honor, pride, cheerfulness, joy and long life (Ecclus. 1,11–12,17–18). In ensuing chapters, however, Ecclesiasticus is clearer about a personal view of Wisdom which sees Her as Mistress and Teacher:

> Wisdom raises her sons to greatness. . . . He who holds fast to her will gain honor; the Lord's blessing rests on the house she enters. . . . the Lord loves those who love her (Ecclus. 4,11,13,14).

It is befitting that the wise person serve Wisdom, for in serving Wisdom one serves the Holy One (Ecclus. 4,14) and one's efforts bear fruit: "If you cultivate her . . . soon you will be enjoying the harvest" (Ecclus. 6,19). The author goes so far as to recommend:

> Put your feet in Wisdom's fetters and your neck into her collar. . . . Do not let her go. . . . she will transform herself for you into joy. . . . You will put her on like a splendid robe and wear her like a garland of joy (Ecclus. 6,24,27–28,31).

She will be to him "like a mother and young bride" and crown him "with joy and exultation" (Ecclus. 15,2,6). She is "the mother of honourable love" (Ecclus. 24,18).[4]

In Ecclesiasticus one finds Wisdom and happiness by fulfilling the Law. Wisdom is "the law laid on us by Moses" (Ecclus. 24,23). The life-giving strength of this Law is compared with the rivers of Paradise and with the most beautiful trees and scented bushes (24,13–15,25). Wisdom's happiness in Ecclesiasticus consists of paradisical abundance and splendor.

The *Book of the Wisdom of Solomon* is the most recent of the Wisdom Books to appear, and it resolves the enigma of life in an essentially new way. It leaves behind an earthly pursuit of happiness and opens the door to a vision of the eternal life which the soul reaps as its reward: "to keep her laws is a warrant of immortality; and immortality brings a person nearer to God" (Wisd. 6,18–19). Wisdom leads the way to eternity and the transcendent order, and this fundamentally new perspective questions previously held values and points to the resolution of hitherto unresolved problems.

References to life after death in the Book of Wisdom (and in Proverbs also) evinces an Egyptian influence. Descriptions of Wisdom's cosmological dimension ("She is more beautiful than the sun, and surpasses every constellation. . . . She spans the world in power from end to end, and gently orders all things"—

---

[4] Ecclesiasticus 24,18 is lacking in some manuscripts (see note 17).

7,29; 8,1) also recalls the Egyptian goddess Isis,[5] though in a more Hellenistic form.

THE HISTORICAL MILIEUX OF THE WISDOM BOOKS

The events of Jewish history help to date the composition of the Wisdom Books and also provide an understanding of the unique features of each individual book (for an overview of the historical placement of the Wisdom Books see Appendix I).

Job's subject matter and reproachful manner reflects its appearance during the time of the Babylonian captivity, when faith in Yahweh was challenged. Commentators date the book's final form to the time around 400 B.C.E.,[6] in the epoch following exile, when the struggle to restore the old homeland and the temple provided a source of hope and strength to those who returned (Job is the first of the Wisdom Books to achieve a final form).

Ecclesiastes (or *Kohelet*) is named for a teacher who speaks before an assembled community (Hebrew *qahal* and Greek *ekklesia* both mean church or community). The author of Ecclesiastes lived in Jerusalem when Palestine was under the rule of Ptolemaic Egypt and Hellenistic influence was steadily increasing.

---

[5] The similarity between Wisdom's cosmological dimension and the portrayal of Isis is evident in the following prayer:

Prayer to Isis, Wife of Osiris and Mother of Horus

Goddess! Holy, eternal preserver of the human race! You, who do not cease to give protection to weak mortals; you who allow a mother's mild tenderness to be bestowed upon the distressed! Not a single day or night or moment, however small, is devoid of your good deeds. You protect humanity on land and water, you keep them far from life's every danger and extend your helping right hand, disentangling the entangled web of fate; you silence the storms of misfortune and hold in check the injurious course of the stars. You are worshipped by the gods above and the gods below. You swirl the earth in circles round and round, enkindling the light of suns, ruling the world. . . . At your command the winds blow, clouds form, seeds sprout and the grass grows. *Gebete der Menschheit* (Cologne: Inselverlag, 1977), p. 314.

[6] H. Junker indicates that Job is certainly older than Ecclesiastes: *Echter Bible* (Wurzburg: Echter Verlag, 1959), Introduction to the Book of Job, vol. 4, p. 317.

The philosophies of Epicurus (the enjoyment of life) and Pyrrho of Ellis (the founder of skepticism) were especially popular. The author of Ecclesiastes seems to have been influenced by both, for on the one hand he is a skeptic ("Futility, utter futility . . . everything is futile"—Eccles. 1,2) and on the other he is the Bible's Epicurean:

> It is good and proper for a man to eat and drink and enjoy himself in return for the fruits of his labors here under the sun, throughout the brief span of life (Eccles. 5,18).

> Do not be over-righteous and do not be over-wise (Eccles. 7,16).

> The light of day is sweet, and pleasant to the eye is the sun. . . . Delight in your youth, young man, make the most of your early days. . . . . Banish vexation from your mind, and shake off the troubles of your body (Eccles. 11,7–10).

The composition of Ecclesiastes is dated to the middle of the third century (around 260 B.C.E.).[7]

Most of *Proverbs* represents the oldest portions of the Wisdom Books. The dates of the book's first and final forms are the most uncertain of all the Wisdom Books (estimates range from 538 B.C.E., around the time of the return from Babylon, to the composition of the Septuagint around 250 B.C.E.[8]). Thus the approximate time of its final composition can be set around 330 B.C.E.

Eccesiasticus was written by a teacher named Sirach or Sira. It was composed in Hebrew around 180 B.C.E. and translated approximately fifty years later into Greek (around 130 B.C.E.) by his nephew Jesus Sirach (Joshua ben Eleasar ben Sira)[9] during a turbulent time in Jewish history. The Seleucids had driven the Ptolemies out of Palestine and replaced them as rulers. Around 190 B.C.E. the Seleucid king Antiochus III had lost his war against

---

[7] Father Notscher, *Echter Bible*, Introduction to Ecclesiastes, vol. 4, p. 537.

[8] V. Hamp, *Echter Bible*, Introduction to the Book of Proverbs, vol. 4, p. 423.

[9] V. Hamp, *Echter Bible*, Introduction to the Book of Ecclesiasticus, vol. 4, p. 571.

the Romans and had to pay off enormous war debts. In a brutal and treacherous manner he exacted these sums from his peoples, not hesitating to rob temples and sanctuaries.[10] His son and successor Antiochus IV, was no better. In 170 B.C.E. he took Jerusalem by storm and desecrated the temple, compelling the Jews to hand over temple treasures and to take up Greek practices and customs. This resulted in resistance and lead to the successful revolt of the Jews inspired by the Maccabees. Something of this critical and troubled time is reflected in Ecclesiasticus, particularly in the emphasis on the "Law," or the call to be faithful to the Law. Toward this end, the "Law" or Torah was identified with Wisdom, who had taken up Her dwelling in Israel. The book aimed to bolster self-confidence and thereby help the Jews survive the identity crisis occasioned by the confrontation with Hellenism. One of the fruits of this effort can perhaps be seen in the heroic death of the Maccabean brothers (2 Macc. 7,1–42) who, rather than betray the Law, were martyred in faithfulness to it.

The *Book of Wisdom* was written in Greek by a Jewish wisdom teacher around 100 B.C.E. in Alexandria, the main center of Hellenism.[11] This was a time when Greek culture was so widespread among the upper classes that the Jews were in danger of falling away from their traditional faith. The author of the Book of Wisdom was familiar with Greek philosophy and understood that it contained much that was true and beautiful. He was impressed by conceptions like the soul's immortality, the world's creation through the mutual action of the *Nous* and *Sophia* (the Father and Mother of the cosmos), and by the devotion to individual deities like Demeter and Isis in the mystery cults. In all such conceptions and practices he perceived the working of Wisdom ("age after age . . . she enters into holy souls, and makes them friends of God and prophets"—Wisd. 7,27) and understood the possibility of using Greek teachings to help explain unresolved questions for the Jews. (Until that time, for example, the concept of the soul's immortality was only known in the Jewish

---

[10] John Bright, *Die Geschichte Israels* (Dusseldorf: Patmos, 1966), p. 443.

[11] Johann Fischer, *Echter Bible* (Introduction to the Book of Wisdom), p. 722. The author speculates that the book was composed between 146–117 B.C.E. However he also mentions those who think that the book could have been composed between 80–30 B.C.E.

tradition in a very rudimentary form.) The teaching about the *Nous* and *Sophia* also appeared to relate to Sophia's portrayal in the Wisdom Books as the mediator between Yahweh and creation and humanity.[12]

Inspired by God, the unknown author of the Book of Wisdom took a courageous and necessary step. Recognizing that knowledge in other cultures comes from Wisdom and complements belief in Yahweh, he concluded that it was justified to incorporate such teachings into the Jewish faith. Yet he was also critical about the weaknesses and imperfections of Greek philosophy (such as the worship of Egyptian gods which had been Hellenized). Thus an attempt was made to synthesize what was good and true with traditional Jewish faith and thereby help the Jews in the struggle to come to terms with Hellenism and the religious myths of neighboring peoples like the Egyptians. (One can add that the situation then has much in common with the challenge to Christianity today by the other world religions and that a similar, more powerful synthesis is demanded.)

The Book of Wisdom and Ecclesiasticus were both taken into the scriptural canon of the Catholic and Orthodox Churches (the fixed inventory of the Bible) but not into the canon of the Jewish tradition. For even though they were valued and used in the synagogue, they were not considered to be of "canonical age." Luther and the Reformation also did not recognize them as canonical, although Luther included them in his translation of the Bible and held them in high esteem.[13]

THE PERSONAL CONCEPTION OF WISDOM

Holy Wisdom (*Chokmah* or *Sophia*) was generally understood as the key to happiness and soon came to be viewed as a virtue and capacity given by God for recognizing what leads to happiness and achieving it. Gradually Wisdom begins to be revealed as a

---

[12] Burton Lee Mack, *Logos und Sophia, Untersuchungen zur Weisheitstheologie im Hellenistischen Judentum* (Goettingen: Vandenhoeck & Ruprecht, 1973).

[13] Luther considered the Book of Ecclesiasticus and the Book of Wisdom to be noncanonical Books of Holy Scripture, "which are not the equal of the Holy Scripture, but which are, nevertheless, useful and good to read."

mysterious being in God, created before all time, who works to-gether in the creation and counsels God, sharing the throne as God's Beloved (Prov. 8,22–31; Wisd. 8,3–4; 9,4). Because of Her role in creation She mediates between God and the world, com-ing from God and leading back to God.

A dawning sense of Wisdom's independent nature had appeared in the Book of Job (28,27); but She is clearly recognized for the first time in Proverbs, where She is poetically proclaimed as the Teacher and Guide to happiness who hosts the banquet of understanding and life (Prov. 8,32–36; 9,1–6).

Ecclesiastes does not take up Wisdom's personal aspect, which perhaps would not have interested its unspeculative au-thor whose concerns are more practical. Ecclesiasticus does pre-sent Her in personal terms, depicting Her proceeding from the mouth of God, Her rulership over the world and its nations, and Her particular relationship to the people of Israel. What is espe-cially emphasized is Wisdom's function as the universal Law (Torah) of God and the world which orders and directs all things. Following the Law becomes the path to happiness, though this happiness is still defined in worldly terms (Ecclus 24,1–12; 23–26).

The Book of Wisdom takes a further step toward unveil-ing the mystery of Holy Wisdom. What was tentatively per-ceived in the previous Wisdom Books is glimpsed more fully: that She proceeds from God, and Her divine dignity and life at God's side, assisting and counseling God. All of this is depicted in a clear language which would seem to go beyond a poetic personification (Wisd. 7,25–28; 8,3–4; 9,4).

She is presented in Her relationship to creation and the cosmos also, as the spiritual power which creates, permeates, en-livens, and renews all things (Wisd. 7,22–24). "Who more than wisdom is the artificer of all that is?" (Wisd. 8,6). She cares for humanity by always and everywhere providing friends and prophets of God (Wisd. 7,27).

• • •

It is a grandiose picture of Wisdom that emerges from every-thing that is said about Her in the Wisdom Books. As will be discussed in the chapters which follow, some Church Fathers understood Her as the Logos and some as the Holy Spirit.[14] Others have called Her the Mother of Creation and the Soul of the World and have identified Her as Mary,[15] the Mother of the Logos Son of God who assisted Him in the work of salvation. This latter understanding is reflected in the liturgy of the Church, whose epistle readings for Marian feast days are taken from the Books of Wisdom (see Appendix II).

The question of the validity of understanding Wisdom-Sophia as a person will be discussed in more depth in chapter 6.

The following verses[16] from the Books of Wisdom are some of the most significant, and help to characterize the figure of "Lady Wisdom." They are arranged according to subject, beginning with Wisdom's origin and culminating with the prophet Baruch's prophecy of Wisdom's appearance on Earth.

WISDOM'S ORIGIN

Ecclus. 1,1–9—Wisdom's Nature and Lineage

1   All wisdom is from the Lord; she dwells with him for ever.[17]

2   Who can count the sands of the sea, the raindrops, or the days of unending time?

---

[14] Athanasius, Gregory of Nazianz and Augustine, among others, understood Wisdom as the Logos. Irenaeus and Theophilus of Antioch understood Wisdom as the Holy Spirit.

[15] Vladimir Soloviev, Pavel Florenski, Sergei Bulgakov; Jacob Boehme also viewed Sophia as a person related to Mary. Teilhard de Chardin refers to Wisdom's relationship to Mary in the poem "The Eternal Feminine" (chapter 15) where he views Wisdom as the Soul of the World. He defends the concept of the World Soul in the essay "The Soul of the World" (chapter 15) asserting that it does not contradict Catholic teaching.

[16] Unless otherwise indicated, all Bible passages are from: *The Revised English Bible* (Oxford University Press and Cambridge University Press, 1989).

[17] Ecclesiasticus 1, 5, and 7 are not included in the main body of text but are rendered as footnotes with the remark that "some witnesses" add them (*The Revised English Bibie*, "The Apocrypha," p. 90.)

3 Who can measure the height of the sky, the breadth of the earth, or the depth of the abyss?

4 Wisdom was first of all created things; intelligent purpose has existed from the beginning.

5 The fountain of wisdom is God's word on high, and her ways are eternal commandments.

6 To whom has the root of wisdom been revealed? Who has understanding of her subtlety?

7 Who has discovered all that wisdom knows, or understood her wealth of experience?

8 One alone is wise, the Lord most terrible, seated upon his throne.

9 It is he who created her, beheld and measured her, and infused her into all his works.

Prov. 8,22–31—Wisdom Witnesses to Her Creation

22 The LORD created me the first of his works long ago, before all else that he made.

23 I was formed in earliest times, at the beginning, before earth itself.

24 I was born when there was yet no ocean, when there were no springs brimming with water.

25 Before the mountains were settled in their place, before the hills I was born,

26 when as yet he had made neither land nor streams nor the mass of the earth's soil.

27 When he set the heavens in place I was there, when he girdled the ocean with the horizon, when he fixed the canopy of clouds overhead and confined the springs of the deep,

29 when he prescribed limits for the sea so that the waters do not transgress his command, when he made earth's foundations firm.

30 Then I was at his side each day, his darling and delight, playing in his presence continually,

31 playing over his whole world, while my delight was in mankind.

Ecclus. 24,1–9—I Am the Word Spoken by the Most High

1 Hear the praise of wisdom from her own mouth, as she speaks with pride among her people,

2 before the assembly of the Most High and in the presence of the heavenly host:

3 "I am the word spoken by the Most High; it was I who covered the earth like a mist.

4 My dwelling-place was in high heaven; my throne was in a pillar of cloud.

5 Alone I made a circuit of the sky and traversed the depths of the abyss.

6 The waves of the sea, the whole earth, every people and nation were under my sway.

7 Among them all I sought where I might come to rest: in whose territory was I to settle?

8 Then the Creator of all things laid a command on me; he who created me decreed where I should dwell. He said, "Make your home in Jacob; enter on your heritage in Israel."

9 Before time he created me, and until the end of time I shall endure.

Ecclus. 24,10–18—I Took Root Among an Honorable People

10 In the sacred tent I ministered in his presence, and thus I came to be established in Zion.

11 He settled me in the city he loved and gave me authority in Jerusalem.

12 I took root among the people whom the Lord had honoured by choosing them to be his own portion.

13 There I grew like a cedar of Lebanon, like a cypress on the slopes of Hermon,

14 like a date-palm at En-gedi, like roses at Jericho. I grew like a fair olive tree in the vale, or like a plane tree planted beside the water.

15 Like cinnamon or camel-thorn I was redolent of spices; like a choice myrrh I spread my fragrance, like galbanum, aromatic shell, and gum resin, like the smoke of frankincense in the sacred tent.

16 Like a terebinth I spread out my branches, laden with honour and grace.

17 I put forth graceful shoots like the vine, and my blossoms were a harvest of honour and wealth.

18 I give birth to honorable love, to reverence, knowledge, and holy hope; all these my eternal progeny I give to God's elect.[18]

WISDOM AS THE TORAH

Ecclus. 24,23–29; Bar. 4,1–4—Wisdom is the Torah or Law of God

23 All this is the book of the covenant of God Most High, the law laid on us by Moses, a possession for the assemblies of Jacob.

24 Never fail to be strong in the Lord; hold fast to him, so that he may strengthen you. The Lord Almighty is God alone, and beside him there is no saviour.[19]

---

[18] Ecclesiasticus 24,18 is similarly lacking from the main body of text and rendered as a footnote (see note 17) with the additional remark that this is the probable meaning of an obscure Greek text. In the Latin Vulgate verse 18 reads: "Ego mater dilectionis et timoris et agnitionis. In me omnis gratia viae et veritatis, in me spes omnis vitae et virtutis."

[19] Ecclesiasticus 24,24 is also lacking from the main body of the text and is rendered as a footnote (*The Revised English Bible*, "The Apocrypha," p. 112).

25 It sends out wisdom in full flood like the river Peshon or like the Tigris at the time of first fruits;

26 it overflows like the Euphrates with understanding or like the Jordan at the harvest season.

27 it pours forth instruction like the Nile, like the Gihon at the time of vintage.

28 No one has ever known wisdom fully and from first to last no one has fathomed her,

29 for her thoughts are vaster than the ocean, her purpose more profound than the great abyss.

Bar. 4,1–4

1 She is the book of God's commandments, the law that endures forever.

2 Return, you people of Jacob, and lay hold of her; set your course towards the radiance of her light.

3 Do not yield up your glory to another or your privileges to a foreign nation.

4 Happy are we, Israel, for we know what is pleasing to God!

WISDOM'S FUNCTIONS AND CHARACTERISTICS

Job 28,12–27—Wisdom Transcends Time and Space

12 But where can wisdom be found, and where is the source of understanding?

13 No one knows the way to it, nor is it to be found in the land of the living.

14 "It is not in us," declare the ocean depths; the sea declares, "It is not with me."

15 Red gold cannot buy it, nor can its price be weighed out in silver;

16 gold of Ophir cannot be set in the scales against it, nor precious cornelian nor sapphire;

17 gold and crystal are not to be matched with it, no work in fine gold can be bartered for it;

18 black coral and alabaster are not worth mention, and a parcel of wisdom fetches more than red coral;

19 chrysolite from Ethiopia is not to be matched with it, pure gold cannot be set in the scales against it.

20 Where, then, does Wisdom come from? Where is the source of understanding?

21 No creature on earth can set eyes on it; even from birds of the air it is concealed.

22 Destruction and Death declare, "We know of it only by hearsay."

23 God alone understands the way to it, he alone knows its source;

24 for he can see to the ends of the earth and observe every place under heaven.

25 When he regulated the force of the wind and measured out the waters in proportion,

26 when he had laid down a limit for the rain and cleared a path for the thunderbolt,

27 it was then he saw wisdom and took stock of it, he considered it and fathomed its very depths.

Wisd. 7,22–28—Wisdom's Power and Transcendence

22 In wisdom there is a spirit intelligent and holy, unique in its kind yet made up of many parts, subtle, free-moving, lucid, spotless, clear, neither harmed nor harming, loving what is good, eager, unhampered, beneficent,

23 kindly towards mortals, steadfast, unerring, untouched by care, all-powerful, all-surveying, and permeating every intelligent, pure, and most subtle spirit.

24 For wisdom moves more easily than motion itself; she is so pure she pervades and permeates all things.

25 Like a fine mist she rises from the power of God, a clear effluence from the glory of the Almighty; so nothing defiled can enter into her by stealth.

26 She is the radiance that streams from everlasting light, the flawless mirror of the active power of God, and the image of his goodness.

27 She is but one, yet can do all things; herself unchanging, she makes all things new; age after age she enters into holy souls, and makes them friends of God and prophets,

28 for nothing is acceptable to God but the person who makes his home with wisdom.

Wisd. 6,12; 7,29–30; 8,1–2—The Splendor and Magnificence of Wisdom

12 Wisdom shines brightly and never fades; she is readily discerned by those who love her, and by those who seek her she is found.

29 She is more beautiful than the sun, and every constellation. Compared with the light of day, she is found to excel,

30 for day gives place to night, but against wisdom no evil can prevail.

1 She spans the world in power from end to end, and gently orders all things.

2 Wisdom I loved; I sought her out when I was young and longed to win her for my bride; I was in love with her beauty.

Wisd. 8, 3–9,16–18,21—The Riches of Wisdom

3   She adds luster to her noble birth, because it is given her to live with God; the Lord of all things has accepted her.

4   She is initiated into the knowledge that belongs to God, and she chooses what his works are to be.

5   If riches are a possession to be desired in life, what is richer than wisdom, the active cause of all things?

6   If prudence shows itself in action, who more than wisdom is the artificer of all that is?

7   If someone loves uprightness, the fruits of wisdom's labours are the virtues; temperance and prudence, justice and fortitude, these are her teaching, and life can offer nothing of more value than these.

8   If someone longs, perhaps, for great experience, she knows the past, she can infer what is yet to come; she understands the subtleties of argument and the solving of hard questions; she can read signs and portents and foretell what the different times and seasons will bring about.

9   So I determined to take her home to live with me, knowing that she would be my counsellor in prosperity and my comfort in anxiety and grief.

16 When I come home, I shall find rest with her; for there is no bitterness in her company, no pain in life with her, only gladness and joy.

17 I turned this over in my mind, and I perceived that there is immortality in kinship with wisdom,

18 and in her friendship there is pure delight; that in doing her work is wealth inexhaustible, to be taught in her school gives understanding, and an honourable name is won by converse with her. So I went about in search of some way to win her for my own.

21 but I saw that there was no way to gain possession of her except by gift of God—and it was itself a mark of understanding to know from whom that gift must come.

WISDOM'S TEACHING:
A MESSAGE OF LIFE AND SALVATION

Prov. 9,1–6; Ecclus. 24,19–22—Wisdom Sends an Invitation

1 Wisdom has built her house; she has hewn her seven pillars.

2 Now, having slaughtered a beast, spiced her wine, and spread her table,

3 she has sent her maidens to proclaim from the highest point of the town:

4 "Let the simple turn in here." She says to him who lacks sense,

5 "Come, eat the food I have prepared and taste the wine that I have spiced.

6 Abandon the company of simpletons and you will live, you will advance in understanding."

Ecclus. 24,19–22—Wisdom Sends an Invitation

19 "Come to me, all you who desire me, and eat your fill of my fruit.

20 To think of me is sweeter than honey, to possess me sweeter than the honeycomb.

21 Whoever feeds on me will hunger for more; whoever drinks from me will thirst for more.

22 To obey me is to be safe from disgrace; those who make me their business will not go astray."

Prov. 1,20–28,33—Wisdom Issues a Warning

20 Wisdom cries aloud in the open air, and raises her voice in public places.

21 She calls at the top of the bustling streets; at the approaches to the city gates she says:

22 "How long will you simple fools be content with your simplicity?

23 if only you would respond to my reproof, I would fill you with my spirit and make my precepts known to you.

24 But because you refused to listen to my call, because no one heeded when I stretched out my hand,

25 because you rejected all my advice and would have none of my reproof,

26 I in turn shall laugh at your doom and deride you when terror comes,

27 when the terror comes like a hurricane and your doom approaches like a whirlwind, when anguish and distress come upon you . . .

28 When they call to me, I shall not answer; when they seek, they will not find me.

33 But whoever listens to me will live without a care, undisturbed by fear of misfortune."

Prov. 4,1–9—Wisdom is the Guide to Happiness and Salvation

1 Listen, my sons, to a father's instruction, consider attentively how to gain understanding;

2 it is sound learning I give you, so do not forsake my teaching.

3 When I was a boy, subject to my father, tender in years, my mother's only child,

4 he taught me and said to me: "Hold fast to my words with all your heart, keep my commandment, and you will have life.

5 Get wisdom, get understanding; do not forget or turn a deaf ear to what I say.

6 Do not forsake her, and she will watch over you; love her, and she will safeguard you;

8 cherish her, and she will lift you high; if only you embrace her, she will bring you to honour.

9   She will set a becoming garland on your head; she will bestow on you a glorious crown."

Prov. 4,20–23—Wisdom's Words Bring Health and Life

20 "My son, attend to my words, pay heed to my sayings;

21 do not let them slip from your sight, keep them fixed in your mind;

22 for they are life to those who find them, and health to their whole being.

23 Guard your heart more than anything you treasure, for it is the source of all life."

Prov. 8,1,12–21—Wisdom Teaches Wise Men and Kings

1   Hear how wisdom calls and understanding lifts her voice.

12 "I am wisdom, I bestow shrewdness and show the way to knowledge and discretion.

13 To fear the Lord is to hate evil. Pride, arrogance, evil ways, subversive talk, all those I hate.

14 From me come advice and ability; understanding and power are mine.

15 Through me kings hold sway and governors enact just laws.

16 Through me princes wield authority, from me all rulers on earth derive their rank.

17 Those who love me I love, and those who search for me will find me.

18 In my hands are riches and honour, boundless wealth and prosperity.

19 My harvest is better even than fine gold, and my revenue better than choice silver.

20 I follow the course of justice and keep to the path of equity.

21 I endow with riches those who love me; I shall fill their treasuries."

Wisd. 6,17–20—Wisdom Leads to Immortality and God

17 The true beginning of wisdom is the desire to learn, and a concern for learning means love towards her;

18 the love of her means the keeping of her laws; to keep her laws is a warrant of immortality;

19 and immortality brings a person near to God.

20 Thus desire for wisdom leads to a kingdom. If, therefore, you value your thrones and your sceptres, you rulers of the nations, you must honour wisdom so that you may reign for ever.

SOLOMON: ARCHETYPE OF A WISDOM-SEEKER

Wisd. 8,21; 9,1–18—Solomon Prays for Wisdom

21 So I pleaded with the Lord, and from the depths of my heart I prayed to him in these words:

1 God of our forefathers, merciful Lord, who made all things by your word,

2 and in your wisdom fashioned man to have sovereignty over your whole creation,

3 and to be steward of the world in holiness and righteousness, and to administer justice with an upright heart:

4 give me wisdom, who sits beside your throne, and do not refuse me a place among your servants.

5 I am your slave, your slave-girl's son, weak and with but a short time to live, too feeble to understand justice and law;

6 for let someone be never so perfect in the eyes of his fellows, if the wisdom that comes from you is wanting, he will be of no account.

7 You chose me to be a king of your own people and judge of your sons and daughters;

8 you told me to build but a temple on your sacred mountain and an altar in the city which is your dwelling-place, a copy of the sacred tabernacle prepared by you from the beginning.

9 With you is wisdom, who is familiar with your works and was present when you created the universe, who is aware of what is acceptable to you and in keeping with your commandments.

10 Send her forth from your holy heaven, and from your glorious throne bid her come down, so that she may labour at my side and I may learn what is pleasing to you.

11 She knows and understands all things; she will guide me prudently in whatever I do, and guard me with her glory.

12 So my life's work will be acceptable, and I shall judge your people justly, and be worthy of my father's throne.

13 How can any human being learn what is God's plan? Who can apprehend what is the will of the Lord?

14 The reasoning of mortals is uncertain, and our plans are fallible,

15 because a perishable body weighs down the soul, and its frame of clay burdens the mind already so full of care.

16 With difficulty we guess even at things on earth, and laboriously find out what lies within our reach; who has ever traced out what is in heaven?

17 Who ever came to know your purposes, unless you had given him wisdom and sent your holy spirit from heaven on high?

18 Thus it was that those on earth were set on the right path, and mortals were taught what pleases you; thus they were kept safe by wisdom.

Wisd. 7,4–22—Solomon's Life with Wisdom

4   [T]hey wrapped me up and nursed me and cared for me.

5   No king begins life in any other way;

6   for all come into life by a single path, and by a single path they go out again.

7   Therefore I prayed, and prudence was given me; I called for help, and there came to me a spirit of wisdom.

8   I valued her above sceptre and throne, and reckoned riches as nothing beside her;

9   I counted no precious stone her equal, because compared with her all the gold in the world is but a handful of sand, and silver worth no more than clay.

10 I loved her more than health and beauty; I preferred her to the light of day, for her radiance is unsleeping.

11 So all good things together came to me with her, and in her hands was wealth past counting.

12 Everything was mine to enjoy, for all follow where wisdom leads; yet I was in ignorance that she is the source of them all.

13 What I learnt with pure intention I now share ungrudgingly, nor do I hoard for myself the wealth that comes from her.

14 She is an inexhaustible treasure for mortals, and those who profit by it become God's friends, commended to him by the gifts they derive from her instruction.

15 God grant that I may speak according to his will, and that my own thoughts may be worthy of his gifts, for even wisdom is under God's direction and he corrects the wise;

16 we and our words, prudence and knowledge and craftsmanship, all are in his hand.

17 He it was who gave me true understanding of things as they are: a knowledge of the structure of the world and the operation of the elements;

18 the beginning and end of epochs and their middle course; the alternating solstices and changing seasons;

19 the cycles of the years and the constellations;

20 the nature of living creatures and behaviour of wild beasts; the violent force of winds and human thought; the varieties of plants and the virtues of roots.

21 I learnt it all, hidden or manifest,

22 for I was taught by wisdom, by her whose skill made all things.

Prov. 3,13–26—Happy are Those Who Find Wisdom

13 Happy is he who has found wisdom, he who has acquired understanding,

14 for wisdom is more profitable than silver, and the gain she brings is better than gold!

15 She is more precious than red coral, and none of your jewels can compare with her.

16 In her right hand is long life, in her left are riches and honour.

17 Her ways are pleasant ways and her paths all lead to prosperity.

18 She is a tree of life to those who grasp her, and those who hold fast to her are safe.

19 By wisdom the LORD laid the earth's foundations and by understanding he set the heavens in place;

20 by his knowledge the springs of the deep burst forth and the clouds dropped dew.

21 My son, safeguard sound judgement and discretion; do not let them out of your sight.

22 They will be a charm hung about your neck, an ornament to grace your throat.

23 Then you will go on your way without a care, and your foot will not stumble.

24 When you sit, you need have no fear; when you lie down, your sleep will be pleasant.

25 Do not be afraid when fools are frightened or when destruction overtakes the wicked,

26 for the LORD will be at your side, and he will keep your feet from the trap.

> *Ecclus. 51,13–21—Wisdom Brings Happiness and Joy to Seekers*

13 When I was still young, before I set off on my travels, in my prayers I asked openly for wisdom.

14 In the forecourt of the sanctuary I laid claim to her, and I shall seek her to the end.

15 From the first blossom to the ripening of the grape she has been the delight of my heart.

16 I had hardly begun to listen when I was rewarded, and I gained for myself much instruction.

17 I made progress in my studies; all glory to God who gives me wisdom!

18 I determined to practise what I learnt; I pursued goodness, and shall never regret it.

19 With all my might I strive for wisdom and was scrupulous in whatever I did. I spread out my hands to Heaven above, deploring my shortcomings;

20 I set my heart to possessing wisdom, and by keeping myself pure I found her. With her I gained understanding from the first; therefore I shall never be at a loss.

21 Because I passionately yearned to discover her, a noble possession was mine:

WISDOM'S BENEFICENT EFFECTS

Wisd. 1, 6–7,12–15—Wisdom's Friendliness

6   The spirit of wisdom is kindly towards mortals, but she will not hold a blasphemer blameless for his words . . .

7   For the spirit of the LORD fills the whole earth, and that which holds all things together knows well everything that is said.

12 Do not court death by a crooked life; do not draw disaster on yourselves by your own actions.

13 For God did not make death, and takes no pleasure in the destruction of any living thing;

14 he created all things that they might have being. The creative forces of the world make for life; there is no deadly poison in them. Death has no sovereignty on earth,

15 for justice is immortal;

Wisd. 6, 13–16—Wisdom is Found by Those Who Seek Her

13 She is quick to make herself known to all who desire knowledge of her;

14 he who rises early in search of her will not grow weary in the quest, for he will find her seated at his door.

15 To meditate on her is prudence in its perfect shape, and to be vigilant in her cause is the short way to freedom from care;

16 she herself searches far and wide for those who are worthy of her, and on their daily path she appears to them with kindly intent, meeting them half-way in all their purposes.

Wisd. 10,9–19; 11,1–5—Wisdom in Israel's History

9   But wisdom brought her servants safely out of their troubles.

10 When a good man was a fugitive from his brother's anger, she it was who guided him on straight paths; she gave him a

vision of God's kingdom and a knowledge of holy things; she prospered his labours and made his toil fruitful.

11 When others in their rapacity sought to exploit him, she stood by him and made him rich.

12 She kept him safe from his enemies, and preserved him from treacherous attacks; after his hard struggle she gave him victory, and taught him that godliness is the mightiest power of all.

13 It was she who refused to desert a good man when he was sold into slavery; she preserved him from sin and went down into the dungeon with him,

14 nor did she leave him when he was in chains until she had brought him a kingdom's sceptre with authority over his persecutors; she gave the lie to his accusers, and bestowed on him undying fame.

15 It was wisdom who rescued a god-fearing people, a blameless race, from a nation of oppressors;

16 she inspired a servant of the Lord, and with his signs and wonders he defied formidable kings.

17 She rewarded the labours of a godfearing people, she guided them on a miraculous journey, and became a covering for them by day and a blaze of stars by night.

18 She brought them over the Red Sea, leading them through its deep waters;

19 but their enemies she engulfed, and cast them up again out of the fathomless deep.

Wisd. 11,1–5

1 Wisdom working through a holy prophet, gave them success in all they did.

2 They made their way across an unpeopled desert and pitched camp in untrodden wastes;

3 they stood firm against their enemies, and fought off hostile assaults.

4 When they were thirsty they cried to you, and water to slake their thirst was given them out of the hard stone of a rocky cliff.

5 The selfsame means by which their oppressors had been punished were used to help them in their hour of need.

Prov. 8,32–36—To Find Wisdom is to Find Life

32 "Now, sons, listen to me; happy are those who keep to my ways.

33 Listen to instruction and grow wise; do not ignore it.

34 Happy the one who listens to me, watching daily at my threshold with his eyes on the doorway!

35 For whoever finds me finds life and wins favour with the LORD,

36 but whoever fails to find me deprives himself, and all who hate me are in love with death."

Prov. 31,10–31—The Strong Woman, Symbol of Wisdom's Works

10 Who can find a good wife? Her worth is far beyond red coral.

11 Her husband's whole trust is in her, and children are not lacking.

12 She works to bring him good, not evil, all the days of her life.

13 She chooses wool and flax and with a will she sets about her work.

14 Like a ship laden with merchandise she brings home food from far off.

15 She rises while it is still dark and apportions food for her household, with a due share for her servants.

16 After careful thought she buys a field and plants a vineyard out of her earnings.

17 She sets about her duties resolutely and tackles her work with vigour.

18 She sees that her business goes well, and all night long her lamp does not go out.

19 She holds the distaff in her hand, and her fingers grasp the spindle.

20 She is open-handed to the wretched and extends help to the poor.

21 When it snows she has no fear for her household, for they are wrapped in double cloaks.

22 She makes her own bed coverings and clothing of fine linen and purple.

23 Her husband is well known in the assembly, where he takes his seat with the elders of the region.

24 She weaves linen and sells it, and supplies merchants with sashes.

25 She is clothed in strength and dignity and can afford to laugh at tomorrow.

26 When she opens her mouth, it is to speak wisely; her teaching is sound.

27 She keeps an eye on the conduct of her household and does not eat the bread of idleness.

28 Her sons with one accord extol her virtues; her husband too is loud in her praise:

29 "Many a woman shows how gifted she is; but you excel them all."

30 Charm is deceptive and beauty fleeting; but the woman who fears the LORD is honoured.

31 Praise her for all she has accomplished; let her achievements bring her honour at the city gates.

WISDOM HAS APPEARED ON EARTH

Bar. 3,9–14—Wisdom, the Fountain of Life

9 Israel, listen to the life-giving commandments; hear, and learn understanding;

10 Why is it, Israel, that you are in your enemies' country, grown old in a foreign land? Why have you shared defilement with the dead

11 and been numbered among those that lie in the grave?

12 Because you have forsaken the fountain of Wisdom!

13 If only you had walked in God's ways, you would have lived in peace forever.

14 Where is understanding, where is strength, where is intelligence? Learn that, and you will know where are length of days and life, where happiness and peace.

Bar. 3,29–32,36–37—Wisdom Appears on Earth

29 Has anyone gone up to heaven and gained wisdom and brought her down from the clouds?

30 Has anyone crossed the sea and found her, or obtained her for fine gold?

31 No one can know the path or conceive the way that will lead to her.

32 Only the omniscient God knows her; the mind of God discovered her. He who established the earth for all time filled it with four-footed animals.

36 Every way of knowledge he found out and gave to Jacob his servant, to Israel whom he loved.

37 After that, wisdom appeared on earth and lived among men.

2

Sophia
According to
Philo of Alexandria

PHILO OF ALEXANDRIA[1] (13 B.C.E.–45 C.E.) was a key figure in the religious world of his time. He was a Jew familiar with Greek philosophy and the religious and Gnostic teachings of Egyptian Hellenism, and he used all of this knowledge in his approach to Jewish revelation.

The concepts of Sophia (Wisdom) and the Logos play an essential role in the religious and philosophical ideas of Philo. Research has shown that Philo initially distinguished between them but later confused their boundaries, understanding them as almost identical and thereby anticipating a development that continued into Christianity and climaxed with the Church Fathers.

---

[1] Some important works on Philo are: *The Works of Philo*, C. D. Yonge, trans. (Peabody, MA: Hendrickson, 1993); E. R. Goodenough, *An Introduction to Philo* (London: Oxford University Press, 1962).

PHILOSOPHICAL CONCEPTS
RELATING TO SOPHIA

Philo repeatedly uses concepts from Greek philosophy like *Logos, Sophia, Idea, Nous, Demiourgus* and *Eikon*. It will be helpful to review their meanings before attempting to clarify how they were used philosophically.[2]

Logos: The word "Logos" means word and speech, and used figuratively, sense and reason (the sense or meaning of spoken words and the reason that conveys meaning). "Logos" also signifies a thinking, perceiving and volitional spirit, and as a conveyer of ideas, the Logos is the first cause and bearer of the "Ideas."

Idea: The word "idea" originally meant the act of perceiving, but later came to signify the inner configuration of the object which reveals itself. Things are formed according to their "Ideas"; the "Idea" of each and every thing descends and incarnates into the material world. The descending "Idea" is called *Logos noetos* and the materialized idea *Logos aisthetos*, indicating the close relationship between "Logos" and "Idea" (*noetos* is related to the word *Nous* below and means conceivable; *aisthetos* means perceptible and is the base of words like "aesthetic"). The individual Ideas come from an *Idea idearum* (Idea of ideas) which is contained in, or is identical with, the *Nous* (who is also called Logos).

Nous: Nous comes from the verb *noein*, which means "to think" or "reflect." "Nous" signifies sense, understanding, reason, thought, spirit, and intellect. It is usually understood as the spirit which permeates and orders everything, the foundation and bearer of the Ideas, and the *Demiourgus*, the master builder of the world.

Demiourgus: This word is made up of *demios* which means "common" and "of the people," and *ourgos* which means "active" or "creative." *Demiourgus* signifies the universal creator, artisan or master builder of the world.

Eikon: Derived from a verb meaning "the same," and signifies an image or likeness.

---

[2] Johann Hirschberger, *A Short History of Western Philosophy*, Jeremy Moiser, trans. (Guilford, England: Lutterworth Press, 1976).

Sophia: "Sophia" derives from the adjective *sophos*, which means wise, reasonable, adept, intelligent, and artful. "Sophia" signifies wisdom, cleverness, adeptness, and artistic skill. In the Greek world, "Sophia" later took on a philosophical content: understood as the "World Soul," She became the artful and intelligent Helper of the Demiourgus. As the World Soul, She contained the Ideas from which the cosmos is formed, Herself being the "Idea idearum," the Idea of ideas (Chokmah, or Wisdom, also took on a cosmological significance in the Old Testament alongside its original ethical and practical meaning).

Heraclitus is the first to mention the word "Logos" around 500 B.C.E. The Logos, whose symbol is fire, is the wise and active World Reason who rules everything and yet is not understood by humanity.[3]

For Plato (ca. 400 B.C.E.)[4] and Aristotle (ca. 350 B.C.E.)[5] the cosmic aspect of the Logos recedes into the background and is superseded by the logical dimension encompassed by "Nous" and "Idea." According to Plato, in the beginning there is the Nous and the "Idea of ideas" containing all other ideas. The Nous then directs the primordial Idea to descend into matter where, as the World Spirit or World Soul (together with its *Pronoia*—providence, wisdom and power), it forms all things which constitute its body. The cosmos is the materialization of the "Idea of ideas" (and is good and beautiful, as Plato solemnly assures us at the end of his dialogue *Timaeus*). Aristotle subsequently coins the word *Entelechy* (the dynamic power residing in things which brings their goal to realization; intended sense and purpose) and substitutes it for the Platonic sense of "Idea."

Stoicism,[6] founded by Zeno of Cyprus (ca. 300 B.C.E.) and developed further by Chrysippus of Cilicia (ca. 250 B.C.E.), takes

---

[3] Olaf Gigon, *Untersuchungen zu Heraclit* (Leipzig: Dieterich, 1935).

[4] G. C. Field, *The Philosophy of Plato* (New York: Oxford University Press, 1949); O. Apelt, *Platons Werke* (Leipzig: F. Meiner, 1920).

[5] W. Jaeger, *Aristotle: Fundamentals of the History of His Development*, Richard Robinson, trans. (Oxford: Clarendon Press, 1955).

[6] Max Pohlenz, *Stoa und Stoiker, Selbstzeugnisse und Berichte* (Zurich: Artemis Verlag, 1950).

up the Logos concept of Heraclitus and makes it fashionable within Hellenistic philosophy. The cosmos is understood as material substance upon which the immanent Logos works throughout the universe. The Logos has different aspects and is named according to the manner of its working. As *Fatum*, the Logos brings matter into existence; as *Nomos*, the Logos structures matter (providing it with laws).

As *Pneuma*, which is understood as spiritual power (and symbolized by fire), the Logos enlivens matter and is actively creative in various ways: as the general "principle of life" in the organic world and in plants; as "soul" in animals; as "spirit" in human beings and as the "World Soul" in the cosmos.

In its function as World Soul, the Logos/Pneuma enlivens the cosmos; and as Pronoia (providence) or Logos spermatikos (seed Logos) the World Soul guides the cosmos, assisted by the Logoi spermatikoi, or the seed-like ideas contained in the Logos spermatikos which descend into things. In this guiding function the World Soul joins the various levels of existence together into a unity which includes humanity. This is brought about by *symphyia* or the nature that everything has in common, and is actualized by *sympatheia*, the common feeling and sympathy that all beings have for one another.

What is important not to lose sight of in all of these descriptions is that the Pneuma (whose highest manifestation is the World Soul) and the cosmic Logos are virtually *identical* (although the Pneuma can also be understood as dependent on the Logos).

The Stoics also attached great importance to "right logos" (*logos orthos*) which consisted of right speech and right life based on the right kind of understanding of the various aspects of the Logos (*Fatum, Nomos* and *Pneuma*). The wise person lived in *symphyia* and *sympatheia* with the Logos and the world, thereby possessing unshakable equanimity (i.e., a stoical attitude). Today this kind of spirituality would be called a nature-oriented and pantheistic monism.

Stoicism was the leading philosophy during the Hellenistic period. Through the influence of people like Philo, Clement of Alexandria, Origen, and Augustine it has continued to exert a lasting influence on Christian thinking in the West.

PHILO'S TEACHING ABOUT SOPHIA

As the previous section has attempted to indicate, Stoicism began to imperceptibly shift the significance of various Greek philosophical concepts through the use of different names. The significance attached to the Nous was replaced by the Logos; the Idea idearum was replaced by concepts like Pneuma, World Soul, and Logos spermatikos (the seed-like Logos); and the Ideas by the Logoi spermatikoi (plural). Thus the Logos concept was being used to describe all of the functions within the cosmos. The three cosmogonic concepts Nous, Idea idearum and Ideae, which previously had specific meanings, could all be expressed with various forms of the one word "Logos," resulting in a nominal identification between them. Johann Gottsberger notes the change that took place in the following way:

> At first the Logos was identified with Zeus, Greek mythology's father of the gods. When Zeus was replaced by Hermes, the Logos of Stoicism took on features which qualified it more as a double of the Old Testament's Wisdom [the Idea idearum and World Soul] as far as the position of the Logos between God and the world was concerned.[7]

Ruling over the entire realm of existence, the Logos became the leading philosophical concept during the Hellenistic period.

Philo was a devout Jew who was thoroughly familiar with Hebrew Scripture but also versed in Stoicism. It is understandable that he might have preferred to use the word "Logos" and even verbally identified Wisdom-Sophia with the Logos, but not in a real sense.[8] Although the opinion arose that Philo considered the two to be identical, this point of view does not hold up to a nuanced investigation.

---

[7] Johann Gottsberger, "Die Goettliche Weisheit als Persoenlichkeit" in *Biblische Zeitfragen*, IX/1–2 (Muenster, 1919), p. 71. Tr: Translation mine.

[8] Burton Lee Mack, *Logos und Sophia: Untersuchungen zur Weisheitstheologie pulchrae im Hellenistischen Judentum* (Goettingen: Vandenhoeck & Ruprecht,1975).

Philo's Sophia teaching is based on the Books of Wisdom. He developed it further in his own way by using concepts like the Logos in particular. This was possible because the Old Testament did ascribe creative and redemption–bringing powers to God's Word (the *Dabar* or *Memra* of Yahveh). For example, Psalms indicates that "The word of the Lord created the heavens" (Ps. 33,6), and other Old Testament verses state:

> ... so is it with my word issuing from my mouth; it will not return to me empty without accomplishing my purpose and succeeding in the task for which I sent it (Isaiah 55,11).

> God of our forefathers, merciful Lord, who made all things by your word, and in your wisdom fashioned man (Wisd. 9,1).

Philo's explanation of the act of creation is that Yahweh creates Sophia at the beginning of creation and then together with Her creates the entire universe:

> At all events we shall speak with justice, if we say that the Creator of the universe is also the father of his creation, and that the mother was the knowledge of the Creator (*epistemene tou pepoiekotos*) with whom God uniting, not as a man unites, became the father of creation. And this knowledge having received the seed of God, when the day of her travail arrived, brought forth her only and well-beloved son, perceptible by the external senses, namely this world. Accordingly wisdom is represented by some one of the beings of the divine company as speaking of herself in this manner: "God created me as the first of his works, and before the beginning of time did he establish me" (Prov. 8,22–23). For it was necessary that all the things which came under the head of the creation must be younger than the mother and nurse of the whole universe.[9]

---

[9] *The Works of Philo*, "On Drunkenness," 30–32, p. 209.

The universe is the Son whose Father is Yahweh and whose Mother is Sophia. Sophia is God's Spouse and the Mother of the world. In line with Platonic thinking, the universe consists of its "Idea" and the substance in which it has materialized; in line with Stoic understanding, Philo names the "Idea" of the universe the Logos noetos and the visible form of the cosmos the Logos aisthetos (thereby using the Logos concept for his own cosmological system). The Idea of the universe is contained in the "Idea of ideas," i.e., in Sophia, who comes directly from Yahweh. This is mythologically expressed by the relationship between Mother and Son (the Logos noetos and aisthetos contained in the "Idea idearum" or Sophia). Yahweh has given creation to Sophia to care for maternally, which is why Philo calls Her the "Mother, Nourisher and Nurse of the universe."[10] The Books of Wisdom describe Her similarly. Philo recalls that She is the "Mother, Wife, Teacher and Guide" of the sages, including Abraham, Jacob and Moses.[11]

The Mother subsequently transfers many of Her caring attributes and functions to the Son. As the Son He is already similar in nature to Her and the Father. He is Sophia's *Eikon* or image and therewith Yahweh's also. Like Her, He is the beginning (*Arche*)[12] and is also the "second God" (*deuteros Theos*).[13] His nature is also light; for as God is the first light and the archetypal model of every light, so is God's most perfect word the light.[14]

---

[10] *The Works of Philo*, "On Drunkenness," 31. Philo was apparently also thinking of the maternal attributes and functions of the goddess Isis "who fills heaven and earth with Her beauty . . . who is great in heaven, powerful on earth . . . from whom everything came into being and through whom everything exists and lives" (Burton Lee Mack, *Logos und Sophia*, p. 66). This task was given over to Isis by Her Father Re: "Her Father Re gave Her His mountain of light and His throne that She might rule His kingdom in heaven and on earth" (*Logos und Sophia*, p. 65).

[11] *The Works of Philo*, "On Flight and Finding," 52; "Questions and Answers on Genesis," III, 21–32; Burton Lee Mack, *Logos und Sophia*, p. 157.

[12] *The Works of Philo*, "On Flight and Finding," 101, 109.

[13] *The Works of Philo*, "Questions and Answers on Genesis," II, 62; Burton Lee Mack, *Logos und Sophia*, p. 108.

[14] *The Works of Philo*, "On Dreams—Book I," 75; Burton Lee Mack, *Logos und Sophia*, p. 109.

These are some of many examples which show how Philo transferred various attributes and functions to the Logos.[15]

B. Lang has indicated that though Philo by and large substituted the Logos or divine Word for Wisdom, he also continued to speak of Wisdom-Sophia's independent existence.[16] Gottsberger also indicates that on the one hand Philo uses the words "Logos" and "Wisdom" in an identical way but on the other hand places them beside each other; and that he did not proclaim their identity but only their relationship.[17]

Philo presented his Sophia teaching through the use of Greek (and Egyptian) concepts. He used the concept of the Demiourgus by first eliminating objectional elements from it (in this case pantheistic and emanationist traces); and in this way he similarly incorporated other ideas into his own philosophical system. Though he used Greek expressions, he remained firmly grounded in the Jewish tradition.

THE CONSEQUENCES
OF PHILO'S SOPHIA TEACHING

It is said that Philo exerted a unique influence on Christianity.[18] His magnificent reflections about God and the spiritual path were taken up without hesitation by the Church Fathers. Because he had transferred Sophia's functions and attributes to the Logos, it was possible for the viewpoint to arise that he understood the two of them to be identical. As will be seen in chapter 5 on the Church Fathers, identifying Sophia with the Logos be-

---

[15] Philo wrote up to forty-three works. In addition to the works already cited, some of the best known are: *On the Contemplative Life or Suppliants, Hypothetica: Apology for the Jews, On the Life of Moses I, II, On Providence: Fragments I & II, Allegorical Interpretation,* I, II, III. He also wrote several commentaries to the Pentateuch (about the creation of the world, Abraham, Joseph, the Ten Commandments, the Laws, the virtues, and reward).

[16] B. Lang, *Frau Weisheit: Deutung Einer Biblishen Gestalt* (Dusseldorf: Patmos, 1975), p. 161 ff.

[17] Johann Gottsberger, "Die Goettliche Weisheit Als Persoenlichkeit im Alten Testament," in *Biblishe Zeitfragen,* IX 1/2 (Munster, 1919), p. 71 ff.

[18] *Lexikon fur Theologie und Kirche* (Freiburg: Herder, 1960), see: Philo.

came a dominant perception; and this is attributable at least in part to the influence of Philo. By identifying the two with each other, Sophia's independent existence was denied, which caused confusion and stagnation as far as the development of Sophiology was concerned.

It is necessary today to strive for a new orientation about Sophia and to take up the many indications given by persons like Augustine, Hildegard of Bingen, Jacob Boehme, Godfrey Arnold, Soloviev, Florenski, Bulgakov, and Teilhard de Chardin. Their contributions toward a new understanding of Sophia will be discussed in the chapters ahead (for a chronological overview of Greek philosophy until Philo, see appendix III).

3

Significant Sophia Texts in the New Testament

JUST A FEW TEXTS IN THE New Testament speak directly about Sophia-Wisdom. However some others can also be indirectly related to Her. One of the most important passages that refer specifically to Her (1 Cor. 1,23–24,30) insinuates the kind of Christological understanding that identifies Wisdom with the Logos. As the previous chapter has indicated, Greek philosophy and the writings of Philo had begun to blur the distinctions between Sophia (the Idea of the ideas) and the Logos, and some Old Testament texts also placed God's Word and God's Wisdom in close proximity to one another (Ps. 33,6; Is. 55,11; Wisd. 9,1). The Corinthians passage further contributed to identifying Sophia with the Logos among some Church Fathers and theologians.

WISDOM'S DEEDS

God's wisdom is proved right by its results (Matt. 11,19).

Some interpret the Wisdom that is mentioned in the above passage as the person of Christ (i.e., Wisdom is understood in a Christological sense). This is, however, not the only interpretation. It is more likely that Wisdom is to be understood here as the mode and characteristic of God's working. Perhaps the text's meaning can best be paraphrased as follows: the Wisdom evidenced in the deeds (in the working) of God is proved right, has shown itself to be right. The wise working of God cannot be characterized as false or incorrect, as the Pharisees complained to John about Jesus—that He was a friend of sinners (tax collectors and whores). Those who work in and from the Wisdom of God act correctly; their deeds are always right.

THE WISDOM AND POWER OF GOD

> . . . but we proclaim Christ nailed to the cross; and though this is an offense to Jews and folly to Gentiles, yet to those who are called, Jews and Greeks alike, he is the power of God and the wisdom of God. . . . By God's act you are in Jesus Christ; God made him our wisdom, and in him we have our righteousness, our holiness, our liberation (1 Cor. 1,23–24, 30).

The first part of the above passage ("he is the power of God and the wisdom of God") could be indicated as proof that Christ is the incarnated Wisdom of God. Such a Christological interpretation, however, does not really make sense. A better interpretation is that Christ is not personally the incarnated Wisdom, but instead the incarnated Word which brought forth Christ—the effect of the power and Wisdom of God.

The second part of the above passage ("God made him our wisdom") must also not necessarily be interpreted Christologically. For here also Wisdom is not to be understood personally but instead effectively—as wisdom-filled life resulting from the incarnation. We are in Christ who God made our proclaimer of Wisdom—the wisdom-filled and God-pleasing way of life—and the one who effects our righteousness, holiness, and liberation. In this way it becomes clear that Wisdom is not to be understood personally and Christologically, but as God's or Christ's manner of working. Wisdom effects and brings forth wisdom-filled life and righteousness, holiness and liberation.

SOPHIA POLYPOIKILOS

> To me, who am less than the least of all God's people, he has granted the privilege of proclaiming to the Gentiles the good news of the unfathomable riches of Christ, and of bringing to light how this hidden purpose was to be put into effect. It lay concealed for long ages with God the Creator of the universe, in order that now, through the church, the wisdom of God in its infinite variety might be made known to the rulers and authorities in the heavenly realms. This accords with his age-long purpose, which he accomplished in Christ Jesus our Lord . . . (Eph. 3,8–11).

This text is perhaps the clearest passage in the New Testament which understands and proclaims Wisdom in a personal manner as Sophia. For this reason it was also used to prove that Christ is the incarnated Sophia. But here also a Christological interpretation is not compelling. And especially because Wisdom is connected to the Church, a Sophian, Marian and ecclesiological interpretation of this important passage is appropriate.

The unfathomable riches of Christ, the mystery hidden since eternity in God the Creator, was realized in the course of time so that the infinite variety of God's wisdom might be made known. In what way? Through the Church in Jesus Christ—the Church as the Bride of Christ.

The mystery of Sophia-Wisdom is that She is the Bride of the Son of God. The betrothal of Wisdom with the Logos-Son of God is revealed by the fact that He ordained and took the Church as His Bride. When we consider that Mary is the beginning of the Church and its Mother, and that Mary is the incarnated Wisdom from whom the Son of God incarnated, then the mystery of Wisdom before history and Her relationship to the Son of God becomes clear. That mystery becomes visible and this passage makes sense. From the earthly reality we are able to infer conclusions about the eternal archetype and prehistoric existence.

The forms of Wisdom's unfathomable riches will become apparent in the following chapters which speak of the Sophian tradition and the other ways in which Sophia has been revealed.

"The unfathomable wisdom of God is to be made known through the Church"—this is a short summary which clearly expresses the relationship of Wisdom to the Church. It does so because the Church is Wisdom incarnate—personally in Mary and collectively in the Body of Christ (the Church), whose spiritual mother is Mary. The explanation of this incarnation of Sophia is given by the *ecclesiological context* of Pauline theology: the Church as the Body of Christ and the Bride of Christ. The *Mariological connection* is indicated by the theology of Luke (the Annunciation of Mary and the childhood of Jesus) and the theology of John (Wedding at Cana, Mary under the cross, the woman clothed with the sun).

The Sophian texts of the Old and New Testaments exercised an important influence on the religious thinking of their times. It is interesting and significant for Sophiology to understand how Wisdom-Sophia was consequently seen and interpreted. This becomes apparent in the chapters which show how Sophia was understood (for example by Philo of Alexandria and the Church Fathers, in particular Athanasius and Augustine).

THE WOMAN OF REVELATION

God's sanctuary in heaven was opened, and within his sanctuary was seen the ark of his covenant. . . . After that there appeared a great sign in heaven: a woman robed with the sun, beneath her feet the moon, and on her head a crown of twelve stars. She was about to bear a child, and in the anguish of her labour she cried out to be delivered. Then a second sign appeared in heaven: a great, fiery red dragon with seven heads and ten horns. . . . The dragon stood in front of the woman who was about to give birth, so that when her child was born he might devour it. But when she gave birth to a male child, who is destined to rule all nations with a rod of iron, the child was snatched up to God and to his throne. . . . the dragon . . . went in pursuit of the woman who had given birth to the male child. But she was given the wings of a mighty eagle, so that she could fly to her place in the wilderness where she was to be looked after for three and a half years out of reach of the serpent.

Furious with the woman, the dragon went off to wage war with the rest of her offspring . . . (Rev. 11,19; 12,1–5,13–14,17).

This vision of St. John is one of the most important and well-known visions of the Apocalypse. Who is this mysterious woman who is represented surrounded by classical and biblical symbols full of meaning: the Old Testament symbol of the Ark of the Covenant and the cosmic symbols of sun, moon and stars; and who is pregnant, giving birth to a ruler-son, and then threatened and pursued with Her son and Her offspring by a dragon?

Most commentators justifiably interpret this mysterious woman in a Mariological sense, i.e., as Mary the Mother of Christ and/or in an ecclesiological sense as the archetype and Mother of the Church. Considering this, it is permissible to summarize these interpretations through a Sophian synthesis and to understand this woman as Sophia Mary. Several reasons can be given to support this point of view:

1. The mention of the Ark of the Covenant in direct relation to the woman. The Ark of the Covenant is where God's presence—the "Schekinah"—is to be found, which in the Jewish mystical tradition of the Cabbala is often identified with Chokmah or Wisdom (see chapter 9).

2. In the liturgical tradition Mary is understood as the Ark of the Covenant; for example in the famous Akathist Hymn (to the Blessed Virgin) of the Orthodox Church where She is praised as the "vessel of God's wisdom" and the "tabernacle of God" and in the Litany of Loreto (a litany to our lady) where Mary is expressly praised as the "Ark of the Covenant" (see appendix IV). The Ark of the Covenant was the repository of the tablets of law which are the symbol for the Torah or Wisdom (see page 16, Wisdom as the Torah).

3. The woman is clothed with the cosmic symbols of sun, moon, and stars. We are reminded of the Wisdom Book passages in the Old Testament where Sophia says of Herself: "The LORD created

me the first of his works long ago" (Prov. 8,22) and ". . . when he made the earth's foundations firm. Then I was at his side each day, his "Amon" (i.e., his beloved counselor, co-worker and master worker—Prov. 8,29–30). The sun with which She is robed, the moon at Her feet and the stars with which She is crowned are indications of Her cosmic dignity and function which goes back to primordial times. In this sense Sophia says of Herself:

> My dwelling place was in high heaven; my throne was in a pillar of cloud. Alone I made a circuit of the sky and traversed the depths of the abyss. The waves of the sea, the whole earth, every people and nation were under my sway (Ecclus. 24, 4–6).

In the figure of Sophia as She is proclaimed to us in the Book of Proverbs and Ecclesiasticus this "great sign" of the Apocalypse finds its prophetic and cosmic explanation. A Sophian interpretation of this vision of John's Revelation truly places upon the head of the apocalyptic figure, who represents Mary and the Church, a cosmic crown.

THE DESCENT OF
THE HOLY CITY—NEW JERUSALEM

> I saw the Holy City, new Jerusalem, coming down out of heaven from God, made ready like a bride adorned for her husband. I heard a loud voice proclaiming from the throne: "Now God has his dwelling with mankind! He will dwell among them and they shall be his people, and God himself will be with them. . . ." One of the seven angels . . . spoke to me, "Come," he said, "and I will show you the bride, the wife of the Lamb." So in spirit he carried me away to a great and lofty mountain, and showed me Jerusalem, the Holy City, coming down out of heaven from God. It shone with the glory of God (Rev. 21,2–3,9–11)

The above passage from Revelation also does not speak about Wisdom, yet it too is mentioned because of the associations that can be made to Wisdom-Sophia.

First, it is traditionally understood to refer to the Church ("Now God has his dwelling with mankind"), and the Church can be related to Wisdom (Eph. 3,8-11). But perhaps more importantly, the images of the Holy City and New Jerusalem recall Augustine's designations for "Created Sophia," whom he calls God's City and Dwelling in heaven, Mother Jerusalem and Holy Zion[1] (see chapter 5); and similar to the way in which the Holy City is described as shining with God's glory, in the Old Testament Wisdom is described as an "effluence from the glory of the Almighty" (Wisd. 7,25–26).

It is also important to note that the Holy City is designated as the "Bride of the Lamb." This is an image that is usually applied to the Church; and if one accepts linking the Holy City to Sophia, then it can be applied to Her as well, and parallels Her description in the Old Testament as Yahweh's "Amon" and "Pareda"—the Beloved who shares the throne (Prov. 8,30; Wisd. 8,4). It can be added that the image of Sophia as the Bride also recalls the Cabbala's description of the Schekinah (Sophia) who is the partner in the *Hieros Gamos* or Sacred Marriage[2] (see chapter 9).

CHRIST AND SOPHIA: SIMILARITIES OF EXPRESSION

The boundaries between Sophia and the Logos had began to merge in Greek philosophy and with Philo. As the following chapter will discuss, many Church Fathers and theologians began to identify Christ the Logos with Sophia; and this identification took place, at least in part, on the basis of apparent similarities between New Testament passages about Christ and Old Testament passages about Sophia. It will be helpful to compare some of these texts in order to illustrate the similarity.

---

[1] Augustine, *Liber Meditationum*, XIX, *Patrologiae cursus completus*, J. P. Migne, ed. Series latina (Paris, 1844–1855), vol. 40, pp. 915–916.
[2] Gershom Scholem, *On the Mystical Shape of the Godhead: Basic Concepts in the Kabbalah* (New York: Schoken, 1991), pp. 183–185.

Table 1. Similarities between New Testament (Christ) and Old Testament (Sophia).

CHRIST (THE LOGOS)	SOPHIA
1. He is the image of the invisible God; his is the primacy over all creation (Col. 1,15).	She is . . . an image of his goodness (Wisd. 7,26).
2. In him everything . . . was created . . . through him and for him (Col. 1,16). All things were made by the Logos and without the Logos was not anything made that was made (John, 1,3).	God of our forefathers . . . who made all things by your word and in your wisdom fashioned man (Wisd. 9,11). Her . . . skill made all things (Wisd. 7, 22).
3. He exists before all things, and all things are held together in him (Col. 1,17). In the beginning was the Logos, and the Logos was with God, and the Logos was God (John 1,1).	The LORD created me the first of his works long ago, before all else that he made. . . . I was born when there was yet no ocean, when there were no springs brimming with water (Prov. 8,22, 24). I was at his side . . . his darling and delight (Prov. 8,30). She spans the world in power from end to end, and gently orders all things (Wisd. 8,1). . . . it is given her to live with God (Wisd. 8,3). . . . wisdom, who sits beside your throne (Wisd. 9,4). I am the word spoken by the Most High (Ecclus. 24,3).

Table 1. Similarities between New Testament (Christ) and Old Testament (Sophia) (*continued*).

CHRIST (THE LOGOS)	SOPHIA
4. He is the radiance of God's glory, the stamp of God's very being (Heb. 1,3).	Like a fine mist she rises from the power of God, a clear effluence from the glory of the Almighty . . . She is the radiance that streams from everlasting light, the flawless mirror of the active power of God, and the image of his goodness (Wisd. 7,25–26).
5. In him was life; and the life was the light of humanity (John 1,4). But as many as received him, to them he gave power to become the sons of God (John 1,12).	For whoever finds me finds life and wins favor with the Lord (Prov. 8,35).
6. The Logos was made flesh, and dwelt among us (John 1,14).	She has built an everlasting home among mortals (Ecclus. 1,15). Make your home in Jacob (Ecclus. 24,8). . . . wisdom appeared on earth and lived among men (Bar. 3,14).

The above New Testament texts do seem to show a close similarity between Jesus Christ the Logos and Sophia as She is described in the Old Testament; and it is understandable that on the basis of such texts the impression could arise that the Logos and Sophia were identical. However several points are worth noting.

First, the New Testament texts were composed after the distinction between the Logos and Sophia (the Idea idearum) had begun to become blurred. In fact both Wisd. 9,1 and Ecclus. 24,3, which could be used to support an identity between Wisdom and God's Word, themselves appeared in books that were composed during the time when Stoicism was changing the significance of the Logos concept (see appendices I and III).

Secondly, John specifically identifies Jesus Christ as the Logos (Word) and not as Sophia (Wisdom), despite the fact that Sophia-Wisdom was such a well-known figure in the Jewish tradition. It can also be said that there are important features to John's description of the Logos which do not coincide with how Sophia is portrayed. The Logos *is* God and gives the power to become sons of God (John 1,1 and 12), whereby Sophia is created and makes friends and prophets of God (Prov. 8,22; Wisd. 7,27); and John specifically contrasts the grace and truth brought by Jesus Christ with the Law of Moses (John 1,16–17), whereby the Law is an image of Sophia (Ecclus. 24,23; Bar. 4,1).

A similarity between the Logos and Sophia can be affirmed in the sense of Philo, but not an identity between them.

Understanding Sophia as someone different from the Logos and related to Mary does not represent a breach with Christology, and it may help to illuminate the full significance of Mary's dignity and function.

4

Sophia According to the Church Fathers

THE CHURCH FATHERS HAD inherited a philosophical and religious milieu that was conducive to identifying the Logos with Sophia. Yet this point of view was not unanimous, for some understood Her as the Holy Spirit; and there were other nuanced perspectives about Sophia-Wisdom also. Theodoret (393–466), one of the most significant theologians of the fifth century, wrote:

> There are three Sophias. One through whom we are gifted with understanding, reason and knowledge of what is to be done, through whom we practice art, pursue science and know God; another who is seen in creation; and a third who appeared in our Redeemer which unbelievers call foolishness.[1]

Thus in line with the various perceptions about Wisdom presented in the Old Testament a distinction was made between

---

[1] Theodoret, *Patrologiae cursus completus*, J. P. Migne, ed. Series graeca (Paris, 1857–1866), 3, 171. Theodoret was Bishop of Cyrrhus in Syria and one of the most significant theologians in the fifth century. Translation from German. Further references to *Patrologiae cursus completus, Series graeca*, shall be abbreviated as PG.

Wisdom as a human capacity (but also as a special spiritual capacity presented by God and as a divine attribute of God), Wisdom in creation, and Wisdom as a person identified with the Holy Trinity (either as the Son of God or Holy Spirit).

THE CAPACITY OF WISDOM

Concerning Wisdom's most basic manifestation as the kind of human capacity evident in philosophy and the pursuit of knowledge, Clement of Alexandria (ca. 140–216) writes:

> Philosophy is a form of the practice of wisdom; wisdom is the scientific understanding of things divine, things human, and causes.[2]

Gregory of Nazianz (330–390) indicates that the well-known saying "Know thyself" (*Gnothi seauton*) is a fruit of wisdom: "Wisdom is knowing oneself."[3]

In their commentaries on Isaiah 11,2, Origen (ca. 185–254),[4]

---

[2] Clement of Alexandria, *Stromateis*, John Ferguson, trans. The Fathers of the Church, vol. 85 (Washington, DC: Catholic University Press, 1991), pp. 43–44; PG 8, 721B. According to Clement of Alexandria in Greek philosophy the Logos was preparing Christian revelation. Clement founded a school in Alexandria (ca. 200 C.E.) and was the teacher of Origen. His works are: *Protreptikos, Paidagogos* and *Stromateis.*

[3] PG 36, 200A. St. Gregory of Nazianz was a humanist and poet and was also called the "theologian." He was the most powerful rhetorician of the three Cappadocians (Gregory of Nyssa, his brother Basil the Great and Gregory of Nazianz) and a defender of traditional faith.

[4] Origen was one of the most significant teachers of early Christendom. He was a pupil of Clement of Alexandria and led the Catechumen school in Alexandria and in Caesaria where he died. Origen lived a life of poverty and dedicated himself to the pursuit of knowledge. His best-known work, the *Hexapla*, deals with different versions of Holy Scripture. He also wrote many Biblical commentaries and works against Gnosticism. His systematic work is titled *Peri Archon* or *De Principiis*. Origen was the first one to make significant progress in the development of a theology. He was strongly influenced by Platonism. Some of his ideas provoked controversy. The Cappadocians looked to him to support their own positions and collected his sayings in the famous *Philokalia*.

Cyril of Alexandria (died 444)[5] and Gregory of Nazianz all speak of Wisdom in the special sense of a spiritual capacity given by God. Clement of Alexandria also touches upon this aspect of Wisdom in the following quotation:

> The Apostle had good reason to call God's wisdom "variegated," "working in many forms and many ways" through technical skill, scientific knowledge, faith, prophecy; it shows us its power to our benefit . . .[6]

The Shepherd of Hermas (an apocryphal New Testament book) speaks of Wisdom as a divine attribute of God: "Behold the mightly Lord, who by his invisible power, and with his excellent wisdom made the world."[7] Dionysius the Areopagite (ca. 500) also says: "Divine Sophia knows all in knowing Herself."[8]

WISDOM IN THE TRINITY

Concerning Sophia's personal aspect in relation to the Trinity, Theophilus of Antioch (died ca. 186) understands Her as the Holy Spirit:

---

[5] PG 2, 193B. St. Cyril of Alexandria was a teacher and the Patriarch of Alexandria. He gathered together the teachings of the Church Fathers (especially those of his predecessor Athanasius). According to Cyril, Christ is God and man, a divine Person in two natures. He was a determined opponent of Nestorius and was responsible for Mary's recognition as *Theotokos* (Mother of God) at the Council of Ephesus.

[6] Clement of Alexandria, *Stromateis*, p. 41; PG 8, 717A.

[7] *The Lost Books of the Bible*, "The Shepherd of Hermas," vision I, 28 (New York: Bell Publishing, 1979), p. 199. This work appeared around the middle of the second century C.E. Its "visions" provide insight into the asceticism and penitant practices of the early Church.

[8] PG 3, 869B. Dionysius the Areopagite (the name is considered a pseudonym) exerted a great influence on the mystics and scholastics of the Middle Ages. Dionysius is known for his teaching on the heavenly hierarchies. According to Dionysius, God cannot be known. Dionysius was strongly influenced by Neoplatonism (Plotin and Proclus).

God the Father, who brings forth from Himself before everything else His own inner (endiatheton) Logos with His own Sophia.[9]

Theophilus understands the first three days of creation as an image of the Trinity defined as "God, His Logos and His Sophia"[10]; and in explaining the Genesis passage "Let us make human beings" (Gen. 1,26) Theophilus writes that the words "Let us make" signify God with God's Logos and Sophia.[11]

Irenaeus (died ca. 202) thinks similarly about Sophia, writing: "Begetting and creating (progenies et figuratio), the Son and the Holy Spirit, i.e., the Logos and Sophia."[12] He also interprets the first words of Genesis in the same way as Theophilus, and clearly distinguishes between Sophia and the Logos:

> The Logos and Sophia, the Son and the Spirit, are always together with the Father, and the Father says to them: "Let us make."

> God made everything through His Logos and made everything beautiful through His Sophia. . . . Through His Logos He made everything firm and through His Sophia He brought everything together.[13]

A Christological understanding of Sophia is held by Origen, Methodius, Epiphanius of Salamis, Gregory of Nyssa, Arius and

---

[9] PG 6, 1064C. Theophilus of Antioch was Antioch's fourth Bishop. His best-known work is *Ad Autolycum*. According to Theophilus philosophy leads to Christianity which is "God's Wisdom." He is the first to mention the Trinity and the first to identify Sophia with the Holy Spirit.

[10] PG 6, 1077B.

[11] PG 6, 1081B.

[12] *Patrologiae cursus completus*, J. P. Migne, ed., Series latina (Paris, 1844–1855) vol. 7, 993A. St. Irenaeus came from Asia Minor and was a pupil of Polycarp. He was the Bishop of Lyons and was martyred around 202 c.e. In his work *Adversus Haereses* he set down the fundamentals of Christian teaching and warned of the dangers of false Gnosis (knowledge). He was the first to draw parallels between Adam and Christ, and Eve and Mary. In his teaching on the Trinity Irenaeus refers to the Holy Spirit as Sophia. Translation from the German. Further references to *Patrologiae Cursus Completus*, Series latina, will be abbreviated as PL.

[13] PL 7, 1032B, 1038B.

Athanasius, Sophronius and John of Damascus. Origen (ca. 185–254) writes that: "Christ is the highest Wisdom and the Logos of God, our Father"[14]; Methodius (died ca. 311) and Gregory of Nyssa (334–394) speak of: "God's First-Born Sophia, who created all things"[15]; Epiphanius (315–403) talks of: "The Father's Sophia, the Only-Begotten God Logos"[16]; Sophronius (died ca. 638) adds: "You alone carried in Your bosom the Only-Begotten Wisdom. O Bearer of God"[17]; John of Damascus (ca. 650–750) states: "God's Only-Begotten Sophia, God's Son, overshadowed Her (the Virgin Mary)."[18]

The Christological understanding of Sophia becomes especially common after the Arian controversy (first quarter of the fourth century) whose primary opponents were Arius and Athanasius.

THE ARIAN CONTROVERSY

The following statement of Paul of Samostata (died ca. 272) shows that Sophia had been the focus of unresolved questions during the first Christian centuries:

---

[14] PG 17, 28.

[15] PG 18, 288C; vol. 44, 641A. St. Methodius was the Bishop of Olympos in Lycia. He was influenced by Clement of Alexandria, Origen, and Plato. Drawing on Plato's *Symposium*, he wrote his own famous *Symposium*. Methodius was an active proponent of the ideals of monasticism. St. Gregory of Nyssa was a Church teacher and one of the three Cappadocians (with his brother Basil the Great and Gregory of Nazianz). He taught the divineness of the Logos and Holy Spirit, and defended the Nicean doctrine of *homoousios* (that the Son was of the same substance as the Father). His main work was *Oratio Catechetica Magna*, which treats all of Christian theology. Gregory was influenced by Origen and took over Origen's teaching about the restoration of all of creation (Apokatastasis Panton).

[16] PG 42, 296. Epiphanius of Salamis founded a cloister in Egypt and was its abbot. He opposed Origen, the Arians and worshiping images.

[17] PG 87, 388A. St. Sophronius was the Patriarch of Jerusalem. During the Monothelite controversy he supported orthodox teaching. Sophronius copied sacred manuscripts and composed poetry.

[18] PG 94, 985B. St. John of Damascus was a Church teacher who defended the tradition of faith and Chalcidonian Christology.

If God's Son, Jesus Christ, is the Son and Sophia, why Sophia and why Jesus Christ? Are there two Sons?[19]

The issue became acute through the teaching of Arius (ca. 260–336).[20] He taught that the Logos, the Son of God, is created by the Father and is therefore not identical, but essentially dissimilar in nature to the Father. Athanasius (295–373)[21] opposed this point of view by stating that the Son is begotten of the Father, not created, and is therefore identical to Him in nature. (One of the controversies of the time concerned whether the Son is identical in nature to the Father—*homoousios*; similar in nature—*homoiusios*; different in nature—*heteroousios*; or dissimilar in nature—*anomoiousios*.)

To support his position, Arius pointed to the figure of Sophia. It was generally assumed that She was a person[22], and Arius identified Her as the Logos as had other Church Fathers like Origen before him. But because of the indications that She is

---

[19] PG 86, 139B. Paul of Samosata (on the Euphrates) was the temporary Bishop of Antioch. His Trinitarian teaching was "Monarchian," and he opposed the teaching that the Son was of the same substance as the Father (the *homoousios* position). The Arians often cited him to support their own position.

[20] Arius was a student of Lucianus of Antioch and was ordained to the priesthood in Alexandria by Bishop Alexandrus. He taught that the Son of God is not eternal but created. His teaching was condemned by a synod in Alexandria and later by the Council of Nicea in 325 C.E. Emperor Constantine banished him to Illyria but later allowed him to return. He died in Constantinople in 336. Arianism was widely influential for a time due to the favor of the emperor, especially Constantius (337–361 C.E.). Arianism finally declined due to inner dissention, withdrawal of the Emperor's favor, and consistant rejection on the part of orthodox theologians, such as Athanasius and Pope Liberius. The Council of Constantinople in 381 C.E. brought a definitive end to this turbulent era in Church history which served to clarify doctrine.

[21] St. Athanasius was a Church teacher and the Patriarch of Alexandria. He was committed to establishing the correct form of Trinitarian belief, defended his views against the Arians and was banished several times. His most famous works are: *History of the Arians*, *Discourse against the Arians*, *The Council of Nicea* and *History of the Monks*.

[22] Justinus, *Dial. C. Tryph.* 61,1 PL 6, 613C; Clement, *Protreptikos* in PG 8, 192A; Origen, *Expos. Prov.* PG 17, 185B; *Comm. Joh.* 1,34 PG 14, 89B and C.

created (Prov. 8,22; Ecclus. 1,4,9; Ecclus. 24,9)[23] Arius deduced that the Logos was created.

Athanasius energetically opposed Arius, but not by arguing that Sophia was a separate individuality. He accepted the assumption that She and the Logos were identical, and took on the challenge of proving that Sophia was not created in spite of Scripture's witness to the contrary.[24] Arius writes:

The Son is a creature, essentially dissimilar to the Father.

The Son is created by the will of God before time and before the eons . . . and He was not before He was created.

We have learned and so also we think, that through the will and resolution of the Father the Son existed before time and the eons and that He, before He was begotten or created or determined or established just not was. . . . We are being condemned because we say that the Son has a beginning, while God is without beginning.

The Son was created and established by the Father before the eons He was not before He was begotten. . . . He is not eternal or uncreated like the Father, and also does not have the same manner of being as the Father.[25]

---

[23] "The Lord created me the first of his works long ago, before all else that he made" (Prov. 8,22); "Wisdom was first of all created things" (Ecclus. 1,4); "It is he (Yahweh) who created her (Sophia), beheld and measured her, and infused her into all his works" (Ecclus. 1,9); "Before time began he created me" (Ecclus. 24,9).
[24] See *Des Athanasios' Rede Gegen die Arianer*, Bibliothek der Kirchenvater (Munich: Kosel, 1913), pp. 23 ff., *Bibliothek Ecclesiae Patrum et Scriptorum*, vol. 30 Wien: 1974), pp. 126–127. Translation from German (hereafter abbreviated as BEPES). See also Athanasius, *The Second Speech against the Arians*, PG 25, 433 ff.
[25] Arius, *Thalis*, PG 25, 433B; Arius, *Ekthesis*, BEPES vol. 37, pp. 102 ff; Arius, BEPES 37, p. 95, lines 25–30. This is in a letter written to his friend Eusebius of Nicomedia. Eusebius (died 341 C.E.) was the Bishop of Nicomedia in Syria. He was a pupil of Lucianus of Antioch, had studied with Arius and was influential at the Emperor's court. During the Arian controversy he supported Arius, who fled to him. He was an opponent of Athanasius and led the opposition against the formulas of the Council of Nicea; Arius, *Ekthesis Pisteos*, BEPES 37, p. 103, lines 20–24.

In his speech against the Arians, Athanasius quotes some passages from Arius himself:

> God was not always Father, for there was once (a time) when God was alone and not yet Father . . . the Son was not always, there was once (a time) when He was not. And He was also not, before He existed, before He was there at the beginning of the act of creation. . . . For there was only God alone and not yet the Logos and Sophia. When He then wanted to create us, then He made Someone and called Him Logos and Sophia and Son, in order to create us through Him. . . . There are, he says, two Sophias: the actual One who exists with God; and in this Sophia the Son came into existence, who only because of His participation in Her is called Sophia and Logos. For this (second) Sophia, he says, came about through the (first) Sophia according to the will of God who is wise.[26]

(It is interesting to note that this description of two Sophias, one of which is the Logos, recalls Philo's transfer of functions and attributes from Sophia to the Logos.)

As for Athanasius' own texts, the following passages are especially illuminating:

> [T]he Son of God ought not to be called a creature . . . it is written, "the Lord created me a beginning of His ways, for His works." . . . it is necessary to unfold the sense of what is said, and to seek it as something hidden, and not nakedly to expound as if the meaning were spoken "plainly," lest by a false interpretation we wander from the truth. If then what is written be about Angel, or any other of things originate, as concerning one of us who are works, let it be said, "created me"; but if it be the Wisdom of God, in whom all things originate have been framed, that speaks concerning Itself, what ought we to understand but that "He created" means nothing contrary to "He begat"?

---

[26] BEPES 37, p. 126, lines 15–18.

. . . "He created" does not necessarily signify the essence or the generation, but indicates something else . . . and not simply that He who is said to be created, is at once in His Nature and Essence a creature.[27]

Athanasius tries to prove his assertions by quoting Scriptural passages like "put on the new nature created in God's likeness" (Eph. 4,24). His intention is to show that Arius cannot prove that the expression "He created me" means that Sophia is a creature.

Athanasius then goes on to interpret the expression "He created me" as signifying Christ's human nature and rebukes the Arians for thinking of Christ as a human being:

[A]ccordingly let "He created" be understood, not of His being a creature, but of that human nature which became His, for to this belongs creation. . . . neither His being Framer of all has had any weight with you, nor have you feared His being the sole and proper Offspring of the Father, but recklessly, as if you had enlisted against Him, do ye fight, and think less of Him than of men.

. . . For the Proverbs say "He created," but they call not the Son creature, but Offspring.

For if He is Offspring, how call ye Him creature? for no one says that He begets what He creates, nor calls His proper offspring creatures.[28]

The position of Athanasius is clear, yet still one must ask how he can equate the expression "He created" (Greek: *ektise*) with "He begot" (*egennese*)—i.e., how can "created" be understood in a generative sense? Moreover, Prov. 8,22 speaks not of the Son but about Sophia. Both Arius and Athanasius assume the identity between Sophia and the Logos which is not found in Proverbs.

Despite Athanasius' verbal skill and knowledge of Scripture his orations give the impression that what should be proven

---

[27] Athanasius, *Select Works and Letters*, Nicene and Post-Nicene Fathers, vol. 4 (Peabody, MA: Hendrickson, 1994), Discourse II, chap. xix, 44–45, pp. 372–373; PG 37, 44–45.

[28] Athanasius: *Select Works and Letters*, 46–48, pp. 373–374; PG 37, 46–48.

is already presupposed. He presupposes the identity between Sophia and the Logos; and also presupposes that Sophia is divine and uncreated. Arius, on the other hand, starts with Sophia's createdness, and on the basis of his own presupposed identity between Sophia and the Logos asserts the createdness of the Logos.[29]

IDENTIFYING SOPHIA WITH THE LOGOS

The Council of Nicaea effectively ended the Arian controversy in 325 by condemning Arius' views. Although the primary issue for the Council was preserving Christ's divinity, the assumed identity between Sophia and the Logos was thereby effectively reinforced.

As has been indicated, the tendency to identify them as the same person can be traced from some New Testament texts back to Philo of Alexandria, some Old Testament texts and the changes that took place in the conceptions of Greek philosophy.[30] It seems that the influence of Philo, who was held in high esteem by many Church Fathers, was crucial. By transferring many of Sophia's attributes to the Logos he contributed to the notion that they were identical, even though research has shown that he maintained Sophia's personal independence.[31]

In challenging the identification between Sophia and Jesus Christ the Logos which took place, it can be noted once again that the Gospel of John did not revert to Sophia to ex-

---

[29] The essential dissimilarity of Sophia to God is based on Her createdness. See note 23 above.

[30] A more comprehensive investigation of the origins and reasons for identifying Sophia and the Logos is warranted. See also: Burton Lee Mack, *Logos und Sophia, Untersuchungen zur Weisheitstheologie in Hellenistischen Judentum* (Goettingen: Vandenhoeck & Ruprecht, 1973). This is a thorough work with abundant references. See in addition: Felix Christ, *Jesus Sophia* (Zurich: Zwingli Verlag, 1970).

[31] See: B. Lang, *Frau Weisheit, Deutung Einer Biblischen Gestalt* (Dusseldorf: Patmos, 1975), p. 161 ff; also Johann Gottsberger, "Die Gottliche Weisheit als Personlichkeit im Alten Testament," in the journal *Biblische Zeitfragen*, IX, 1/2, Munster, 1919, pp. 71 ff.

plain the Son of God's nature; he only used the Logos concept. The point is made that John used the Logos to appeal to the Greeks; but this does not explain why he would not also use Sophia, a figure who was thoroughly familiar to the Jewish tradition.

The identification between Sophia and the Logos was developed by the Church Fathers into a theologoumenon (a nonbinding theological statement resulting from an effort to clarify faith) at a time when it was important to articulate the mystery of the Son of God and the Trinity.[32] It is understandable that Sophia seemed to serve this purpose. Yet by identifying Her with the Logos the nature of Her own identity and essence were concealed for centuries[33] and brought confusion to Sophiology.[34] As a result the development of an unambiguous Sophian spirituality has been hindered; and where such practices have appeared they have been burdened with the stigma of heresy and unorthodoxy. It can even be said that the exclusion of Sophiology from official theology left a vacuum within theology which heretical movements consistently tried to fill.[35]

---

[32] See Gerhard Ruhbach and Josef Sudbrack, *Christliche Mystik: Texte aus Zwei Jahrtausenden* (Munich: C.H. Beck, 1989), pp. 215 ff.

[33] Insufficient attention has been paid to Sophia's relation to the cosmos (i.e., to Her functions as the "Arche" or beginning and "Entelechia" or goal of creation) and to Her function as the Mother and Soul of the World. Verses like: "The Lord created me the first of his works" (Prov. 8,2) and "She (Sophia) spans the world in power from end to end, and gently orders all things" (Wisd. 8,1) point to Her cosmological function.

[34] Many Sophia icons in Russia portray Her as an angel-like female figure despite the fact that in such depictions She is usually interpreted as Christ (see Sophia in Russian iconography in chapter 16).

[35] Gnosticism has produced an abundant body of Sophianic speculation. See the Coptic papyrus Berolinensis 8502, which contains three Gnostic works from the fifth century: the *Gospel According to Mary*, the apocryaphal *Gospel of John*, and the *Sophia of Jesus Christ*, in *Die Gnostischen Schriften des Papyrus Berolinensis*, edited by W. C. Till (Berlin: Akademie Verlag, 1955).

See also the Gnostic manuscript: *Pistis Sophia: A Gnostic Gospel*, G.R.S. Mead, trans. (Blauvelt, NY: Spiritual Science Library, 1984) [according to the codex Askewianus and Brucianus].

In the *Gospel According to Phillip* (111, 30–112, 5), Sophia is designated as "Mother of the Angels and Companion of Christ" [in the image of Mary

Great religious spirits and visionaries, however, have always been inspired by Sophia and have tried to unveil Her mystery. It will be the task of the chapters ahead to explore their contributions and so to contribute to the development of a new Sophian spirituality.

﹡

Magdalene] Robert Haardt, *Die Gnosis: Wesen und Zeugnisse* (Salzburg: D. Mouller, 1967), p. 207.

Irenaeus reports about the Sethians who designate Sophia as "Sister of Christ" and "Bride of Christ." The Barbelo Gnostics knew of a "Sophia prounikos" [the word *prounikos* apparently means "Bearer of Burdens"] Irenaeus, *Adversus Haereses*, III, 29 and 30; R. I. Haardt, op. cit., pp. 65, 76. See also his more specific remarks on pp. 307 and 337.

5

Sophia
According
to Augustine

S T. AUGUSTINE[1] (354–430) is the Church Father who occupied himself the most with Sophia. According to him, there are two Wisdoms: "Uncreated Wisdom" (Sapientia Increata) and "Created Wisdom" (Sapientia Creata). In his many references to Wisdom,[2] Augustine is speaking almost without exception about "Uncreated Wisdom" whom he identifies, along with many other Church Fathers, as the Logos Son of God.[3] When he does, however, turn his attention to "Created Sophia" he dedicates profound medita-

---

[1] St. Augustine was a Church teacher and the greatest among the Latin Church Fathers. He was first involved with Manichaeism but converted to Christianity, became a priest and later the Bishop of Hippo. Alongside his pastoral duties, he wrote about theological problems and gathered around himself a monastic community which was the archetype for the founding of other monasteries. As a philosopher and theologian, he played an essential part in the transition from antiquity to the Middle Ages and had a great influence on the philosophy and theology of the Church. By christianizing Neo-Platonism he made it into a useful tool of evangelization; and yet maintained Holy Scripture and tradition as the source of his teaching. The Cappodocians were his model.

[2] Augustine was the Church Father who wrote the most about Sophia in *De Incarnatione Verbi* (PL 42, 1175 ff); *De Civitate Dei* [The City of God] (XI 10, 3 and 24; PL 41,326,3); *De Doctrina Christiana* (PL 34,22 ff); *Confessiones* (PL 32, 831 ff.);

tions and prayers to Her, using images like "heavenly Jerusalem" and "our Mother from above" and relating Created Sophia to the eternity of God and to the temporality of created things.

SOPHIA INCREATA—UNCREATED SOPHIA

In his treatise on the incarnation (*De Incarnatione*) Augustine clearly expresses his Christological understanding of the Sophia who is uncreated:

> Sophia must be understood as God's Logos. . . . Whatever we have said of Sapientia is also true of the Son of God.[4]

Augustine bases this interpretation on the following verses from the Book of Wisdom on which he comments:

> Like a fine mist she rises from the power of God, a clear effluence from the glory of the Almighty. . . . She is the radiance that streams from everlasting light, the flawless mirror of the active power of God (Wisd. 7, 25–26).

He understands these verses in a theogonic sense, interpreting Wisdom as a part of God and not as something created: "This Sapientia is called Only-Begotten because She is Herself the Only-Begotten Son."[5] Further on Augustine continues to emphasize this Wisdom's relationship to Christ: "For this Wisdom is Christ . . . God's Wisdom, who is the only-begotten Son"[6] (an al-

---

and *Liber Meditationum* (PL 40, 915 ff.). The *Lexikon fur Theologie und Kirche* (Freiburg: Herder, 1960), vol. 1, columns 1095 and 1101, indicates that Augustine dedicated himself to Divine Wisdom and that for him the highest stage of Christian life is Wisdom and the loving experience of God and divinity; and yet none of the writings about Augustine speak about his teaching on Sophia.
[3] In identifying Uncreated Sophia with the Logos Augustine quotes primarily Origen's *Peri Archon*, Book 1, chap. 2, and Athanasius' *Contra Arianos* I,9. PL 17, 185B, and vol. 26, 145 ff.
[4] Augustine, *De Incarnatione*, PL 42, 1178.
[5] PL 42, 1178.
[6] PL 42, 1181.

ternative interpretation of Wisd. 7, 25–26 will be discussed later in the chapter).

In his work *De Civitate Dei* (The City Of God) Augustine says the following about Wisd. 7,22 ("In wisdom there is a spirit . . . made up of many parts . . ."):

> [T]he Spirit of wisdom is called "manifold" because it contains many things in it; but what it contains it also is, and it being one is all these things. For neither are there many wisdoms, but one, in which are untold and infinite treasures of things intellectual, wherein are all invisible and unchangeable reasons of things visible and changeable which were created by it.[7]

This is a passage which recalls the Greek conception of the Idea idearum in which is contained the Ideas of all things. The entire cosmos is contained in Sophia by means of Her "treasures of things intellectual" and in beholding them God brings about creation.

In other passages about Sophia which identify Her with the Logos Augustine repeatedly emphasizes that the Genesis verse "In the beginning God created the heavens and the earth" (Gen. 1,1) refers to creation through the Logos: "In the beginning" means: "In the Logos (understood as Sophia) God created the heavens and the earth"[8]; through the Sophia-Logos, His Son, with whom and through whom He created everything, as is said in the Prologue to the Gospel of John: ". . . and through him all things came to be; without him no created thing came into being" (John 1,3).

Augustine seems to have overlooked the fact that understanding the Genesis verse "in the beginning" to mean "in the Logos" leads to a tautology for the first verse of John: "In the beginning the Word (Logos) already was" (John 1,1) becomes "In the Logos the Logos already was." It seems to make more sense

---

[7] Augustine, *The City Of God*, Rev. Marcus Dods, trans. (Edinburugh: T. & T. Clark, 1871), vol. 1, Book XI, 10,3, pp. 449–450; PL 41, 326, 3.

[8] Augustine, *Confessions*, E.B. Pusey, trans. (New York: E.P. Dutton, 1975), Book XII, 28–29, pp. 293–295; PL 32, 836/28–29.

if Gen. 1,1 is understood to refer to creation through Sophia who is not the uncreated Logos but instead a separate, created individuality as She is repeatedly proclaimed in the Books of Wisdom (Prov. 8,22; Ecclus. 1,4,9; Ecclus. 24,9). "In the beginning" then means "God created in and with and through Sophia" (and John's "In the beginning the (Logos) already was" consequently means "With Sophia the Logos already was and the Logos was with God"). Rabbinical commentators have actually explained the first verses of Genesis in this sense.[9] Yet such a viewpoint requires understanding Wisdom in the Old Testament to always refer to a created Sophia.

SOPHIA CREATA—CREATED SOPHIA

For Augustine, Sophia who is depicted in Wisd. 7,25–26, is the uncreated Logos Son of God, and this "Uncreated Wisdom" is eternal, unchanging and unchangeable. The Sophia who is otherwise depicted in the Old Testament, however, is generally to be understood as "Created Wisdom": "because She is not without beginning, namely, She is created."[10] And Augustine has difficulty describing Her relationship to the temporal order. Though She has a beginning and is not eternal like God, She is eternal in Her own way:

> Is not the *house* of God, not coeternal with God, yet after its measure, *eternal in the heavens,* when you seek for changes in time in vain. . . . For that . . . surpasses all extension, and all revolving periods of time.[11]

In referring to Ecclus. 1,4 ("Wisdom was first created of all things") Augustine continues by saying that Created Wisdom participates in God's eternity because She was created "before

---

[9] Compare what is said in the *Zohar*, "Die Thora und die Erschaffung des Menschen" in: Ernst Müller, *Der Zohar, das Heilige Buch der Kabbala* (Dusseldorf: Diederich, 1984), p. 36; see also Targum on Jeremiah 2 and Neofiti on Gen. 1,1.

[10] Augustine, *Liber Meditationum*, PL 40, 915.

[11] Augustine, *Confessions*, Book XII, 22, p. 290; PL 32, 834/22.

everything"; and Prov. 8,22 explains this further by adding: "the first of his works long ago." In effect Augustine is distinguishing between three modes of existence: co-eternal being, the absolute and everlasting eternity of God signifying "simultaneous being and knowing"[12]; participatory eternity; and temporality with its dimensions of space and time.

Augustine also distinguishes Uncreated Sophia and Created Sophia by differentiating between "illuminating light" and "illuminated light" or brightness existing through the light of the sun:

> However just as the illuminating light is differentiated from the illuminated light, so great is the difference between You, the highest, creating Sapientia and that Sapientia which is created.[13]

He also calls Created Sophia a "rational and intellectual mind" (mens rationalis et intellectualis) and "Our Mother Jerusalem who is above and free . . . eternal in heaven" (referring to Gal. 4,26). He again tries to explain Her mode of eternity by repeating that She was the first created long ago and is eternal because there is no time before Her. She was not the beginning in a temporal sense but because of "Her own condition."[14] He also says that She is the "pure and most harmoniously single mind (mens pura, concordissime una), the place of peace of blessed spirits, in heaven and above the heavens indicating that She is the principle of unity and peace (recalling Jacob Boehme's words of praise which also speak of peace in Sophia[15]).

Augustine's subsequent statements are very important because they speak of Created Sophia in an individual and personal way:

> This Sophia is from You, O God, but something quite different from You. Although we do not find temporality in

---

[12] Augustine, *Confessions*, Book XIII, 19, p. 323; PL 32, 853/19.

[13] Augustine, *Liber Meditationum*, XIX; PL 40, 915.

[14] Augustine, *Liber Meditationum*, XIX.

[15] Jacob Boehme, *The Way to Christ* (New York: Paulist Press, 1978) I/50, pp. 61–62.

Her, nevertheless She is able to change, whereby She could turn away from God. But She does not do that, for She is bound to God with a great love. . . . Although She is not equally eternal to You, She is not constrained by transitions in time, and experiences no difference of time and is not extended in time, but instead rests in eternal contemplation of Your being.[16]

The above passage raises the question of whether Augustine understood Sophia as a personification or as an actual person. Clearly he understood Uncreated Sophia as a person (identifying Her as the Logos Son of God), but whether he also thinks of Created Sophia as a person is less clear. He says little about Her in a direct way; and when he does refer to Her he uses phrases like "House of God," "City of God," "Jerusalem," "Our Mother Zion," or "Daughter Zion," which are ambiguous.

Other examples of universal notions that are portrayed in personal terms are the myth of Adam Cadmon,[17] the *Anthropos Macros* who contains all individual human beings and things; the parable of the vine and the branches in the Gospel of John ("I am the vine; you are the branches"—John 15,5); and the mysterious Body of Christ made up of Christ as the head and the faithful as the members (1 Cor. 12,12–28). Teilhard de Chardin similarly spoke of Christ in a universal way defining him as the "Omega Point" or goal of the universe[18]; and Soloviev under-

---

[16] Augustine, *Liber Meditationum*, XIX; PL 40, 916.

[17] Adam Cadmon; see also: *Lexikon fur Theologie und Kirche* (Freiburg, 1960), vol. 10, 564.

[18] See Adolf Haas, *Teilhard de Chardin Lexikon* (Freiburg: Herder, 1971), vol. 2, under "Person," pp. 244 ff. Haas indicates that uniting the universal and the personal is the primary concern for Teilhard who does not think that they are opposed to one another (pp. 246, 251). According to Teilhard, the concepts "personal" and "individual" must not be confused:

What constitutes an individual essence is the fact that it is different from other essences which surround it. What constitutes its "personalness" is the fact that in its deepest nature it is itself (Ibid., p. 249).

How can the individual human personality be saved and how can one think about a Personality of the universe? . . . In order to place at the apex or summit of evolution the possibility and even the necessity of some

stood Sophia as the personal "Hen-kai-pan," or the One and All of humanity and creation.[19] Such examples suggest that Augustine's phrases can be understood to refer to a person, albeit a person of a higher order.

What gives more credence to the hypothesis that Augustine viewed Her as a person is the fact that he attributes personal characteristics, qualities and functions to Her. He says, for example, that though She is changeable She never turns away from God because She is attached to Him with "great love" and rests "in eternal contemplation of His being"; also, that She is a spiri-

---

thing personal that is universal, we have presumed that an ultra-concentration of elements which are personal and human can and must take place in a higher consciousness (Ibid., p. 252).

Let us seek our essential satisfaction in the thought that through our struggles (efforts) we serve a personal universe (Ibid., p. 254). [Translation mine.]

[19] For Soloviev, Sophia was "the personal incorporation of the primary foundations of the world in a feminine form of transcendental beauty." See *Solowjews Leben in Briefen und Gedichten*, Rudolf Muller, trans. (Munich: Rudolf Muller, 1977), p. 23. In this supplementary volume to the German complete edition he says:

Sophia is not only the object of divine activity, as the primordial Cosmos which includes all ideas and created beings in itself; She is Herself an active, living Being who is the spiritual foundation of the world, the Soul of the World, representing nothing other than the first created, undivided, living Creature, the ideal Personality of the world and, above all, of humanity. She is simultaneously the individual and the universal, primordial human being, or (which means the same thing) the individual and universal organism of all of humanity, actually containing in Herself all individual human beings, and in whom every human being as a creature of nature has his or her home and metaphysical roots. She is truly the great Mother of all persons and creatures. K. Pfleger, *Die Verwegenen Christozentriker* (Freiburg: Herder, 1964), p. 86. [Translation mine, tr.]

See also the introduction in Pfleger's book to the chapter "Solowjew" which refers to Edith Klum's *Natur, Kunst und Liebe in der Philosophie Wladimir Solowjews, Eine Religionsgeschichtliche Untersuchung* (Munich: Otto Sagner Verlag, 1965). Paul Florenski says that Sophia is "all of humanity, the higher and complete form (of the world), the living Soul of nature and of the universe" (Florenski, *La Colonne et le Fondement de la Vérité*, Constantin Andronikov, trans. (Lausanne: L'Age d'Homme, 1975), p. 253.

tual nature "who in contemplating the light is light"; and that She is a "blessed, elevated creature, the greatest of all created beings" who is "happy, indeed bountifully felicitous, heaven of heaven, God's dwelling in heaven above the heavens."[20] Thus She is more elevated than all other creatures and spiritual beings such as Angels, occupying a unique position of dignity (God's heaven of heavens).

Calling Her the "rational and intellectual mind of your City, Our Mother, who is eternal" is another clear indication of Her personal nature, for only an individuality that has understanding and reason and is able to exercise intellectual functions. Augustine also says that She is "capable of beholding continually the countenance of God."[21]

In a lovely prayer ("O House, luminous and beautiful") Augustine fervently requests that he "be carried on the shoulders of the Good Shepherd to Her" as if to a comforting Mother.[22] He also speaks of Her in personal terms by saying:

> Therefore may You say, may You ask (O Sophia), that He (God) make me worthy to participate in Your splendor . . . may Your assistance help me . . . may Your holy, pious and most pure prayers stand by me, for in no way could they be ineffectual with God. . . . Driven out of the paradise of joys, I cry in the land of my exile, when I think of You, O Mother Jerusalem, O Holy and Beautiful (Bride) Zion.[23]

All of the various statements cited above combine to give the impression that Augustine also understands Created Sophia as a personal individuality.

In conclusion it can be noted that the expressions "God's City," "Bride Zion," and "Mother Jerusalem" directly relate to the following passage in Revelation:

---

[20] Augustine, *Liber Meditationum*, XIX; PL 40, 916, 915.

[21] Augustine, *Liber Meditationum*, XIX; PL 40, 915, 916.

[22] Augustine, *Liber Meditationum*, XIX; PL 40, 916.

[23] Augustine, *Liber Meditationum*, XIX; PL 40, 916.

I saw the Holy City, new Jerusalem, coming down out of heaven from God, made ready like a bride adorned for her husband. . . . "Come," he (an Angel) said, "and I will show you the bride, the wife of the Lamb. So . . . he . . . showed me Jerusalem, the Holy City, coming down out of heaven from God (Rev. 21,2,9–10).

These passages are usually interpreted to relate to the Church and Mary (who is the Mother of the Church); and by using such expressions to refer to his Created Sophia, Augustine relates Her to the Church and Mary, defining Created Sophia's ecclesiological and Mariological dimensions. The expressions "God's House and City" can also be said to represent an idealized creation, defining Created Sophia's relationship to creation and the cosmos.

INTERPRETING WISDOM 7,25–26

Augustine refers to the verses below from the Book of Wisdom in order to justify the view that "Uncreated Sophia" (*Sophia Increata*) is to be understood as God's Logos:

> For she is a breath of the power of God, and a pure emanation of the glory of the Almighty. . . . For she is a reflection of eternal light, a spotless mirror of the working of God, and an image of his goodness (Wisd. 7,25–26).[24]

He interprets these passages about Sophia to express the process of procreation by the Father and resultingly identifies Sophia with the Logos, who is the Son of God:

> It is to be believed that Sophia was begotten and must be understood as the Word of God. . . . Wisdom who is called the Only-Begotten Son of God . . . our Lord Jesus Christ who is God's Wisdom.[25]

---

[24] From *The New Oxford Annotated Bible with the Apocrypha*, Revised Standard Version (New York: Oxford University Press, 1977).
[25] Augustine, *De Incarnatione Verbi*, Book I, 8, 10, 14; PL 42, 1178, 1179, 1182.

Yet as has been indicated Augustine also speaks of "Created Sophia" (*Sapientia Creata*) who is distinguished from Uncreated Sophia by differentiating between the "light which illuminates, and the light which is illuminated"[26]; and following Augustine many commentators and theologians have continued this distinction between Uncreated and Created Sophia.[27]

Recently, however, some have broken with this tradition and no longer acknowledge any difference between them. They recognize only Created Sophia conceived as an attribute of God and deny Sophia's personal individuality: Lady Wisdom is only an allegorical personification.[28]

Such a nonpersonal understanding of Sophia is also not traditional. Uncreated Sophia has been understood as either the Holy Spirit or the Son of God; and though Augustine did not explicitly understand Created Sophia as a person, he nevertheless referred to Her with personal conceptions ("House of God," "City of God," etc.) and otherwise spoke of Her in personal terms.

The present work supports the point of view of one Sophia who is created and personal but who is not Jesus Christ the Logos; and in order to defend this viewpoint it is important to examine the passages in Wisdom 7,25–26 which are Augustine's basis for identifying Sophia with the Uncreated Logos.

A theogonic interpretation of Wisdom 7,25–26 identifies the source of breath, emanation, reflection, mirror, and image (God) with what is breathed out, emanated, reflected and mirrored (Sophia).

That She is a "breath of the power of God" raises the question, however, of whether the process of breathing, or the

---

[26] Augustine, *Liber Meditationum*, XIX, PL 40, 915.

[27] Practically the entire exegetical tradition throughout the Middle Ages up to modern times. See R. Cornely, *Commentarius in Librum Sapientiae* (Paris: Sumptibus P. Lethielleux, 1910), p. 280; and Andreas Eberharter, *Das Buch Jesus Sirach* [i.e. Ecclesiasticus] (Bonn: P. Hanstein, 1925), pp. 89 ff.

[28] For example in Herbert Haag's *Bibel-Lexicon* under "Weisheit" (Einsiedeln: Benzinger, 1956, column 1701 ff.); *Echter-Bibel* (Wurzburg: Echter Verlag, 1959); V. Hamp, *Einleitung und Kommentar zum Buch der Spruche und zum Buch Sirach* (Ecclesiasticus); and J. Fischer, *Einleitung und Kommentar zum Buch der Weisheit*; and also B. Lang, *Frau Weisheit, Deutung Einer Biblischen Gestalt* (Dusseldorf: Patmos, 1975), pp. 168 ff, in which are contained extensive and valuable references.

breath itself, must necessarily be equated with the breather. It can be said that breath is brought forth or produced by the breather in act of breathing; and that in this case, the relationship of God to Sophia (breath) is a relationship of cause and effect.

The significance of "emanation" in the passage "(She is) a pure emanation of the glory of the Almighty" is less clear. The historical context of the Latin word for emanation (*emanatio*) usually signifies the act of flowing out and not the emanation itself.[29] In addition there are two forms of an emanation: something which flows from a willful source; or a natural physical process which takes place without the willful participation of the source (the sap of plants and the resin of trees). Yet in both cases the emanation is created by a superior source. In the above passage Sophia is this emanation, and the entire tenor of the Books of Wisdom is that She is created by a superior source who is God.

In turn a reflection ("For she is a reflection of eternal light") such as the sun on a window pane does not signify an identity between the source and the image. This verse also can be understood in a "creationist" sense—that the source creates the reflection.

The words "spotless mirror" and "image of his goodness" ("she is . . . a spotless mirror . . . and an image of his goodness") also do not necessarily imply a theogonic significance, for the image that is mirrored is not identical with its source, even if it is allowed that the source is present to some extent in the image.

Consider by way of analogy the expressions "participation in divine nature" (*participtio divinae naturae*) and "kinship' with God" (*filiatio*—sonship or daughtership). They cannot be interpreted in a strict theogonic sense, for one has to remember that participation in divine nature and kinship with God takes place analogously on a human level (*per modum creaturae*, and *per analogiam*). Someone who participates in divine nature experiences something of this nature, but the person cannot be identified with God. Just as expressions like "kinship" do not relate to human beings in a theogonic sense, the symbolic expressions of

---

[29] On the concept *emanatio*, see *Lexikon fur Theologie und Kirche*, vol. 3, column 841.

Wisdom 7,25–26 do not necessarily relate to Sophia in a theogonic sense either.

Faced with the challenge of articulating an understanding of Christ and Christ's relationship to the Father, it is understandable that Church Fathers understood images like those in Wisdom 7,25–26 to signify the Son's generation; but such conclusions were premature. The images can also be understood to refer to an elevated category of creation; and this kind of interpretation preserves the integrity of Sophia's created nature which is different from the Logos. Yet because such a point of view has far-reaching exegetical and theological implications a more thorough investigation is warranted.

In summary it can be said that Augustine's reflections about Sophia undoubtedly served as a stimulus for others to devote themselves to the mystery of Sophia. St. Bonaventure and Nicholas Cusanus occupied themselves with Her.[30] The adoration and love of Heinrich Suso (Seuse) for his "Exalted Lady"[31] recalls Augustine's prayer "O House, luminous and beautiful." His intimations about Sophia's relationship to creation laid the foundation for understanding Her universal dimension which later becomes visible in the works of Hildegard of Bingen, Jacob Boehme, the Russian Sophiologists and Teilhard de Chardin (and will be taken up in the chapters ahead).

---

[30] St. Bonaventure in his *Breviloquium*, Erwin Essei, trans. (St. Louis: Herder, 1947), and Nicolas of Cusa in his treatise *De Venatione Sapientiae*, German/Latin, Paul Wilpert, trans. (Hamburg: F. Meiner, 1964).

[31] Heinrich Suso (Seuse) in his *Little Book of Eternal Wisdom* and *Little Book of Truth*, James M. Clark, trans. (New York: Harper & Row, 1953). He called himself *Ego servulus, ipsa Domina* (I am the servant, She is the Lady) recalling the minnesinger devotion of the Middle Ages. See *The Exemplar: Life and Writings of Blessed Henry Suso*, complete edition, Sister M. Ann Edward, trans. (Dubuque, WI: Priory Press, 1962).

6

Sophia–
Personification
or Person?

THE PREVIOUS CHAPTER addressed the issue of whether Augustine understood "Created Sophia" as a person. However the question of whether Sophia is to be understood at all as a person, or instead as a personification or quality of God, has been the subject of debate and has been variously answered. It is a question which deserves a more in-depth treatment, which first necessitates defining some terms.

PERSONIFICATION, HYPOSTASIS, AND PERSON[1]

The usual understanding of the word "personification" is thinking of or representing something inanimate or abstract as a person. A synonym for personification is allegory. Depicting the earth as "Mother Earth" and representing ideas like harmony, fertility, and love as the goddesses Concordia, Ceres, and Amor are examples of personifications. In this sense "Lady Wisdom"

---

[1] Concerning the words personification, hypostasis, and person, see Alfred Bertholet, *Woerterbuch der Religionen* (Stuttgart: Kroener 1976).

as She is depicted in the Old Testament could be understood as the personification of God's quality of wisdom.

The word "hypostasis" is generally used in religion to refer to a quasi-independent divine or divine-like being who manifests a higher divinity. Examples are the Egyptian Maat and the Hebrew Schekinah, who personify the presence of God. In a more specific theological sense, an hypostasis signifies something personal and individual which is a part of a larger whole, as in the Three Persons of the Holy Trinity.

The word "person," however, signifies a specific individual endowed with reason and free will, who bears the fullness of its spiritual identity independently. In this sense human beings, Angels, and God can all be called persons.

It will also be helpful to say something about the terms "Old Testament" and "Old Covenant." They are Christian designations and presuppose the "New Testament" and "New Covenant," which are understood as fulfillments of the previous revelation (the Jewish tradition refers to its Holy Scripture as the Tenach[2]—the "written teaching" which encompasses the Law, the Prophets, and all the other books).

For Christians, Old Testament revelation represents a veiled prophecy which becomes clarified through the New Testament (thus the phrase: *Novum in vetere latet, vetus in novo patet*—the New is latently contained in the Old, the Old becomes open and accessible in the New).

"Old Testament" exegesis or interpretation is thus by definition "Christian" exegesis. While Jewish exegesis does not interpret Jewish Sacred Scripture on the basis of Christian revelation and teaching, it is necessary for Christian Old Testament exegesis to always bear in mind the Christian perspective on the Old Testament revelation. This distinction is crucial to the discussion of the various commentaries on the figure of Wisdom as She is presented in the Wisdom Books which follow.

---

[2] According to Rabbi Paul Eisenberg in *Alle Meinen Denselben Gott, Lesungen aus den Heiligen Buechern der Weltreligionen*, selected and translated by Heinz Gstrein (Wien, 1981), p. 19.

UNDERSTANDING
WISDOM AS A PERSONIFICATION

Vincent Hamp indicates that Wisdom cannot be considered a personal hypostasis because this would contradict the fundamental monotheistic conception of the Old Testament. He writes:

> A critical review of all Wisdom passages leads to the conclusion that a personal hypostasis in or even next to God beyond a lively, oriental, dramatic personification is no more present than a personal wisdom who is preaching before the gates of the city. . . . As Proverbs 8 indicates, wisdom is introduced as a personified speaker. To consider Her a personal hypostasis goes too far and would contradict the strict monotheistic thinking characteristic to the Old Testament. The roll She plays as divine Wisdom only befits, in all seriousness, the God who is all-wise.[3]

Johann Fischer also interprets Wisdom as a personification, adding that She could not be considered a person in God such as the Logos, with whom She has been identified:

> Wisdom's strong personification (in the Book of Wisdom) is greatly significant, although the opinion that this strongly personified Wisdom is identical to the Logos of John's Gospel cannot be recognized as correct. The author goes no further than a strong personification of Wisdom; She is for him a divine quality or even the nature itself of God, but not an individual person in God.[4]

The above quotes understand Lady Wisdom in an allegorical and poetic sense and reject a personal interpretation. At the most, She might be accepted as a hypostasis in a general reli-

---

[3] *Echter Bibel* (Wurzburg: Echter Verlag, 1959), vol. 4, pp. 418, 568.
[4] *Echter Bibel*, p. 718.

gious sense, which is the understanding conveyed by many reference works.[5]

A. Strobl, a professor of Old Testament exegesis, quotes Hamp and Fischer and takes a position similar to them. He writes:

> . . . it can be said that the author (of the Books of Wisdom) was not thinking of a hypostasis . . . the manner of expression which borders on a hypostasis belongs to God's way of teaching.[6]

Strobl admits that many commentators do understand Sophia as a real person different from God who works independently of God; and he also refers to those who think She is portrayed as a "subsistent being," though he adds that such a description does not remove the veil that mysteriously surrounds Her.[7]

He names Gregory the Theologian, Ambrose, Augustine, Bernhard of Clairvaux, and Bonaventure among those who understood Sophia as a person and the Logos. Strobl remarks, however, that "this conclusion is unreliable"; for if Sophia is a person, then "foolishness," which is also depicted in personal terms in the Books of Wisdom, must be a person, too. He concludes that "Wisdom cannot be a person in or next to God at all!"[8]

UNDERSTANDING WISDOM AS A PERSON

Johann Gottsberger is one commentator who supports understanding Wisdom as a person; and what is especially interesting is his notion that the contours of a personal perception of Wisdom only gradually emerge in the course of the various Wisdom Books.

---

[5] *Handbuch Theologischer Grundbegriffe* (Munich: Heinrich Fries, 1962); Herbert Haag, *Bibellexikon* (Einsiedeln; Benziger, 1956).
[6] A. Strobl, "Die Weisheit Israels," in the encyclopedia *Der Christ in der Welt*, (Ascaffenburg: Pattloch, 1967), p. 12.
[7] A. Strobl, "Die Weisheit Israels," pp. 10, 12.
[8] A. Strobl, "Die Weisheit Israels," p. 444.

In Job She is viewed as a kind of thing which is somehow objectively independent (Job 28, 27ff.). Proverbs takes the first step toward introducing Wisdom as a person, depicting Her as Yahweh's Amon or Darling and the beginning of His works. In Ecclesiasticus She is depicted as the Queen of the universe, ordained by God, whose throne is in the clouds and whose dwelling place is Israel, where She appears as a Teacher who is identified with the Torah or Law. In the Book of Wisdom Her most elevated dignity and function is portrayed—She shares God's throne and chooses from among God's plans. She is the one who fashions creation and is the renewing principle of life which permeates all things. Her intimate relationship to humanity is also shown by depicting Her as Mother, Teacher and Bride of those who seek Her.

Gottsberger writes:

[T]he fragments of the Old Testament story of Wisdom show the growth and development of a personal understanding of Wisdom; at first Her independence is indicated in an almost hesitant manner, but by the end She is fully and clearly recognized as a person.[9]

Referring to Wisdom's description in Prov. 8,22 ff., he writes:

This is a very unique personification of Wisdom which cannot be simply called bold. The personification is so powerfully and sensitively elaborated that most commentators feel compelled to admit that whoever presented Wisdom in this manner had more in mind than a mere abstraction or divine quality or attribute which human beings can ideally participate in. Looked at logically and humbly, a mere personification cannot be absolutely ruled out. However the enthusiasm which is evident here cannot be sparked by empty words but must have a deeper basis. If the words are meant as mere poetry, why does no other concept show such an extended degree of personifi-

---

[9] Johann Gottsberger, "Die Goettliche Weisheit als Persoenlichkeit," in *Biblischer Zeitfragen* IX/1-2 (Munster, 1919), p. 6. Tr: Translation mine.

cation? Others show hints of hypostasization; but there is no other hypostasization in the Old Testament which could distantly compete with our concept of Wisdom.[10]

As for the Proverbs passage about "Lady Foolishness" (Prov. 9,13–18) to which some point in order to justify understanding Wisdom as personification, Gottsberger writes that "the personification of foolishness does not detract from the independence of Wisdom, which is very real."[11]

Ecclesiasticus adds more detail to the picture of a personal Wisdom:

> Here we see Wisdom consciously and independently determining Her path in life and unfolding a manifold activity within the circles alloted to Her. In 24,9, Wisdom's pre-worldly existence is emphasized and it is clear that She appears separate from God and the world. She is created by God (24,9) and He commands Her; She is with Him and external to Him (24,3f.). And thus it makes sense that She is not dependent on human beings. Just as She relates to the works of creation as an individual work among them, She appears amongst peoples and individuals also as an individual personality (24,19 ff.). As in Proverbs, a mere poetic portrayal cannot be absolutely excluded, and several commentators have gone no farther. But the majority have not rejected the impression that it is not quite correct to understand Wisdom merely in a poetic way.[12]

The development of Wisdom's description as person culminates in the Book of Wisdom:

> In Wisd. 6–9, we arrive at the conclusion of the Old Testament's development of an idea which results in under-

---

[10] Johann Gottsberger, "Die Goettliche Weisheit als Persoenlichkeit," p. 28. Tr: Translation mine.

[11] Johann Gottsberger, "Die Goettliche Weisheit als Persoenlichkeit," p. 32.

[12] Johann Gottsberger, "Die Goettliche Weisheit als Persoenlichkeit," p. 45. Tr: Translation mine.

standing Wisdom as a person. The end of this process of development is synonymous with its apex. Those for whom it would be necessary to see this idea developed within the Old Testament cannot deny the impression given in Wisd. 6–9 that Wisdom is a real person.[13]

Gottsberger summarizes the key features of Sophia's personal nature in the following way:

> Where does Wisdom fit as She is depicted in the Old Testament in the conceptual world of theology? Wisdom understood as a person is a mediator between God and the world, Her nature is independent in both directions in spite of the fact that Her nature and activity is closely related to both poles of existence. Her origin in God is mysterious. The level-headed call it creation and others go beyond this and call it emanation. She appears before created time and is close to the existence before time of the One from whom She originated. As creator and co-genitor, She participates in the creation of things. Standing at God's side, She appears to be woven into Divine Providence which constantly preserves the world and guides humanity. Thus can Wisdom be understood. Those who want to name Her with a single word will have to be satisfied with analogies, for Wisdom has no equal. They would have to borrow the Platonic "Idea" from Greek philosophy and put Wisdom aside.[14]

As for specifying more exactly who the person of Sophia might be, Gottsberger is cautious:

> Some commentators think that an independent Wisdom is identical to the personified Word of God. But an ex-

---

[13] Johann Gottsberger, "Die Goettliche Weisheit als Persoenlichkeit," p. 59. Tr: Translation mine.

[14] Johann Gottsberger, "Die Goettliche Weisheit als Persoenlichkeit," p. 60. Tr: Translation mine.

pression that is only occasionally used cannot be interpreted as the personified Word of God.[15]

Although these remarks refer specifically to Wisd. 9,1, it can be
assumed that Gottsberger does not think that an identification
between the Logos and Sophia is justified because he gives no
such indication in his commentaries on the Wisdom Books. As
for the passages in Paul which seem to support identifying the
two, Gottsberger remarks that they are not decisive and unequivocal proofs.[16] And according to him what is important
about the position of the Church Fathers is not the general identification of the Logos with Sophia but that the recognition of
Wisdom's personhood had been irrevocably achieved.[17] Though
he admits that the Wisdom Book texts do not decisively answer
whether She is a personification or person, he argues that when
everything is considered, there are more compelling reasons for
accepting Sophia's personhood than for rejecting it.

Another commentator who understands Wisdom as a
person is Reinhold Stecher. Like Gottsberger, Stecher also rejects
the notion that the depictions of Lady Wisdom and Lady Foolishness can be equated:

> Lady Foolishness and Wisdom must not be understood as
> personifications of equal value. . . . nothing can be validly
> placed along side of (Wisdom's) personification. . . . there
> are no profound speculations attached to the personifica-
> tion of foolishness, nor does she appear again within the
> whole breadth of Wisdom literature.[18]

Stecher notes that Proverbs 8 is generally understood as an indication of Wisdom's participation in creation, which leads to ask-

---

[15] Johann Gottsberger, "Die Goettliche Weisheit als Persoenlichkeit," p. 58. Tr:
Translation mine.
[16] Johann Gottsberger, "Die Goettliche Weisheit als Persoenlichkeit," p. 77.
[17] Johann Gottsberger, "Die Goettliche Weisheit als Persoenlichkeit," p. 78.
[18] Reinhold Stecher, "Die Personliche Weisheit in den Proverbien Kapitel 8," in
Zeitschrift fur Katholische Theologie (Innsbruck: Herder, 1953), p. 414. Tr: Translation mine.

ing whether the composer really imagined Her as an independent person next to God. He notes that other commentators have understood Her in this way, and he poses the question of whether a holy scribe is simply an instrument of revelation or actually initiated into the Scriptural message.[19] He comes to the conclusion that the author of Proverbs could not have accepted Sophia as a person, as this would have contradicted the author's monotheistic belief. He sees further proof of this in the fact that there is no mention of a cultic devotion to Sophia. (Stecher's first assertion, which is the general view of most recent commentators, cannot be refuted; as for the absence of a cult of Sophia, no cults of Angels existed in Judaism even though Angels were clearly recognized.[20])

The line of reasoning that Stecher takes (along with others) implicitly supposes that Sophia is a divine hypostasis or person next to Yahweh, which is a viewpoint that clearly no Israelite could accept. This perhaps explains why many commentators understood Sophia as a personification instead of as a person (though it must be pointed out that understanding Her as a created person eliminates any apparent difficulty).

Though Stecher does not share the opinion that Wisdom is a personification, he proposes a novel alternative view that is more in keeping with traditional Jewish faith—by designating "Wisdom" (Chokmah), "Word" (Dabar Yahweh) and "spirit" (Ruach Yahweh) as "dynamic concepts."[21]

Ultimately, however, Stecher is a proponent of the Christological interpretation of Sophia which has been dominant in traditional theology from Patristic times until the present:

> The figure of a personal Wisdom is the Old Testament's anticipation of the New Testament's revelation of the Logos . . . the Holy Spirit (the inspiration) beholds in the depiction of Wisdom the Verbum Divinum (Divine

---

[19] Reinhold Stecher, "Die Personliche Weisheit in den Proverbien Kapitel 8," pp. 424, 437–438.

[20] See: Herbert Haag, *Bibel-Lexikon*, under "Engel," p. 390 ff.

[21] Reinhold Stecher, "Die Personliche Weisheit in den Proverbien Kapitel 8," p. 446.

> Word). We are assured of this . . . by the clear statements in the New Testament which indicate that Christ has become our Wisdom from God (1 Cor. 1,21, 24, 30) . . . and we want to eschew the idea that a human composer is necessarily initiated into the intentions of the Divine Author and would understand the Trinitarian sense of what he writes.[22]

Though Stecher's last statement can be completely affirmed, this book's point of view is that the apparent similarity between Sophia and the Logos does not mean that they are identical. With Stecher one can also affirm that Sophia is a person, but a *created* person (as stated in Prov. 8,22), which precludes identifying Her with the Divine Logos.

• • •

In summary it can be said that understanding Sophia-Wisdom as a person is legitimate for the following reasons:

1. In Holy Scripture She is proclaimed as a spiritual nature with the qualities, attributes, and functions of a person (such as reason and free will).

2. She is described as a created female who is different from God and who acts independently:

a) with respect to God: She dances before God, advises God, and actively participates in the work of creation with God;

b) with respect to creation: She guides, renews, and rules everywhere with reason, power, and goodness;

c) with respect to humanity: She admonishes, leads, and assists as Mother, Teacher, and Beloved.

(Because She is characterized as independent She must at least be recognized as a dynamic hypostasis in a religious sense, but not as an allegory or personification.)

---

[22] Reinhold Stecher, "Die Personliche Weisheit in den Proverbien Kapitel 8," pp. 450 ff. Tr: Translation mine.

3. The Christian tradition from the Church Fathers to the present has always understood Sophia as a person, even if interpretations have varied (She is understood as the Holy Spirit and the Logos; and some indications relate Her to Mary, the Church, and to all of humanity or creation).

In the chapters that follow many contributions from theologians, saints, mystics, philosophers, and artists will be considered, for they all reflect a personal understanding of Sophia.

PART II

PORTRAITS
AND VISIONS
OF SOPHIA

7

Sophia in Art of the Middle Ages

THE LATIN MIDDLE AGES did not bequeath very many images of Sophia, but the few that do exist possess a vigorous power.

THE CODEX ROSSANUS

The oldest known depiction of Sophia is found in the Codex Rossanus, a sixth-century Biblical manuscript from the Italian town of Rossano in Calabria which is kept in the library of the Arch Bishop.[1] The person depicted in figure 1 (page 94), who is Mark the Evangelist's source of inspiration (She is touching the manuscript on which he is writing), is generally interpreted as Sophia.

---

[1] See: Fairy of Lilienfeld, "Frau Weisheit in Byzantinischen und Karolingischen Quellen" in *Typos, Symbol und Allegorie bei den Oestlichen Vaetern und Ihren Parallelen im Mittelalter*, Internationales Kolloquium Eichstatt 1981 (Regensburg, 1982), pp. 156, 160, and the picture (Codex Rossanus) and references.

Figure 1. Sophia appears to St. Mark the Evangelist. Tracing by Maria Brandhofer. Codex Rossanus.

THE CODEX SYRIACUS

The Codex Syriacus in the National Library of Paris is another ancient Biblical manuscript (from either the seventh or eighth century) which contains an interesting image of Sophia. Sophia is depicted in a royal garment with a blue veil. She is standing to the right of Mary the Mother of God, who is holding an image of the Christ Child, and King Solomon stands to the left of Mary. Sophia is holding a crosier (a staff with a cross on top) and both Sophia and Solomon have books in their hands (figure 2, page 95).

Fairy of Lilienfeld rejects (justifiably) the customary interpretation which speaks of a depiction of Sophia and King

Figure 2. Sophia,
Solomon, and Mary
with the Christ Child.
Codex Svricus, sixth
or seventh century.
Bongers
Recklinghausen.

Solomon as the two authors of the Books of Wisdom.[2] In her
view, Sophia and Solomon relate typologically to Mary and the
Christ Child, but she interprets Sophia Christologically as a pre-
figuration of Jesus Christ. However for such an interpretation
the significance of Solomon remains unclear.

An alternative interpretation is that Sophia relates to
Mary and Solomon to Jesus Christ.

Understanding Solomon as a symbolic depiction of the Son
of God is not inappropriate, for parallels exist in the ancient world
and in Scripture.[3] In ancient Egypt, Sumeria, and Babylon the king
was considered the adopted son of God; and in Holy Scripture
King David is referred to as God's son ("I shall be a father to him,
and he will be my son"—2 Sam. 7,14). Solomon himself was called
"Jedidiah" or God's favorite (2 Sam. 12,25) and is thus an appropriate symbolic figure for the Son of God or the Logos.

---

[2] Fairy of Lilienfeld, "Frau Weisheit in Byzantinischen und Karolingischen
Quellen," p. 159.
[3] Manfred Lurker, *Woeterbuch Biblischer Bilder und Symbole* (Munich: Kosel,
1973), pp. 294 ff.

Holy Scripture portrays Solomon taking Sophia as his Bride (Prov. 8,2 and 9); and a New Testament parallel to this idea can be seen in the descent of the Holy City Jerusalem as the Bride of the Lamb (Rev. 21,2, 9–10). The image of the Holy City is traditionally related to the Church (and to Mary as the Mother of the Church); however this image also relates to Sophia, for Augustine calls Her "God's City" and "Mother Jerusalem."[4] The relationship of Sophia to the "Hieros Gamos" or Sacred Marriage will be taken up in chapters 9 and 25.

Thus this Syrian miniature can also be interpreted as a depiction which relates Sophia to Mary.

SOPHIA AND BOETHIUS

This portrayal of Sophia with Boethius (480–524) in prison is thought to have been made in St. Alban's Abbey in England around the 12th century. It is kept today in Oxford's Bodleian library.

Sophia is dressed in royal clothing and wears a crown. With Her right hand She instructs Boethius (the index finger is disproportionately long) and in Her left hand She appears to be holding a seed from which a three-leafed flower blossoms up on a long slender stem. Boethius[5] holds a book in one hand; the other hand is close to his ear (figure 3, page 97). He wrote of this experience in jail in 524:

> It seemed as if a dignified-looking woman appeared to me; Her eyes sparkled and Her gaze was more penetrating than is usual with people; Her face glowed with life, unwithered in its power of youth, yet at the same time

---

[4] Augustine, *Liber Meditationum*, XIX; Patrologiae cursus completus, J. P. Migne, ed. Series latina, (Paris, 1844–1855), vol. 40, 916. Further references to this volume will be abbreviated as PL.

[5] Boethius was a theologian, philosopher and statesman. See: Gunter Stemberger, *2000 Jahre Christentum* (Salzburg: Andreas, 1983), p. 252, and the picture and references.

Figure 3. Sophia visits Boethius in prison. Book illustrations from the 12th century. Andreas & Andreas, Salzburg.

She seemed aged; no, one could not believe that She belonged to our time. Her stature could not be clearly distinguished; for at one moment She was not larger than normal, but at the next the crown of Her head seemed to reach up towards heaven. Had She lifted Her head still higher, She would have towered up to heaven itself, and one would have gazed after Her in vain.[6]

THE HILDESHEIM MISSAL

Famous codices and missals appeared in the *scriptoria* (writing rooms) of older Orders like the Benedictines, and newly formed reform Orders like the Cistercians and Praeminstratens when book illustration was flourishing during the 12th century. The Hildesheim missal is one example, and it contains an impressive miniature of Sophia that bears witness to the Sophian stream that existed in the Middle Ages.

The missal comes from St. Michael's in Hildesheim and is now in the possession of the estate's executor, Graf Egon von Furstenburg-Stammheim, in Cologne-Muehlheim. See figure 4, page 99. Albert Boeckler describes the missal's miniature in the following way:

Sapientia as "Creatrix" of the world. She carries a bust of God and on Her scarf is the inscription: "I created the world with Him." Persons from the time of the Old Covenant are shown on both sides of Her who point to Christ. In creating the world Divine Wisdom also takes into account the plan of redemption.[7]

Wisdom (Sapientia) is royally dressed and wears a mason's crown which symbolizes Mother Earth and the "polis" or city

---

[6] Boethius, *Consolatio Philosophiae*, chap. 1, PL 64; Eugen Biser, *Christus und Sophia, Die Neuentdeckung Jesu im Zeichen der Weisheit* (Augsburg: Katholische Academie, 1987), p. 40. Tr: Translation mine.

[7] Alfred Boeckler, *Deutsche Buchmalerie in Vorgotischer Zeit* (Koenigstein im Taunus: K.R. Langewiesche, 1976), picture p. 53 and text p. 79. Tr: Translation mine.

Figure 4. Hildesheim Missal Miniature. From Albert Boeckler, *Deutsche Buchmalerei in vorgotischer zeit,* *Koenigstein/Taunus.*

(i.e., the civilized human community). She is holding up a bust of the Logos, or from another point of view, She is receiving the Logos and presenting Him to humanity (She is connecting the world and humanity with God as the bridge and way to the Logos and God).

The figures next to and beneath Her symbolize redemption, i.e., the plan to redeem and divinize humanity and the world. Many of them can be identified by the banners that they carry. The banner: "In your offspring all nations will be blessed" (*In semine tuo omnes gentes benedicentur*—Gen. 22,18) identifies Abraham. "The fruit of your body I will set on the throne" (*De fructu ventris tui ponam super sedem*—Ps. 132,11) identifies David. The prophet Bileam is identified by the verse: "A star will come forth out of Jacob" (*Orietur stella ex Jacob*—Num. 24,17); and the verse from Isaiah: "Behold the Lord of Hosts will come" (*Ecce veniet Dominus exercituum*—Is. 3,1) probably identifies the prophet Isaiah. The central figure in the lower portion of the picture is most likely Zechariah, whose banner reads: "The one who comes with the dawn from heaven has visited us" (*Visitavit nos oriens ex alto*—Luke 1,78). To the left of Zechariah is apparently Matthew the Evangelist whose banner reads: "Behold, God himself will come who incarnates" (*Ecce veniet Deus et Homo*). The banner on the right is undecipherable (perhaps the young man carrying it is John the Evangelist). Under Zechariah is the Patriach Jacob.

All of these figures point to Christ, i.e., to the incarnation of the Logos Son of God. What, however, is the significance in this composition of "Sapientia," Holy Wisdom, who is entirely surrounded by these Biblical figures that point to the incarnation of the Logos?

The answer to this obvious and essential question lies in the well-known fact that in Eastern liturgy and iconography, and then through its influence in the Byzantine-Russian and Roman-German Church of the Middle Ages, Holy Wisdom was understood to be intimately related to Mary. On Marian feast days, for example, the readings were taken from the Wisdom Books of the Old Covenant. Our ancestors intuitively sensed the close and essential connection between Sophia and Mary which is the basis of the Russian Sophia icons in particular. The Russian Sophiologists, especially Soloviev and Florenski, later tried to theologically articulate this deep conviction of the people with the concise formulation: *Sophia appeared in Mary, Sophia became human in Mary.*

Compare what the Russian Sophiologist, Father Paul Florenski, says about Sophia in describing the Novgorod Sophia icon which is a faithful copy of the original in Constantinople:

> There can be no doubt that a religious unity between
> Sophia and Mary the Mother of God exists which is ex-
> pressed in liturgical practice and in religious devotion. . . .
> It is proven that Sophia is Mary the Mother of God. . . .
> Again and again, Mary the Mother of God is Sophia . . .
> the saints adored in Mary the Mother of God the Bearer of
> Sophia, the visible appearance on earth of Sophia Herself,
> and felt that Her (Mary's) dignity and nature has its basis
> in Sophia.[8]

Paul Florenski is thereby formulating the ancient Sophia teaching and devotion of the Eastern Church (he died for his faith in a
Siberian concentration camp).

Beginning with such theological presuppositions, which
somehow also found their way into the Western Church or at
least were felt afterward, and which are possibly the basis for the
Hildesheim Missal miniature, we can proceed to the correct interpretation of this unique, Western icon of Sophia.

The Logos and Sophia are depicted in their *pre-incarnational* existential forms. Sophia's scapular states: "I created the
world *with Him*"—a clear reference to Prov. 8,22 which reveals
Sophia in Her pre-existential, aeonic existence. The figures and
their banners, however, point to the *incarnational*, salvational
destiny and mission of the Logos within time and therewith of
Sophia also. The Logos takes on human form from the Virgin
Mary. Why, then, is not Mary but Sophia depicted? Because
Mary's basis is in Sophia; because She is Sophia in human form,
the incarnated Sophia. Sophia incarnated in Mary and from
Mary the Logos took on flesh, i.e., human nature. The incarnation of Sophia in Mary and of the Logos from Mary are the presuppositions for justifying and understanding the figures and
the contents of their banners. They all point to Christ who was
promised as Abraham's and David's descendant, who according
to Isaiah would be born from a virgin (Is. 7,14) and who was introduced by Zacharias and his son John the Baptist as the one to
come and proclaimed by the Evangelists Matthew and John as

---

[8] Pavel Florenski, *La Colonne et le Fondement de la Vérité*, chapter 10 "Sophia,"
pp. 351–388, quoted from Nikolai Bubnoff and Hans Ehrenberg, *Ostliches Christentum* (Munich: C.H. Beck, 1925), pp. 22–194. Tr: Translation mine.

the Son of Man (the Son of Abraham, David and Mary—Matt. 1,1-2, 12) and the Son of God (John 1,1–18).

Sophia and the Logos are shown on this image as two clearly separated figures who are, however, connected in a most intimate vertical unity. A clear distinction is made between Sophia and the Logos and between Christ and Mary. This clearly contradicts the difficult-to-understand opinion of some Church Fathers (for example Athanasius) according to which Christ is understood as the incarnated Sophia. Such a Christological interpretation and transformation of Sophia's function, which was a reaction against Arianism, has contributed greatly to unclarity and confusion with respect to theological knowledge about Sophia. Fortunately the sense of faith (*sensus fidei*) of the Christian people intuitively understood in the Sophia churches and icons the correct significance of this secret and carried it through the ages; namely, the most apparent and best intelligible Christian interpretation: Sophia has an individual, personal, created-before-all-time and therefore pre-existent stature, the Bride of the Logos. In order to execute the plan of salvation She incarnated in Mary, from whom the Logos then incarnated. Just as both, Sophia and the Logos, were intimately connected before time, so, too, were they in time as Christ and Mary, and will be inseparable for all of eternity.

On the basis of its theological statement, this *Sapientia* miniature of the Hildesheim Missal belongs to the clearest and most impressive Sophia images that are known. Though its artistic value does not compare with the Russian Sophia icons, the Sophiological meaning is clearer and more unequivocal than its Russian sisters.

SOPHIA—QUEEN OF THE SEVEN LIBERAL ARTS

This is a depiction from around the 12th century of Sophia as the Queen of the Seven Liberal Arts. Herrad von Landsberg put it in his famous *Hortus Delicarium* (Garden Of Delights).[9] Sophia is

---

[9] E. Neumann, *The Great Mother: An Analysis of the Archetype*, Ralph Manheim, trans. Bollingen Series XLVII (Princeton: Princeton University Press, 1955, 1963), plate 165.

sitting on a royal throne in the center of the picture surrounded by the Seven "Artes Liberales" or Seven Liberal Arts. See figure 5, page 104. Three small heads protrude from the top of Her own head, and She holds a banner with the inscription: "All Wisdom is from God, and only those become wise who yearn for Her." A stream of water pours from each of Her sides. Beneath Her are the philosophers Plato and Aristotle. The Seven Liberal Arts—Grammar, Rhetoric, Dialectics, Music, Mathematics, Geometry, and Astronomy—are depicted as women and positioned around Her inner circle.

The three heads protruding from Wisdom's head are designated as "Ethica," "Logica," and "Philica." Some understand them to represent the inclusion of the more elevated subjects of theology, law, and medicine within the circle of the Seven Liberal Arts of philosophy (represented by Wisdom). However they can be understood to represent the three higher functions of Wisdom: logic and rational knowledge; love or the affective experience of valuing what is known; and ethics or the commitment to recognized values and their realization.

This kind of viewpoint suggests a holistic understanding of what Wisdom is and what Sophia as Wisdom effects. Wisdom is an amalgam of logical knowledge, heartfelt experience and decisive commitment, which combine to form a harmonious and unified whole. Concord between intelligence (Logica), feeling (Philica) and will (Ethica) are the fruits of Wisdom.

The two streams of water pouring forth from Her sides symbolize the "water(s) of wisdom" (Ecclus. 15,3)—the life and vivifying strength that She gives to those who revere Her. Socrates and Plato represent the "philosophers," or friends of Wisdom, who are under Her guidance and inspiration.[10] The Seven Liberal Arts surrounding Wisdom point to Her role as Mother of the arts and sciences. This is an aesthetically pleasing portrait that is able to concretely convey a wealth of insight into the identity of Wisdom.

---

[10] Socrates and Plato also represent polar streams in philosophy, the one more rational, the other more intuitive, etc.

Figure 5. Sophia—Queen of the Seven Liberal Arts. From Erick Neumann, *The Great Mother: An Analysis of an Archetype*, Ralph Manheim,
trans. Bollingen Series vol. 47 (Princeton: Princeton University Press,
1964), plate 165, "Philosophia Sophia," from the 12th-century manuscript *Hortus deliciarum* of Herrad of Landsberg.

SOPHIA—THE NOURISHING MOTHER

The inscription at the top of this picture: "This is a depiction of
Wisdom" (*Hic depingitur imago Sapien(ti)ae*) explicitly identifies
Sophia as its subject.[11] See figure 6, page 105.

Sophia is presented as a royal Lady seated on a throne
under a canopy. She wears a broad cloak that is lined with a lux-

---

[11] E. Neumann, *The Great Mother*, plate 174, Sophia-Sapientia.

Figure 6. Sophia—the Nourishing Mother. From Erich Neumann, *The Great Mother: An Analysis of an Archetype*, Ralph Manheim, trans. Bollingen Series, vol. 47 (Princeton: Princeton University Press, 1964), plate 174. "Sophia-Sapientia," from a medieval Italian manuscript.

urious ermine fur. Her arms are around two kneeling men who suckle from Her breasts. The image recalls the Old Testament passages:

> She will come out to meet him like a mother; she will receive him like a young bride. For food she will give him the bread of understanding and for drink the water of wisdom (Ecclus. 15,2–3).

> Lord . . . you give them to drink from the streams of your delights (Ps. 36,5,9).

The Lord effects this through Sophia the Mother. The two men can be understood to represent the wise of the Old and New Testaments, or the wise of the Judao-Christian tradition and the other religious traditions. They portray the family that rests at Sophia's maternal bosom and is nourished by Her milk. Both are clasping hands, indicating the close connection between all of Sophia's children.

SOPHIA PAREDRA—
YAHWEH'S THRONE COMPANION

This portrayal of Sophia, from around 1400, is found in Guyart des Moulins' *Historical Bible* in the Royal Library of Brussels.[12] Sophia is seated on an overly-large throne that is meant for two persons (see color Plate 1, page 109). She is dressed in blue with a royal purple cloak lined with white ermine fur and wears a crown on Her head. In Her left hand She holds a lily scepter, and in the right hand, a banner with the inscription: "I was formed in earliest times at the beginning" (*Ab initio et ante saecula creata sum*—Prov. 8,23).

This is an image which directly relates to Wisdom 8,3 and 9,4 which speak of Sophia living with God and sharing God's throne; and when Proverbs 8,22–30 is also considered, then it is clear that something important is being expressed: Sophia is

---

[12] Gunter Stemberger, *2000 Jahre Christentum*, p. 116, picture and text.

Yahweh's Beloved who participates in the work of creation, ruling together with Him.

THE ALTAR OF GHENT

The Altar of Ghent was created around 1432 by Jan van Eyck, and has been called "the greatest masterwork of Old Netherlands art."[13] It is a work that bears witness to the fact that in those times Mary's relationship to Sophia was understood. The illustration, Plate 2, has been reproduced in color on page 110.

The middle portion of the altar is divided into two parts. The lower portion depicts the veneration of the Lamb of God and above are the figures of God the Father (or Jesus Christ as King and Pantocrator) with Mary and John the Baptist.

Mary is royally dressed in a wide blue cloak and wears a radiant crown. In Her hand She is holding a book and above Her head are the words:

> She (Sophia) is more beautiful than the sun. . . . Compared with the light of day, she is found to excel (Haec [Sapientia] speciosior sole—Wisd. 7,29).

The juxtaposition of this verse about Sophia with the figure of Mary is a telling indication of the mystery of their relationship.

---

[13] *Das Grosse Lexikon der Malerei* (Braunschweig: Westermann, 1982), p. 204.

PLATE 1 □ 109

Plate 1. Sophia Paredra—Yahweh's throne companion. From Guyart des Moulins, *Bible Historiala*. Andreas & Andreas, Salzburg.

Plate 2. The Ghent Altar (middle portion), Jan van Eyck, 1432. Westermann Braunschweig.

PLATE 3 □ 111

Plate 3. The Cosmiarcha, Co-Creator and Mother of the World and Humanity. From the *Book of Divine Works*, Vision 2. Otto Mueller Verlag, Salzburg.

Plate 4. Sophia Mary—Icon of the Holy Spirit. From the *Book of Divine Works*, Vision 9. Otto Mueller Verlag, Salzburg.

PLATE 5 □ 113

Plate 5. Sophia with the Law Tablets. From the *Book of Divine Works,*
Vision 10. Otto Mueller Verlag, Salzburg.

Plate 6. Sophia Wisdom and Her Seven-Pillared Temple of Virtues.
From *Scivias*, Vision 9. Otto Mueller Verlag, Salzburg.

PLATE 7 □ 115

Plate 7. Sophia Mary with the Lamb of God—Mother and Bride of the Lamb. From the *Book of Divine Works*, Vision 1. Otto Mueller Verlag, Salzburg.

Plate 8. Sophia Mary—Bride of Christ and Mother of the Church. From *Scivias*, Vision 3. Otto Mueller Verlag, Salzburg.

PLATE 9 □ 117

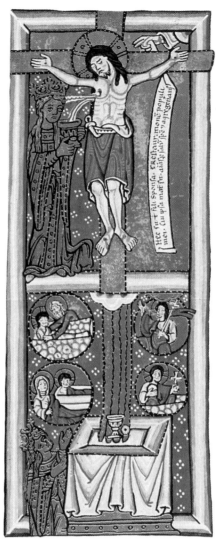

Plate 9. Left: The Holy Spirit and Sophia Mary as Mother of the Church; Right: Sophia Mary as the Co-Redemptrix and Mediator of Graces. From *Scivias*, Visions 4 and 6. Otto Mueller Verlag, Salzburg.

Plate 10. Sophia-Mary—the Omegarcha of Creation and the Church. From *Scivias*, Vision 5. Otto Mueller Verlag, Salzburg

PLATE 11 □ 119

Plate 11. Detail from Michelangelo's "The Creation of Adam." Herbig, Munich.

Plate 12. Isenheim Altar Tabernacle Picture (middle panel, left side). Matthias Gruenewald. Musee de Unterlinden, Colmar.

PLATE 13 □ 121

Plate 13. Isenheim Altar Tabernacle Picture (detail). The "Blue Lady" within the Aureole. Primordial Sophia beholds the Logos becoming human. Inspired, She flies down to Earth. From Emil Spath, *Geheimnis der Leibe: Die Isenheimer Altar von Matthias Gruenewald*, Freiburg: Edition Muensterturm, 1991, p. 48.

Plate 14. Church of Maria de Victoria. Inside ceiling fresco. C. D. Asam. Top left corner: a beam of light descends from God the Father and is reflected by a woman to Mary. Schnell & Steiner, Munich.

PLATE 15 □ 123

Plate 15. Church of Maria de Victoria. Ceiling fresco (detail). The Annunciation. Mary is depicted as a life-giving spring (see also the Russian icon, "The Mother of God, the Fount of Life" in chapter 17. A ray of light descends from above, via Mary, to the Queen of Saba (on the right) and to Pallas Athena (on the left). C. D. Asam. Schnell & Steiner, Munich.

Plate 16. Entrance hall mural in the Loreto Church in Birkenstein (central portion). Schnell & Steiner, Munich.

Plate 17. Novgorod Sophia Icon. Sophia's color is indigo red, the color with which She is portrayed in both East and West. In the East, the Angel with the fire-red face is also called "the Angel of Good Counsel," similar to Mary's appellation in the West as "Mother of Good Counsel." According to the Church Fathers, the "Good Counsel" or *Euboulia* is the loving God's *entire* resolution and plan for creation's salvation, which is very nicely realized personally and visibly in Mary. Alkannin Museum, Recklinghausen, Germany.

Plate 18. Stroganov Sophia Icon. Alkannin Museum, Recklinghausen,
Germany.

Plate 19. Apsis and Iconostasis. Sophia Cathedral in Kiev (1032).
Patriarchat, Moscow.

Plate 20. Apsis Mosaic. Sophia Cathedral in Kiev (1032).
Patriarchat, Moscow.

Plate 21. Russian Icon. The Mother of God, the Fount of Life. From
Tausend Jahre Marienverehrung in Russland und in Bayern. Munich:
Schnell & Steiner, 1988, p. 87.

Plate 22. Sophia—God's Wisdom. "Wisdom Has Built a House." Kiev, 19th century. Patriarchat, Moscow.

Plate 23. The Mother of God of Vladimir. Patriarchat, Moscow.

Plate 24. Icon of the Mother of God. "Mary Protectress." Mary is standing in the middle of the heavenly and earthly Church, surrounded by the saints, in particular those who are venerated in Russia. Beneath Her is St. Romanus, a composer of hymns, to whom the "Akathist Hymn" (appendix IV) is ascribed.

Plate 25. Arya Tara—the Noble Tara. Rhein Verlag, Zurich.

Plate 24 (cont'd). At the bottom right is St. Andreas, the "fool for Christ's sake." He understands the unity between heaven and earth, and points this out to his pupil. At the far right, Mary appears to St. Romanus the Melodist and teaches him the Marian song "Axion Estin." Patriarchat, Moscow.

Plate 26. Mother Earth (Rumanian). This image of Mother Earth is from Rumania and was conceived according to Marxist ideology: Mother Earth brings forth the earth and its products from herself. Because of its symbolism, however, this image can be more deeply understood as a symbolic representation of Sophia in Her role as the Mother of the cosmoś, who is the basis and the ideal for "Mother Earth" and "Mother Nature." Monsignor Rauch, Ostkirchliches Institut, Regensburg.

PLATE 27 □ 135

Plate 27. Prayer for Peace, Assisi, October 26, 1987. Pope John Paul II and representatives of the World Religions. Photo.

Plate 28. Mary's Coronation. Depicting the Trinity together with Mary's Coronation is a frequently occurring theme in traditional Christian art. Mary represents the entirety of the Trinity's plan of salvation, from creation's beginning to its perfection. Mary and the Holy Spirit are always vertically connected, which is very nicely portrayed here by the aureole that they share. Dieric Bouts. Westermann Braunschweig.

PLATE 29 ☐ 137

Plate 29. Mary's Dormition and Assumption. Modern icon. Anton Wollenek, private collection.

Plate 30. Mary's Dormition and Assumption (Coptic). Aries Verlag, Munich.

PLATE 31 □ 139

Plate 31. Trinity Icon (Russia, 19th century). An angel with the figure and color (indigo red) that is typical for Sophia is included in the circle of the Trinity. This angel is often called the "Angel of Good Counsel," which means the good resolution (*Eubolia*) of God's *entire* salvational work with God's beloved creation, from creation's beginning to its perfection. Aries Verlag, Munich.

Plate 32. Mary is depicted amid symbols for the cosmos and the world religions. Harald Reitterer, after a picture in the Church of Mary, Eben-Maurch, Lake Achen, Tirol: "Lady of all Nations."

8

Holy Wisdom According to Hildegard of Bingen

HILDEGARD OF BINGEN was born in 1098 (apparently in the German town of Bermersheim). She was taught by Jutta, the Mother Superior of the Benedictine convent on Mt. Disibode, and succeeded her as leader after Jutta's death in 1136. Between 1147 and 1150 Hildegard founded a cloister on Mt. Rupert in the vicinity of Bingen, and in 1165 another one in Eibingen near Rudesheim.

She experienced visions which began in her childhood. She was chronically ill, but still undertook major journeys to Cologne, Trier, and southern Germany in order to hold Lenten sermons. Her many letters indicate that she was an adviser to popes, bishops, and princes, as well as to people of every class. In her works she writes of the soul's mystical path of ascent by means of contemplation and suffering. Considering the time in which she lived, Hildegard possessed an astonishing knowledge of medicine and the sciences. She died at the ripe age of 81 on September 17, 1179 on Mt. Rupert. Her remains are found in the former cloister church at Eibingen.

Her most significant written works are: *Scivias* (Know the Ways), *Liber Vitae Meritorum* (Book of Life's Merits) and *Liber Divinorum Operum* (Book Of Divine Works). They contain a record of her visions pertaining to religious, scientific, and medical subjects, which she was accustomed to behold in a paranormal light. St. Hildegard is renowned for her cosmic vision of the world which is portrayed in profound and significant symbolic images. Hildegard herself provided lengthy commentaries to these symbolic images, which were illustrated by skilled craftsmen; although her commentaries were naturally made according to the level of her understanding. Thus there is much in her images that lies hidden, which a modern-day knowledge of symbols (symbology), supported by psychology and the science of religion, is able and ought to recognize and explain in a more comprehensive way.

One such discovery appears to be Hildegard's Sophian world conception. She sees the universe as a cosmos that is ensouled and directed by an extraordinarily wise power. Several times she expressly names this power "Wisdom" (Sophia). She presents visions and images in which it seems that Sophia is clearly meant and portrayed, alone as well as in relation to God, Jesus Christ, the Church, creation, or even to the individual human in his or her being, activity, purpose, and goal.

THE SOPHIA PICTURES OF ST. HILDEGARD

St. Hildegard of Bingen, who was intuitively and mystically talented in an extraordinary way, was also strongly affected by the Sophian stream coming out of the Eastern Church which we have already seen expressed in the Hildesheim Missal (chapter 7). She consequently lent strength and depth to this stream, and infused it with grandiose theological and cosmological relationships through her Sophian visions and images. Long before Jacob Boehme (chapter 11) and Vladimir Soloviev (chapter 15), she illustrated and presented the mystery of Sophia through an archetypical symbolism and cosmological breadth of vision. Unfortunately this Sophian background to her visions has not been sufficiently acknowledged, and as a result, the interpretation of her pictures has remained fragmentary and unsatisfactory in essential points.

The most powerful of her Sophian depictions will be presented from the two works *Scivias* (*Know the Ways*) and *Book of*

Divine Works (*Liber Divinorum Operum*). Several pictures represent Sophia from an Old Testament point of view as "Chokmah Yahveh" (Yahweh's Wisdom), i.e., the Co-Worker at creation and the Mother and Soul of the World. Others present a New Testament perspective, depicting Her as Sophia Mary, i.e., the Bride of Christ and the Mother of the Church; and some combine both aspects.

Figure 7. St. Hildegard and her faithful helper P. Volmar of Mt. Disibode. From *Scivias*. Vision 1. Otto Mueller Verlag, Salzburg.

Sophia Amon—Cosmiarcha, Co-Creator and Mother of the World and Humanity (Book of Divine Works, Vision 2)

The figure of a woman, crowned with a man's head, holds in her hands and carries in her womb a circle in which a man stands, who is the object of rays streaming forth from symbolic animals and nature figures. What is the meaning of this mysterious picture, which St. Hildegard received according to an Old Testament manner of conception? See Plate 3, page 111.

The head above the head of the woman signifies Yahweh, the Creator; and the woman's figure below shows Wisdom Sophia, who is His *Amon* (Hebrew: "Beloved, Darling, Confidant, or Co-creator," see Prov. 8,30), the first of created beings, Darling and the one who stands by His side during creation and the world's preservation (see Prov. 8,22–30).

Sophia encircles the world, which is represented by symbolic animals and nature figures, and She carries it in Her womb. At the world's midpoint stands the human being. Various vital energies emanating from Sophia stream out to the human being standing in the middle through the symbolic figures.

Under and with Yahweh, Sophia is the *Cosmiarcha* (Greek: *Kosmos*—cosmos; *Arche*—beginning), the Co-Creator and Mother of the cosmos. In Her motherly concern She is also the world's *Eubiarcha* (Greek: *eu*—"well" *Bios*—"life" *Arche*—"beginning")—Fount of salvation and Mother of a thoroughly whole life—especially for the human being, which is indicated by the human being depicted within Her womb.

Plate 3 on page 111 is an extraordinarily expressive image of unfathomably deep cosmological and anthropological symbolism. One of its essential statements is that nature and humanity form an organic unity with Sophia. Sophia is Mother and Soul of this unity, the Mother and Soul of the World, the "Cosmiarcha." She is, however, also the "Eubiarcha," especially for humanity. The following Biblical verses help bring this to expression:

> She spans the world in power from end to end, and gently orders all things (Wisd. 8,1).

Do not forsake her (Wisdom), and she will watch over you (Prov. 4,6).

From me come advice and ability; understanding and power are mine. . . . In my hands are riches and honour, boundless wealth and prosperity (Prov. 8,14,18).

For whoever finds me finds me finds life and wins favour with the LORD, but whoever fails to find me deprives himself (Prov. 8,35–36).

This fascinating picture contains a wealth of deep and cosmic symbolism about life, whose full interpretation is unfortunately not possible within the present framework.

Sophia Mary—Icon of the Holy Spirit (Book of Divine Works, Vision 9)

This fascinating and mysterious picture shows two figures (Plate 4, page 112). Hildegard calls the one on the left "Wisdom" and the one on the right "God's Omnipotence." Describing the figure on the left she says:

> I saw close to the northern corner a figure facing to the east. Its face and feet shone with such brilliance that they dazzled my eyes. It wore a gown of white silk and over it a green mantle richly adorned with the most varied precious stones. There were pendants on its ears, a collar on its breast, and coils on its arms. . . .[1]

Heinrich Schipperges[2] summarizes what Hildegard says about the first figure in the following way:

> The figure in the northern corner indicates the Wisdom of true rapture, a Wisdom whose beginning and end are be-

---

[1] Hildegard of Bingen, *Book of Divine Works*, Matthew Fox, ed. Robert Cunningham, trans. (Santa Fe: Bear & Co., 1987), vision 9:1, p. 210.
[2] *Book of Divine Works*, translator's note, p. 2.

yond human reason. The silken garment indicates the virgin birth of the Son of God; the green cloak indicates the world of creation along with the human species associated with it. . . .[3]

This interpretation of the vision in which Hildegard expressly beholds and declares Wisdom is extremely revealing. The figure of Wisdom is radiant with a wonderful and blinding brilliance. The statement "the silken garment indicates the virgin birth of the Son of God" is extremely profound and significant, because Sophia is related to the birth of the Son of God, and therefore to Mary, the Mother of Jesus. What is this relationship? The explanation near at hand is the thesis that runs throughout this book like a golden thread: Sophia incarnated in Mary, from whom the Son of God took on flesh and was virginally born. In other words, Sophia took on human form in Mary, and Mary is the true dwelling place of Wisdom, which is the basis for Her participation in Sophia's splendors. This Sophiological thesis has far-reaching implications for Mariology and ecclesiology.

Plate 4 (page 112) shows that over Her garment of white silk, the figure of Wisdom is wearing a green cloak which is richly decorated with all kinds of precious stones:

> [T]he green cloak indicates the world of creation along with the human species associated with it; the adornment, too, is a symbol of the order of creation that is subordinate to humanity. But we humans are responsible for the whole of creation.[4]

This declaration is of cosmic significance. The cloak and jewels are related to creation and the jewels to humanity in particular. Creation is therewith *the cloak of Wisdom and She is decorated with humanity, Her favorite and most precious possession.* Just as a woman wearing a garment is the mistress, indeed the soul of the

---

[3] *Book of Divine Works*, 9:2, p. 212.
[4] *Book of Divine Works*, p. 212.

garment, Sophia is the Mistress and Soul of creation, which is Her garment.

A woman's jewels emphasize and perfect her beauty. In the same way humanity is Sophia's masterpiece and primary decoration. Yet the person wearing the jewelry lends the jewels their brilliance, bringing out the full effect. In the same way, Sophia is the inner brilliance of humanity, helping humanity achieve the fullness of its radiance and dignity.

White is a color containing all other colors. In the same way, Sophia's orientation to the Logos, and Her bridal and maternal relationship and cooperation with the Logos become human, is the basis for all aspects of Her dignity and beauty: the entire rainbow of Her splendor. Green is the color of life and hope. Sophia is the essence of *viriditas* (Latin: *viridis*—"green" *viriditas*—"greenness" a primary concept of Hildegard's nature teaching), the essence of nature's and humanity's power of life. Gold is the most precious of all metals and signifies the elevated nobility of Sophia as well as humanity.

One could deduce still more comparisons and insights from this image of Sophia. One thing is certain: this vision is fundamental and the key to understanding and interpreting the others. For it reveals Sophia in Her relationship to Mary as the Mother of the Son of God (Sophia became a human being in Mary in order that the Son of God might become man from Her), as well as in Her relationship to creation (creation is Her garment and decoration, She is Herself the bearer of creation and creation's Mistress, Soul and Power).

Hildegard indicates that the vision's second figure, in the form of a winged being, is a symbol of "almighty God, invincible in majesty and marvelous in power."[5] This apparition has the form of a six-winged Seraph, hands upraised in prayer, with a garment of fish scales and the feet of a lion. In the figure's bosom is the head of an old man. A fascinating and remarkable image!

Perhaps it is not erroneous to relate Hildegard's words about the figure's symbolic relationship to Almighty God to the Holy Spirit in particular, i.e., the figure is a symbol of the Holy Spirit in its dignity and powers. In Sacred Scripture, the Holy

---

[5] *Book of Divine Works*, 9:3, p. 213.

Spirit is often portrayed as a being with wings—in Genesis, for example, as a brooding mother bird: "the spirit of God hovered over the surface of the water." (Gen. 1,2). In the New Testament the Holy Spirit descended upon Jesus in the form of a dove at the baptism in the Jordan (Matt. 3,16, as well as the other Evangelists report this). The Seraph's six wings point to the Holy Spirit, who is the spirit of love. The number six is the symbolic number of bounteous love, and Seraph means "burning in love." The hands of the Seraph figure are stretched out in supplication. The Holy Spirit pleads and sighs for us (Rom. 8,26). The garment of fish scales perhaps points to the water of baptism: "no one can enter the kingdom of God without being born from water and spirit" (John 3,5).

Water is also the symbol of life and wisdom—water of life, water of wisdom. The feet of the lion may be an indication of the "power of the Holy Spirit" (*virtus spiritus sancti*). The figure's head radiates like the sun. The essence of the Holy Spirit is absolute light, sun, warmth, and life. The six wings—six is the symbolic number of love, the six Works of Mercy—point to the Holy Spirit, who is entirely love and mercy, and to the power of love which "soars" to more elevated states.

Perhaps the presence of this symbol next to the image of Wisdom means to indicate that *Wisdom is especially "involved" with the Holy Spirit and that She is the image or perfect mirror of the Holy Spirit*:

> She [Wisdom] is the radiance that streams from everlasting light [i.e., the Holy Spirit], the flawless mirror of the active power of God (Wisd. 7,26).

If Sophia is the most perfect image of the Holy Spirit, perhaps we can draw conclusions about Sophia's characteristics based on those of the Holy Spirit. She participates in all the qualities and powers of the Holy Spirit, to the extent that this is possible for a creature (Wisd. 7, 22–29 says: "In wisdom there is a spirit intelligent and holy . . .").

Thus can we understand this Seraphic spirit-figure as a symbolic interpretation of Sophia Herself. The wings point to Her perfectly spiritual nature which is elevated beyond space and time. Eastern Church icons almost always represent Sophia with wings. The garment of fish scales points to Her relationship to water. Water is the symbol of life and wisdom: water of life, water of wisdom. The head of the old man within Her womb perhaps indicates that She effects everything in connection with Yahweh, guiding it to completion. The head of the old man is depicted above the head of Sophia in the picture of the cosmos and in the picture of the Lamb of God (Plates 3 and 7, pages 111, 115). This is another reason for thinking of Sophia here and for understanding the depiction as a symbol of Her. The outstretched arms signify that Sophia is always open for God and the world; She is the intercessor praying for the world, the world's praying and intercessionary Guardian Angel, as Florenski (chapter 15) calls Her.

The figure's head radiates like the sun: i.e., Sophia's thinking and willing works like the sun; Sophia is indeed the sun that illuminates, warms and animates the world, causing it to grow and ripen; She is the Soul of the World. The Book of Wisdom says: "She is more beautiful than the sun, and surpasses every constellation" (Wisd. 7,29). The lion's feet indicate Wisdom's power and might.

From head to foot Sophia is light, beauty, power, might, and love. The figure of the Seraph with the six wings testifies to this. Six is the symbolic number of proliferous love. The five spheres within the wings, however, also emphasize this. In symbology five is well known as the number of the magical love and power of the feminine. Five is also the number consecrated not just to Ishtar, the goddess of life and love, but to Venus, the goddess of love. The five-sided Venus temple in Balbek is a clear sign of this. In Christian symbolism Mary is represented with the symbol of the pentagram or five-pointed star as *Stella Matutina*. Five appears as a magical number in connection with the power of *eros* and the feminine.[6] Accordingly, the five spheres within the Seraph's wings signify Sophia's magically inspired and inspiring power of love.

---

[6] Franz Carl Endres and Annemarie Schimmel, *Das Mysterium der Zahl* (Cologne: Diederichs, 1984), pp. 122–124, 136.

This extraordinary and intensely expressive Wisdom-symbol next to Wisdom's figure intends to declare to us the nature, function, and characteristics of Sophia—which cannot be expressed by the depiction of a human image.

Perhaps it is just through the juxtaposition of Sophia and the Spirit-symbol that the vision intends to show Sophia's dignity, power, and splendor in an original, subtle, and genial manner, and above all that She is the most perfect icon of the Holy Spirit.

Sophia Torah—Heart, Soul, and Focal Point of the Kingdoms of Nature, Time and Creation (Book Of Divine Works, Vision 10)

This vision of Sophia with the tablets of law also has its basis in the revelation of the Old Testament, where Sophia is seen as the Torah or the cosmic order of nature. The Book of Ecclesiasticus expressly identifies Sophia as the Torah (law, order of nature):

> All this is the book of the covenant of God Most High, the law (the Torah) laid on us by Moses (Ecclus. 24,23).

The prophet Baruch confirms that the Torah is Wisdom Herself:

> She [Wisdom] is the book of God's commandments, the law that endures for ever. All who hold fast to Her will live, but those who forsake her will die (Bar. 4,1).

Hildegard beheld this Torah as a woman with the tablets of law, in the middle of a wheel divided into four parts. She says of this figure:

> And behold! In the midst of this wheel I saw again . . . the figure that at the outset was named to me as "Love". . . .[7]

> In these arrangements the eternity of God's perfect power indicates what should occur in the total fullness of

---

[7] *Book of Divine Works*, 10:1, p. 222.

creation. It is, so to speak, the greening power of generation in a shoot as it sprouts forth. For heaven and earth
were not yet in existence. . . .[8]

Hildegard explains this figure as "Love" but identifies Her with
"God's far-sightedness":

God's far-sightedness is shown in the view of Love because Love and God's providence are in total agreement
with each other. . . .[9]

Thus, on the basis of Hildegard's own explanation we can understand the figure that is shown as "Wisdom" or Sophia. See
Plate 5, page 113.

The figure in the middle of this picture splendidly
dressed is therefore Sophia as the ordering focal point, Teacher
of the entire creation. Her eyes and ears are fully attentive to the
Creator and His intentions for creation. She watches, listens, and
obeys. She is holding the tablets of law, i.e., She demonstrates
and teaches the order of creation, the order of nature, the "law,"
the sense and fulfillment, the "fullness" (Greek: *pleroma*) of creation. She is the personal Torah—order and harmony in person.
With the hand that is open and raised upward She receives,
rules, and teaches.

What do the wheel and its five parts (or eight parts—one
of the fields is itself divided into four parallel parts) signify, in
whose center Sophia is depicted? In her explanation of the picture, Hildegard mentions the kingdoms of nature and also
speaks at length of five or eight world eras.[10] Perhaps they are
meant to be symbolically depicted by the wheel's divisions: nature's inorganic kingdom of four elements and the world of
plants, animals, humanity, and spirits. As for the world ages she
enumerates five or eight: that of the dog, the lion and the horse,
which she again divides into four parts, and then the ages of the
pig and wolf.

---

[8] *Book of Divine Works,* p. 225.
[9] *Book of Divine Works,* p. 226.
[10] *Book of Divine Works,* pp. 224–225, 229, 240–252.

This is a simple illustration but one that conceals in an unexpected manner a wealth of information about nature and the world's historical eras, which all have their foundation in the figure of Sophia Torah.

Sophia Wisdom and Her Seven-Pillared Temple of Virtues (Scivias, Vision 9)

This vision is based on the verse of the Book of Proverbs: "Wisdom has built her house; she has hewn her seven pillars" (Prov. 9,1). From there She calls out to humanity: "Let the simple turn in here" (Prov. 9,4).

In this vision (Plate 6, page 114) Hildegard sees Wisdom as a woman dressed in golden vestments standing on a domed temple with seven pillars. Her description indicates:

> [O]n top of this dome I saw a beautiful figure. . . . Her head shone like lightning. . . . Her hands were laid reverently on her breast. . . . She had on her head a circlet like a crown, which shone with great splendor. And she was clad in a gold tunic, with a stripe on it from the breast to the feet, which was ornamented with precious gems; they glittered in green, white, red and brilliant sky-blue. And she cried out to the people of the world, saying: O slow people, why do you not come? Would not help be given you, if you sought to come?[11]

This corresponds with Sophia'a words in Sacred Scripture where She calls:

> "Let the simple turn in here. . . . Abandon the company of simpletons and you will live, you will advance in understanding." (Prov. 9,4-6).

This seven-pillared temple, upon which Wisdom is standing, symbolizes Her Church for which She prays and intercedes and

---

[11] Hildegard of Bingen, *Scivias*, Mother Columba Hart and Jane Bishop, trans. (New York: Paulist Press, 1990), vision 9, 9:1, p. 452.

which She teaches and protects through Her gifts and powers. The latter are symbolically portrayed by the three figures to the left and right of Her, whom Hildegard herself interprets in the following manner. The woman with the banner symbolizes justice; the man holding a sword above a dragon signifies strength; the middle head of the three-headed figure with a sword and cross signifies holiness coming from the cross on the chest, i.e., from humility; the right head symbolizes the root of all goodness, which is faith; the left head above the sword signifies self-control; and the sword spiritual discernment. These are the seven main virtues and gifts (justice, strength, holiness, humility, faith, self-control, and spiritual discernment) with which Wisdom armors and strengthens Her own, individually and in the community of the Church. These virtues are also represented in the seven pillars of the temple and in the seven towers of the church standing next to it. The church is in danger of collapsing due to the attacks of its enemies, and yet remains strong and unassailable in the strength of its towers.

Wisdom's radiant and ornamental appearance proclaims Her beauty and dignity. The sparkling halo crowning Her head symbolizes Her dignity as the first created and Yahweh's Co-Worker at creation (in Plate 3—Sophia Yahweh's Amon, Cosmiarcha, Co-Creator and Mother of the World—Wisdom is crowned by the head of Yahweh). The golden tunic in which She is dressed signifies Her beauty as Yahweh's Amon (Prov. 8,30). The four-colored gems on the banner which stretches from Her breast to Her feet signify that She is the archetype, mother, mediator, and saviour of the virtues. This picture affords a truly deep insight into Sophia and Her Church, which can only be described here in their most essential features.

Sophia Mary with the Lamb of God—The Mother and Bride of the Lamb (Book of Divine Works, Vision 1)

This extraordinarily expressive picture shows a man's head above the figure of a winged woman, who is holding at Her breast a Lamb with a cross. See Plate 7, page 115. On Her imposing wings can be seen the heads of a human being and an eagle. Beneath Her feet a snake is entwined who surrounds a human figure.

Hildegard writes about this image:

> For what you see as a marvelously beautiful figure in God's mystery . . . similar to a human being—signifies the Love of our heavenly Father. . . . Love appears in a human form. . . .[12]

This "Love in human form" can be understood as Sophia Wisdom, in the sense of Hildegard's identification between Love and Wisdom (see the remarks which follow about Plate 10). As these remarks show, Love and Wisdom are often identical for Hildegard in her visions and in what she says. Considering the entire context of her visions, and especially the explanation of the preceding image of Yahweh's "Amon," it is therefore permissible to understand this figure with the Lamb as Wisdom who became human in Mary, Sophia Mary.

After the above introduction, interpreting the picture is not difficult. The head above the winged figure of a woman represents undoubtedly God the Father. Since the Lamb with the Cross can be recognized as the true Lamb of God or Jesus Christ, this leads to the analogous interpretation that the Woman carrying the Lamb in Her hands is Sophia who became human, or Sophia Mary. The figure's large, majestic wings also point to such a Sophian interpretation. The Eastern Church's Sophia icons always portray Her with wings. Thus the picture shows God the Father, the Lamb of God Jesus Christ who is the Logos Son of God become man, and Sophia Mary who has become human, the Mother and Co-Worker of Jesus Christ the Lamb of God in the redemptive work of the entire plan of salvation.

On the wings are a human head and an eagle. The human head, symbol of the first Evangelist Matthew, and eagle, symbol of the last Evangelist John, stand for the entirety of the Gospels, which proclaim to us the mystery of the Son's incarnation and Sophia Mary's assistance.

The snake beneath the woman's figure, trampled by Her feet, signifies Mary Sophia's power over the snake. That is to say, She conquers the evil which holds humanity captive and there-

---

[12] Hildegard of Bingen, *Book of Divine Works*, 1:3, pp. 11–12.

with frees human beings so that they can elevate themselves again and return to their original place at the center of creation, i.e., within the womb of Sophia Mary, as Plate 3 so impressively depicts.

Thus according to a Sophian interpretation, Plate 7 is a New Testament fulfillment of the previous Old Testament picture of Yahweh's Amon—Cosmiarcha (Plate 3), i.e., God's Sophia in Her pre-existence as God's Co-Worker in the work of creation. Here the very same Sophia is depicted in Her incarnation as Sophia Mary and Co-Worker of the Logos Lamb of God become human in His work of redemption.

Sophia Mary—Bride of Christ and Mother of the Church (Scivias, Vision 3, Top-Half)

Hildegard provides a transition to a Marian and ecclesiological view of Sophia with the previous picture of Sophia Mary with the Lamb of God. In the present vision from *Scivias* (see Plate 8, page 116), as well as in those that follow (*Scivias*, visions 4 and 6), she beholds Sophia Mary as the Bride of Christ and Mother of the Church.

These images are grandiose illustrations and commentaries full of symbolism about Chokmah-Sophia of the Old Testament and Sophia-Mary-Church of the New Testament. They illustrate with a visionary and genial originality the Sophian verses of Holy Scripture, particularly those in the New Testament about the revelation of the connection between Christ and Sophia-Mary, between Sophia-Mary and the Church, and between Christ and the Church. They strongly suggest that Sophia incarnated in Mary—from whom the Logos Son of God became man and with whom He built, as out of a maternal and original cell, the Church whose head is Christ and whose bosom and heart is Mary. In this sense these images have been selected, reproduced and discussed.

Right Side: Sophia-Mary is shown as the Bride of Christ who is Teacher and "Pantocrator" (Ruler of All). Christ, the Logos become human, has a golden halo and is sitting on a rock-like golden throne. One hand is raised in blessing and the other rests upon Holy Scripture (the Bible). Sophia-Mary is completely gold and wears a crown and royal garments. She is embracing the throne with Her hands. Mary's intimate connection to Christ is being depicted here. Christ is Teacher, King and "Pantocrator"; Mary is the Queen and Bride holding on to Christ's throne, but also carrying him. The throne decorated in gold symbolizes the Church, whose head is Christ and which Mary carries. Mary is the Church's archetype and primary cell. Sophia-Mary-Church stands in virginal, bridal readiness to become the Mother of the Church.

Left Side: Now the mothering process and state are shown. The same woman in the same golden, regal garments and decoration is depicted. A new element is the banner in Her right hand, which reads: "I must conceive and bear." With Her other arm She clasps three figures to Her bosom, one of whom is playing the zither. To the right and left of the woman, Angels (according to Hildegard's own words) are carrying chairs, stairs with six steps, and a ladder with six rungs. Of the four chairs, two are simple in style and the two others more elegant. This is the picture of Sophia-Mary-Church as the Mother, organizer, and fulfillment of the Church, leading it ever higher.

The Holy Spirit and Sophia Mary as the Mother of the Church (Scivias, Vision 4); Sophia Mary as Co-Redemptrix and Mediator of Graces (Scivias, Vision 6)

Left Side: Sophia-Mary-Church is illuminated by a tower of light with three windows, from which seven beams are radiating. See Plate 9, page 117. At the bosom of the crowned woman are Her children, whom She protects from attacks and for whom She prays (She is presented in a praying position). She is shown here as Mother of the Church and Mediator of Life. The three windows symbolize the three divine persons of the Trinity, and the seven beams of light the seven gifts of the Holy Spirit.

Right Side: This is a depiction of Sophia-Mary-Church with the crucified Jesus Christ. In her commentaries Hildegard says that "by the will of the Heavenly Father, she was joined with Him in happy betrothal"[13]; and she also hears a voice from heaven which says: "May she, O Son, be your Bride for the

---

[13] Hildegard of Bingen, *Scivias*, vision 6, p. 237.

restoration of My people."[14] She stands by Jesus under the cross, catching His blood. She is the intercessor and mediator of the graces earned by Jesus. The four pictures above the altar present the Lord's birth, burial, resurrection, and ascension.

Sophia Mary—Omegarcha of Creation and the Church (Scivias, Vision 5)

This monumental picture depicts a majestic woman in silver and gold towering up out of wine-blue mountain peaks (see Plate 10, page 118). She is surrounded by a golden mantel, Her arms are spread wide and Her hands are raised up in prayer. She is carrying a golden chalice or calyx with twelve outer and three inner petals, in whose midst is a small, praying figure surrounded by eight persons. The woman's head wears a crown that is only partially painted with gold. Her countenance gazes majestically, knowingly and with concern into the distance.

This vision, whose artistic depiction for unknown reasons remained incomplete, is extensively commented on by Hildegard, even if various parts of the picture are not mentioned. In the first section of her description she says:

> After this I saw that a splendor white as snow and translucent as crystal had shone around the image of that woman . . . and in this brightness . . . appeared a most beautiful image of a maiden. . . .
>
> And I heard the voice from Heaven saying, "This is the blossom of the celestial Zion, the mother and flower of roses and lilies of the valley. O blossom, when in your time you are strengthened, you shall bring forth a most renowned posterity."
>
> And around that maiden I saw standing a great crowd of people. . . .
>
> And again I heard the voice from on high, saying, "These are the daughters of Zion, and with them . . . the voice of all gladness, and the joy of joys."[15]

---

[14] *Scivias*, vision 6, p. 237.
[15] *Scivias*, vision 5, p. 201.

The crystalline, silver brightness surrounding the woman would seem to signify Sophia in Her purely spiritual, pre-existential form; while the gold seems to symbolize the stages of Her realization and fulfillment in time and space, and in the supernatural dimension of salvation. Sophia incarnates into creation. The symbol for this is the wine-blue mountain. Sophia incarnates and fulfills Herself personally in Mary. The symbol for this is the "little maiden" who is praying in the calyx. Together with Christ She brings to completion Herself and everything in the New Jerusalem, in Zion, in the Church. The symbols for this are the eight figures surrounding Her within the calyx.

In summary and conclusion, this picture is a grandiose, monumental, and yet enchantingly charming depiction of the great mysteries of creation, the Church, nature, and the supernatural realm. We can understand Sophia Mary here as the one who fulfills and brings to completion these mysteries, and therefore call Her "Omegarcha" with respect to Teilhard de Chardin's expression "Omega Point" which refers to Christ. Teilhard de Chardin explains this expression in the following way. Creation, humanity and the world have a natural as well as a supernatural future. Viewed theologically, this future has begun in Christ. It works on in history and is above all the distant, certain point of the historical development of salvation. Teilhard de Chardin simply names this point with the last letter of the Greek alphabet—*omega*. He sees this crystallization- and end-point as realized through and in Christ.[16] Since Sophia Mary accompanies Christ and works together with Him in everything, She also participates in the process of the coming into existence of the "Omega Point." In this sense She can be called *Omegarcha* (Greek: *Arche*—beginning; *Omega*—end; i.e., the beginning of the process leading to the "Omega Point").

THE IDENTITY BETWEEN SOPHIA AND HILDEGARD'S SYMBOLIC FIGURE FOR LOVE

St. Hildegard sometimes uses the word "Love" to designate the figure which is interpreted as Sophia in Plates 3–7. To this it can be

---

[16] Adolf Haas, *Teilhard De Chardin Lexikon* (Freiburg: Herder, 1971).

said that *Hildegard's symbolic figure of "Love" is actually Chokmah-Sophia-Wisdom.* This viewpoint is held for the following reasons:

1. From the context of Sacred Scripture. The deeds and virtues which St. Hildegard ascribes to the figure "Love" are spoken of in relation to Wisdom, in particular in Holy Scripture. One example is the indication that Holy Wisdom is praised as the "Mother of honorable love" (Ecclus. 24,18).

2. In reference to the teaching that Holy Wisdom is the most perfect image of the Holy Spirit. The Holy Spirit is the "spirit of love," the personal love between the Father and the Son. In the Book of Wisdom Sophia is called the "image of God's goodness" (Wisd. 7,26). She is, in fact, often equated with the Spirit of God. Examples are:

> Who ever came to know your purposes, unless you had given him wisdom and sent your holy spirit from heaven on high? (Wisd. 9,17).

> In Wisdom there is a spirit intelligent and holy . . . (Wisd. 7,22). Compare also Wisd. 1,4–7; and Wisd. 12,1.

3. From the fact that Holy Wisdom is loved by Yahweh most of all. She is "Yahweh's Amon," i.e., Yahweh's Darling or Beloved (Prov. 8,30).

4. In reference to the *Scivias* vision of Hildegard herself (vision 9, here Plate 6, where Holy Wisdom is beheld as the Queen of virtues). "The greatest . . . is love" (1 Cor. 13,13).

Holy Wisdom is an all-embracing virtue which radiates love in particular as its most beautiful jewel. In the providential and solicitous help which She provided to the people of Israel and its best leaders (Wisd. 10,1 ff.) this great, wise Love shines in a particularly concrete way. "The spirit of Wisdom is kindly towards mortals" (Wisd. 1,6; 7,23).

It can be seen that all of the above reasons support the claim of the identity between Hildegard's figure of Love and Holy Wisdom. It can also be seen that equating them can therefore prove useful to interpreting her visions, especially on the additional basis of other symbolical and exegetical reasons and when such an interpretation leads to a deeper and clearer understanding of the pictures, i.e., they become more intelligible. (In her article "Sophia in the Mysticism of the Middle Ages" Barbara Newman says: "Wisdom and Love are practically identical figures which appear in place of the Biblical Sophia as God's spouse, co-creator and world regulator."[17])

In summary, although only a few of Hildegard's visions specifically depict Wisdom, many of them do relate to Her and reveal important aspects of Her identity. While Hildegard does not speak directly of a relationship between Sophia and Mary, there are hints in her visions and commentaries which mysteriously link them, providing a basis for considering indications from persons like Jacob Boehme and the Russian Sophiologists who do speak directly of their relationship.

If the interpretation that is given to Hildegard's visions is accepted, then it can be said that they portray the full scope of Sophia's identity and functions—from the creation of the universe and humanity to Her role in the history of salvation through Mary and the Church.

---

[17] Verena Wodtke, *Auf den Spuren der Weisheit* (Freiburg: Herder, 1991), p. 87.

9

Sophia and the Schekinah of the Cabala

THE MYSTERIOUS FIGURE of the Schekinah plays an important role in the Talmudic and Cabalist traditions (the Talmud is a collection of ancient Rabbinical writings considered authoritative; the Cabala refers to Judaism's esoteric and mystical teachings and the form of devotion attached to them, which first appeared in France around the 12th century and subsequently spread to Spain).[1]

The well-known Cabalistic scholar Gershom Scholem has noted that researchers have focused for some time on the connection between the Schekinah and Chokmah-Sophia of the Old

---

[1] The Cabala is based on the Bible, the Talmud and an oral tradition. It includes the teachings of great Talmudic figures like Rabbi Nehunya ben Ha-Kanah (first century C.E.), Rabbi Akiva ben Joseph (55–135 C.E.) and Simeon ben Yohai (second century C.E.) to all of whom are ascribed various pseudo-epigraphic Cabalist works. The Cabala was significantly influenced by Greek, Jewish, and Christian Gnosis.

The first summary of its teaching was the *Book of Yetzirah* (Book of Creation) which appeared in the eighth century—although the Cabala itself did not appear until between 1150–1250 in Provence (in the south of France). It was then that the first classical work of Cabala, the *Bahir* ("what is bright or clear"), appeared which is ascribed to Rabbi Nehun-ya ben Ha-Kanah.

From France, the Cabala spread to Spain, where Moses de Leon composed its second classical work, the *Zohar* ("splendor of light") between

Testament (*Chokmah* is the Hebrew word for Wisdom).[2] A discussion of the figure of the Schekinah is thus an important aid to a fuller understanding of Sophia.

THE CABALA'S TEACHING ON THE SCHEKINAH

It is noteworthy that Scholem repeatedly emphasizes that Sophia is created in spite of those who designate Her as a Divine Hypostasis. She is the first created being and older than the rest of creation; but younger than God and not co-external with God.[3]

Scholem defines the Schekinah as "the personification and hypothesis of God's 'in-dwelling' or 'presence' in the world" and says that this idea has accompanied the Jewish people for two thousand years.[4] He further characterizes the Schekinah as corresponding to the biblical idea of "God's glory," which is at the same time the throne of the Holy Spirit; and he quotes Judah Halevi who believes that the Schekinah is a fine and creaturely substance which follows God's will, and Mai-

---

1275–1290, which he attributed to the famous Rabbi Simeon ben Yohai.

After the Jews were driven out of Spain in 1492, the Cabala became a folk movement within Judaism. Its most famous teachers (called Cabalists) gathered in Safed in Palestine. Among them were Isaac Luria (1534–1572) and Moses Cordovero (1522–1570) who was a pupil of Solomon Halevi.

Many people outside of Judaism were also influenced by the Cabala, like J. Reuchlin, Agrippa of Nettesheim, Knorr of Rosenroth (who wrote the book *Kabbala Denudata*—The Cabala Unveiled), and Jacob Boehme and Soloviev. The Cabala's influence also extended to the Freemasons and Rosicrucians as well as to other theosophical and humanitarian-oriented groups.

Gershom Scholem is one of the most prominent among Cabala researchers. His primary works are: *The Book Of Splendor* (Zohar) (New York, 1949); *On the Kabbalah & Its Symbolism* (New York: Schoken, 1969); *On the Mystical Shape of the Godhead: Basic Concepts in the Kabbalah* (New York: Schoken, 1991).

[2] Gershom Scholem, *On the Mystical Shape of the Godhead: Basic Concepts in the Kabbala*, p. 144.
[3] Gershom Scholem, *On the Mystical Shape of the Godhead*, p. 142.
[4] Gershom Scholem, *On the Mystical Shape of the Godhead*, p. 141.

monedes, who speaks of the Schekinah as descended, created light.[5]

The *Bahir* and *Zohar* (the Cabala's two classical works) and the sayings of the Cabalist masters depict the Schekinah in various ways (but especially in connection with the teaching about the Tree of the Sephiroth).[6]

Similar to the first Old Testament texts about Sophia, the Schekinah is also understood as the origin and source of creation. She is the origin of all created beings, from the highest Angels to the creatures of the earth. She is the Mother of "Metatron," the highest angelic potency "who emerged from between Her legs"; and She is also depicted as the "wisdom of Solomon."[7]

Various parables allude to the Shekhinah in mysterious ways. One old midrash depicts a king traveling through the land who has a herald proclaim that no one may see his face until they have seen the face of the Queen or "Matrona."[8]

---

[5] Gershom Scholem, *On the Mystical Shape of the Godhead*, pp. 154–155.

[6] According to the Cabala, the Sephiroth (singular: Sephirah) are the primary dynamic powers of the manifesting Godhead; and they are also the transcendent archetypes and divine ideas according to which the world is created and formed. They are also referred to as the light by which the human being really knows God and creation; and the gates by which the human being enters into the mystery of God. Creation (and the human being) is a mirror image of the God who manifests and reveals Godself in the ten Sephiroth. "En Soph" is the divine, unknowable, uneradicable primordial ground, the "Deus Absconditus" or Hidden God. The ten Sephiroth are named: Keter (Crown); Chokmah (Wisdom); Binah (Intelligence); Chesed (Mercy); Din or Gebura (Justice or Power); Tipheret (Beauty); Netzach (Victory, Duration); Hod (Glory); Yesod (Foundtion); and Malkuth (Kingdom). The ten Sephiroth are polar powers but fully and dynamically harmonious. The ones that are designated with uneven numbers are masculine (Keter, Binah, Gebura, Netzach, Yesod); and those with even numbers are feminine (Chokmah, Chesed, Hod, Tipheret, and Malkuth); however, some Cabalists think differently, and view, for example, Chokmah (Wisdom) as a masculine Sephirah (which is difficult to comprehend). Pairs of Sephirah form polar and harmonious unities (Keter and Malkuth, Chokmah and Binah, Chesed and Geburah, Hod and Netzach, Tipheret and Yesod). The tenth Sephirah "Malkuth" is often identified with the Schekinah.

[7] Gershom Scholem, *On the Mystical Shape of the Godhead*, p. 191.

[8] Gershom Scholem, *On the Mystical Shape of the Godhead*, p. 162.

Another midrash speaks of the Schekinah as the 32 paths of Sophia and the spiritual foundations of the world, and as a king in the innermost chamber of his apartments of 32 rooms. The king concentrates all the paths in her, his daughter; and to enter the interior, one must look at her. She is given to a king as a gift and married to him. Sometimes he calls her sister (they are from one place), but sometimes daughter (for she is) and sometimes mother.[9]

She is Matrona, the Queen, hidden in her chambers, whom everyone is seeking, the synthesis who points out the ways that lead to the King, the medium of access to the King that facilitates knowledge of the King's splendor (by means of the jewels which sparkle on Her dress). She is the Daughter of the King Himself, sent to the earth from far away. Thus Her light shines into the world and She also has Her dwelling on earth. The *Bahir* does not say that She is in exile but implies that it is Her destiny to rule here below.[10]

Another passage calls the Schekinah the "principle or essence of this world," and "the brilliance taken from the primal light"; God has incorporated the paths of Wisdom in this radiance and given it to the world; it works as the "secret law . . . which is equated with the Oral Law . . . the mystical substance of tradition"; this is the sphere where the Schekinah resides and has its foundation.[11]

Understood as the "Daughter," She is "the blessing that God sent into the world"; She is Abraham's daughter, whom a Talmudic passage calls "Bakol" (literally: "in or with everything"), a vessel of precious jewels given to Abraham: "And God blessed Abraham *with everything*" (i.e., with Bakol, which means with the Schekinah).[12]

Another parable speaks of a king's beloved vessel that is beautiful and fragrant:

Sometimes he placed it on his head . . . sometimes he placed it on his arm . . . sometimes he loaned it to his son,

---

[9] Gershom Scholem, *On the Mystical Shape of the Godhead*, pp. 162–163.

[10] Gershom Scholem, *On the Mystical Shape of the Godhead*, p. 167.

[11] Gershom Scholem, *On the Mystical Shape of the Godhead*, p. 167.

[12] Gershom Scholem, *On the Mystical Shape of the Godhead*, p. 168.

that he might sit with it; and sometimes it was called his throne.[13]

The Cabala often identifies the Schekinah with the tenth Sephirah of the Sephiroth Tree called "Malkuth." From this perspective the Schekinah is "a mystical hypostasis of the divine immanence in the world."[14]

In a widely circulated text about the tenth Sephirah or the Schekinah, Rabbi Moses Nahmanides of Gerona (died in 1270) says that it symbolizes this world and is called "angel" and "angel of God." It is also called:

> *Beth-El* [House of God], because it is a house of prayer; and it is the *bride of the Song of Songs*, who is called "daughter and sister"; and it is *Kenesseth Yisra"el* [literally, "Gathering of Israel"], in which everything is in-gathered. It is the supernal Jerusalem, and in prayers it is known as Zion [i.e., depiction, representation, emergence], for it is that in which all potencies are represented.

> This lower Shekhinah is designated as *"Malkhuth,"* "the Kingdom"—i.e., God's dominion or power in the world. This term . . . became generally accepted from the time of its earliest appearance, shortly after the redaction of the *Bahir.* . . . This dominion is symbolically represented by the body of *Kenesseth Yisra'el*—"Israel forms the limbs of the *Shekhinah*," says a later popular Kabbalistic epigram.[15]

The appearance of the proposition that the individual forms of things are prefigured in the Schekinah is especially significant. This idea is particularly emphasized in the Spanish Cabala which comes after the *Bahir*, although its influence is also evident in the *Zohar*. Not only are all things in nature formed from the Schekinah; they are also already contained and prefigured in Her. A text from around 1250 speaks of all things entering the Schekinah shapeless but exiting from it with "matter and image

---

[13] Gershom Scholem, *On the Mystical Shape of the Godhead*, p. 169.
[14] Gershom Scholem, *On the Mystical Shape of the Godhead*, p. 171.
[15] Gershom Scholem, *On the Mystical Shape of the Godhead*, p. 172, 175.

and shape"; the Schekinah is "the form which embraces all forms" where every unique form is prefigured.[16]

The manner in which the Schekinah's form prefigures creation relates to the Schekinah's garments. The "upper and lower beings" and the shapes and names of the Sefiroth have their form in it; and in this are also engraved "all the souls and angels and holy beings."[17]

This idea is illustrated by a parable about the different garments in which the King dresses the Schekinah. All of the creatures that God creates have always been prefigured in these garments, which are the Schekinah's attributes and forms of activity. When God is guiding the development of the world He does not behold creatures in Himself but beholds them prefigured in the garments of the Schekinah.[18]

THE SCHEKINAH AND THE SACRED MARRIAGE

The *Zohar* commonly speaks of the Schekinah as "the world of the female" but also calls Her the "celestial Donna" (*ha-isha ha'elyonah*) or the "Woman of Light," who is the basis of the mystery of everything feminine in the world. Joseph Gikatilla says that during the time of Abraham She was called Sara; during Isaac's time Rebecca; and during Jacob's time Rachel.[19] Scholem then continues that the primary role of the feminine Schekinah is as the partner in "zivuga kaddisha" or sacred union where "the unity of the divine potencies is realized."[20] This is the marriage of the "holy king and queen," the holiness of procreation finds its understanding in this sacred union and only when it is abandoned does sexuality become "impure, profane, demonic and depraved."[21]

The *Zohar* is the first work to describe the inner divine marriage, and does so by referring back to Sacred Scripture. The stages leading to "union" or *yihuda* are presented as sexual "cou-

---

[16] Gershom Scholem, *On the Mystical Shape of the Godhead*, pp. 178–179.

[17] Gershom Scholem, *On the Mystical Shape of the Godhead*, p. 179.

[18] Gershom Scholem, *On the Mystical Shape of the Godhead*, p. 180.

[19] Gershom Scholem, *On the Mystical Shape of the Godhead*, p. 183.

[20] Gershom Scholem, *On the Mystical Shape of the Godhead*, pp. 183–184.

[21] Gershom Scholem, *On the Mystical Shape of the Godhead*, pp. 183–184.

pling" or *zivuga*, according to a naturalistic interpretation of the Song of Songs (Song of Songs, 2,6). Other Biblical verses are also understood as hymns to the Holy Marriage or *tush-bahta de zivuga*.[22] Scholem writes:

> The entire dynamics of the Zoharic notion of God is based upon this doctrine, in which the oneness and the unity of the divine life are realized in the sacred marriage; under no circumstances can these dynamics be separated from this doctrine.[23]

This hierogamous (referring to the *Hieros Gamos* or Sacred Marriage) understanding of the oneness between God and His Schekinah is graphically encountered in the Cabala of Safed in the 16th century. There it is described how the ritualistic formula: "for the sake of the unification of the Holy One, blessed be He, and His Schekinah" (in use since Rabbi Moses Cordovero) accompanied every religiously prescribed act.[24] This same understanding is solemnly reflected in the development of the rites of the "Hieros Gamos" which are elsewhere described by Gershom Scholem.[25]

PARALLELS AND SIMILARITIES BETWEEN THE SCHEKINAH AND SOPHIA

The preceding indications about the Schekinah can be summarized in the following way:

1. The Schekinah is not a Divine Hypostasis, but is created. She is a creature, the first and most perfect, with whom God creates all other creatures and things (God remains separate from Her).

2. God is active in creation and dwells in it through the Schekinah (according to such an idea, God is immanent in the world through the Schekinah, but at the same time transcendent to the world, and one).

---

[22] Gershom Scholem, *On the Mystical Shape of the Godhead*, p. 184.
[23] Gershom Scholem, *On the Mystical Shape of the Godhead*, p. 185.
[24] Gershom Scholem, *On the Mystical Shape of the Godhead*, p. 192.
[25] Gershom Scholem, *On The Kabbalah and Its Symbolism*.

3. The Schekinah is intimately related to God (She is variously referred to as the King's Mother, Queen, Daughter, Sister, and Bride. She is worthy of recognition and praise, for through Her access is found to God's inner mysteries (to the King's innermost chambers).

4. Creation and the natural world make up the Schekinah's garments. She is the "Bakol," in and with, but yet more elevated than everything, the Mother of creation and creation's inner Law (the Torah).

5. She is the blessing of abundance to God's chosen ones (the Bakol blessing supplying Abraham with everything).

6. She is "Malkuth," the Kingdom of God, which manifests God's power and rule.

7. She is God's Throne and House, Zion, supernal Jerusalem, and the Congregation of Israel (to which belong all of those who know, honor, and praise Her).

8. She is the Angel of God who protects and guides the world and those who belong to God.

9. She is the primordial ground and principle of life. Everything is prefigured in Her and takes its form from Her. She is the form that encompasses all forms.

10. She is the Celestial Donna (*ha-isha ha'elyonah*), the Woman of Light (the Eternal Feminine).

11. She appears in various manifestations and forms—as Sara, Rebecca and Rachel (Eph. 3,10: "Sophia polypoikilos"—Wisdom in its infinite variety).

12. She is God's partner in the Sacred Marriage (the "Hieros Gamos").

Many of these themes about the Schekinah have already been sounded about Sophia; and as will be seen, they are themes which recur in the contributions which follow. The correspondence is rooted in the similarity of knowledge and inspiration of those who consecrate themselves to Wisdom, who, in the mystical tradition of the Cabala, is known as the Schekinah.

10

Sophia in Art After the Middle Ages

THE CELEBRATED ARTIST Michelangelo Buonarotti is best known for renovating and completing St. Peter's Dome, for the Pieta sculpture, and "The Creation of Adam" in the Sistine Chapel.[1] See Plate 11, page 119.

The Sistine Chapel ceiling contains this famous portrayal of the creation of Adam in which there appears the figure of a woman next to God the Father (who has His arm around Her).

The woman is usually interpreted as Eve, who watches Adam's creation with interest. Yet according to the Bible Eve was created after Adam, having been formed from his side. An alternative interpretation which readily suggests itself is that the woman is Sophia or Holy Wisdom, who was created by God before the creation and who was with God as Counselor when God created the world:

> The LORD created me the first of his works long ago, before all else that he made. I was formed in earliest times (Prov. 8,22–23).

---

[1] Holles Kunstgeschichte (Baden-Baden: Holle Verlag, 1971), p. 161.

SOPHIA-MARY AND THE ISENHEIM ALTAR

The depiction of Sophia on the Isenheim Altar of Matthias Grue-newald deserves special consideration. The fact that we have here before us not just a "momentary glimpse" of Sophia, but a synoptic representation of Her salvational and historical phases justifies, or even demands, a closer examination of this *Sophian work of art* (first primordial Sophia is depicted as the *Reschit*, *Arche* or beginning of creation, and Bride of the Logos Son of God; then Her incarnation in Mary and the proclamation of the incarnation of the Son of God from Bethlehem to Golgotha; and finally the Coronation of Sophia-Mary, the true Bride, Mother and Co-Worker of Christ in the work of redemption and divinization).

History of the Isenheim Altar

St. Anthony's Isenheim cloister and hospital in France's Elsas region was an important settlement of St. Anthony's Hospice Order, which was founded in France around 1095 to care for the sick. Its rules were taken from the Order of the Knights.[2] The Order had in its possession up to 370 hospitals throughout Europe and also had the privilege of caring for the Pope in Rome.[3]

The leaders of the Isenheim convent were some of the Order's most significant individuals from all of Europe. In Grue-newald's time, two Italians were the cloister's preceptors: Jean Orliaco of Savoy and his successor Guido Guersi from Sicily. Orliaco, who had come from St. Anthony's convent in Ferrara, was acquainted with the Italian Renaissance and therewith with Platonism also, whose center at that time was the Platonic Academy in Florence, numbering among its members famous people like M. Ficino and Pico della Mirandola. Orliaco's origins and Platonic inheritance are important to keep in mind for a deeper un-

---

[2] The Order of Knights followed the Augustinian rules.
[3] See: *Lexikon fur Theologie und Kirche* (Freiburg: Herder, 1965), see entry "Antoniter Hospitalorden."

derstanding of the Isenheim Altar and especially its middle panel.[4]

Orliaco, who commissioned the altar, certainly conceived the altar as a whole. His successor Guido Guersi conscientiously held to this conception and lived to see the altar's completion through Gruenewald.

Matthias Gruenewald, whose actual name was Mathis Gothart Nithart, was born around 1460 in Wurzburg. He was given the name of Matthias Gruenewald by Joachim of Sandrart (1606–1668), to whom we are indebted for the few existing biographical facts about Gruenewald's life.[5]

Gruenewald was a talented artist who founded a studio in Aschaffenburg. This is why he was also known as Mathis of Aschaffenburg. He received commissions from the court of the Archbishop of Mainz and ultimately became the court artist of Cardinal Albrecht von Brandenburg, the Archbishop of Mainz and the Bishop of Halle, where Gruenewald died in 1528.

The Isenheim Altar is Gruenewald's most prominent work and was created during the years 1512–1516 (his other important works are the Tauberbischofsheim Altar and the Stuppach Madonna, to name only the most significant). When

---

[4] Marsilio Ficino (1433–1499) was a contemporary of Orliaco and Gruenewald and the leader of the Academia Platonica in Florence. He translated the works of Plato and Plotinus, successfully attempted to synthesize Platonic and Neoplatonic philosophy with Christian theology, and exerted a great influence on the intellectual life of his time. He was also a significant humanist. His best-known work is *Theologia Platonica* (New York: Olms, 1975, reprint of Paris 1559 edition). See also: Walter Dress, *Die Mystik des M. Ficino* (Berlin: W. de Gruyter, 1929).

The concept of the World Soul is fundamental to Platonism and Neo-platonism. Christian Patristic theology related the concept of the World Soul to Wisdom, i.e., the Sophia of Revelation. Perhaps Orliaco obtained the impulse to portray Sophia on the Isenheim Altar in Italy, for he was from St. Anthony's convent in Ferrara and was certainly familiar with the spiritual movements of his time. He wanted, in fact, to present a vision of the whole of Christian theology, which Georg Scheja also emphasizes. (See Georg Scheja, *The Isenheim Altarpiece*, Albert Erich Wolf, trans. (New York: Harry N. Abrams, 1967) pp. 65–66.

[5] See: *Das Grosse Lexikon der Malerie* (Braunschweig: Westermann, 1982), under the entry "Gruenewald," p. 269.

Gruenewald began the Isenheim Altar, Michelangelo had just completed the Sistine Chapel (1508–1512).

Art history reckons Matthias Gruenewald as the greatest colorist among the German painters of his time, who included Lucas Cranach, the Elder, Albrecht Altdorfer, Albrecht Durer, and Hans Holbein, the Elder. Related as he was to the best artistic traditions of his time, he was able to depict the earthly world, as well as divine mysteries, in a vivid and penetrating manner like no other German painter using color as the medium of expression.[6]

The Altar's Conception and Purpose

As previously indicated, those who were responsible for commissioning the altar were leading figures in the spiritual tradition of St. Anthony's Order and of the times. Situated in the Hospice Order's church, the altar was to give comfort and strength to the sick from the life and suffering of Jesus and the saints. Onlookers were to receive instruction in the fundamental mysteries of Christian faith through a comprehensive presentation of the most essential and important contents of faith. The primary saints and patrons of the Order were also to be depicted and their veneration promoted. This was certainly the assignment that Gruenewald was given, and he fulfilled it in a masterful, moving, and comprehensive way with a triptych altar (a central altar with folding sidewings) which afforded him the best means. Gruenewald thereby created one of the greatest art works of his time.

A Brief Overview of the Altar's Pictures

The altar consists of three panels of pictures with folding sidewings.

1. *Front Panel—The Panel of Suffering*: This is the altar in its closed position, which was apparently how it was viewed on

---

[6] *Das Grosse Lexikon der Malerie*, p. 271.

weekdays and ordinary Sundays. The middle panel shows a large and impressive picture of Jesus' death on the cross with Mary, the Apostle John, Mary Magdalena, and John the Baptist. A picture on the left shows St. Sebastian after withstanding his ordeal, and on the right another picture shows the patience of St. Anthony. We see below on the predella Jesus being mourned, the sorrowful Mother of God with Her dead and martyred Son before the grave. John the Beloved and Mary Magdalena accompany the Mother of Sorrows.

2. *Middle Panel—The Panel Of Divine Redemption*: This is the altar with the first set of wings open, as it was apparently viewed on the solemn feast days of the Lord and Mary. In this position we see on the left side of the central panel the temple or tabernacle picture[7] depicting the *mysteries of the entire plan of salvation*, while the other pictures (Christmas, the Annunciation, and Easter) portray *the work of salvation's individual events and deeds*.

3. *Rear Panel—The Panel of the Order's Saints*: This panel was opened on feast days of the saints. In the middle is St. Anthony with St. Augustine and Hieronymus. The two sidewings portray the temptation of St. Anthony and his visit with St. Paul Eremita.

Interpreting the Temple or Tabernacle Picture

In this study we are particularly interested in the left side of the middle panel—the so-called temple or tabernacle picture (Plate 12, page 120) where is shown the mystery of the resolution and preparation of the Son's incarnation in Mary. A closer examination of the picture's depiction reveals the following:

1. In the typanon image above the crowned "little Madonna," a patriarch asks God's blessing for his people. This is a symbolic

---

[7] The picture is called the temple, chapel, or tabernacle picture because it appears composed within a framework that looks like a chapel or tabernacle. The name "tabernacle picture" is preferred by those who understand the "little Madonna" as a depiction of Mary in the temple. The designations "chapel" or "tabernacle" picture come closer to the mysterious intimacy of this picture.

representation of the Son of God asking the Father's blessing for His work. The Father gives this blessing and sends Him out into the world.[8]

2. In the mysteriously dark portion above the concert of Angels, we see the figure of a woman, surrounded by a circle and various figures in blue, who is gazing reflectively up to the typanon image just mentioned. Who is this primordial figure of a woman? She is Sophia in Her pre-existent state—"eternal Mary," as many commentators have interpreted. She is enraptured, gazing up to the scene where the Son of God is asking the Father's blessing for His incarnation and work on earth.

As the Son's Bride and "Amon" who had already assisted Him at creation (Prov. 8,22–30), She can not and will not leave Him alone now. Flames of love ignite within Her and She decides to descend to earth with Him, to also become a human being and to help Him with the work of redemption and the divinization of creation. In the radiant and winged Angel figure,[9] from whose head a cascade of light shines forth, we see Her, full of enthusiastic love, descending to earth in order to become a human being in Mary and to help the Son of God in His incarnation and work.[10]

---

[8] Scheja also interprets the figure with a halo on the throne as God the Father; but he considers the figure without a halo to be a patriarch or prophet. However, considering the golden fullness of the entire tympanon, it is fair to assume that this kneeling figure is God the Son who is expressing to God the Father His readiness for emptying Himself and incarnating.

[9] The Russian Sophia icons portray Sophia with wings (for example, the Sophia icon of Novgorod in chapter 16).

[10] Perhaps these passages of Holy Scripture provide access to what Matthias Gruenewald intended by the mysterious blue circle above the choir of Angels, which shows a naked and powerful woman who takes up half of the circle's area. Gruenewald certainly wanted to indicate something important with this.

A possible interpretation is that the nakedness symbolizes the pure spirituality of this woman and Her immaterial, pre-incarnational essence—in contrast to being clothed, which visually symbolizes Her incarnation. She is primordial Sophia, the primordial Mother in the vitality of Her power and greatness. She sits sovereignly at rest, holding one hand loose in Her lap and gazing meditatively above to the tympanon image of the other circle, where the Father blesses and sends the Son. She is reflecting about Her origin from God and about the Son of God, who is Her Spouse and who is now declaring His

3. Her incarnation in Mary is depicted by the image under the typanon. In this mysterious picture of the "little Madonna" the incarnated Sophia—Sophia-Mary—is depicted in Her readiness to become the Mother of the Son of God, but also in the supernatural splendor which She will receive as a result. Her head is crowned and surrounded by a halo in the same colors as that of the resurrected Lord (the right sidewing picture). All of creation joins in jubilation. This is shown to us by the concert of Angels in a fascinating and convincing way.[11]

---

readiness to incarnate, and to redeem and divinize the world after the initial plan of creation was ruined by the fall of the Angels and Adam and Eve. God's incomprehensible love wants to effect something even more beautiful: not just the restoration of the original state of dignity, but the divinization of humanity and, in fact, of the entire cosmos.

Movement now arises in this peaceful, powerful, and sovereign woman as She reflects on all of this. Her bridal love for the Son results in Her decision to help Him with His plan of incarnation by also incarnating and becoming His bodily Mother. Her love becomes inflamed and Her élan radiant. She receives four wings, folds Her hands and descends to earth, chooses Her parents Joachim and Anna and incarnates from them. Sophia-Mary is born. Perhaps the golden Angel flying in front of Her is the Archangel Gabriel.

Her radiant, blue color signifies the profound and as yet concealed mystery of Sophia, which even then was shrouded in mystery. Blue is Sophia's color and is also found in the dress of Sophia-Mary under the golden tympanon. The Madonna wears a red cloak over Her dress, symbolizing Her readiness to become the Son's dear Mother. Her folded hands point toward the Christ Child in the arms of the Christmas Madonna, and Her gaze is directed to the Child's cradle. Her head is enveloped with golden light surrounded by a red, radiant circle. This light's essence and colors are identical to the halo of light surrounding the Resurrected Christ (right sidewing), symbolizing that Sophia-Mary participates in the splendor of Her Son as a reward for working together with Him. The fiery crown on Her head indicates that Her corporeality will be crowned. The crown of pearls above it, carried by two Angels who are led by a blue Angel, indicates that Mary will receive a crown in Her identity as Sophia. Sophia (who is Mary's soul) is also rewarded and crowned for Her readiness and cooperation. She is taken up into heaven body and soul and crowned there. The scepter of lilies emphasizes Her royal dignity. The triangle which is difficult to recognize with the circle next to the coronating Angel on the right, and the nine (three times three) flames of Her fiery crown probably indicate Her relationship to the Trinity, i.e., Mary's special participation in the Trinitarian mystery as Daughter of the Father, Bride of the Son and Icon of the Holy Spirit. This Trinitarian understanding of Mary's coronation is a favorite motif. Compare, for example, the coronation pictures where Mary stands in the center above

Thus are the Sophian and Marian mysteries of the history of salvation prophetically and symbolically depicted. The concrete realization is shown in the rest of the panel's pictures.

The assumption that Sophia is mysteriously depicted in the entire tabernacle picture, and especially in its blue aureole, is supported by the fact that the most renowned interpreters of the altar assume that "Mary of the Divine Resolution," or "Mary idealis," or "Mary aeterna," the "image of Mary's essence" is being depicted here:

> The key and "virtually geometrical central point" of the interpretation is the "mysterious figure" beneath the baldachin. She is the *Maria aeterna*, "Mary as Idea." The entire mystery of salvation is presented in these pictures as "the ideal and real progress of Mary through all the millennia of the history of salvation." The scene under the baldachin is "her election in the bosom of the Father, her salutation by the angels on the morning of the Creation . . .[12]

H. Feurstein thought that St. Bridget of Sweden's *sermo angelicus* had served as the inspiration for the entire middle panel of the Isenheim altar; and her text does suggest comparisons between the "Madonna of the divine decree" [Divine Resolution] and Sophia (Wisdom) of Proverbs: .

---

the Holy Spirit and is given the crown by the Father and Son together.

The luxurious decanter, the little golden pillars, the elegantly arched bows, and the entire decor of this sacellum all emphasize the festiveness concealed within this mystery.

[11] The "concert of the Angels" also has a deep, symbolic significance. The three large Angels are closely connected to the three primary mysteries. The one with wings gazes directly up to the Sophia with four wings and the cascade of light and to the tympanon picture. The white Angel looks directly over to the Madonna with the crown of fire, and the Angel in red garments gazes meditatively downward to the washtub. All of their faces are full of reverence, admiration, and a mysterious joy. The other figures, with and without halos, winged and nonwinged, also have symbolic significance. The purpose of the entire group is to express joy about the plan of salvation in a downright ecstatic way.

[12] Georg Scheja, *The Isenheim Altarpiece*, pp. 74–75. Tr: Translation mine for this and subsequent quotations.

In accord with the general context of Proverbs 8:22–36, the pre-existent eternal wisdom is understood to be the Madonna of divine providence . . .[13]

For Feuerstein, the uncreated Madonna of divine providence is "the central idea of the left half of the middle panel."[14] This left side is also justifiably called the temple or tabernacle picture.

Scheja is quite correct in saying that "the baldachin would be a symbolic representation of the 'old marriage' of the Old Testament."[15] This conception points to the "Sacred Marriage" (Greek: *Hieros Gamos*; see chapters 9 and 25) between God and Sophia as it is revealed in the Book of Proverbs (Prov. 8,30) and in the Book of Wisdom (Wisd. 8,3). W. Niemeyer, along with Feuerstein, describes Mary as:

Idea, eternal thought, awakening, germinating, growing, Mary before time, on the threshold of time, who gazes on herself as the fulfillment of time.[16]

W. K. Zuelch emphasizes:

There can be no doubt that here, created out of the vast body of Marian poetry, we have kneeling before us the *Mary aeterna*, the bearer of God, who was created by divine decree before the creation of the world and who is shown in the state of expectation and as foremost among all those who wait.[17]

One can add: not just as a summary of Marian poetry but of Marian teaching, especially in the Eastern Church. Even Scheja admits of the possibility of a Sophian interpretation. For in the history of the associations relating to Mary she became:

---

[13] Georg Scheja, *The Isenheim Altarpiece*, p. 75; St. Bridget of Sweden, *Sermo angelicus* (Uppsala: Almquist & Wiksells, 1972).
[14] Georg Scheja, *The Isenheim Altarpiece*, p. 75.
[15] Georg Scheja, *The Isenheim Altarpiece*, p. 41.
[16] Georg Scheja, *The Isenheim Altarpiece*, p. 43.
[17] Georg Scheja, *The Isenheim Altarpiece*, p. 76.

the Madonna of Divine Providence, the wisdom created
before the Fall of Man, the vaster allegory of the Madonna
as a participant in the work of Redemption.[18]

Not just as image of Her essential nature or as idea, but as the
personal, original plan for realization which was also realized. In
his *Divine Comedy* Dante writes in the Song of Paradise:

> So there, that oriflame of peace on high
> Was quickened at the heart. . . .
> About the heart . . . on outstretched wing
> More than a thousand angels jubilant,
> Distinct in radiance and functioning.[19]

Dante calls the Madonna here "la coronata fiamma." This is a
further indication that the radiant Angel with the four wings in
the blue aureole is to be recognized as Sophia before time as She
is descending to incarnation on the earth. In Scheja's opinion this
fiamma portrayal of Sophia goes back to Byzantine influences.
This remark supports the assumption of Sophian influences
coming from Byzantium, i.e., from the Eastern Church, which in
fact had a deep relationship to Sophia, as evidenced by the
Sophian churches and icons.

The vision that the Isenheim altar presents is fascinating
and grand. It was conceived by Orliaco and Gersi and executed
in an artistically unique manner by Gruenewald. Much of it recalls Jacob Boehme's visionary descriptions of Sophia (see chapter 11). Both Orliaco, via the Platonic Academy in Florence, and
Boehme, via Paracelsus who had become familiar with Platonism in Italy, are closely connected with the Italian Renaissance.
This is why Scheja emphasizes the necessity of using Platonic
and Neoplatonic thought for interpreting the altar[20] (for example, the Neoplatonic theory of an absolute primordial being, the
Nous (Logos), and a Soul of the World (Sophia)—concepts
which penetrated Western intellectual and theological thought

---

[18] Georg Scheja, *The Isenheim Altarpiece*, p. 77.
[19] Dante, *The Divine Comedy*, Dorothy Sayers and Barbara Reynolds, trans. (Baltimore: Penguin, 1962), Canto XXXI, lines 127–132, pp. 330–331.
[20] Georg Scheja, *The Isenheim Altarpiece*, p. 40.

along with Platonism. The "luminous corporeality" of the Isen-heim Altar, as it is so felicitously and effectively portrayed, also comes from Platonism:

> Transfigured corporeality is to be understood here as the transubstantiation of flesh into light, as propounded by the Neo-Platonic current in theology.[21]

THE "BLUE LADY"—PRIMORDIAL SOPHIA

The blue figure of a woman in the blue aureole (Plate 13, page 121) can probably be best explained from a Sophian context by the Biblical, primordial figure of Sophia before time, mysterious and hidden. The Book of Job says of Sophia:

> But where can wisdom be found . . . no one knows the way to (Her). . . . God alone understands the way to (Her), he alone knows (Her) source. . . . he considered (Her) and fathomed Her depths (Job 28,12–27).

Other passages about Wisdom speak of God making Her His "Amon" (intimate friend), Workmaster, and Co-worker at creation (Prov. 8, 22 ff).

In that God created Sophia as the "beginning" (Greek: *Arche*; Hebrew: *Reschit*) and then with Her the rest of the things and beings of creation, God made Her creation's primordial Mother. This blue and peaceful, primordial figure can truly serve as a symbol of primordial Mother-Sophia. She is gazing comtemplatively up to Her spouse in the tympanon picture who is asking the Father's blessing for His incarnation. The decision not to let Him do this alone becomes firm in Her. She hovers down to the earth as an Angel sending forth flames of fire.

The Flaming Angel

To the right of the "Blue Lady" the artist has depicted a winged, angel-like exalted being in the midst of accompanying Angels.

---

[21] Georg Scheja, *The Isenheim Altarpiece*, p. 66.

Flames of fire shoot out from its head lighting up its countenance and the surrounding Angels with a golden glow; its hands
are folded and it looks as if it is about to fly off, its glance directed yearningly toward a very definite goal.

Who and what did the artist intend to depict? In the sense
of a Sophian understanding of the entire tabernacle picture, this
winged being who shoots forth flames can be interpreted as
Sophia. In gazing upon the Son of God, who has just obtained
the Father's blessing for His incarnation, She has enthusiastically
decided not to let Him, Her spouse, do this alone, but to descend
to earth with Him and help Him with His work, i.e., to incarnate
in Mary and to become His Mother and Co-worker with the
work of redemption and divinization.

If, in the "Blue Lady," the pre-existent, primordial Mother
Sophia, who was created in the beginning—"Sophia Archaia"—
is being symbolized, then here in this angelic figure sending
forth flames of fire "Sophia Descendens" is being depicted—
Sophia who is descending to earth. Her folded hands and the
flames that issue from Her head testify to the enthusiasm and
love with which She undertakes this "departure," accompanied
by Angels.

The "Little Madonna" or the "Gloriosa Madonna"

Below and to the right of this dramatic depiction, where the
tabernacle opens to the right, and exactly under the tympanon
image where the Son asks and receives the Father's blessing for
His incarnation, we see the image which represents the fulfillment of all the previous images: Sophia who has become a
human being in Mary—Sophia Mary in Her pregnancy and
splendor at the end of time, the Queen of heaven and of the
earth and the "Omegarcha." Strangely enough this image is often
called the "little Madonna" (perhaps in comparison to the larger
Christmas Madonna opposite to it). In the context of the entire
tabernacle picture we can perhaps also call this image the
"Madonna of Glory."

J. Bernhart sees in this figure "Maria in exspectatione,"
i.e., Mary awaiting birth, but also the temple Virgin and the
apocalyptic Woman of the Book of Revelation. This seems con-

tradictory, yet perhaps the interpretation is quite profound and valid, when it is not understood in an "historical" manner, but in a symbolic and synoptic sense; when the Virgin with the blessed body is understood as a symbol of Her readiness to work together with the incarnated Logos in the work of redemption, i.e., Her readiness for a messianic pregnancy; and when the temple Virgin is viewed as a symbol of Sophia, who says of Herself:

> Before time began he created me. . . . In the sacred tent I ministered in his presence (Ecclus. 24,9–10).

Mary's time in the temple is a symbol for Her readiness and preparation for working together on God's plan of salvation. The halo of light around Her head is a prophesy of The image of Her being clothed with the sun, with the divine light-filled splendor of the Resurrected One (see: Rev. 12,1ff, "a woman robed with the sun").

Corresponding to his theological, visionary, and artistic genius, Gruenewald depicted in this tabernacle image a symbolic and synoptic summary view of Sophia's dignities, functions, and cooperation in all three phases and manifestations of Her existence: before time as Sophia, in time as Mary, and at the end of time as She who is taken up into heaven and crowned. The "little Madonna" symbolically contains and portrays all of Mariology, including its Sophiological aspect and basis: Her preexistence as Sophia-Wisdom, Her becoming human in Mary, Her working together as Mary with the incarnation of the Logos and His work of salvation (redemption and divinization) in time, and Her glorification with Christ (Assumption and Coronation) as Sophia-Mary-Church in eternity at the end of time.

As for the image of Mary's Coronation, the following can be said. She is crowned with two crowns—with a crown of flaming fire on Her head and a crown of pearls carried by the Angels. With the crown of flames, Her corporeality is being crowned with the resurrection splendor of Christ; with the crown of pearls, Her Sophian nature is being crowned and rewarded for becoming human. The blue Angel behind the two figures carrying the crown of pearls points to the Sophian significance of this crown.

The Angels in the Tabernacle Picture

As for interpreting the Angels, the following can be said. The Angels in the blue aureole jubilate and accompany the ecstatic readiness (symbolized by the cascade of flames shooting up from Her head) of Sophia for becoming human and cooperating with the plan of salvation. The concert Angels sing and exult over the various phases of the plan of salvation and its realization. The dark, feathered Angel gazes up to the blue gloriole of the time before history; the red Angel gazes at Mary with Her symbols of the child's bed; and the white Angel looks up to the "little Madonna" who is the symbol of the Sophian-Marian totality. The other Angels and figures could be interpreted as symbolic representations of different peoples (Bernhart) or of the various functions and aspects of Sophia-Mary.

• • •

There are two possible explanations for the origin of the profound symbolism contained in the Isenheim Altar. The author either beheld everything in spirit, understood it and consciously composed and arranged it into a whole; or he did not so much understand everything but was led and inspired by a higher hand and worked everything in de facto. A higher manner of observation and meditation will succeed in discovering the hidden treasures which are depicted and indicated in the altar's symbols.

Orliaco, the spiritual and ideational author of the Isenheim Altar, can be credited with the former explanation for the altar's symbolism, on the basis of his universal disposition, spirituality, and his education and connection with the leading figures of his time. In Matthias Gruenewald he had the great and rare fortune of finding a genial artist able to depict his Sophian conception in masterful and incomparable forms and colors.[22]

---

[22] Drawing on Sophia in order to interpret the "most enigmatic picture" of the middle panel is a preliminary hypothesis. It is supported by the assumption that Orliaco, who conceived and commissioned the altar, knew the Old Testament's Wisdom Books and the Platonic idea of Sophia as the World Soul (he was connected with the Academia Platonica in Florence) and wanted to work its Christian expression into his work. That such a hypothesis would explain

In the Isenheim Altar we undoubtedly have the most genial and complete artistic portrayal of Sophia in the entirety of Her identity and mission.

THE CHURCH OF MARIA DE VICTORIA

The Church of Maria de Victoria in Ingolstadt, Germany was constructed for the student congregation of the University of Ingolstadt between 1732–1737. Its frescoes were painted by Cosmas Damien Asam in 1734.

The ceiling fresco in the entrance hall portrays Wisdom sitting on a throne amidst royal insignia. Behind Her is a temple-like building with a round dome. (See figure 8, page 184.) Beneath Her throne is a banner with the inscription: "Wisdom has built her house" (*Sapientia aedificavit sibi domum*—Prov. 9,1).

What is especially significant about the fresco is that while Asam usually portrayed Wisdom as one of the Seven Gifts of the Holy Spirit, here She is portrayed as an individual person along with Her house (the domed temple behind Her).

Wisdom's throne is surrounded by six lions playing with the royal insignia (the imperial orb, crown, sword, scepter, and cornucopia). Depicted as a Queen, Sophia carries a staff and also a scepter in the form of a snake. Above the throne hovers a dove (the Holy Spirit) and above the dove there is a triangle with an Eye of God. An Angel is reflecting the dove, triangle, and Eye of God with a mirror from which a beam of light descends to Sophia.

Taken together the many symbols provide a comprehensive vision of Sophia-Wisdom. She is depicted as a wise, powerful, and benevolent Queen. The throne, staff, six lions, and insignia all point to Her royal dignity. The two cornucopias point to Her benevolent and maternal abundance which pours

---

these enigmatic pictures in a satisfying and eloquent way speaks in its favor. It is surprising that Scheja did not stumble upon this intepretative key. Sophiology still represents largely unexplored territory for the Western Church (which is not the case for the Eastern Church). Teilhard de Chardin's essay "The Soul of the World," and especially his classic "Hymn to the Eternal Feminine" provide an access to Sophiology (see chapter 17).

Figure 8. Entrance hall fresco. Church of Maria de Victoria. C.D. Asam. Schnell & Steiner, Munich.

forth gifts upon the earth. The scepter in the form of a snake symbolizes Sophia's healing and salvation-bringing power (the snake is a symbol of wisdom and healing).

The round, domed temple, Wisdom's House, can be understood as a symbol of the cosmos which Wisdom created, thereby revealing Her role as the Master Builder (*Technitis*) and

Mother (*Genetis*) of the universe (the Soul of the World). The temple can also be understood as a symbol of the Church, thereby connecting Sophia to Mary, the Mother of the Church.

Sophia's special relationship to the Trinitarian God (and to the Holy Spirit in particular) is also suggested in that the triangle, Eye of God, and dove (the Holy Spirit) are reflected down to Her on the throne (very nicely expressing that She is God's mirror image). She reveals the perfections and virtues of God in their pristine, original form. In Her we behold the beauty, majesty, and wisdom of God, whom we cannot behold face to face. Sophia is the means for knowing God, God's Trinitarian nature (the triangle) and especially the Holy Spirit (the dove). Her relationship to the Holy Spirit is a subject that will be taken up in chapter 26.

The entrance hall fresco represents a kind of "prologue" to the ceiling fresco inside the church. See Plate 14, page 122. There one sees a beam of light descending from God the Father to a woman dressed like the Sophia in the entrance hall painting (top left corner). From Her another beam descends down to Mary (see detail in Plate 15, page 123), who is kneeling in assent to the message that She is to be the Mother of God. By Her "fiat mihi" ("May it be as you have said"—Luke 1,38) Mary agrees to partake in the incarnation of the Son of God and the work of redemption.

The woman who reflects the beam of light to Mary has been interpreted as the "love of God." Understanding Her as Sophia, however, adds a new measure of insight to Her interpretation, for as Scripture says of Sophia: "Then I was at his (Yahweh's) side each day, his darling and delight" (Prov. 8,30).

She can be interpreted to represent Sophia in Her prehistoric existence, and the beam of light that She reflects to Mary mysteriously connects the two of them. The link between them is also suggested by the presence of certain symbols in the ceiling fresco (the Ark of the Covenant, house, and tower) which are also found in the Litany of Loreto and the Akathist Hymn to the Blessed Virgin Mary.[23]

---

[23] The Litany of Loreto to the Blessed Virgin Mary draws upon symbols from the Old Testament and especially the Wisdom Books, including the Song of Songs. Among its invocations are: Ark of the Covenant, House of Gold, Tower of Ivory, Gate of Heaven, Health of the Sick, and Help of Christians (see appendix IV). The Akathist Hymn attributed to St. Romanus the Melodist, which is sung in Orthodox Lenten services, uses many of the same titles (appendix IV).

Figure 9. Detail of The Annunciation. Church of Maria de Victoria. C. D. Asam, Schnell & Steiner, Munich.

It is further interesting to note that the beam of light re-flected to Mary is in turn reflected by Her down to the Queen of Saba, who symbolizes Wisdom and the Wisdom-seeker; and Pallas Athena, the Greek goddess of Wisdom (see figure 9, page 186). Such indications strengthen the idea of an intimate, albeit unspoken, relationship between Sophia and Mary.

THE MURAL OF THE LORETO CHURCH IN BIRKENSTEIN

The Loreto pilgrim's Church in Birkenstein, near Fischbachau in the Bavarian Alps, can also be cited as a witness to the relation-ship that exists between Sophia and Mary.[24]

In the first place, Loreto Churches are related to the Litany of Loreto to the Blessed Virgin (appendix IV), whose invocations draw upon the Old Testament's Wisdom Books. In addition there is a magnificent and enigmatic mural (German: "Lehrtafel" or teaching panel) in the entrance hall painted by Josef Franz Zaver Gross in 1761, which lends further support to the idea of a connection between them (Plate 16, page 124).

At the top of the mural is the figure of a woman sur-rounded by Angels. Beneath Her, several Angels hold open a large protective cloak, revealing the figure of the Madonna and Child. The primary inscription of this central portion of the mural reads: "I want to fulfill (German: *erhoeren*) heaven which is Mary and Mary will fulfill the earth." What is interesting about this inscription is that heaven is equated with Mary. Yet according to St. Augustine, God's heaven is "Created Sophia."[25]

---

[24] *Tausend Jahre Marienverehrung in Russland und in Bayern*, published by Albert Rauch and Paul Imhof, commissoned by the Spiritual Academy in Sagorsk/Moscow and the Eastern Church Institute of Regensburg (Munich/Zurich: Schnell and Steiner, 1988).

[25] Augustine, *Liber Meditationum*, XIX; Patrologiae cursus completus, J. P. Migne, ed., Series latina (Paris, 1844–1855) vol. 40, 916.

Of further interest is the inscription (in red) beneath the Madonna from Ecclesiasticus: "I give birth to honorable love, to reverence, knowledge, and holy hope" (Ecclus. 24,18). This verse about Holy Wisdom appears three times in the mural and sets the tone of the church, which is dedicated to Mary as the Mother of Honorable Love and Helper of the Afflicted.

The mural's Sophian tenor is further enhanced by the depictions on the pedestals of the oblisks. The left pedestal depicts King Solomon, the seeker of Wisdom. With trusting love, he gazes upon a young woman who embraces him and gives him a bowl of fruit. The right pedestal also depicts a king, but one who is turning away. The pedestals seem to symbolically portray the words:

> Come to me, all you who desire me, and eat your fill of my fruit (Ecclus. 24,19).
>
> But because you refused to listen to my call. . . . your doom approaches (Prov. 1,24, 27).
>
> If only you embrace her, she will bring you to honor. . . . she will bestow on you a glorious crown (Prov. 4,8–9).

The entire mural's Sophian significance is also suggested by other depictions (not shown) of Old Testament scenes where according to Scripture Sophia intervened, fulfilling the promise of assistance given in Ecclus. 24,18 to those who revered Her (Noah is rescued from the flood; Joseph from starvation; Moses from servitude and slavery; David from defeat in war; Elijah from infertility, drought, shipwreck, and the labyrinth; and the poor and the sick who seek help and health are also portrayed).

11

Jacob Boehme—
The Father of
Western Sophiology

J ACOB BOEHME (1575–1624) deserves to be called the Father of Western Sophiology because, through his visionary power, he achieved a far greater knowledge of Sophia than many others. Boehme's literary style is often awkward and his thoughts difficult to understand. Some statements seem to contradict others as he attempts to work out the opposition of polarities in a manner that sometimes seems incompatible with rational thought. Yet in spite of such problems, there is much of value to be found in his works.

In order to better understand Boehme's ideas and his teaching about Sophia an overview will first be provided of his life and works.[1]

---

[1] The source of biographical information about Boehme are the sketches provided by friends and contemporaries who knew him. Of particular value is the "Gruendliche und Wahrhafte Bericht von dem Leben Jacob Boehmes" (A Thorough and True Report of the Life of Jacob Boehme) which was published by Abraham von Frankenberg, his aristocratic friend, shortly after Boehme's death (reprinted in: *Jacob Boehme Saemtiche Schriften*, facsimile printing of the edition of 1730 in 11 volumes, newly published by Will-Erich Peukert, Stuttgart 1955, 11 volumes plus a one-volume index).

LIFE AND INFLUENCE

Jacob Boehme was born as a poor farmer's son in Altseidenberg near Gorlitz in the region of Germany then known as Schlesia. He was brought up in the Lutheran faith at a time when the contours of Protestant theology were becoming firmer, which would prove to be difficult for him because of his mystical inclinations.

Already as a youth Boehme was deeply religious. He learned the cobbler's trade and became a journeyman apprentice, which was customary at the time. The experience of injustice and evil weighed heavily on his sensitive nature and stood in the background to the mystical experiences that began during his journeyman period. During his first mystical experience he felt himself bathed in a supernatural light and blessed sense of peace which lasted for seven days. Eventually he returned home to Gorlitz (around 1594) and opened a cobbler's shop, and shortly thereafter married a woman from Gorlitz who bore him four sons.

Around 1600 he had a second mystical experience. While watching the splendid glow of sunlight on a pewter jug, it seemed that he became aware of forces active within the jug that gave him insight into the foundations of things and into questions which had troubled him for some time. After this second experience, he had a number of visions and realizations which seemed to deepen his insight. Yet his experiences seemed disjointed and he remained silent about them until a third experience (around 1610), which seemed to pull everything together. At this point he began to record his experiences and visions. This resulted in his first work, *Aurora* (Dawn Rising).

Some of the contents of this work, full of the freshness and originality of youth, were made public in 1612, before its completion, by some of Boehme's friends. This resulted in much grief and suffering for him. Gregor Richter, the orthodox Lutheran Monsignor of Gorlitz, attacked the work from the pulpit in Boehme's presence, branding him a heretic and an instigator. The magisterium subsequently silenced Boehme and forbade him to write. Boehme honored this prohibition for a long while, but in 1619 he began to write again, urged on by friends and his own inner voice to write down his visions. Until his death he composed the rest of his life's works.

JACOB BOEHME—THE FATHER OF WESTERN SOPHIOLOGY □ 191

During Boehme's life Dr. Balthasar Walter, a physician and the head of the chemical laboratory in Dresden, was especially helpful to him. Dr. Walter was a student of Paracelsus, and like Paracelsus, he had traveled much. He had spent six years in the Near East pursuing Wisdom, but found what he had sought with Boehme. He went to live with Boehme for three months in order to learn from him. Walter, in turn, provided Boehme with the basic knowledge of many subjects that were unfamiliar to him (perhaps it was Walter who introduced Boehme to the teachings of Paracelsus, alchemy, astrology and the Cabala).

A report from this time relates that on hearing the Greek word "Idea," Boehme was filled with joy and said that it awakened in him the image of a "beautiful, pure Virgin and Goddess elevated in spirit and body."[2] Boehme's occupation with Sophia, whom he had not mentioned in his first work, dates from this period. His love for Sophia subsequently appears in works like *The Way to Christ*, which portrays conversations between Sophia and the soul.

In 1624 he was invited to the provincial capital of Dresden, where he was warmly received by the advisors to the Kurfurst, and even received an audience with the Kurfurst himself. Yet he was not able to gain unequivocal support and returned home disappointed. He later died after a short illness. It is reported that on his deathbed he heard music and singing and asked that the door be opened wider that he might hear everything better. A beautiful cross was erected on his grave but was subsequently desecrated through the instigation of his opponents.

Among Boehme's friends were prominent persons like aristocrats and physicians; and yet others, led by Gregor Richter, fanatically rejected him. However Richter's son was so impressed by Boehme's teachings that together with Frankenberg he published the first edition of Boehme's works (the so-called Thorner edition) between 1651–1660. The first edition of his collected works, carefully edited and elaborately engraved, was published

---

[2] Abraham von Frankenberg, *Gruendliche und Wahrhafte Bericht von dem Leben Jacob Boehmes*, p. 20.

in 1682 by Georg Gichtel. While Gichtel's own extreme views and interpretations served more to damage Boehme's reputation, the renowned theologian, Gottfried Arnold (see chapter 12), was inspired by Boehme and contributed greatly to his proper evaluation in the theological and scientific worlds.

Boehme's writings were soon translated into Russian. They also became known in England after King Carl I sent learned men to Gorlitz to research Boehme's life and to translate his works into English. Within forty years after Boehme's death, three editions of his works were published in England. John Pordage wrote some noteworthy interpretations and commentaries and Lady Jane Leade founded the "Philadelphia Society" in Boehme's honor. In France, Louis-Claude de Saint Martin became an enthusiastic follower of Boehme and also translated his most important works (for more on Pordage, Leade and Saint Martin see chapter 13).

Boehme's influence in Germany also continued to prevail. Hegel became acquainted with him through the Romantics (especially Novalis, Fichte, Schelling and Schlegel); and though valuing him greatly, he found Boehme's thought difficult to grasp and called his language usage and literary style barbaric.[3] Franz Baader and Christoph Oetinger were also influenced by Boehme and incorporated his ideas into their own philosophical systems, thereby making his thought more comprehensible to modern times.

BOEHME'S TEACHING ON EXISTENCE

Boehme's primary concerns were philosophical and existential. He wanted to understand the origin and purpose of the world, humanity, suffering, and evil. He pursued these questions to their roots, which led him to the absolute and primordial ground of existence.

---

[3] In his *History of Philosophy* Hegel calls Boehme a "powerful intellect," but also speaks of the "impossibility when reading his works of pausing and trying to grasp his thoughts without one's head spinning around with qualities, spirits, and Angels." See Julius Hamberger, *Die Lehre des Deutschen Philosophen Jacob Boehme* (Munich: 1844; new edition Hildesheim: Gerstenberg, 1975), pp. lxxv ff.

For Boehme this absolute primordial ground of all existence cannot itself be talked about. He calls it the "abyss" (German: *Ungrund*), and it is motivated by a primordial, latent will for self-experience and self-enjoyment. Beginning from a condition of absolute freedom and subjectivity, it moves toward absolute form and objectivity. The abyss perceives, as if in a mirror, the possibility of unfolding and giving birth to itself. Through the agency of this mirror, primordial will transforms the possibility of unfolding itself into a reality.

The mirror through which this occurs is called the eternally Divine "Science" or "Mother of the Word of all of life"[4] when the self's image is reflected "ad intra" into the mirror's interior. Boehme prefers to call it the eternally Divine Wisdom. When what is reflecting itself turns "ad extra," outside to external possibilities in creation, a created image of the eternally Divine Mirror is produced and this created mirror is created Wisdom, or Sophia. Creation is the result, which is itself mirrored in Her. In this way Sophia is the Mother of all that is created (She is the "Idea of the ideas," the "Entelechy" of entelechies, and the "Arche" or Beginning of creation).

God's self-becoming and self-begetting in the abyss, and creation's coming into existence within God, are activated by latent qualities within the abyss. Boehme calls them source spirits, qualities, nature characteristics, or simply qualities, whereby (linguistically incorrect, but in his own sense justifiable) he relates the German word *Qualitaet* (quality) with the words *Quelle* (source or spring), and *quellen* (gush forth). These qualities gush forth from the abyss and contain all the possibilities of existence

---

[4] The etymological derivation of the word *Science* (German: *Scientz*) is the Latin word *scientia* (knowledge). It means knowledge of the primordial ground and knowledge coming from the primordial ground, which is exactly how "Wisdom" is defined. This understanding of *Science* is the bridge to Boehme's other concepts for the Holy Spirit (Wisdom and Mirror). Boehme uses the same concepts for Created Sophia. The two Sophias are only distinguished by "createdness" or "uncreatedness" and by the relationship *ad intra* or *ad extra* to the Divine Nature. Thus Sophia is the perfect image of the Holy Spirit (the Spirit Mother). She is the "out-spoken Substance, where through . . . the spirit of God manifesteth . . . Forms . . . and Shapes . . ." (Jacob Boehme, *The Second Apologie to Balthazar Tylcken*, John Sparrow, trans., (London, 1661), II/64, p. 16) and "the Mother, wherein the Father worketh" (Ibid., II/65, p. 16).

in the form of polarities (including evil). Good and evil are born here, since in the abyss, itself, everything is beyond polarity (and good and evil). Thus Boehme says that evil is not a reality existing next to God (as, for example, in a dualistic worldview like Manichaeism or India's Sankya philosophy) but has its foundation in God's primordial ground of existence which Boehme identifies with absolute freedom. Spiritual creatures like Angels and human beings also participate in this divine freedom, which defines part of their God-like image. Evil and suffering results from the misuse of freedom, i.e., by separating and activating the polarities of something that is whole; and by disengaging oneself from the full order of existence. The solution lies in the correct separation and the correct reuniting of the polarities in nature (suffering, error, and sin do, however, have a ultimate purpose; they are signs of experiences that must be learned from, and even the sense of guilt can be understood as something fortunate and an effect of God's special mercy).

THE SOURCES OF BOEHME'S SOPHIA TEACHING

The two sources for Boehme's conception of Sophia are his own effervescent mystical experience and the historical tradition (the latter of which he mentions infrequently).

Boehme's personal mysticism was based on his visionary power and his drive to investigate the essence of things and to understand their relationships. In a report about Sophia's appearance to him he states:

> I rely upon her faithfull promise, when shee appeared to mee, that shee would turne all my mournings into great joy: and when I lay upon the mountaine towards the North . . . and all the stormes and winds beate upon me . . . then shee came and comforted mee, and married her selfe to mee.

> For the virgin [the wisdome of God] hath graciously bestowed a Rose upon us . . . in the hand of the virgin, which shee reacheth forth to us, in the same place, where shee came to us in the Gate of the Deepe, and proffered us

her love: when wee lay on the Mountaine towards the North, in the strife and storm . . . [5]

This particular mystical experience took place during the time of Gregor Richter's attacks against Boehme and the years of his silence (1612–1618). After reporting it, he begins to increasingly mention Sophia, and the individual texts indicate that his knowledge of Her increased and that he became more successful in his ability to portray Her (Boehme himself ascribed his visions to direct illumination by the Holy Spirit and Sophia).

As for historical sources of knowledge about Sophia, Luther's translation of the Bible was readily available to him. The verses which may have especially influenced him are Proverbs 8,22–31, Ecclesiasticus 24,1–6 and chapters 7–9 of the Book of Wisdom.

The Proverbs and Ecclesiasticus passages, for example, clearly portray Wisdom as a person and also Her mediating role between God and creation and God and humanity. Boehme's seven qualities or characteristics of Sophia (keen, soft, firm, serious, clear, pure, and persuasive) reflect the description in Wisdom 7,22–24; and like the description in Wisdom 7,25–26 She is for him God's power which is breathed out, and God's mirror and the image of God's goodness. Echoing Wisdom 8, She is transcendent and present in all things. She dwells in pious souls and is Friend, Betrothed, Bride, Mistress, and Teacher to those who seek Her in an upright manner. She gives immortality to those who unite themselves with Her. She is the source of joy and pure desire and is sent by God to mediate between God and humanity, and to help and comfort. Boehme ascribes all of these characteristics and functions to Sophia and infers important consequences from them: She is truly his spiritual Friend and Bride, Mother and Teacher.[6] Although commentators are not unanimous about whether Wisdom 7 and 8 depict Sophia as a person or merely as a per-

---

[5] Jacob Boehme, *The Second Book Concerning the Three Principles of the Divine Essence*, John Sparrow, trans. (London, 1648), chapter 14/52, p. 142; chapter 18/58, p. 228.
[6] Jacob Boehme, *The Way to Christ* (New York: Paulist Press, 1978), I/45–51, pp. 56–62.

sonification, for Boehme She is clearly a person: "the noble, pure and divine Virgin Sophia."[7] (What is, however, remarkable about Boehme's perception of Sophia is that he sometimes speaks of Her as a Bridegroom, i.e., as a man; one possible explanation is the Christological view of Sophia, and another is the influence of the Cabala where the Sephirah Chokmah, or Wisdom, is sometimes understood as masculine; in any case, Boehme's primary view of Sophia is feminine.)

Another possible historical source of knowledge about Sophia was the Sophia tradition of the Middle Ages visible in portrayals like the Hildesheim Missal, and Sophia with the Seven Liberal Arts (chapter 7), a depiction of Her with the Seven Gifts of the Holy Spirit,[8] the visions of Hildegard of Bingen (chapter 8), and the mysticism of Heinrich Suso or Seuse (1295–1366).[9] Some of Boehme's ideas may also have been influenced by the Cabala.[10]

BOEHME'S SOPHIOLOGY

According to Boehme, Sophia's origin is found in the "abyss," the most profound ground of existence. The abyss is pure potentiality. In the act of establishing itself it unfolds to a ground or

---

[7] Henri Plard, *La Médiatrice Cosmique—La Vierge Sophie de Jacob Boehme: L'Univers à la Renaissance, Microcosme et Macrocosme* (Bruxelles: Presses Universitaires de Bruxelles, 1970), pp. 145 ff.

[8] Erich Neumann, *The Great Mother: An Analysis of the Archetype*, Ralph Manheim, trans., Bollingen Series XLVII (Princeton: Princeton University Press, 1955, 1963), "Sophia Ecclesia," plate 175.

[9] Heinrich Suso (Seuse) was a Dominican father from Constance and an example of Sophian mysticism in the Middle Ages. As the result of an experience at age 18, he devoted himself to Eternal Wisdom, whom he thereafter served as a knight to his Lady. He perceived Sophia as the Queen with a golden cloak at God's throne and understood himself as Her Lover. His dictum was: *Ipsa Sponsa et ego eius servulus* (She is my Bride and I am Her servant). His servitude was a "service of love" in the sense of the "Minnedienst" of the Middle Ages (Henri Plard, *La Médiatrice Cosmique*), p. 156.

[10] Henri Plard, *La Médiatrice Cosmique*, p. 156 ff; see also: Thomas Schipflinger, "Die Sophia bei Jacob Boehme—Die Sophiologie Boehmes" (paper for the seminar "Naturmystik und Naturwissenschaft in der Renaissance" at the University of Munich, Professor H. B. Gerl-Falkovitz, winter semester 1985/1986), p. 34 ff. (manuscript).

foundation called the absolute and divine "Ens a se," or Divine Nature. This Nature consists of will and knowing (Science, Wisdom) and the product of the two. This aspect of the Divine Nature involves its life in and to itself (*ad intra*) and represents the three principles of the Trinity.[11]

The Trinitarian God wills to extend its life outside of itself (*ad extra*) and beholds an opportunity to do this in an archetype of creation—created Wisdom or Sophia—the special image of uncreated, Divine Wisdom. God beholds the ideas of creatures and the things of creation in Her. Thus She is synonymous with the beginning and is the one with whom God creates the heavens and the earth, as indicated by Holy Scripture: ". . . in the beginning (by means of Wisdom) God created heaven and earth" (Gen. 1,1). In this way Sophia is the Co-Creator and Mother of the universe and the Mediator between God and creation.[12]

With respect to redemption, She is the Co-Worker of the Son who incarnates for this purpose. Her cooperation involves Her own incarnation by becoming the Son's bodily Mother in Mary.

The above is an overview of Boehme's Sophia teaching whose details will be reviewed in the sections which follow.

Divine and Eternal Wisdom in the Holy Trinity

Boehme's single, divine ground ("abyss") of Divine Nature becomes a polarity of Will and Science-Wisdom; and they in turn unfold the third element which is their product. This suggests a Trinitarian conception composed of Will (the Father), Science-Wisdom (the Spirit Mother or Holy Spirit) and their product who is the Son. Such a conception does not correspond to the traditional understanding of the Trinity, whereby the Holy Spirit proceeds from the Father and the Son (or in the Eastern Church, from the Father through the Son). Although Boehme actually held to the literal sense of traditional Trinitarian understanding, his consistent use of the schema Will, Science-Wisdom, and their

---

[11] Alexandre Koyré, *La Philosophie de Jacob Boehme* (New York: B. Franklin, 1968).
[12] Henri Plard, *La Médiatrice Cosmique* (note #9), p. 153.

product suggests interpreting them as Father, Holy Spirit (Spirit Mother) and Son:

> For the Nothing causeth the willing, that *it is* desirous; and the desiring is an *Imagination*. . . . Wherein the will, in the Looking-Glass of Wisdome, discovereth it selfe . . . and impregnateth it selfe with the Imagination out of the wisdome, viz: out of the Virgin-like Looking-Glass which there, is a *Mother*. . . . For, the will, viz: the Father, *speaketh* . . . in the Looking-Glass of the wisdom. . . . and openeth the word of life.[13]

As for Boehme's understanding of *Science* (Wisdom), he affirms its Latin derivation (knowledge); but adds that he also understands it in the sense of "the true Ground,"[14] and in the sense of the word "draw":

> The Eternall Science in the Will of the Father draweth the Will (which is called Father) into it selfe, and shutteth it selfe into a Center of the Divine Generation of the Trinity, and by the Science speaketh it selfe forth into a word of understanding.[15]

For Boehme, however (as with Augustine), there is a second Wisdom next to the previous eternal, divine Science *ad intra*—a Science *ad extra* related to creation[16]:

> Now this Science is the Root to the fiery Mind, and it is in briefe the Root of all Spirituall beginnings, it is the true Root of Soules and proceedeth through every Life, for it is the Ground from whence Life commeth.[17]

---

[13] Boehme, *Incarnation of Jesus Christ*, John Sparrow, trans. (London, 1659), chapter 2/4–5, 13–14.

[14] Boehme, *The Clavis or Key*, John Sparrow, trans. (London, 1647), p. 210.

[15] Boehme, *The Clavis or Key*, p. 217.

[16] The distinction between the *processiones naturae divinae ad intra* (processes of the Divine Nature to itself, or toward the inside) and *opera Dei ad extra* (God's works toward the outside in creation) is important and epistemologically helpful. Yet Boehme often blurs the boundaries.

[17] Boehme, *The Clavis or Key*, p. 215.

"Science" in the above quotation means the image of the eternal, Divine Science—created Wisdom or Sophia.

It almost seems that in speaking of a second "Science," Boehme introduces a fourth divine principle next to the Trinity of the Divine Nature. He was accused of having done so, but such a notion is ultimately based on a misinterpretation. Apart from the fact that Boehme adhered to traditional Trinitarian teaching, the supposition of a fourth divine principle would contradict his fundamental ontogenetic schema which proceeds from unity, to a polar duality and then to a trinity. He consistently held to this schema, and when this is kept in mind the unclarity resolves itself.

Interpreting Boehme's Divine Science or Wisdom as the Holy Spirit raises the question of whether the Holy Spirit embraces a feminine dimension of the Godhead.[18] This is a subject that will be taken up in more detail in chapter 26.

Wisdom-Sophia in Creation

Wisdom-Sophia in creation is the Wisdom in whom the Divine Nature beholds, as if in a mirror, the wonders of creation and then calls them into existence through the Word:

> . . . shee is the wonderfull Wisdome . . . in her hath the Holy Ghost discovered the Image of Angells, as also the Image of Man, which the *Verbum Fiat* hath created.
>
> Shee is the *Great* secret *Mystery* in the Counsell of God . . . and openeth the Wonders in the hidden seales or formes of Nature. . . .[19]

> This Wisdome of God (which is the Virgin of Glory . . . and an Image of the number Three) is (in her figure) an

---

[18] See Christa Mulack, *Die Weibichkeit Gottes, Matriarchale Voraussetzungen des Gottesbildes* (Stuttgart: Kreuz, 1983), p. 9 ff; Leonardo Boff, *The Maternal Face of God: The Feminine and its Religious Expressions*, Robert R. Barr and John W. Diercksmeier, trans. (San Francisco: HarperSanFrancisco, 1987).

[19] Boehme, *The Threefold Life of Man*, John Sparrow, trans. (London, 1650), chapter 5/44–45, p. 70.

Image, like Angells and Men . . . like a blossome of a branch, out of the Spirit of God.

For, shee is the *Substantiality* of the Spirit, which the Spirit of God putteth on as a Garment, whereby he manifesteth himselfe, or else his forme would not be knowne: for shee is the Spirits Corporeity, and though shee is not a corporeall palpable substance, like us, Men, yet shee is substantiall and visible, but the Spirit is *not* substantiall.

For wee, Men, can in Eternity, see no more of the Spirit of God, but onely the *Glance* of the Majesty; and his glorious *power* wee feele in us, for it is our life, and conducteth us.[20]

In this Looking-Glass, hath been seen from Eternity, the substance of this world, *viz.* the Third Principle. . . .

In this Eternall Looking-Glass of the wisdome of God, hath also the soul of Man . . . been discovered *in the Essence*, which with the beginning of the first Moving in the *Fiat* of God, became formed into a Creature. . . .[21]

The Eternall Virgin of Wisdome, stood in Paradise as a Figure, in which all the *Wonders* of God were knowne, and was in its figure an Image in it selfe . . . and in that Virgin, God created the Matrix of the Earth, so that it was a visible *palpable* image in substance; wherein Heaven, Earth, Starres, and Elements stood in substance, and all whatsoever liveth and moveth was in this one Image.[22]

. . . she is his . . . *Cabinet,* or Body, she is the Holy Spirits Corporeity, *in her* lye the Colours of the Vertue, for she is the Out-spoken Substance. . . .

She is the highest Substantiality of the *Deity* . . .[23]

Boehme explains how She gives life to the world and guides it

---

[20]Boehme, *The Threefold Life of Man*, chapter 5/49–51, p. 71.

[21] Boehme, *The First Apologie to Balthazar Tylcken*, John Sparrow, trans. (London, 1662), Part II/142, 148, pp. 20–21.

[22] Boehme, *The Threefold Life of Man*, chapter 11/12, p. 161.

[23] Boehme, *The Second Apologie to Balthazar Tylcken*, II/67, p. 16.

by using the image of the soul in the body. Corresponding to the three levels of the human soul (the spiritual soul, the soul of the senses and the vegetative or life soul) Wisdom also animates and guides the universe and creation on three levels. The *Spiritus Majoris Mundi* is the Spirit of the entire cosmos; the *Archaeus* is the inner ground from which the starry heavens and the four elements arise; and the *Spiritus Mundi* is the World Spirit or Soul of the World. These three levels of soul[24] correspond to three bodily regions upon which they work. The body of the *Spiritus Majoris Mundi* is the entire universe; the body of the *Archaeus* is the starry heavens (the sun, planets and stars); and the body of the *Spiritus Mundi* are the four elements themselves out of which all creatures and things come into existence.

In summary, God creates Sophia as the Mirror in which God's ideas of creation and possibilities *ad extra* are beheld. She is Herself the "Idea of the ideas" in whom is contained all ideas. She transforms these ideas into reality, providing them with the raiment of visible corporeality and begetting and sustaining all creatures. They are Her Body, and She is the Soul—of the universe and of the world. In beholding creation we behold Her power and beauty, and through Her, the power and beauty of the Creator.

This grandiose vision of creation as Sophia's Body is the basis for Boehme's nature mysticism. It is a perception that has the potential today of preventing a devotionless attitude and exploitative behavior against the earth, promoting instead a genuine love and reverence for nature (Honor Thy Mother!).

Sophia and Mary

The most interesting and original aspect of Boehme's Sophia teaching concerns Her relationship to Mary. According to Boehme, Sophia entrusted Herself to Mary and took on human

---

[24]See Edith Klum, *Natur, Kunst, und Liebe in der Philosophie W. Solowjews, Eine Religionswissenschaftliche Untersuchung* (Munich: Otto Sagnet, 1965), p. 98 ff. "Die Weltseelenlehre Solowjews"; Pierre Teilhard de Chardin, *Writings in the Time of War*, Rene Hague, trans. (New York: Harper & Row, 1968), "The Soul Of The World," pp. 182–190.

form in Her. Mary is the paradise entrance point into the world, and the means for the world to return to an original, divine condition. She is a paradisical womb, making possible the Son's incarnation, the Son who is capable of bringing about the divinization of humanity:

> And the will of the Heart of God in the Father, is from the Heart entred into the will of the Wisdome, before the Father, into an Eternall contract; and the same virgin of the Wisdome of God, in the Word of God, hath in the bosom of the virgin *Mary*, given it selfe into her virgin-Matrix. . . . in that, the Heart of God is become an Angelicall Man, as *Adam* was in the Creation. . . .[25]

> We cannot say that the heavenly virgin of the Mercy of God (*viz.* that which entred into *Mary* out of the Counsell of God) is become Earthly; but wee say that the soule of *Mary* hath comprehended the heavenly virgin: and that the heavenly virgin hath put the heavenly new pure Garment of the holy Element, out of the chast virgin of God . . . on to the soule of *Mary*, as a new Regenerated Man: and in that same shee hath conceived the Savior of all the world, and borne him into this world.[26]

> . . . wee say of *Mary*: shee hath comprehended the Holy Heavenly Eternall Virgin of God, and put on the holy and Pure Element . . . and yet was truly a virgin in this world [generated] by *Joachim* and *Anna*. But shee was not called a holy pure virgin according to her earthly Birth . . . but her holinesse and purity is according to the Heavenly virgin . . .[27]

---

[25] Boehme, *A Description of the Three Principles of the Divine Essence*, John Sparrow, trans. (London, 1648), chapter 18/37.

[26] Boehme, *A Description of the Three Principles of the Divine Essence*, chapter 22/37.

[27] Boehme, *A Description of the Three Principles of the Divine Essence*, chapter 22/34.

> For, when Gabriel . . . brought her the Message . . . and
> she consented thereto . . . then the Center of the Holy
> Trinity, moved it selfe, and opened the Convenant, that is,
> the Eternal Virginity . . . in her in the word of Life.[28]

What was the basis for this teaching about the relationship between Sophia and Mary? Although Valentin Weigel (1533–1588),
a Lutheran theologian and mystic from whom Boehme borrowed some ideas, often spoke about Sophia-Mary,[29] it seems
that historical sources alone (including the Cabala and Scripture)
are insufficient to explain the teaching. The resulting conclusion
is that it originated from Boehme's own visionary power and intimate relationship to Sophia Herself.

Though Boehme's Marian Sophiology has not received
much attention, it may comprise the most important part of his
spiritual legacy. What is known today about Russian Sophiology[30] may help stimulate a closer examination of Boehme's
Sophiology, which can lead to a more profound knowledge of
the mystery of Sophia-Mary.

BOEHME'S PERSONAL RELATIONSHIP TO SOPHIA

Boehme's intimate relationship to Sophia is perceptible in everything that he says about Her. Particularly poignant are the conversations he depicts between Sophia and the soul that venerates
Her. Sophia begins by speaking to the soul:

> O my bridegroom, how good it is for me in your mar-
> riage. Kiss me, then, with your desire in your strength
> and might. Then will I show you all my beauty and bring

---

[28] Boehme, *Incarnation of Jesus Christ*, chapter 8/13, p. 62.
[29] See for example: Hans Maier, *Der Mystische Spiritualismus von Valentin Weigel* (Guetersloh: C. Bertelsmann, 1926), note #1, p. 80.
[30] Fairy von Lilienfeld, "Sophia—Die Weisheit Gottes, uber die Visionen des Wladimir Solowjew als Grundlage Seine 'Sophiologie'," *Una Sancta*, 39, 1984, pp. 113–129.

you joy in your fire-life and sweet love and bright light. All holy angels rejoice with us now that they see us married once more. Now, my dear beloved, remain faithful to me. Do not again turn your face from me. Work your miracles in my love, for which God awakened you. . . .[31]

The Soul Speaks Further to the Noble Sophia:

My beautiful and sweet Spouse, what ought I to say before You? . . . I had wasted Your sweet love, and not kept my faith with You by which I fell into eternal punishment. Yet since You came to me out of love in my hellish anguish, and redeemed me from pain and took me again as a bridegroom, I shall now break my will for Your love and be obedient to You and wait for Your love. I now have enough, since I know that You are with me in all my need, and You do not abandon me. O gracious Love, I turn my fiery face to You. O beautiful crown, take me immediately into You and lead me out of my restlessness. I wish to be with You eternally and nevermore depart from You.[32]

The Noble Sophia Answers the Soul Comfortingly, and says:

My bridegroom, be comforted. I have engaged myself to you in my highest love, and in my faith [have I] bound myself to you. I shall be with you in all the days to the end of the world. I shall come to you and make my dwelling in you in your internal choir. You will drink from my fountain, for I am now yours and you are mine.[33]

As beautiful and moving as this mystical dialogue about Boehme's personal relationship to Sophia is, it gives rise to the question of whether such a relationship of betrothal to Sophia is equally applicable to women. The answer is to be found in Holy Scripture. In the Old Testament, the people of Israel were understood as Yahweh's Bride (Hos. 11,4), just as in the New Testament the Church is understood as the Bride of Christ (Eph. 5,32).

---

[31] Boehme, *The Way to Christ*, I/47, p. 59.
[32] Boehme, *The Way to Christ*, I/50, pp. 61–62.
[33] Boehme, *The Way to Christ*, I/51, p. 62.

Men also were to participate in the espousal of the community to Yahweh and Christ, which symbolizes the wholeness of union with God's higher nature; and in the same way women also are to participate in the graces and splendors that union with Sophia conveys on the soul.

BOEHME'S RELEVANCE TODAY

As difficult as Boehme's thought can be to penetrate, there is much of value to be found in his works. Although a lowly cobbler by trade, he made a deep impression on his contemporaries and significantly influenced the intellectual world after his death. The knowledge that he pursued and discovered is still relevant today, especially his teaching about polarities and nature's life principle, who is Sophia.

Polarities (such as light and darkness, water and fire, hardness and softness) arise from the dynamic abyss, which is the ground of all being. The phenomena of the world come into existence through the intermingling of these polar qualities and elements. Evil itself is the manifestation of an imbalance of elements which are merely a part of existence; and the freedom that is inherent to creatures possessing a soul and spirit also plays into the possibility of manifestations.

Western thinking has lost knowledge of the ontological polarity of existence and the importance of the balancing and synthesis of opposites. As a result, Western culture is ruled by static forms of knowledge which are opposed to a more universal kind of knowledge that represents wholeness. Environmental problems are one example of an inability to synthesize the tension between polarities such as rationality and intuitiveness, material and spiritual concerns, and freedom and limitation.

Boehme teaches that polarities belong to the dynamism of existence, but that they must be harmonized and synthesized. Such a recognition is crucial to communal life and to the evolution of the world and humanity. While it seems that nature on its own is able to achieve a kind of natural balance, problems result primarily through humanity's misuse of freedom. A solution may lie in awareness of polarities and finding the strength to synthesize them, which can be gained through humility (and humble prayer) and good will.

Boehme also teaches that there is an inner principle of life or soul that is inherent to all creatures and the world. The soul is the actual formative force that determines external shapes and configurations. What is visible is the external reflection of an inner spiritual reality, the concrete manifestation of an "idea." Sophia is the Idea or Soul of the entire deeper world, which is Her Body. Such an understanding is the key to an insight into the natural world, but also the key to a feeling of connectedness to nature, for all of nature is ensouled and represents the mighty effects of the workings of Sophia-Wisdom. This is the philosophical and theological basis for a genuine reverence of nature and for a nature mysticism.

Boehme refers to Sophia as the Mirror in which God beholds the reflection of Godself and God's ideas, and upon beholding them God rejoices. It is humanity's task to gaze into creation and to behold and know Sophia, and through Her God's plan for all of creation and humanity. As Sophia says:

> [B]e comforted. . . . I shall be with you in all the days to the end of the world. . . . We shall bring about in this world what God has foreordained for us [to do]; we shall serve Him in His temple which we ourselves are. Amen.[34]

---

[34] Boehme, *The Way to Christ*, I/51, p. 62.

12

Gottfried Arnold—
The Bard of Sophia

GOTTFRIED ARNOLD (1666–1714), authored the following prayer. He was one of Jacob Boehme's most gifted and influential pupils. Arnold was himself a mystic and also an evangelical church historian. He studied theology, became a professor of church history and subsequently worked as an administrator. Arnold was the prolific author of some 52 books and also composed church hymns.[1] The breadth of Arnold's influence stretched from Germany (Herder and Goethe) to Russia (Soloviev and Florenski).

A Prayer

> O God, that I might whisper the wonders of Divine Sophia, give me, O Father, according to your promise, the spirit of Wisdom!

---

[1] Arnold's main works are: *Unpartheyishche Kirchen und Ketzerhistorie* [An Impartial History of the Church and Heretics] (Schoffheusen: Emanuel and Benedict Hurter, 1740–1742), and *Das Geheimnis der Goettlichen Sophia* [The Mystery of Divine Sophia].

And to those who read this, just that very same spirit of faith which You have given me so that I believe and speak of it . . .

Behold Lord, what You allowed me to truly see in spirit and hear with the ears of my heart, and feel and taste in my own essence, let me proclaim that to others, that they too may share in the company of this mystery . . .

For the time has come, and many are to be prepared and led to what was so long hidden, to the stone rejected by the builders as unworthy.

Therefore let me, O God and Father, proclaim the truth of Wisdom and how She came to be.[2]

ARNOLD'S SOPHIA TEACHING

Arnold's Sophiological work is *Das Geheimnis der Goettlichen Sophia* [The Mystery of Divine Sophia]. The first part is theoretical and deals with Sophia as She is described in Holy Scripture and in tradition. The second part is a collection of Arnold's poetry about Sophia.

In the first chapter of Part One, which takes up the question of why Sophia is so little known, Arnold writes:

Unfortunately one experiences daily that the eternal cause of all that is good, Divine Wisdom, is not known by most people and is therefore scorned and not valued very much, and even most of those who are upright do not heed Her sufficiently but accept Her in varying degrees.[3]

---

[2] Gottfried Arnold, *Das Geheimnis der Goettlichen Sophia*, facsimile printing of the Leipzig 1700 edition with an introduction by Walter Nigg (Stuttgart-Bad Cannstatt: Friedrich Frommann Verlag, 1963), part I, p. 1.

[3] Gottfried Arnold, *Das Geheimnis der Goettlichen Sophia*, Part I, p. 1. This and subsequent quotations from this work have been translated from the German.

In the ninth chapter, which deals with attaining Wisdom, he writes:

> Most of those souls on the earth at one time or another experience all of this . . . but human beings can be divided into two groups; the largest which resists Wisdom; and the other that is obedient and therefore becomes overshadowed with a special grace . . . to belong to this last group (speaking plainly) one must simply be obedient and true in and through God to what the spirit of Wisdom . . . testifies in you. There are no further burdens or commands, and it is not necessary for those who pursue Her earnestly and zealously to run hither or thither by the strength of their own efforts.

> . . . I have nothing at all to do with reason, which is despicable, bringing the torment of a plethora of thoughts. As to how Wisdom can simultaneously be a Virgin and Begetter, Mother and Bride . . . the proper understanding is found in Holy Scripture, which tells us that Wisdom is not just called Mother but also Virgin, Bride, Betrothed, and Consort. Solomon himself, who is experienced, assures us that he wanted Her as his Bride, and determined to bring Her home in order to dwell with Her (Wisd. 8,1). Just as his entire song, which is called the "Song of Songs", speaks of the love of the soul and spirit for Sophia.[4]

In speaking about Sophia Arnold often quotes passages from the Church Fathers. One of the most informative is by Augustine:

> . . . there is a certain sublime creature, with so chaste a love cleaving unto the true and eternal God, that although not co-eternal with Him, yet is not detached from Him, nor dissolved into the variety and vicissitude of times, but reposeth in the most true contemplation of Him only . . . This is the house of God . . . partaker of Thy eternity . . . Thou hast made it fast for ever and ever . . .

---

[4] Gottfried Arnold, *Das Geheimnis der Goettlichen Sophia*, I, pp. 57, 111.

> Nor yet is it co-eternal with Thee, O God, because not
> without beginning; for it was made . . . that wisdom
> which is created . . . the intellectual nature, which by con-
> templating light, is light . . . our mother which is above
> . . . the place of the habitation of the glory of my Lord, thy
> builder and possessor.[5]

Arnold responds to this passage:

> With these words Augustine touches upon mysteries
> which are not well known about the eternal Dwelling of
> God and about Wisdom who issued forth from there;
> how She is something different from the eternal Son of
> God and the entire Blessed Trinity on high and yet is to-
> gether with the Trinity a single nature splendid beyond
> splendor, the New Jerusalem, the Mother of us all, etc.[6]

Unfortunately he does not go on to explain fully what he means
(by the "etc."), only adding that reason would like to expose
"these pearls" but would trample them underfoot; thus it is better not to discuss the matter any further.[7]

In other selections from the book's first part Arnold
speaks clearly of Sophia's personal and separate nature:

> From the proceeding it is certain above all that Wisdom's
> nature is spiritual, independent, lasting, and divine and
> heavenly, existing in itself. . . . Wherefore it follows that
> the holy did not understand Wisdom as a mere name, but
> as a divine being, higher than all Angels and human be-
> ings—who is an independent person, just as Anastasius
> Sinaita says.

> Thus She only allows Herself to be moved by the eternal
> spirit of God, whose body She is (speaking in the truest

---

[5] Gottfried Arnold, *Das Geheimnis der Goettlichen Sophia*, I, p. 48; English: *The Confessions of Augustine*, Edward B. Pusey, trans. (New York: Random House, 1949), pp. 280–282.
[6] Gottfried Arnold, *Das Geheimnis der Goettlichen Sophia*, I, p. 50.
[7] Gottfried Arnold, *Das Geheimnis der Goettlichen Sophia*, I, p. 52.

sense of the word). She is in Herself, however, eternally still and at rest, a reflection of the splendor of God. For all eternity Her radiance penetrates only into the center of divine love. . . . Thus She is constantly a recreated image of God's love, in which this love is reflected and has its joy.

Her kiss brings to whomever this Dove (Sophia) takes to Her bosom an olive leaf of untroubled peace and fortified hope. One is free to enjoy Her and to take as much as is desired from Her balsam of life. And once comforted, one may lay at Her breast and suckle to satisfaction, all Her pure powers are there for the taking in this paradisical game of love.[8]

The above statements indicate that Arnold was deeply convinced of the individuality of Created Sophia. Even if in some passages he seens to waver in this belief because of dogmatic considerations, his songs clearly speak of his conviction of Sophia as a person. Again and again he calls Her his queen, friend and bride.

SONGS OF SOPHIA

Arnold's book also contains a collection of "poetical proverbs" (156 in number) in praise of Wisdom which were inspired by Solomon's "Song of Songs" in the Old Testament. The following selections are from his book.

Who Am I
That the Mother of My Lord Should Visit Me?
Dark night had covered everything with darkness
And my soul felt sorrow, hope, love,
Longing, worry and fear about my wish:
That JESUS' roots remain eternally in me.

---

[8] Gottfried Arnold, *Das Geheimnis der Goettlichen Sophia*, I, pp. 30–31; pp. 15, 113. (Anastasius Sinaita was the abbot of the Catharine monastery on Mt. Sinai. He wrote several theological works.)

Then in an instant came before my spiritual eye
WISDOM, Bride of God, but not in Her highest Glory
(in which She otherwise often comes to human beings).
Yet larger than a human form, all glittering with beauty,
Noble to behold, arousing love, lovely and gay,
So that I was reverently filled
With love and joy

I could only say:
O Princess, whoever you are, be merciful to this mote of
    dust,
Who lays under your gaze. What brought You hither?
Who could be allowed to put my lament before You?
But in answer only this I heard: Be content!
And therewith bowed She sweetly down to me,
And layed Her left arm down upon my right
And embraced me (She was so friendly)
And kissed me. Even now I see
Her rosy cheeks before me, Her shining purple mouth,
Where lies suspended loveliness a thousand times
like drops of pearl . . .
The fairness of Her face, the bright roundness of Her eyes.

The reverence lies forever impressed within me,
That I did feel before Her together with sweet love:
As if a king had sent his spouse unto a beggar.
Thus felt I, when my God sent Wisdom unto me.
And so I asked astonished, who am I
That the Bride and Mother of my Lord should visit me?[9]

This poem is an testimony to Gottfried Arnold's experience of
Sophia during a night spent in contemplation. The title of the
poem is a reference to Elizabeth's words to Mary (Luke 1,43);
and by referring to Sophia as the "Mother of the Lord" Arnold is
acknowledging, entirely in the sense of Jacob Boehme, an intimate relationship between Sophia and Mary.

---

[9] Gottfried Arnold, *Das Geheimnis der Goettlichen Sophia*, II, p. 293.

The following poems,[10] which speak about love of Sophia, are inspired by motifs from Solomon's "Song of Songs" in the Old Testament.

O Sophia, My Strength

Let reason laugh
So very much at my simplicity:
Even more will I sing
About the object of my love.

O, Sophia, my Strength . . .
O She is my Heroine,
And everything that I need.
And without Her know I
Myself to be unprepared for battle . . .

Be Thou mine, Thou Heroine, Thou,
God's pure Life.
Let me be suspended unharmed
In peace that is assured.
Hold me tightly to You
Protect me with your cloak!
And when the enemy's power mounts,
So fight and be victorious in me!

Golden Sun

Golden Sun, arise, spread forth Thy rays of light
In me! O Fount of Life, well up in me with power:
Wisdom, Goddess of my love, without whom everything
    is broken,
Behold, how my spirit lifts me up in search of Thy gaze.

---

[10] The poems are from Gottfried Arnold, II, p. 45, 46, 145, 49, 53, 55, 99–100 (verses 10–15, 19, 25), 143. Tr: translation mine.

Come, O come, my Bride, if I may call Thee so.
And if not worthy now, let me but stand as a servant be-
fore Thee.
Come to me from Lebanon, where all the flowers know
Thee.

Sulamith

Sulamith, sugared delight,
Splendor of Light, elevated Sun.
Did Thy arrow not strike me?
Is all of Thee not open to me?

Did Thou Thyself not appear to me,
To serve me personally,
As does a Bride her dearest?
Has my wish not been granted,
When Thou permeated my spirit through and through?
O my incomparable Treasure!

Come, O Dove, come, my Life!
Let me give Thee a thousand kisses.
Because my mouth is devoted to Thine.
Let me press closer to Thy heart,
Until I finally come to lie
Sunk within Thine essence.

Shine on, most beauteous Sun,
Make this small world even brighter.
Let no small cloud enter in.
Let me undisturbed enjoy
What the spirit wants to give me,
Till I may be changed completely.

Next She left a kiss from above,
Which like a mirror straightway filled my spirit:
My heart adoring, my mouth full of praise,
So that I sang this song of glory.

Thou, Mistress Of My Youth

Thou mistress of my youth
My wedlock's Consort
Ruler of my senses
With whom I walk and stand:
My Angel and Companion
I will never leave Thee
When there is no one more to see.

Well Of Joys

O Sister, O most lovely Bride, Thou art to me
A Fountain of Gardens, a Well of joys.
A Pond built on living waters.

Allow, O Queen

Allow, O Queen, Throne Princess of all powers,
Ruler of my senses, whom I also call Friend,
Yea, to be my dear Bride, O do not scorn me.
Allow my poor spirit to bow before Thee.

From Songs Imploring Divine Wisdom:

Give me Wisdom, whom Thou love,
And give to them who love Thee.
Wisdom, who with Her crown
Always appears before Thy throne.

I love Her lovely countenance.
She is my hearts Joy and Light.
She is most beautiful of all, She who holds me
And is most pleasing to mine eyes.

She, most noble, is chosen
By Thee, Most High, Self born.
She is equal to the bright sun
Rich in virtues and gifts.

Her mouth is sweet and comforting
When Her gaze glances on us,
When bowed we are by trouble,
It is She who quickens the heart.

She is all honor and splendor,
Proven in death and great distress.
Those who entreat Her and implore
Remain alive, though they may die.

She is the Creator's closest Friend,
Mighty in word and deed.
Through Her the blind world knows,
What God is thinking in His dwellings.

So send Her from Thy throne,
And give Her to Thy child and son.
Ah, shake and pour Her richly out
Into the dwelling of my poor heart.

So that in all that I may do,
I might increase in Thy love.
For those who keep themselves from Wisdom,
They remain unloved by Thee.

From a Prayer of Gottfried Arnold to Sophia:

Holy Sophia, faithful Sovereign, coax them more towards Thee. . . . O that all, who are intent on riches or
honors in life, would only dare try to follow Thee and
leave all else behind!

Thou showerest Thy friends with all the treasures of
Thy house, so that they can only complain of their
tired, mistrusting, ungrateful, lazy hearts that are too
narrow to contain the abundant waters of the ocean of
Your love.

Gottfried Arnold struggled to come to a clear picture of Sophia. In spite of his zeal for investigating Wisdom, he is not able to move beyond the level of thinking of his time, even though he tries many times to transcend it. His poems to Sophia express his deeply held conviction of Her reality, and on the basis of these poems, he can be called without question a great Sophian teacher and mystic—perhaps the most significant in the West next to Jacob Boehme. Although in his speculative Sophiology he was not able to come to terms fully with the Sophia of Scripture and tradition, his work remains full of affective power and mystical profundity.

13

Significant Sophiologists after Boehme

JACOB BOEHME'S LIFE AND works aroused a lot of attention—from brusque rejection to enthusiastic recognition and acceptance. Many God-seekers, stimulated and encouraged even by Gottfried Arnold, took up Boehme's writings and teaching enthusiastically and spread them further. It would be impossible to relate all of that here. The portraits of a few of these seekers will be presented here, for they exerted a particular influence on their surroundings and times. To these individuals belong, without a doubt, Jane Leade, John Pordage, Johann Georg Gichtel, Louis-Claude de St. Martin, and Johann Jacob Wirz.

It is astonishing to see how much they were seized by Jacob Boehme's ideas, and how they passed on his teachings to others, in particular his Sophia teaching, oftentimes in conjunction with very great sacrifice.

LADY JANE LEADE

After Boehme's works had come to England through the interest of King Carl I, they were taken up by the Londoner John Pordage

(1607–1683), an Anglican clergyman whose commentaries helped to spread awareness of Boehme.[1]

Lady Jane Leade (1623–1704) belonged to Pordage's circle, and she was a woman who proved herself especially receptive to Boehme's teaching. She was born into a prominent family and had received a good education. At age 16, she had heard a beautiful voice during a Christmas celebration that made such a deep impression on her that she began to lead a reclusive religious life. Efforts to divert her attention to other things were in vain. Upon turning 21 she married a relative named William Leade at her family's insistence and bore him two daughters. When her husband died in 1670, she again took up a reclusive life and lived in poverty, having been deprived of her husband's estate due to administrative malfeasance (a vision in 1668 had prepared her for this misfortune).

The Boehme study group that she took part in with Pordage nourished her proclivity for spirituality and mysticism. She seriously tried to shape her life according to Boehme's teaching, which Pordage helped her to understand. She experienced visions and auditions, and those from Sophia were especially significant to her. She wrote them down in sixteen separate works.[2]

Her writings attracted little attention until they were translated into Dutch by Loth Fischer who lived in Rotterdam.

---

[1] John Pordage's main works are: *Theologia Mystica* (London, 1681), *Metaphysica Divina, Sophia,* and *Philosophia Mystica.* Pordage's cosmology and soteriology (salvational teaching) were similar to Boehme's but individual as well. The relationship of Sophia and the Trinity to creation and humanity occupy a special place in his works. Humanity's goal consists of uniting the inner human being with the resurrected and transfigured Christ; this is the condition of resurrection or ascension. It must, however, be proceeded by a condition of renewal, which consists of union and cooperation with Sophia. Through Sophia, Christ must be born and live, suffer, die, and resurrect in us (*Realenenzyklopaedie fur Protestantische Theologie und Kirche* (Leipzig: Hinrichs, 1896), vol. 15, J. Pordage, pp. 553 ff).

[2] The most significant works of Lady Jane Leade are: *The Heavenly Cloud* (London, 1681), *The Revelation of Revelations* (London, 1683), *A Fountain of Gardens* [spiritual diaries in four volumes] (London, 1696–1701), *The Law of Paradise* (London, 1695), *A Message to the Philadelphia Society* (London, 1696), *The Tree of Faith* (London, 1696), *A Revelation of the Everlasting Gospel Message* (London, 1697), *The Ascent to the Mount of Vision* (London, 1698).

As a result she became a celebrated personality; and when the young Oxford scholar Francis Lee traveled through Rotterdam, he heard of her and later sought her out in London. Lee was very affected by her piety and dedicated himself to the task of publishing her work and promoting the Philadelphia Society[3] which she had founded in 1670 with Pordage and led. (The Society was inspired by the teachings of Boehme, became widespread in England and existed on the continent of Europe as well.)

The last years of her life were marked by poverty, dissension among her followers, criticism, and eventually blindness. Francis Lee had been inspired by one of her visions to marry one of her daughters, and he stood steadfastly by her until her death at age 81.

Lady Jane Leade's visions of Sophia began in 1670. One report from her diaries indicates:

Sophia appeared to me in the figure of a woman with a very friendly and dignified demeanor, Her countenance radiated like the sun and She was dressed in a garment of translucent gold.[4]

---

[3] According to its founders the purpose of the Philadelphia Society was: the founding of the kingdom of God on earth by means of a holy life, the struggle against sensuality and the general spread of brotherly love (Philadelphia) which is the beginning and basis of the Immaculate Bride of the Lamb (i.e., of the Church) (*Lexikon fur Theologie und Kirche*, vol. 8 (Freiburg: Herder, 1963), p. 499.

For more on the Philadelphia Society, see: *Realenenzyklopaedie fur Protestantische Theologie und Kirche*, vol. 11, pp. 326 ff. and vol. 15, pp. 553 ff; *Lexikon fur Theologie und Kirche* (Freiburg: Herder, 1963), vol. 8, p. 443; *Dictionaire de Théologie Catholique* (Paris: Letouzey et Ané, 1930), vol. 9, pp. 94 ff; *Zeitschrift fur Historische Theologie* (Leipzig, 1865), vol. 35, pp. 171–290; Nils Thune, *The Behmenists and Philadelphians* (Uppsala: Almquist & Wiksells, 1948); Gottfried Arnold, *Unpartheyische Kirchen- und Ketzergeschichte III* (Schaffheusen: Emanuel and Benedict Hurter, 1740–1742), chap. 20 and 22.

[4] Hutin Serge, "Les Disciples Anglais de Jacob Boehme" (Paris, 1960), p. 85, quoted in: *L'Univers à la Renaissance, Microcosme et Macrocosme* (Brussels: Presses Universitaires de Bruxelles, 1970), p. 145. See also: Thomas Schipflinger, *Die Sophiologie Jacob Boehmes*, seminar thesis for the Institute for Spiritual History and Humanism at the University of Munich, manuscript 1986, pp. 2, 8. Tr: translation from the German.

Sophia says to her:

> Look at me! I am the eternal Virgin Wisdom of God, who you always wished to see just once. I am come to unveil to you my profound treasures of God's Wisdom, and I will be to you what Rebecca was to Jacob, a true and natural Mother, for you will be spiritually begotten in my bosom, conceived and born anew.
>
> You will recognize something active in you which will leave you no rest until Wisdom has been born in the depths of your soul. Think about my words until I come to you again.[5]

Sophia did appear again three days later, radiant and wearing a crown, and said:

> Behold your Mother, and know that you must enter into a covenant with me in order to be in harmony with the laws of the new creation, which will be revealed to you.[6]

Sophia then gave her a golden book, sealed with three seals, containing the mysteries of Divine Wisdom. Six days later She appeared again. This time She invited Jane Leade to come closer in order to see and hear Her better and initiated her into the society of Her "newly born." Sophia explained that from now on Her appearances would not be visible but spiritual and that She would reveal the source of Wisdom and understanding. Jane Leade's Sophia teaching can be summarized as follows:

1. Sophia preserves and reveals the mysteries of God.

2. She is the Mother for those who belong to Her who are spiritually begotten in Her bosom. Through this new birth they become the true children of Wisdom.

3. Sophia expects Her children to live according to the condition of rebirth and this resolve is to be strengthened and confirmed

---

[5] Hutin Serge, "Les Disciples Anglais de Jacob Boehme."
[6] Hutin Serge, "Les Disciples Anglais de Jacob Boehme."

by a covenant with Her. All who enter into this covenant comprise the Sophian community.

4. The goal of the covenant is the restoration at the end of time of a paradisical state of perfection for humanity (the androgynous human being), resulting in bliss (spiritual marriage with Sophia), the reuniting of the churches and peace on earth (turning earth into paradise).

5. Sophia is the Mother, Teacher and Queen to Her children, but also a spiritual and divine seed-like principle that has been implanted into humanity. The essence of this principle is the perfection that humanity is to attain—for humanity's own fulfillment, for Sophia's and ultimately for God's also, who is the foundation of everything.

As the above summary indicates, the primary emphasis of Jane Leade's Sophia teaching is not Sophia's cosmological dimension (as the source of life) but Her function of restoring harmony, union, and bliss. On this path She is the most powerful Helper.

Today it seems that it is finally possible to come to a more objective evaluation of Jane Leade's life and work.[7] She was a gifted visionary who achieved mystical states of elevation. She awaited the coming of a "new spiritual kingdom" in which those who are truly "reborn" will form a community of brotherly love (Philadelphia) and live in matrimonial union with Sophia, and through Her, with Christ.[8]

JOHANN GEORG GICHTEL

Johann Georg Gichtel (1638–1710) came from the German town of Regensburg. After studying law and becoming a lawyer, Gichtel wanted to found an evangelical missionary society, but his efforts were unsuccessful. He thereupon went to Holland, where

---

[7] Ernst Benz mentions her often with respect and calls her a "genuine charismatic visionary." Benz, *Die Vision* (Stuttgart: E. Klett, 1969), p. 513; see also pp. 571–572.

[8] Benz, *Die Vision*, pp. 571–572.

he began to occupy himself with Boehme; and he eventually published an edition of Boehme's complete works in 1682 that was illustrated with costly engravings. Gichtel subsequently founded the "Brothers of the Angels" whose members eschewed marriage. He appears to have had contact with Jane Leade's Philadelphia Society in England, and he knew Gottfried Arnold (who did not approve of all of Gichtel's views). Gichtel's study of Boehme and his own spiritual experiences resulted in his own work about Sophia. It was titled *Theosophia Practica* and was published posthumously in 1722.

Like his teacher Jacob Boehme, Gichtel also understood the created Sophia to be intimately related to the Holy Trinity. She is the Mirror and Matrix (Mother's womb) in which God beholds the ideas and plans for creation and realizes them. Gichtel's primary concern, however, was not speculative but practical: He wanted Sophia's task to be recognized, which is to help humanity reach the goal of participation in the life of Jesus Christ and the Trinity. To achieve this it is necessary to recognize and restore one's holy and essential relationship to Sophia through repentance and rebirth. By increasingly strengthening this "hierogamous" (holy and matrimonial) relationship to Sophia, one comes to Jesus Christ and to the Trinity and participates in their life.

Gichtel's thought touches upon several important points: initial repentance and rebirth; a period of growth and maturation which includes temptation and suffering; the resistance of self-will; and the overcoming of self-will.

Repentance and rebirth are the keys to entering Sophia's kingdom and signify:

> Fiery baptism—the soul is immersed in the fiery sea of God's love and ignited again by the flame of God's love, whereby the noble, gentle light (Sophia) appears in the heart.

> Those who have been reborn, however, go with their magic (with their faithful and active cooperation with the inspirations of Sophia) in themselves, then into the true and holy heaven of the tincture of light (of Sophia's power of light) until they stand before the Holy Trinity.

As long as human beings maintain the holy fire in them through earnest prayer and constantly guard the flame, divine Sophia will continue to illuminate their souls, and the devil will not so easily approach or touch them.[9]

Steady growth, however, must follow the condition of rebirth. Sophia helps to protect and nourish this process but also allows suffering and temptation in order to test and strengthen the soul:

This light (Sophia) does not abide unceasingly in the soul; first the divine Virgin (Sophia) tests Her bridegroom to see whether he will be true to Her in suffering as well as joy, and constantly follow Her in the face of all obstacles.[10]

Yet self-will often resists Her efforts, and faithfulness does not always remain constant in the face of temptation:

Although God intended that the soul rule the body and gave His divine Virgin of Wisdom to help, so that the soul together with divine Wisdom should be active and manifest God's miracles, the soul of fire (the will) separated itself from its lovely helper; it wanted to be its own ruler and to be active and create in this world what it wanted.[11]

As a result "the self-will of created beings can no longer be a spirit with God or a bridegroom with divine Sophia.[12]

When human beings are faithless and do not stand firm when tempted, and Sophia sees that She cannot approach the soul in love:

---

[9] Johann Gichtel, *Theosophia Practica*, trans. into modern German and with an introduction and index by Agnes Klein (Munich: Ansata Verlag, 1979), chap. 5, ¶88; chap. 6, ¶s 18 and 144. Tr: translation from German.

[10] Johann Gichtel, *Theosophia Practica*, chap. 5, ¶90.

[11] Johann Gichtel, *Theosophia Practica*, chap. 2, ¶39–40.

[12] Johann Gichtel, *Theosophia Practica*, chap. 2, ¶56.

Then She is very sorrowful and withdraws, She darkens the fire of the soul and lets him fall into sin and foolishness, giving him an inconstant and foolish wife to hang around his neck.

Then things become grave . . . then the devil comes looking like an angel. . . . Thus beginners must be careful and on guard. They will not be accepted again before they have learned their lesson and overcome the dragon.

Christ's poverty is the fortress of divine Wisdom where She lives protected; those who want to go to Her must first become poor . . . fools scorn Her, but the wise esteem Her greatly. All earthly mammon is mud by comparison.[13]

When self-will has been overcome, however, Sophia returns and clothes the soul in new garments to show that it is worthy again of Her love and participation in the divine life of the Trinity:

Thus when human beings have overcome themselves, divine Sophia goes forth to meet them . . . and quickens their souls with inexpressible sweetness and clothes them once again with Her divine nature.[14]

In addition, Gichtel also understood Sophia Christologically and often identified Her with Christ.

Although some of his viewpoints were not in accord with Boehme or with Sophian teachings in general (he was negatively disposed toward women, sexuality, and marriage), he revered and sought Sophia, and committed his life to Her with admirable faithfulness and constancy. Gichtel achieved a practical knowledge about Sophia, and his contributions certainly merit attention.

---

[13] Johann Gichtel, *Theosophia Practica*, chap. 3, ¶71; chap. 4, ¶101, 110; chap. 2, ¶161.
[14] Johann Gichtel, *Theosophia Practica*, chap. 1, ¶17.

LOUIS-CLAUDE DE SAINT MARTIN

Louis-Claude de Saint Martin (1743–1803) was a French philosopher who published his writings under the pseudonym "the unknown philosopher." He was a friend of Martinez de Pasqualis (1727–1774), the founder of the Martinist Order, with whom he collaborated.[15]

Louis-Claude de Saint Martin is known for his French translation of Jacob Boehme's works. However he is also known for his own works, which are permeated with Boehme's spirit and which popularized Boehme's ideas and developed them further (thereby achieving a clarity of thought and expression that eluded Boehme himself).[16]

Saint Martin focuses in particular on Sophia's function as the *miroir des formes et terre des generations spirituelles*—the Mirror of formational ideas and the Ground of spiritual generation.

She is intimately related to the persons of the Trinity, yet different from them. She is the created Mediator between the Creator and creatures, the Mirror in which God beholds Godself and God's ideas, allowing them to become "essential" or real in Godself as if in a maternal bosom. She is the "Idea of the ideas" (*forme des formes*), the model and formational principle of all things who preserves and develops them. The ideas and the things in which these ideas (forms) are materialized are the radiations, images, and effluence of "primordial Sophia" (*Sagesse primitive*). Sophia is a person, the primordial Ideal of creation. The Sophian form (idea) in the individual person is that person's

---

[15] The Martinists are an esoteric order whose outward form is similar to the Freemasons, but whose teaching, like Martinez de Pasqualis himself, comes from Spain and the verbally transmitted Cabala. Louis-Claude de Saint Martin was for a time the secretary of the order and became its head after the death of Martinez de Pasquali. The order was later resurrected by Papus, the well-known French esotericist and Cabalist (Dr. Gerard Encausse, born in Spain in 1865, died in Paris in 1916). See also: H. E. Miers, *Lexikon des Geheimwissens* (Freiburg: H. Bauer, 1970).

[16] Louis-Claude de Saint Martin speaks about Sophia in the following works: *Tableau Naturel Des Rapports qui Existent Entre Dieu, L'Homme et l'Univers, Le Ministère de l'Homme-Esprit, Le Nouvel Homme, De l'Esprit des Choses, Oeuvres Posthumes*.

ideal image, and the goal is for each person to bring this image to realization. Effort and cooperation are necessary so that the beauty and goodness of Sophia can appear through human beings in the world.[17] Repentance toward Sophia is appropriate because, instead of realizing this ideal, humanity has done much to disfigure it, thereby depriving the world of its Soul.[18]

Such thoughts are particularly relevant to the ecological problems of the present age. They reconnect the world and nature to an immanent and transcendent principle of life and outline the correct kind of attitude toward the Creator, creation, and also religion (understood in the etymological sense of connecting and uniting). Through such a perception a genuinely profound and reverent relationship to nature can thrive. This is the kind of consciousness that is necessary today for the protection of nature and the environment, which makes us realize that Sophiology is not some kind of theological speculation foreign to reality. It contains extraordinarily relevant and practical teachings which are fundamental to overcoming critical problems in our time.

Saint Martin indicates that human beings are a particular idea of Sophia. To the extent that they allow themselves to be inspired and formed by Her they reach the goal of participation in divine nature.[19] Only in connection with Sophia, and above Her with Christ, can human beings truly fulfill the task given them— to be a pure mirror of Sophia and thereby of God, to unite the world again with Her, to adapt themselves to Her ideal, and thereby restore the lost paradise of harmony, beauty, goodness, and love.[20]

The above is an outline of Louis-Claude de Saint Martin's Sophiology, which will be followed by excerpts from his writ-

---

[17] Nicole Jacques-Chaquin, "Sophia, Miroir des Forms et Terre des Generations Spirituelles: Introduction à Quelques Textes de Louis-Claude De Saint Martin sur la Sagesse Divine," in *Sophia et l'Ame Du Mond*, Cahiers de l'Hermetisme (Paris: Albin Michel, 1983), pp. 237,11; 239,14–15. The teaching about the "ideas" stems from Plato. He outlines the fundamental features of this teaching in the dialogue *Timaeus*.
[18] Nicole Jacques-Chaquin, "Sophia, Miroir des Forms . . ." p. 240, ¶20.
[19] Nicole Jacques-Chaquin, p. 239, ¶15, 17.
[20] Nicole Jacques-Chaquin, p. 229; ¶240, 19.

ings. In a letter to his friend Kirchberger, the Baron of Liebistorf, he speaks of Sophia's function and Her mediating role to God:

> She (Sophia) is the true and actual preserver of all spiritual forms (ideas) . . . She always dwells by God, and when we possess Her, or much more when we are possessed by Her, God also possesses us, since both in their union are inseparable, even though their natures are different.[21]

In his works he writes:

> The paths of Wisdom are so manifold that She changes Herself every moment in order to adapt Herself to all of our situations. And though She spans all time and space on the basis of the fullness of Her capacities, She never allows the fountainhead to run dry from which Her gifts come, no matter what situation we find ourselves in.
>
> In bringing forth living creatures, She (Wisdom) gives them an effluence of Her wisdom, that they might be Her image. Thus do all living creatures have in themselves a radiant beam of Wisdom Most High and thereby a radiant beam of Her weight, number and measure (Her proportions).
>
> It was enough for God to contemplate Himself in the mirror of the eternal Virgin or Sophia, into which He carefully engraved forever the model of all living beings.
>
> In regards to Sophia, I do not doubt that She could be born within us, in our heart or in our nature. And just as much I do not doubt that even the divine Logos could be born through this means, as He was born in Mary.
>
> When She has prepared human beings in this manner (directing Her energies and powers into them) and they have not hindered Her in Her plans in any way, then She

---

[21] Nicole Jacques-Chaquin, p. 235, ¶2. Tr: translation from German.

transports them to that place of light where they have their origin and beginning. And there they imbibe fully of the bliss that belongs to their nature. They drink it without fear or disquiet, like Wisdom Herself, for through the grief that She has allowed them to receive, their hearts have become pure like Her and free from the instabilities and uncertainties experienced within the fragileness of time. For them what is elevated and low are in complete accord, they perceive that the peace that they discover in these invisible regions dwells as much in them also . . . they perceive that everything is as one, all things and they themselves appear to be one and the same thing.

There is a natural maternal ground (*terre vegetale*) like that of our fields and vineyards; there is a maternal bosom which is Sophia.

The universe lies on a bed of sorrow, and it is our task to comfort it. The universe lies on a bed of sorrow because since the fall, a foreign substance has penetrated its veins and has not ceased to burden and torment the principle of its life. It is our task to speak words of comfort which are able to help it bear its misfortune. It is our task, I say, to proclaim to it the promise of liberation and the covenant which eternal Wisdom is about to form with it.

That is our part in duty to righteousness, for the head of the family of humanity (Adam) is the first cause of the sorrow of the universe. We can say to the universe that it was we ourselves who caused the loss of its spouse. As long as the sad situation continues does it not wait expectantly moment by moment that its spouse will be returned?

Yes, benevolent sun, we are the primary cause of your unrest and eruptions. The light of your eye shines on all regions of the earth, one after the other, without growing weary. Every day you rise for all human beings. You raise yourself up full of joy, in the hope that they will give you back your beloved spouse, eternal Wisdom, who was robbed from you. You complete your daily course imploring Her back from the entire earth with flaming words, leaving behind the burning of your yearning. But in the evening you descend again in sorrow and tears having sought your Bride in vain, you have implored human beings for Her in vain. They have not given Her back to you at all and they let you tarry in sterile places, in dwellings of shame and disgrace.[22]

As the above passages indicate, like Boehme, Saint Martin also looks at humanity and even the entire universe from the viewpoint of their special relationship to Sophia. With moving words he describes Sophia's bridal relationship to the cosmos and how humanity is responsible for restoring the universe's lost Bride.

It is worth considering the relevance of these ideas to a mechanistic worldview which understands the cosmos as a machine (that neither has nor needs a soul). Without an understanding of Sophia as the World Soul, worldviews indeed become soul-less and unwholesome.

JOHANN JACOB WIRZ

Among those who were inspired by Boehme's Sophiology was Johann Jacob Wirz (1778–1858), a silk weaver from Basel. Wirz was a noble and charismatic figure who founded the "Community of the Nazarenes" composed of his students and followers. He had come from a reformed family, and his teaching combined Protestant and Pietist elements with Catholic teaching and practices. The members of the Community of the Nazarenes lived in a fellowship which shared goods and possessions (some still exist today in Switzerland and in the southern German states of Baden and Wuerttenberg). Many considered him to be a prophet, and it is reported that thinking of him "awakened the holy fear of the presence of God, which visibly surrounded him."[23]

---

[22] Nicole Jacques-Chaquin, "Sophia, Miroir des Forms . . ." p. 235, ¶4; p. 235, ¶5; p. 237, ¶9; p. 239, ¶14; p. 240, ¶17; p. 240, ¶19; p. 240, ¶20.
[23] Kurt Hutten, *Seher, Grubler, Enthusiasten* (Stuttgart: Quell Verlag der Evan Gesellschaft, 1966), p. 444 f.

In Wirz' own opinion he was inspired by God, and the herald of God's third and last kingdom, the kingdom of the Holy Spirit, which had been proclaimed by the Cistercian abbot Joachim von Fiore 700 years before. The revelations that Wirz received were published posthumously in two volumes.[24]

What is of particular interest to the present study is Wirz' view that Sophia took on human form in Mary, a teaching that he perhaps borrowed from Boehme by way of Arnold and Gichtel. He also viewed Holy Wisdom as the Friend, Mother and Spouse of the devout, similar to the depictions in the Book of Wisdom (8,2–18) and Ecclesiasticus (15,2). In a diary entry (dated January 1, 1837) Wirz writes:

> Yesterday evening, at the year's close, you renewed your obligation of obedience to the heavenly Mother. She heard you better than you perceive your own voice. She accepted your vow and answered you as follows:

> Blessed are the souls who do not just obligate themselves to Divine Wisdom, but who through their obedience succeed in becoming entirely Hers. She will be to them everything that some theosophical authors say about Her, the heavenly Sophia.[25]

The "theosophical authors" probably refers to persons like Boehme, Arnold, Gichtel, and those in the Philadelphia Society, as well.

He continues by speaking of Sophia's maternal nature, and goes on to distinguish varying degrees of intimacy in Her relationships and to define what they signify:

---

[24] Johann Jacob Wirz, *Zeugnisse und Eroeffnungen des Geistes Durch J. Jacob Wirz, Heilige Urkunden der Nazarenergemeine,* in commission with W. Langewiesche (Barmen, 1863), in two volumes. Other relevant literature: *Biographie von J. Jacob Wirz, Ein Zeugnis der Nazarener-Gemeinde von der Entwickelung des Reiches Gottes auf Erden* (Barmen, 1862); *Briefe,* three volumes, (Barmen, 1863/1873); Ernst Staehlin, *Der Basler Seidenweber Johann Jacob Wirz als Hellseher und Gruender der Nazarenergemeine* (Basler: Stadtbuch, 1966).

[25] Wirz, *Zeugnisse,* vol. 1, p. 488. This and subsequent quotations have been translated from the German.

First of all, this heavenly Sophia, according to Her maternal character, will take care of the earthly needs of such human beings, and provide them with an abode appropriate to their individual situations which will help to promote the salvation of their souls. They will lose nothing that is essential to them.

Sophia is the fulfillment on earth and in heaven of God's promises. But everything depends on the degree to which She is able to work in an individual soul. . . . Although it is always so that only a few exist who love divine Wisdom and seek Her, nevertheless amongst the vast quantity of human beings on the whole earth, She has quite a large number of friends. The number, however, of those who really accept Her as a Mother and belong to Her as children is very small, and even fewer succeed in attaining to a matrimonial relationship with Her.

Those for whom She is a Mother, are, as already said, truly cared for in body and soul. But those who attain the matrimonial relationship possess so much more, everything that they could ever need in time and eternity, in order to participate in the splendor of the image and likeness of God.[26]

Wirz answers how the Mother can also be Spouse, and how a child can also be husband to his Mother, in a truly mystagogical way: such matters pertain to the grace and mystery belonging to spiritual growth and maturation.

His further explanation of the degrees in which Sophia works in the soul reveals his Sophian Mariology. Sophia is "personified" in Mary (which apparently means "incarnated") and their relationship is like that of the soul to the body:

Understand that in the first degree, Holy Wisdom is to the friend of Wisdom the friend and companion on life's journey.

---

[26] Wirz, *Zeugnisse*, vol. 1, p. 488, 489.

In the second degree, She is a Mother, the actual and true Mother of God, who Catholics without exception adore in the image of Mary. In Mary, Wisdom personified Herself in Her maternal character; but since the one who hallows is always to be esteemed higher than the one who is made holy, so is Wisdom to be esteemed higher than Mary. Yet the two relate to one another precisely like the soul to the body.

In the third degree, Holy Wisdom is a wife to the soul; human beings leave behind their divided nature and become whole human beings. Only then, after the division in human nature is made inactive by union with heavenly Wisdom, and what was lost has been restored, may the human being be called whole.

Thus, accept what little has been given you of this great mystery as a New Year's present from the heavenly Mother, guard it and reflect on it in your heart. Amen![27]

As this diary entry indicates, Wirz felt himself personally related to Sophia. He understood Her as his Mother and committed himself to serving Her; and though acquiescing, She points simultaneously to the higher state of becoming "entirely Hers." This recalls the Perfect Dedication and Devotion to Mary taught by St. Ludwig Marie Grignion of Montfort (1673–1716) which exerted such a great influence on Catholic spirituality and Marian devotion.[28]

The kind of spirituality that is visible in Wirz' Sophia teaching is active, but also passive in a mystical way. For relationship with Sophia progresses along a path—from initial friendship, to maternal care, to matrimonial union, whereby

---

[27] Wirz, *Zeugnisse*, vol. 1, p. 492.

[28] Ludwig Marie Grignon von Montfort, *Das Goldene Buch der Vollkommenen Andacht zu Maria* (Fribourg: Kansius-Verlag, 1918). St. Maximilian Kolbe, who sacrificed his life at Auschwitz for the father of a family, drew the strength for his astonishing life as a missionary, writer, publisher and martyr from the Marian spirituality of Ludwig Marie Grignon's Complete Devotion to Mary. The heraldic motto of Pope John Paul II is *Totus Tuus* or "entirely yours," i.e., entirely dedicated and belonging to Mary, in the sense of Grignon's Complete Devotion.

Sophia is also Herself active to the extent that the soul is open and prepared for Her to enter and work in it. These three steps along a path are clearly reminiscent of the traditional teaching about the mystical way.[29]

Though some of Wirz' statements may seem unusual his genuinely deep devotion and profound insight into spiritual matters make his work worthy of serious attention.

---

[29] The traditional Christian teaching on the mystical way speaks of the stages of purification, illumination, and union. See: Adolphe Tanquerey, *Grundriss der Aszetischen und Mystischen Theologie* (Paris: Tournai Société de Saint Jean l'Evangelist, Desclée and cie, 1931), p. 445 f. Compare also the Bhaki devotion of India (chapter 20) which speaks of three stages in the love of God which are described almost word for word with what Wirz says.

14

Eternal Mary in the Visions of Anne Catherine Emmerich

THE VENERABLE ANNE Catherine Emmerich beheld in her visions someone whom she called "Mary in eternity," but a more exact formulation based on Her descriptions identifies this Mary as Sophia. The story of "Mary in eternity" also merits serious attention despite the fact that the great seer who beheld Her is not well known.

Anne Catherine Emmerich (1774–1824) was born in Flamske near the German town of Coesfeld. At age 28 she entered the Augustinian convent of Dulmen, where she became known for her devotion and the compassion that she showed toward others. In 1812 she received the stigmata, whose genuineness was attested by a Church investigation. The physician who cared for her reports of her exceptionally virtuous life and unusual gifts: She needed no nourishment, was able to discern souls, and evinced great magnanimity.[1] In spite of her own poverty and infirmity, she did sewing work in order to help the poor.

---

[1] J. Seller, *Im Banne des Kreuzes, Lebensbild der Anna Katherina Emmerich* (Wurzburg, 1940); *Lexkon fur Theologie und Kirche* (Freiburg: Herder, 1958), vol. 3, p. 850.

Anne Catherine Emmerich had numerous visions about the life of Jesus Christ and Mary. Her spiritual director, Bernhard Overberg, asked the great German Romantic writer Clemens Brentano (1778–1842) to write about her. Brentano was so affected by her humble personality that he moved to Dulmen and remained there until her death so that she could personally relate her visions to him. He discussed them with her and recorded them as carefully as possible. His labors resulted in the works: *The Dolorous Passion of Our Lord, The Life of the Blessed Virgin Mary* and *The Life of Jesus Christ and Biblical Revelations* which continue to be published and have been translated into several languages.

Anne Catherine Emmerich was one of the greatest visionaries of her time. Her visions report many interesting details about the life of Jesus Christ and Mary which have even helped to clarify exegetical questions (yet how her visions are to be explained is a question for the domains of theology and mysticism and will not be taken up here).

What is of particular interest are the visions which concern Mary's conception and birth. It seems that Anne Catherine Emmerich beholds a kind of pre-existential condition of Mary. Her descriptions and their symbolic content suggest that she perceived the origins of created Sophia and Her relationship to Mary.

VISIONS AND SYMBOLS

I. An Angel Tells St. Anne that She Will Conceive a Holy Child

> After she (Anna) had slept for a short time, I saw a brightness pouring down to her from above, which on approaching her bed was transformed into the figure of a shining youth. It was the angel of the Lord, who told her that she would conceive a holy child; stretching a hand over her, he wrote great shining letters on the wall which formed the name MARY. Thereupon the angel dissolved into light and disappeared. During this time Anna seemed to be wrapped in a secret, joyful dream. She rose half-wak-

ing from her couch, prayed with great intensity, and then fell asleep again without having completely recovered consciousness. After midnight she awoke joyfully, as if by an inner inspiration, and now saw, with alarm mixed with joy, the writing on the wall. This seemed to be of shining and golden-red letters, large and few in number; she gazed at them with unspeakable joy and contrite humility until day came, when they faded away. She saw the writing so clearly, and her joy thereat became so great, that when she got up she appeared quite young again. In the moment when the light of the angel had enveloped Anna in grace, I saw a radiance under her heart and recognized in her the chosen Mother, the illuminated vessel of the grace that was at hand. What I saw in her I can only describe by saying that I recognized in her the cradle and tabernacle of the holy child she was to conceive and preserve; a mother blessed indeed. I saw that by God's grace Anna was able to bear fruit. I cannot describe the wonderful manner in which I recognized this. I saw Anna as the cradle of all mankind's salvation. . . .[2]

II. Anne's Miraculous Conception

They (Joachim and Anne) embraced each other with holy joy, and each told the other their good tidings. They were in a state of ecstasy and enveloped in a cloud of light. I saw this light issuing from a great host of angels, who were carrying the appearance of a high and shining tower and hovering above the heads of Anna and Joachim. The form of this tower was the same as I see in pictures, from the Litany Of Our Lady, of the Tower of David, of the Tower of Ivory, and so forth. I saw that this tower seemed to disappear between Anna and Joachim, who were enveloped in a glory of brightness. . . . I had at the same time an indescribable vision. The heavens opened above them, and I saw the joy of the Holy Trinity and of the

---

[2]Anne Catherine Emmerich, *The Life of the Blessed Virgin Mary* (Rockford, IL: Tan Books, 1970), p. 31. Used by permission.

angels, and their participation in the mysterious blessing bestowed on Mary's parents.[3]

III. Visions about the Preparation of the Incarnation

I saw the Throne of God and the Holy Trinity, and at the same time a movement within that Trinity. . . . I saw a mountain as of precious stones appear before the throne of God; it grew and spread. It was in terraces, like a throne; then it changed into the shape of a tower—a tower which enshrined every treasure of the spirit and every gift of grace. . . . I saw in the sky a figure like a virgin which passed into the tower and as it were melted into it. The tower was very broad and flat at the top; it seemed to have an opening at the back through which the virgin passed into it. This was not the Blessed Virgin as she is in time, but as she is in eternity, in God. I saw the appearance of her being formed before the Most Holy Trinity, just as when one breathes, a little cloud is formed before one's mouth. I also saw something going forth from the Holy Trinity towards the tower. At this moment of the picture I saw a vessel like a ciborium being formed among the choirs of angels. The angels all joined in giving this vessel the form of a tower surrounded by many pictures full of significance. Beside it stood two figures joining hands behind it. This spiritual vessel went on increasing in size, beauty, and richness. Then I saw something proceed from God and pass through all nine choirs of angels; it seemed to me like a little shining and holy cloud which became more and more distinct as it approached the sacramental vessel which it finally entered. . . . I finally saw this blessing in the shape of a shining bean, enter the ciborium, which then passed into the tower.

In this little cloud (for which Elias had prayed) I saw from the first a little shining figure like a virgin. . . . The head of this virgin was encircled with rays, she stretched her arms

---

[3] Emmerich, *The Life of the Blessed Virgin Mary*, pp. 40–41. Used by permission of the publisher, Tan Books, Rockford, IL.

out in the form of a cross, and had a triumphal wreath hanging from one hand. . . . She appeared as if hovering above the whole Promised Land in the cloud as it spread even farther. I saw how this cloud divided into different parts and fell in eddying showers of crystal dew on certain holy and consecrated places inhabited by devout men and those who were praying for salvation. I saw these showers edged with the colors of the rainbow and the blessing take shape in their midst like a pearl in its shell.[4]

IV. *Other Visions about the Incarnation of Mary*

I had a vision of the creation of Mary's most holy soul and of its being united with her most pure body. In the glory by which the Most Holy Trinity is usually represented in my visions I saw a movement like a great shining mountain, and yet also like a human figure; and I saw something rise out of the midst of this figure towards its mouth and go forth from it like a shining brightness. Then I saw this brightness standing separate before the Face of God, turning and shaping itself—or rather being shaped, for I saw that while this brightness took human form, yet it was by the Will of God that it received a form so unspeakably beautiful. I saw, too, that God showed the beauty of this soul to the angels, and that they had unspeakable joy in its beauty. . . . I saw Our Lady's holy mother lying asleep in her bed in her house near Nazareth. There came a shining light above her, and a ray from this light passed into her in the shape of a little shining human figure. In the same instant I saw Our Lady's holy mother raise herself on her couch surrounded by light. She was in ecstasy and had a vision of her womb opening like a tabernacle to enclose a shining little virgin from whom man's salvation was to spring.[5]

---

[4] Emmerich, *The Life of the Blessed Virgin Mary*, pp. 42–43, 49. Used by permission of the publishers, Tan Books, Rockford, IL.

[5] Emmerich, *The Life of the Blessed Virgin Mary*, p. 73. Used by permission.

INTERPRETING THE VISIONS

Anne Catherine Emmerich indicates that the visions which were given to her about the events in the Bible and the lives of the saints:

> were given to me by the grace of God not only for my benefit, as there is much that I could not understand, but to pass on, so that many things which had been hidden and forgotten might be reawakened.[6]

A deeper glimpse into the mystery of Mary's conception and Her relationship to Sophia belongs to what had been hidden and was to be reawakened, particularly in the Western Church (Russian Sophiology preserved the sense of Sophia's relationship to Mary in the Eastern Church—see chapters 15 and 16).

A closer analysis of the visions excerpted above indicate that they relate not only to the conception of Mary's body but most importantly to the mystery of the preparation of Her soul in heaven (IV—"I had a vision of the creation of Mary's most holy soul and its unification with her most pure body"); and to the distinction between Mary in time and Mary in eternity, in God (III—"This was not the Blessed Virgin as she is in time, but as she is in eternity, in God").

The process of incarnation from "eternity" to "time" is depicted through various symbols: mountain, throne, tower, cloud, bean, and pearl.

Before the throne of God a movement takes place within the Trinity which produces a mountain of precious stones that grows and is terraced and like a throne; it becomes a tower full of spiritual treasure and grace; the virgin "in eternity" appears from out of the Trinity as a small cloud of breath and merges with the tower (III). A similar but different description of the same process speaks of a mountain movement and human form

---

[6] Anna Katherina Emmerich, *Leben der Heiligen Jungfrau Maria*, recorded by Clemens Maria Brentano, Paul Pattloch (Aschaffenburg, 1980), 6th edition, p. 449.

in the Trinity which exits as a kind of brightness and is formed into a beautiful human soul (IV).

Other details in the visions speak of "many pictures full of significance" which surround the tower; a little shining cloud from God and a bean that enter into the tower; and a virgin inside the little cloud that hovers over the Promised Land, falling in showers on holy places and then taking shape "in their midst like a pearl in its shell" (III). Finally the tower hovers between Joachim and Anne and disappears in their midst (II).

Of particular interest are the images which speak of the origin of Mary in eternity from out of the Trinity. She is described as a kind of breathlike cloud before the mouth of the Trinity and as a shining brightness which proceeds up out of the midst of the Trinity and from its mouth. The similarity between this description and that of Sophia in the Book of Wisdom is striking:

> For she is a breath of the power of God, and a pure emanation of the glory of the Almighty (Wisd. 7,25).

This breathlike cloud of brightness which becomes Mary's soul is then formed before God, recalling the words of Proverbs:

> The LORD created me the first of his works long ago, before all else that he made. I was formed in earliest times, at the beginning, before earth itself . . . (Prov. 8,22).

Other images from the visions also relate to Sophia. The tower into which the virgin passes is described as throne-like. The throne image is reminiscent of several Old Testament passages which relate the throne, a symbol of royal power and might, to Sophia:

> My dwelling-place was in high heaven; my throne was in a pillar of cloud . . . (Ecclus. 24,4).

> Give me wisdom, who sits beside your throne . . . (Wisd., 9,4).

> She adds luster to her noble birth, because it is given her
> to live with God; the Lord of all things has accepted her
> (Wisd. 8,34).

The figure of the little virgin within the cloud hovering above
the Promised Land is also described. It divides into parts which
shower dew onto certain holy places, and then takes shape as a
blessing "in their midst like a pearl." The first part of this description recalls Sophia's words:

> My throne was in a pillar of cloud. . . . every people and
> nation were under my sway. Among them all I sought
> where I might come to rest. . . . Then the Creator of all
> things laid a command on me. . . . "Make your home in
> Jacob" (Ecclus. 24,4–8).

Sophia took up Her special abode in the Promised Land of Israel; but as the Book of Wisdom indicates, She also dwells in
other places (upon which She showers dew) where the devout
pray to Her:

> Wisdom . . . is readily discerned by those who love her,
> and by those who seek her she is found. . . . he who rises
> early in search of her will not grow weary in the quest, for
> he will find her seated at his door. . . . she herself searches
> far and wide for those who are worthy of her, and on their
> daily paths she appears to them with kindly intent, meet-
> ing them half-way in all their purposes (Wisd. 6,12,14,16).

Wisdom inspires the wise of all peoples and nations, but Her relationship to the Promised Land is special. As various parts of
the visions describe, a bean enters the tower, a blessing takes
shape in the Promised Land "like a pearl in its shell," and the
tower disappears between Joachim and Anne. These are all symbolic representations of the unification of the soul of "Mary in
eternity," who is Sophia, with the body of "Mary in time," which
is conceived through Joachim and Anne ("I had a vision of the
creation of Mary's most holy soul and of it being united with her
most pure body"—IV).

It appears that in her own way Anne Catherine Emmerich beheld the mystery of the incarnation of Sophia, Holy Wisdom, in Mary. Even though she does not speak directly of Sophia, the relationship of Sophia in the Old Testament to key elements of her description of the creation and incarnation of "Mary in eternity" is unmistakable. Anne Catherine Emmerich was unique in her ability to preserve this mystery and deserves to be held in high esteem among Sophiologists in the West and in the East.

The visions described above took place between 1819–1822, and two years later Anne Catherine Emmerich died in 1824. She had fulfilled her destiny of revealing through her visions "many things that had been hidden," earning her, and Clemens Brentano who preserved them in written form, the gratitude of posterity.

15

Sophia
According to the
Russian Sophiologists

SOPHIOLOGY DID NOT RECEIVE much attention in the West, but the situation was different in the East. A Sophian tradition and devotion flourished in Russia and nourished the development of prophets of Sophia like Vladimir Soloviev who can be considered the Father of Russian Sophiology. His works stimulated others to take up the study of Sophiology, such as Pavel Florenski and Sergei Bulgakov, who are among the most prominent of those who followed.

SOPHIA ACCORDING TO VLADIMIR SOLOVIEV

Soloviev (1853–1900) grew up in the spiritual tradition of the Russian Orthodox Church, but as a youth he had become attached to an atheistic and materialistic outlook. After much searching he returned to Christianity, yet his religious views were permeated by philosophical and mystical considerations. Of particular interest is his teaching about Sophia.[1]

---

[1] Soloviev's *Collected Works* published in Russian, 1901 and 1911, St. Petersburg (an expanded edition published in Brussels, 1966–1969). Many titles were cited

Soloviev's devotion to Sophia had been nurtured by the tradition visible in the Russian icons and churches dedicated to Sophia, and this tradition was itself rooted in an intimacy with and devotion to nature and "Mother Earth." In 1862, at age 9, Soloviev experienced his first of three visions of Sophia.

The Sophian philosophy and theology that Soloviev developed were grounded in the Wisdom literature of the Old Testament and its traditional Christian interpretation. However, Soloviev was familiar with Gnostic speculations about Sophia; and he knew the works of Boehme, Arnold, and Gichtel, and was influenced by Swedenborg, Oetinger, Baader, and Schelling as well. After traveling to London in 1875 he became familiar with the "Cabbala denudata" of Baron Christian Knorr von Rosenroth. During this time in London he had a second vision of Sophia, and thereupon traveled to Egypt where, in the same year, he had his third and decisive vision inside a pyramid.

Soloviev's primary writings about Sophia are found in his *Lectures About the Divine Human Being, Russia and the Universal Church, Sophia*, and also in his poems.[2]

In his lyrical and intuitive poems, Soloviev celebrates Sophia and tries to impart a comprehensive vision of Her. His philosophical and theological works, which are more analytical, attempt to portray his understanding of Sophia's dignity and function.

---

in the German edition; however, English readers may want to explore Egbert Munzer *Solovyev, Prophet of Russian Western Unity* (New York: Philosophical Library, 1956).

[2] In Cairo in 1876 Soloviev wrote the work *Sophia* while still affected by his third vision of Sophia inside a pyramid. In a letter to his father Soloviev characterizes this work as "fundamental to his life and efforts." The book was written in French; and although Soloviev was unable to find a French publisher, the work was published a hundred years later by François Rouleau (Lausanne: L'Age d'Homme), 1978; see pp. xii ff. Soloviev's *Sophia* clearly shows the Sophian direction of all of his thought and efforts. Sophia is depicted as the ontological and epistemological principle of unity within multiplicity and the synthesis of the polar forms of life. This work has not been reviewed, which would require a detailed study.

Theoretical Sophiology

In his philosophical and theological works Soloviev refers to Sophia as: "the intelligible collective Soul of humanity which comprises the many selves of individual human beings."[3] She is:

> One and Everything—"hen kai pan". . . . As the living center or Soul of all creatures. . . She includes the manifoldness of living souls, She is all of humanity together in one, or the Soul of the World. She is ideal humanity, containing all individual living creatures or souls and uniting them through Herself. . . . Her task is to mediate and unify the manifoldness of living creatures, who constitute the actual content of Her life and the absolute unity of God.[4]

Sophia, the "Soul of the World," has three parts which allow Her to unify, connect and direct everything: a higher, divine part, a lower earthly part, and a middle portion which creates space, time, and causality, and directs them (Soloviev's tripartite division is an attempt to explain the complexity of Her function).[5] The function which preserves the world and allows it to unfold through trial and error belongs to the middle and lower parts of Sophia's soul. About this activity Soloviev writes:

> If the Soul of the World were to stop unifying everything through Herself, all created beings would lose their common relationship, the union of the cosmos would fall apart into a multiplicity of individual elements, and the organism of the world would transform itself into a mechanical mass of atoms.[6]

---

[3] Edith Klum, *Natur, Kunst und Liebe in der Philosophie Wladimir Solowjews, Eine Religionsgeschichtlichte Untersuchung* (Munich: Otto Sagnet, 1965), p. 101.
[4] Edith Klum, *Natur, Kunst und Liebe*, p. 105. This and subsequent quotations have been translated from the German. Tr.
[5] Edith Klum, *Natur, Kunst und Liebe*, p. 269.
[6] Edith Klum, *Natur, Kunst und Liebe*, p. 107.

In the same vein he writes in a lecture about the work of August Compte:

> Humanity or nature is neither the sum of individual human beings or things, nor an abstract concept or empirical aggregate, but an actual, living being, a transpersonal being, not a personified principle, but an essential person or person-principle, not a personified idea, but the idea of a person. Compte ascribes complete reality, power, and wisdom to this principle, and also gives it the identity of a feminine being.[7]

In the same lecture, Soloviev mentions the famous icon of Divine Wisdom in the Sophia cathedral in Novgorod (see chapter 16), exclaiming:

> Who is it who sits there in royal dignity on the throne, if not Holy Wisdom, the true and pure ideal of humanity itself, the highest and all-inclusive "morphe" (Greek: form) as well as the living soul of nature and the cosmos, eternally bound to God, who unites everything existing in the temporal world with Her.[8]

Elsewhere he remarks:

> Every conscious effort of the human being that is based on the idea of universal harmony and syzygy (appearances in pairs), and every effort whose goal is the manifestation of the all-unifying ideal (Sophia), creates spiritual and even physical vibrations. These vibrations gradually spiritualize the surrounding material world and manifest one image or another of the all-inclusive unity.[9]

These are encouraging words for those desiring to promote a deeper understanding of the unity between humanity and nature with the Soul of nature who is Sophia. The force of these ef-

---

[7] Edith Klum, *Natur, Kunst und Liebe*, p. 262.
[8] Edith Klum, *Natur, Kunst und Liebe*, p. 273.
[9] Edith Klum, *Natur, Kunst und Liebe*, p. 216.

forts are very real and will eventually have their unerring effect. Such ideas exerted a tremendous influence on Soloviev's contemporaries and on the 20th century as well. Recent scientific thought about the way the world works closely parallels the formulations of Soloviev's Sophia teaching, making him the prophet of present-day hypotheses (see the Gaia Hypothesis in chapter 18). Soloviev's Sophiology deserves to become better known to today's scientists as well as theologians.

Sophia Poetry

Some selected poems depicting Soloviev's experiences of Sophia, in which he repeatedly proclaims Her as his Mistress, Queen and Friend, now follow.

> *Today I Saw Her*
> Today I saw her with my eyes
> My queen, all bathed in radiance,
> Rejoicing, my heart stopped beating.
> This happened at the golden light of dawn,
> A miracle divine.
> All earthly desire vanished,
> Seeing her alone, her alone, only her.[10]

The above poem was written in Cairo at the end of November 1875 when Soloviev was still affected by his third vision of Sophia under the pyramid.

> *My Queen's Castle*
> My queen's castle shimmers with gold,
> Seven pillars are in the hall.
> The diadem of my lovely queen
> Shines with radiant jewels untold.

---

[10] Ludwig Mueller and Irmgard Wille, *Solowjews Leben in Briefe und Gedichte* (vol. 9) (Munich: Wewel Verlag, 1977), p. 198/2; for the biographical remarks which follow the poem, see p. 323. This and subsequent quotations have been translated from the German.

And in the green garden of my queen,
Blooms a rainbow of lilies and roses,
The deep waters of a silver brook
Mirror her countenance, lovely and pure.

But she does not see the dance of the waves,
Nor does my queen glance at the flowers.
Sadness surrounds her eyes' bright gaze
Her heart heavy and grave.

She watches afar, in the land of the night,
Where mist covers the sun,
How her friend with the power of darkness fights,
But parted from her, has not won.

She sets aside her crown of pearls,
And leaves the palace of gold
And comes down to her faithless friend
As an unexpected guest.

Like a blossoming spring after winter's might
She comes with a radiant wreath.
Her gracious form bends down to him,
Surrounds him with glittering veils.

At once dark power is vanquished,
Her friend's fire burns pure with light.
With eternal love her eyes smile to him,
And he hears her softly speak:

"Ah, your will was weak. And you swore to be true,
Yet your deed showed not any faith.
Yes, you broke your oath, but only you:
I will not betray, but be true."[11]

This poem was written between November 1875 and March 1876 in Cairo, and also shows the influence of Soloviev's vision of

_____

[11] Mueller and Wille, *Solowjews Leben in Briefe und Gedichte*, p. 198/3; biographical remarks, see p. 323.

Sophia, which provokes self-reflection. The poem's castle and palace with seven pillars recalls Sophia's house of seven pillars in the Old Testament (Prov. 9,1).

> *O Earth, My Mistress!*
> O earth, my mistress, since the days of youth
> I have felt your sweet breath,
> Heard the beat of your heart in the veil of your blossoms
> And touched the pulse of all life.
>
> At noon heaven's mercy descended upon me
> In a shimmering form with the same tenderness,
> The banks of the blue sea, the song of the beating waves
> And the trees bristling in the forest
> Sent their joyful kiss to Her.
>
> The soul of the earth wants to bind itself,
> Mysteriously, with the fountain of light.
> What luck that I chance upon this covenant!
> All the world's suffering becomes as nothing.[12]

The earth that Soloviev celebrates in this poem from May of 1886 actually signifies the earth's soul, or the Soul of the World, whose bodily garment nature forms. The poem reveals Soloviev's profound vision of nature and his close relationship to the earth which is a special characteristic of the Russian soul that perceives nature as "Mother Earth" (evident in poets like Dostoyevsky, Gogol, and Tutschov). This mystical and nature-related sensibility helps to explain Sophian devotion in Russia.

> *O Earth, My Mistress!*
> O Earth, my Mistress! I do not tire of harkening
> To your song, before and now again it moves my heart,
> Eternally fresh strains sing to me of rushing waters,
> And the ancient beauty of dark forests.

---

[12] Mueller and Wille, *Solowjews Leben in Briefe und Gedichte*, p. 213/22; biographical remarks, see p. 330.

On that day, the light from the vaults of heaven
Flowed down differently, clear and unclouded;
Between the old familiar trees of earth
Appeared mysteriously pale eyes, so blue.[13]

The above poem from June 29, 1898, is also titled: "O Earth, My Mistress." Soloviev again speaks of Sophia's eyes, which is a favorite topic and attests to his love and devotion.

O Splendid, Tender Beauty How I Love You
O splendid, tender beauty, how I love you,
Regardless if the day is bright or dark and oppressing.
I love the look of your eyes shining brightly;
But when grief surrounds them, I am also in ecstasy

O most tender and beloved, who would deny me nothing,
O tell me, could you also, like others, be untrue?
No, proclaims my heart, often uncourageous faltering,
Now comes its final yearning.

O, splendid, tender beauty, love me!
Regardless if the day is bright or dark and oppressing.
O love me fervently, tell me: "I love thee!"
Then will I life-long blessed and happy be.[14]

Slumbering In Winter in a Blanket of Snow
Slumbering in winter in a blanket of snow
You lie before me, resting, sleeping
Not death, but fullness of life
Wafts out to me from your blanket all aglow.

My inner eye perceived
How fine You look, wreathed about in cliffs and pines.

---

[13] Mueller and Wille, *Solowjews Leben in Briefe und Gedichte*, p. 266/98; biographical remarks, see p. 350.

[14] Mueller and Wille, *Solowjews Leben in Briefe und Gedichte*, p. 244/66; biographical remarks, see p. 341.

Lovely mistress of the fairies' kingdom,
Royally resting, how your beauty shines.

Immaculata, snow-white, unvanquished,
Deep in thought like the mid-winter's night,
Resplendent, come out of the dark and chaos,
Bright as the northern light in all its flaming might.[15]

The two poems above, written in the autumn and winter of 1894, manifest an almost ecstatic love of nature which comes from the conviction that Sophia loves and is loved through nature. They also testify to Soloviev's belief that not lifeless, mechanical laws but instead spiritual powers and "ideas" are at work in nature; and that Sophia, the Soul of the World, is the Queen and Mistress of all.

I Am Always There, Both Day and Night
Between the dawn and dreams, always
You are there, both day and night.
Your gaze streams through me, to the deepest ground,
Full of splendor, full of might.

The ice is melting, clouds yield to light,
Flowers blooming all around me,
Silent tones in ether of transparent sounds,
I sense you everywhere.

Sin's sting has been extinguished in the soul
And fear at the face of death.
Without concern I can look into the darkest depths,
Nothing can harm me there.

All around just water and light, afar in the blue
All flows into one.
But her eyes remain, shining like stars
When all that seems to be fades away.[16]

---

[15] Mueller and Wille, *Solowjews Leben in Briefe und Gedichte*, p. 245/68; biographical remarks, see p. 342.
[16] Mueller and Wille, *Solowjews Leben in Briefe und Gedichte*, p. 276/102; biographical remarks, see p. 351.

This poem, written November 21, 1898, again reflects Soloviev's deeply mystical relationship to Sophia. He constantly feels Her merciful presence and the loving gaze of Her eyes, seeing Her in everything. Union with Sophia loosens the effect of evil and banishes fear.

Soloviev's Encounters with Sophia

Soloviev says of the poem in which he movingly depicts his three visions of Sophia:

> The experiences that were the most significant in my life up until then are presented in the form of light-hearted verses. For two whole days my consciousness was flooded with memories and consonances, and on the third day I completed this little autobiography, which has been well received by some poets and ladies.[17]

[Some verses have been excluded from the version which follows.]

A Poem
Before death's advent I have conquered death
And—through love—the power of time.

O, Eternal Friend, so weakly praised by me,
Accept, what my muse now hallows to you . . .

Three times you showed yourself to me.
You were not my mind's invention;
No, profoundly real was your presence:
You heard the call of my heart and came.

I.

The first time was thirty-six years ago—
So long that I hardly recall!

---

[17] Mueller and Wille, *Solowjews Leben in Briefe und Gedichte*, p. 350.

My child's soul perceived
An uneasy dream of love's yearning . . .

Ascension Day's high mass. A beautiful morning!
My heart was seething, the mass was long.
"O let us . . . forget . . . all woe,"—
Sang the choir's cherubinal song.

Suddenly my eyes could not focus,
Without a trace the earth disappeared.
Passion's storm faded away,
I was surrounded with heavenly blue.

You too are radiant blue! A blossom
Of supernatural beauty in your hand.
With gracious goodness you smiled at me,
Nodding—then the heavenly image was gone . . .

II.

Years passed. My first foreign journey,
As a private teacher. Swiftly
Flying through Germany on the rails of a train,
Berlin—Hannover—Cologne: rolling along.

Prado, Notre Dame, the Coliseum,
Aja Sophia—nothing interests me,
But then the British Museum beckoned,
And there my dream was fulfilled.

Never will I forget that wonderful time.
No earthly beauty drew me.
Nor was I possessed with passion,
You ruled my soul, only you . . .

Mostly alone in the reading room,
Reading what I found about you.
Hidden powers were at play
Guiding the best into my hands . . .

Then one day—towards the evening of the year—
I whispered: "I feel you near:
You are here, just as when I was young. Show,
O Flower of God,—show yourself to me."

Scarcely spoken, I felt myself surrounded
By golden light and radiant blue
And I saw her again, all full of light,
Only her countenance, ah!—only her countenance.

Long did I drink from this hour's happiness,
Blind and dumb again to the earth.
And when I thought of all that was written,
Hopeless and empty it seemed.

III.

I said to her: "Yes, I saw you,
But only your countenance, heavenly radiant.
O Eternal Friend, hear my plea,
And reveal all of your self, as once to the child, to me!"

"On to Egypt!" echoed within me.
Was it recklessness to act?
No matter—listening, without doubting,
Soon I was in a train for Paris.

Lyons, Turin, Ancona, Bari,
Everything flew past, mattering little.
Soon I embarked from Brindisi through the waves
Bound on a British steamer to the land of the Nile.

In Cairo I found welcome
In the lovely hotel Abbat.
Russians were there aplenty,
From Moscow too, city of my birth . . .

Watching all the while for her sign.
And lo—in night's stillness.

She gently wafted through my room:
"On to the desert! I await you!" . . .

Thus day found me wandering
Penniless, trusting luck
Towards the desert
Unconcerned about provision . . .

The sun was sinking,
And duskless darkness followed.
Black was the star twinkling night,
All was silent, still and deep . . .

Long I lay, half sleeping
When I heard: "Poor friend, sleep on!"
And so slept on;—and on awakening
The world was glowing with early dawn.

Springtime broke from the morning sky's
Purple glow, and there you were!
A new Radiance shining in your eyes
Like day's light at dawn's creation.

What is and was, and will come in eternity,
The rich, multitudinous forms—I saw them all:
Shimmering blue beneath me, the depths of the sea,
White mountain tops and distant forest.

I saw all, and all was one,
The precious image of my Eternal Friend,
A reflection of heaven's radiance
Was all around—my heart was full.

Radiant Light, your words do not deceive:
In the desert I saw all of you.
Wherever fate may lead me
This happiness will not fade away.

And yet in an instant, all was gone.
On the horizon was rising the sun.

> Stillness was in the desert. But in the morning light
> I heard within the echo of distant bells . . .
>
> The world is vain. But matter's phantom no longer hides
> The eternal, primordial ground of all;
> While still in this world I glimpsed God's fullness,
> Saw the eternal oneness of being.
>
> Through the mystic dream, I feel, even now,
> Death vanquished, and, too, the power of time.
> O Eternal Friend, whom I so weakly praise.
> Grant me pardon for what my muse hallows to you.[18]

Soloviev wrote this revealing poem at the end of September in 1898, two years before his death.

SOPHIA ACCORDING TO PAVEL FLORENSKI

Pavel Florenski was born in 1882 in Tiflis in the republic of Georgia of a Russian father and Armenian mother. Florenski's father taught mathematics and biology, and Florenski shared his father's scientific interests, writing an article as a school youth about phosphorescence in lightning bugs. After graduating, Florenski enrolled at the University of Moscow, where he studied mathematics and occupied himself with classical Greek thought. He later attended the Theological Academy in Moscow and received a teaching degree in 1908, and in 1909 began attending lectures on the history of philosophy. He wanted to become a monk but his confessor advised him to marry, which he did in 1911. Not long afterward, he was ordained as a priest of the Orthodox Church.[19]

---

[18] Mueller and Wille, *Solowjews Leben in Briefe und Gedichte*, p. 267/100; biographical remarks, see p. 350.

[19] For more complete biographical information on Florenski see L. L. Hammerich, *Phillipians 2,6 and P. A. Florenski* (Copenhagen: Munksgaard, 1976), p. 13 f; Fairy von Lilienfeld, "Sophia—Die Weisheit Gottes" in *Una Sancta, Zeitschrift für Okumenische Begegnung* (Freising, 1984/2), p. 126 and 129, notes 34–36; *Die Religion in Geschichte und Gegenwart, Handwoeterbuch für Theologie und Religionswissenschaft* (Tübingen: Mohr, 1957–1965), vol. 3, "Florenski."

In the years that followed, Florenski taught at the Theological Academy and wrote diverse articles and essays. In 1914 his principle theological work appeared, *The Pillars and Foundations of Truth*, which comprehensively expresses his thought and religious philosophy. It reveals that he was a disciple of Soloviev and a representative of the so-called renaissance in Russian religion which took place around 1900.

After the Communist Revolution of 1917, the Theological Academy in Moscow where he taught was closed. Since Florenski was known as a capable scientist, he received a teaching position in mathematics and physics at the Polytechnical College in Moscow.

In time his reputation grew to the extent that he was consulted about the proposed electrification of the Soviet Union. He also became the principle editor for important parts of the Soviet Encyclopedia of Technology, which provided him with the opportunity to occupy himself with the latest currents of scientific thought (such as quantum mechanics, the theory of relativity and particle physics).

Though belonging to the middle class, Florenski's professional standing guaranteed his personal safety during the 1920s; and when many scientists, artists, and academicians left Russia in 1922 (including Berdyayev and his personal friend Bulgakov) he chose to stay behind.

His appearance in priestly garb at a celebration of the Society of Physics in 1926 was tolerated but not forgotten. When Stalin began to persecute nonconformist academicians and scientists in the years which followed, Florenski's fortunes also began to diminish. His name was eliminated from textbooks and lexicons and was not allowed to appear in the press. His close association to Bucharin,[20] who had sought Florenski's advice in scientific matters, proved to be disastrous. Following Bucharin's execution, Florenski was deported to a concentra-

---

[20] Nikolai Bucharin (1888–1938), one of the leading figures who worked with Lenin, was an important Communist economist and the editor-in-chief of Pravda. He eventually opposed Stalin's forced collectivization and industrial plans. He was ostracized and removed from all posts, arrested in 1937, and executed in 1938 after a mock trial.

tion camp in Siberia, and after 1937 nothing more was heard from him.

Florenski's colleague and friend Sergei Bulgakov,[21] himself a pioneer theologian, spoke of the lasting impression of Florenski's powerful personality. He also said that Florenski was a congenital genius whose life was marked by spiritual and intellectual endeavor, and compared him to a work of art. Konstantin Andronikov, the French translator of Florenski's *The Pillars and Foundations of Truth*, considered this work as the synthesis of all of Russian culture and spiritual thought.

After being forgotten for some time, the Russian Orthodox Church has begun to celebrate Florenski's memory, commemorating the anniversary of his 100th birthday in 1982.[22]

Florenski's Sophia Teaching

In writing about the Russian Sophia icons Florenski says:

> This sublime, royal and feminine nature, who is not God or the eternal Son, nor an Angel or one of the saints . . . is she not the true synthesis of all humanity, the higher and more complete form (of the world), the living soul of nature and the universe? . . . our forefathers, the devout

---

[21] Sergei Bulgakov was a theologian and philosopher of religion. He had studied economics and become a Marxist, but later returned to the Orthodox faith and the Church with his friend Berdyayev. He was ordained to the priesthood in 1918, but was expelled from Russia in 1922. Beginning in 1925, he was the deacon of the Russian Orthodox Theological Institute in Paris. Sophia is central to his thought, and in his own Sophiology he builds on the work of Soloviev and Florenski (see the section in chapter 15 on Bulgakov).

[22] Zurnal Moscovskoj Patriarchii [Journal of the Moscow Patriarchs] 1982/4. This issue commemorated the 100th anniversary of Florenski's birth. The first article "Fundamental Characteristics of the Person, Life and Works of the Priest Pavel Florenski," by his nephew Andronik (a monk and priest) is a contribution to Florenski's biography. It is followed by a report about the commemoration of Florenski's 100th birthday at Moscow's Spiritual Academy. Another issue of this journal (1981/9) includes an article about Bishop Antony Florensov, Florenski's spirtual advisor and confessor.

builders of the Sophia churches and painters of the Sophia icons deeply sensed her existence.[23]

Florenski also says that Sophia is a monad or personal unity in which the Creator encompasses all of creation. Recognizing the person of this monad of creation does not come from intellectual reflection, but is instead the result of an actual spiritual experience:

> The monad of which I speak is for me a fact of living experience. She is a religious reality, not something accepted a priori but a posteriori, not by arrogantly constructing Her, but in humble devotion to Her. . . . I am compelled to use metaphysical terminology, but the concepts in my expositions do not serve a strictly technical purpose . . . but a more symbolical one. They are the colors with which one paints feelings.[24]

Further on he writes:

> I said a monad, i.e., a unity that is very real . . . which takes its place among other such monads, excluding them from its own sphere; for if it were to lose its singularity, the other monads would force it to merge with them into an indeterminate, elementary union. But in the spiritual realms of which I speak, nothing loses its individuality. All things are understood and experienced as organically and inwardly bound and wedded to one another by a

---

[23] Pavel Florenski, *La Colonne et le Fondement de la Vérité*, translated from the Russian by Constantin Andronikov (Lausanne: L'Age d'Homme, 1975), p. 253 (a partial translation in German of this work is found in: Nikolai Bubnow and H. Ehrenberg, *Oestliches Christentum* (Munich, 1925), pp. 24–194). Translator's note: Although Florenski does not say so, he is paraphrasing here the words of Vladimir Soloviev. See Soloviev's previous remarks in this chapter about the works of August Compte. I am indebted to the Soloviev scholar Professor Leonid Sytenko for this clarification. This and the following quotations are translated from German.

[24] Pavel Florenski, *La Colonne et le Fondement de la Vérité*, p. 212.

> process of voluntarily realized self-emptying, as a nature
> that is intimately and essentially one and whole . . . in
> short, they are all a manifold but single nature, every-
> thing is essentially one and everything is personally dif-
> ferent. This is a union realized by an eternal act . . . a
> suspended balance of hypostases . . . an eternal exchange
> of energies . . . eternal motion at rest and eternal rest in
> motion.[25]

In the above passage Florenski is attempting to explain the nature and life of the Trinity, which is one and consubstantial but
individual in three hypostases as the model for a life together in
love of many different "persons." The Trinity is a whole composed of individuals, and this "sublime nature" is Sophia, God's
Wisdom. He continues:

> Sophia is the Grand Root of the synthesis of everything
> that is created, i.e., the entire creation and not just all crea-
> tures . . . Sophia is the Guardian Angel, the Ideal Person
> of the world, its formational foundation. . . .
>
> Sophia is the eternal Bride of the Logos. She is manifold
> in the ideas of creation, and She receives the creative
> power for this from Him. She is one in God and many in
> creation. . . . The entirety of these ideas and images is the
> true House of God, the Holy Temple of God, the Holy
> City, Heavenly Jerusalem.[26]

It is worth remarking that in these passages Florenski is quoting
Count M. M. Speransky, a Sophian mystic from the beginning of
the 19th century, whose ideas about Sophia were very profound
and original. Speransky compares Sophia to Eve. Just as Eve issued from the side of Adam, Sophia came forth from the Logos
"by division." This idea was criticized as pantheistic, but it can
be understood in a symbolic and mystical sense (such as the
Holy Spirit's designation as "Costa Verbi" or the Rib of the

---

[25] Florenski, *La Colonne et le Fondement de la Vérité*, p. 213.
[26] Florenski, *La Colonne et le Fondement de la Vérité*, pp. 213, 215–216.

Word). Speransky depicts the relationship of Sophia to the individual persons of the Holy Trinity in a beautiful and profound manner: She is the Daughter of the Father, the Sister and Bride of the Son, and the Image of the Holy Spirit; She is the primordial Idea, the Mother of everything external to God; She is the first being external to God and She is supernatural Eve, the Mother of all "ideas" of creation. Florenski summarizes:

> Except for saying that the Logos is divided, Speransky's point of view does not contradict Biblical teaching or Patristic interpretation of the Bible.[27]

Florenski likes to describe Sophia with images from Holy Scripture and the Church Fathers such as the City of God, Heavenly Jerusalem, Bride of Zion, and the Spouse of the Lamb (the Church who has made herself beautiful for her Husband). He points to the Bride's pre-existence by referring to Clement of Rome and Pastor Hermas in particular. Florenski uses the same expressions that Augustine repeatedly used to describe "Created Sophia."[28]

Florenski also frequently invokes Athanasius, according to whom:

> Sophia impressed Her image in space and time and thus precedes the universe as the pre-existent hypostatical whole of the ideas and prototypes of creation.[29]

However Athanasius was undoubtedly referring to Uncreated, Divine Sophia, or Jesus Christ. Florenski interprets Athanasius to be referring to Sophia as a created person with an individual dignity and function, and not to a Sophia who is the Logos; yet Athanasius actually meant the latter.

---

[27] A. B. Eltchinov, *Le Mysticisme de M. Speransky* (Bogosl. Vestn. 1906), quoted in Paul Florenski, *La Colonne et la Fondement de la Vérité*, Constantin Andronikov, trans. (Lausanne: L'Age d'Homme, 1978), p. 217 and 417 (notes 587, 588).

[28] Florenski, *La Colonne et le Fondement de la Vérité*, p. 218 ff.

[29] Florenski, *La Colonne et le Fondement de la Vérité*, p. 227.

Sophia, Mary, and the Church

In describing the entirety of Sophia's attributes, functions, and titles, Florenski clearly reveals his ecclesiological and Marian understanding of Her. Some of these descriptions are:

> Sophia is the first created and the first redeemed, the center (heart) of redeemed creation. She is the Church, i.e., the whole of everyone who comes to enjoy redemption and makes up the body of Christ.
>
> Sophia is personal virginity, i.e., the power which makes a human being entirely whole. And Mary carries this virginal power in Her par excellence. She is, therefore, the manifestation of Sophia, i.e., Sophia incarnated.[30]

By means of a bold series of inferences, he makes some grandiose statements about Sophia:

> If Sophia is the whole of creation, then She is Humanity par excellence, which is indeed the soul and consciousness of creation. If Sophia is the whole of humanity, then She is the Church par excellence, which is indeed the soul and consciousness of humanity. If Sophia is the Church, then She is par excellence the Church of the saints, for the Church of the saints, the divine Church, is the soul and consciousness of the Church (on earth). And as the Soul of the divine Church, She is our advocate to the Logos, the Judge, for She is also the Mother of God (p. 228).

In the above passage he is clearly identifying Sophia with Mary, the Mother of God. He continues:

> Sophia is truly the Jewel of human existence, Sophia is Beauty. Only Sophia is the Beauty in essence of all of creation. . . . Sophia is the Guardian Angel of all of creation (pp. 228–229).

---

[30] This and the following quotation are from Florenski, *La Colonne et le Fondement de la Vérité*, p. 228.

He continues that Sophia is the:

> Fountainhead of the Church, beautiful and young Bride of God, She is not "prima inter pares" (first among equals) among the saints but above all saints. She is the Bridge that connects God and creation, the Heart and Apex of creation. She is the Church in person. (p. 231).

Florenski adds that what he has said about Sophia is found in the Church's liturgy, in iconography and also in Church writings. He quotes several beautiful liturgical passages which identify Sophia with the Blessed Virgin:

> Let me dare to celebrate Her who interceded for the world, the Spotless Bride, the Virgin . . . who You named Sophia, Wisdom of God. . . . You gave to Her a countenance of fire, from which goes forth the flame of Your divinity, i.e., Your Son.[31]

However, Florenski also quotes liturgical passages which present a Christological view of Sophia, for example: "From all of our hearts let us seek God's Wisdom, who incarnated from the Virgin Most Pure."[32] He explains the apparent contradiction by saying that Sophia is worshipped both as the Logos-Christ and Mary, Mother of God, adding:

> It is beyond the capacity of our theologians to explain and clarify this phenomenon. The devotion of the Russian soul has always understood Sophia to possess a mysterious grandeur of Her own and has correctly related Her to Mary or even identified Sophia with Her.[33]

He goes on to say that official theology is inspired by liturgy and the popular devotion, but often lags behind them. The the-

---

[31]Florenski, p. 252. The text is from the "Office Of Holy Sophia, Wisdom Of God," celebrated in the Holy Sophia Church in Moscow. See also the note on p. 480.

[32]Florenski, p. 481.

[33]Florenski, pp. 252, 474, 478. He mentions Tolstoy, Dostoyevsky, and Soloviev.

ological axiom *Lex orandi est lex credendi* (the law of prayer is the law of faith) expresses this phenomenon and in a sense legitimizes it.[34]

Sophian Iconography

Florenski attributes special significance to Sophian iconography and indicates that its representations do not always accord with the interpretation of Sophia given by the Church Fathers:

> It was from the beginning an authentic religious creation of our folk soul and does not represent something borrowed. . . . What the Church Fathers meant by Sophia does not always correspond with the contents of the icons, which appeared much later; or to express it otherwise, the figure depicted in the icons does not always correspond to their understanding of Sophia.[35]

He expands on this statement by distinguishing between three types of Russian iconographic portrayals of Sophia—which depict Her either as an Angel, the Church, or as Mary. The Novgorod icon (figure 10, page 269) is an example of the first type, depicting Her as an Angel (see also chapter 16). Jesus Christ, or the Logos, is above Her. To Her left is Mary and the Child, and to Her right is John the Baptist. This particular icon is also interpreted Christologically because it is supposed to be a copy of the icon of the Divine Sophia Church in Constantinople, and the dedication date of both the Constantinople and Novgorod churches falls on Christmas. However, is not Christmas also a feast day of Mary, the Mother of God?

The second type of icon (figure 11, page 270) portrays Sophia as the Church or the Body of Christ. Sometimes these depictions show the figure of Jesus Christ on the cross (such as the one in the church of St. John Chrysostomos in Jaroslav). The body of Jesus Christ represents the Church, which is born from

---

[34] Florenski, p. 238.
[35] Florenski, p. 240.

Figure 10. Sophia Icon. Novarod type. Pavel Florenski, *La Colonne et le Fondement de la Vérité*. L'Age d'Homme, Lausanne, 1975.

the wound in the side opened by the lance (i.e., the Church comes forth from Jesus' heart).

The third type of Sophia icon (figure 12, page 271) depicts Her as the Intercessor, or as the Mother of God. Such portrayals

Figure 11. Sophia Icon, Jaroslav type. Pavel Florenski, *La Colonne et le Fondement de la Vérité*. L'Age d'Homme, Lausanne, 1975.

exist in the Sophia Cathedral in Kiev (see also chapter 16), the hermitage of Optina, and the Zion Cathedral in Tiflis[36] (the familiar icons of Mary are most similar to this type).

In addition to the three main kinds of icons outlined above, there are others which combine all three elements that Florenski also discusses.

---

[36] Florenski, *La Colonne et le Fondement de la Vérité*, note 682, p. 475.

Figure 12. Sophia Icon. Kiev type. Pavel Florenski, *La Colonne et le Fondement de la Vérité*. L'Age d'Homme, Lausanne, 1975.

Florenski allows that some iconographic portrayals may have meant to depict Wisdom as an attribute of God. He acknowledges that the original Hagia Sophia Church in Constantinople was perhaps conceived in this way. Emperor Constantine, who built the church, built two others dedicated to Divine Peace (*Eirene*) and Divine Power (*Dynamis*), apparently so that pagans might be able to identify with these churches (Justinian I rebuilt the church in Constantinople after its destruction and dedicated it to the incarnated Logos). Florenski concludes his remarks about Sophia with the words:

> Sophia reveals Herself first of all as a transfigured and spiritualized promise to the world, a vision incomprehensible to others, of the kingdom of heaven on earth.[37]

Pavel Florenski remained true to Sophia and true to his faith and suffered exile and martyrdom as a result. His vision of Sophia's significance has meaning for our time, which hopefully will begin to understand more and more that Sophia—the world's Guardian Angel and creation's Soul and Mother, who intercedes for us and leads us to Christ—can help to save the world from the ecological disaster and threat of destruction caused by humanity.

SOPHIA ACCORDING TO SERGEI BULGAKOV

Sergei Bulgakov (1871–1944) was born in Livny as the son of an orthodox priest.[38] Although he planned to enter the priesthood himself, he left the seminary at age 16 because of a personal religious crisis. He subsequently attended the University of

---

[37] Florenski, p. 253.

[38] Biographical references are taken primarily from the article "Sergej N. Bulgakov" in H. J. Ruppert, *Klassiker der Theologie* (Munich: 1983), H. Fries and G. Kretschmer vol. 2, pp. 263–276. This article does justice to Bulgakov's concern for reclaiming the sense of the world's existential relationship and unity with God that had become lost due to the influence of the scientific worldview. His Sophiology sought to make this possible. See also "Vater Sergej Bulgakov zum 40. Todestag," *Voices of Orthodoxy* (the monthly journal of the Russian Orthodox Eparchates for Middle Europe), Berlin, 86/8.

Moscow from 1890 to 1894, where he studied economics and joined the Marxist movement. He also partook of studies in Berlin, where he met some of the principal representatives of the social democracy movement (Bebel, Adler, and Rosa Luxemburg). Having concluded that materialistic philosophy was incompatible with spiritual ideals, he turned to the kind of socialism that was rooted in Christianity and helped in the attempt to found a Christian Socialist party.

Before World War I, he was closely allied with the spiritual elite of the "Silver Age of Russian culture" (particularly Berdyayev, Mereschovski, and the symbolists A. Blok and A. Belyi); and from 1904–1905 he published the journals *New Way* and *Questions about Life*. During this time he was immersed in religious and philosophical studies. He was deeply interested in the apparent tension between God and the world, and tried to come to terms with liberal Protestant theology and the history of religion. In 1912 his work *Philosophy of Economics* was published. In 1917 his first religious and philosophical work *The Never Fading Light* appeared, and in the same year he was also the representative of the College of Moscow at the Council of the Russian Orthodox Church. The impact of the October Revolution resulted in his decision to become a priest, and he was ordained in 1918 in the presence of friends like Berdyayev, Florenski, and E. N. Trubeckoj.

As civil war tore through Russia, he was expelled in 1923, along with others belonging to the religious intelligentsia, like Berdyayev. He traveled through Constantinople and Prague and finally reached Paris, where, until his death, he was a professor of Dogmatics at the Orthodox Institute of St. Sergius.

Bulgakov's literary output was prodigious. He wrote a dogmatic trilogy about the divineness of humanity: *The Lamb of God* (about Christology), *The Comforter* (Pneumatology), and *The Bride of the Lamb* (Ecclesiology). His work *The Burning Thornbush*, which summarizes his thinking about Mary, shows that he was well versed in Mariology.[39] The leitmotif that is present in all

---

[39] Since the appearance of this work in 1927, Bulgakov has been considered one of the most significant Orthodox Mariologes. His courageous and clear committment to the Mariology of the Orthodox Church created quite a sensation. Titles in English mentioned in text are translations from German titles.

his works, however, is Sophia, and his work *Sophia the Wisdom of God*[40] summarizes his teaching about Her.

Boulgakov's commitment to social welfare and his familiarity with the Sophiological ideas of Soloviev and Florenski led him to Sophia, and She subsequently became the focal point of his thinking. Boulgakov wanted to demonstrate the relationship between the Wisdom inherent to creation and the Wisdom in God. His intention was to oppose Manichaeism by emphasizing creation's unity and value, and to also oppose the prevalent atheism of the time by emphasizing creation's origin in God and significance. He was interested in developing a new "theology of creation" or "theology of nature" which for him was synonymous with Sophiology.[41] Through Sophiology he was attempting to penetrate to the world's hidden meaning, and he believed to have attained this by coming to understand Sophia as the universal, living element at the basis of all existence both created and divine.

His teaching, however, was strongly criticized by the Church; in part because of misunderstandings about his theology and cosmology, but also because of some genuinely problematic formulations.

---

[40] Bulgakov began to express his Sophiological ideas in his *Economic Philosophy* and honed them further in his trilogy about the divinity of humanity. He summarized his thinking about Her in *The Wisdom of God: A Brief Summary of Sophiology*, originally published in English in 1937 (republished Hudson, NY: Lindisfarne Press, 1993). All quoted texts are from the French edition, which the translator claims is based on the original, unpublished Russian text: Serge Boulgakov, *La Sagesse de Dieu, Resumé de Sophiologie*, Constantin Andronikov, trans. (Lausanne: L'Age d'Homme, 1983). The French editon appears to be quite different from the English translation mentioned above.

[41] Boulgakov says that Sophiology is: "a Weltanschauung (worldview), a Christian vision of the world, a theological conception . . . a particular interpretation of the entirety of Christian teaching, beginning with the teachings about the Holy Trinity and the origin of humanity, to the practical questions of Christianity today . . . the relationship between God and the world is the central problem of Sophiology . . . the created world is related with the divine world through Sophia, She is in God . . . Sophiology is an appeal to a spiritual life and to creative activity, in order to save oneself and the world (*La Sagesse de Dieu*, pp. 13, 15). This appeal is particularly relevant today, considering the global ecological crisis which threatens humanity and the world. This translation and subsequent quotations are from the German.

Sophiological Aspects
of Boulgakov's Thought

According to Boulgakov, Sophiology is not well known and recognized in the Church because of the inherited Patristic teaching which usually identifies Sophia with the Logos or Jesus Christ. A similarly dominant Christological interpretation of Sophia had also become entrenched in Byzantine theology, iconography and liturgy.

> Byzantine theology did not answer the question of Sophia . . . the theological significance (of the Sophia churches) remained hidden for a long time. The curtain began to rise not through the efforts of theology but through the development of sacred symbology . . . theologians had considered symbolism to belong to the domain of archeology, or they were hostile towards it, thinking that it signified a misunderstanding of dogma . . . but the time has come to decipher this sacred message (the Sophia icons and churches) and to reawaken the living tradition which has been interrupted.

> What is significant for dogma and historically undeniable is that Sophia churches, which are understood Christologically in Byzantium, are understood Mariologically in Russia . . . Sophia devotion took on a Marian character. The Christosophia of Byzantium was complemented by Sophia Mary, the Mother of God. Russian Sophia churches were consecrated to the Mother of God and their patron feast days were celebrated on feast days of Mary; in Kiev on the feast of Mary's birth, and in Novgorod on the feast of Mary's Assumption, which has a particular Sophian character among Marian feasts . . .

> This change in interpretation also had a visible effect on iconography and liturgy. The characteristics of Sophia icons clearly became Marian . . . even though they were sometimes interpreted Christologically.[42]

---

[42] Boulgakov, *La Sagesse de Dieu*, pp. 8–9; 80–81, notes 56–59.

Boulgakov admits that Russian Sophiology was partially influenced by Jacob Boehme and his pupils in western Europe, and he acknowledges Boehme's contributions by calling him "Germany's most genial thinker" who can undoubtedly be named the Father of Western Sophiology. He also refers to John Pordage's treatises and says that: "The works of Boehme and Pordage have exerted an incredible influence on Russian thinking."[43]

Boulgakov also indicates that Soloviev was responsible for guiding him from Marxism to idealism, and then to the Orthodox Church, but he criticizes Soloviev's gnostic tendencies. His judgment of Florenski's Sophiology is very positive, especially because of its orthodoxy.[44] He regrets that Florenski's work (i.e., his Sophiology) had not been taken up by theologians; and he also complains that in the West the best of Russian ideas are not acknowledged, and says that Sophia represents "an essential figure within Christianity."[45] He continues that not until the mid-19th century through Sophiologists like Soloviev was Sophiology reawakened, and the intimations of the Russian people—expressed in the Sophia icons and churches—elevated to level of philosophical and theological consciousness.[46]

One of his ideas, which became vociferously criticized, was his understanding of Sophia as the universal nature which contains everything that is divine and created. She is *Ousia*, the essential nature of God *and* creation. She is the Divine Nature, and while not a hypostasis, She is hypostasized or personalized in the three persons of the Divine Trinity; and She is also mysteriously the nature of creation and individualized in created beings. Boulgakov summarizes the first part of this teaching by saying:

> In short, by embracing three in one the Holy Trinity *is* Sophia. It *is* the Ousia or Sophia . . . the Trinity has a single Ousia and this Ousia is Sophia.[47]

---

[43] Boulgàkov, *La Sagesse de Dieu*, p. 10.
[44] Boulgakov, *La Sagesse de Dieu*, p. 11.
[45] Boulgakov, *La Sagesse de Dieu*, pp. 12–13.
[46] Boulgakov, *La Sagesse de Dieu*, p. 20.
[47] Boulgakov, *La Sagesse de Dieu*, pp. 35–36.

He defends himself against the criticism that such an idea adds a fourth hypostasis (to the three persons of the Trinity) by saying:

> The three divine persons a life in common, i.e., an Ousia, Sophia. . . . Sophia is not a hypostasis, She is a mode, a quality, an attribute of a divine hypostasis or a hypostatical nature. . . . Understanding the divineness of God to exist in God's Ousia, which is something other than God's hypostases, does not mean transforming the Trinity into a quaternity.[48]

Although he admits:

> It is only natural for discursive reason to hesitate when it is a question of distinguishing between hypostatic and essential nature. . . . God's nature is God's Ousia and God's Ousia is Sophia, and Sophia is everything and the union of everything with everything in everything, a pan-organism of the Ideas of everything in everything. . . . The Sophia-Ousia is itself not a hypostasis, but being and nature which takes on a particular form and modality through different hypostases that are both divine and created.[49]

In other words, Sophia has a divine nature and a created nature, and they are united but also different, which in effect defines Her mystery. This kind of thinking recalls the mystical theology of Meister Eckhart[50] which also supposed a certain identity between divine and created nature, but distinguished between the all-inclusive Godhead and the God of three persons. Such conceptions are difficult for even theologians to understand, and it is understandable that both Eckhart and Boulgakov were accused of heresy. Though one wonders whether Boulgakov really

---

[48] Boulgakov, *La Sagesse de Dieu*, pp. 27, 35, 37.

[49] Boulgakov, *La Sagesse de Dieu*, pp. 37, 38, 44.

[50] Concerning Meister Eckhart (1260–1328) see *Lexikon fur Theologie und Kirche* (Freiburg: Herder, 1959), vol. 3, pp. 645 ff; *Denzinger* (Freiburg: Herder, 32nd edition 1962), num. 950–978; W. Bange, *Eckharts Lehre vom Goettlichen und Geschoepflichen Sein* (Limburg: Pallottiner Verlag, 1937).

deserved to be considered a heretic, it must be acknowledged that expressions like: "Sophia is Ousia" or "Divine Nature" represented a significant departure from the traditional understanding of Her.

It is also clear that from Boulgakov's point of view Sophia could not be a person in the sense that She had been traditionally understood, either as Christ or even as Mary. At most one could perhaps speak of an hypostasized or individualized presence of the principle of Sophia—in Christ, Mary, or in any other individual.

Though one can affirm Boulgakov's rejection of an identity between Sophia and the Logos, this rejection must be viewed critically because it stems from the premise of Sophia's impersonalness. And were She to represent a person for Boulgakov, She would represent a fourth element within God's nature.

In spite of such difficulties, Boulgakov's fundamental purpose was sound: to affirm creation's goodness and the connection between God and nature.[51] It is important to the signifi-

---

[51]Teachings about the world's "Sophian character" are a significant theological response to the modern-day "secularization of the cosmos" and society. Sophiology deals with God's nature and activity in the world by speaking about grace and salvation and the world's preservation and development (H. J. Ruppert, *Klassiker der Theologie*, pp. 269–270).

In Russia before World War I, one of the main concerns of the "new religious consciousness" was overcoming the worldview which separated God from the world and did not, or did not want to, perceive God's activity in the world. A synthesis was sought which could unite religion and life, theology and science, and spirituality and culture. Its representatives criticized the West for neutralizing and secularizing the cosmos. Berdyayev considered Jacob Boehme to be a prophet who warned about what was to come: "The pre-eminent significance of Jacob Boehme and the Christian theosophy of the West is their stand against the de-sacralization of the cosmos. But in spite of everything, the consciousness of the Christian West lost its sense for the divinity of the cosmos and nature" (Ruppert, *Klassiker der Theologie*, p. 272). Boehme's goal was not to justify creation but to explain it. Sophiology is a means to this end.

According to the conviction of Russian devotion as expressed in the famous icons and cathedrals dedicated to Divine Sophia (in Kiev, Susdal, and Novgorod), Mary is Sophia's human form. The Russian Sophiologists all confirm this, from Soloviev to Boulgakov. Boulgakov repeatedly emphasized to opponents of his Sophiology that understanding Mary as Wisdom incarnate has its roots in Eastern Church architecture (the Sophia cathedrals), liturgy, and

cance of Sophiology that Boulgakov emphasized again and again:

> The images of creation, the ideas of things and natures are grounded in Sophia, yes, She is the primordial, all-embracing Idea of everything. She is the ideal of everything, the integral organism, and the ideal unity of all ideas.[52]

He also continually stressed that Sophia is the "Arche" or beginning of everything. She is the beginning in the sense of an ontological principle; and the Genesis words "in the beginning God created heaven and earth" signify "God created the world through Wisdom with Wisdom, and according to the image of Wisdom." In making this statement he is arguing against the view that identifies Sophia with the Logos.[53]

He also characterizes Sophia as the entelechy of the world and of the entire cosmos. For him, entelechy means the principle of the world's actualization and fulfillment. This is a thought which comes close to the idea of the World Soul, but he does not develop it any further.[54]

It is also worth noting that Boulgakov attributes a kind of androgenous nature to Sophia. She is the polar "dyadic revelation of the Logos and the Spirit," She is "raison et coeur," reason and heart together, a harmonious abundance of both aspects are present in Her. And yet Her female nature is dominant. She is and remains a woman.[55]

Mary in Boulgakov's Sophiology

According to Boulgakov, in the realm of creation Mary represents Sophia's hypostasized form (he does not speak of an incarnation), and this hypostasization is the most elevated that occurs

---

iconography. All are genuine sources of knowledge which must be taken seriously. They should not be dismissed as something "paraliturgical" or be considered the product of naive folk devotion.

[52] Boulgakov, *La Sagesse de Dieu*, p. 32.
[53] Boulgakov, *La Sagesse de Dieu*, p. 57, 58.
[54] Boulgakov, *La Sagesse de Dieu*, p. 49.
[55] Boulgakov, *La Sagesse de Dieu*, p. 65.

within creation. Sophia's hypostasis in Mary is also the basis for Mary's cosmological dignities and functions. She is the "Mother of Humanity, the spiritual focus of all that is created, and the Mother and Heart of the World."[56]

When the Holy Spirit descends on Mary at the Annunciation, She becomes the Spirit's bearer and is enabled to become the Mother of the incarnate Son of God. This is the basis for Her theological dignities. She is the:

> Daughter of the Father, Bride and Mother of the Son, the Image (Icon) and human revelation of the Holy Spirit, the Heart and Mother of the Church, the Queen of Heaven, the Wife and Bride of the Lamb.[57]

As Sophia's hypostasized and created form Mary is "the ground of the world, but also the power of its transfiguration."[58]

Boulgakov's expositions about Mary and Sophia's relationship to Her exhibit a great love and a reverence, proving that he was a genuine son of Russian spirituality and devotion.

[56] Boulgakov, *La Sagesse de Dieu*, p. 78.
[57] Boulgakov, *La Sagesse de Dieu*, p. 80.
[58] Boulgakov, *La Sagesse de Dieu*, p. 82.

16

Sophia in Russian Iconography and Architecture

ICONS LIKE THE NOVGOROD Icon reveal how Russian artists perceived Holy Wisdom, as well as showing the extent to which She was embraced and revered by the Russian people. This icon depicts Sophia as a radiant Angel with royal vestments and a crown who is holding a scepter (see Plate 17, page 125). She is sitting on a throne with a globe at Her feet. She has a halo around Her head and is the focal point of three concentric circles. Mary stands next to Her with an aureole containing the Christ Child. On the other side is John the Baptist with a scroll, his right hand raised in a gesture of bearing witness. Above Sophia is an image of Christ, surrounded by concentric circles of light. His halo is imprinted with a cross and contains the Greek words *ho on* ("He who is"). Above Him are three arches with an Etoimasia altar shaped like a throne in the middle. Three Angels hover on each side.

The icons that depict Sophia as an Angel belong to the first type of Sophia icons outlined by Pavel Florenski (chapter 15). As previously indicated, this particular icon has traditionally been interpreted Christologically. This is because it is supposed to be a copy of an icon in the Divine Sophia Church in Constantinople whose consecration date, like the Novgorod Church, falls on Christmas. Pavel Florenski, however, interprets the icon Mariologically and says the following:

> We see here the wonderful icon of God's Sophia, the icon of His most pure Mother. . . . This icon shows us the ineffable purity of the Most Holy Mother of God's virginity; above Her Christ sits on a throne, God's Logos, who loved this Sophia and willed to be born of Her according to the flesh.[1]

Following Florenski, the icon is interpreted to reflect Sophia's individual identity, which is separate from Christ, and Her incarnational relationship to Mary. It can be said to depict both the pre-incarnational and incarnational appearances of Sophia and Christ. Sophia on the throne with Christ above Her depict them in their pre-incarnational forms (Christ's inscription: "He who is" is primarily an indication of the divine nature of the Logos); and Mary with the Child depict their incarnational existence. John the Baptist bears witness to them.

THE STROGANOV ICON

This unusual icon from the School of Stroganov (see Plate 18, page 126) is described as:

> A combination of the Novgorod Sophia and the theme "your consort takes her place at your right hand" [Ps. 45,9]. A fiery angel (Christ) [sits] between Mary and John the Baptist, both of whom have wings. God the Father and an Angel are in the upper part of the picture, David is to the left and Solomon with a verse from Scripture (Prov. 9,1) to the right. Under Solomon are Joachim and Anne, and under David, musicians who are being led to the king. The might of God has thrown some warriors to the

---

[1] Pavel Florenski, *La Colonne et le Fondement de la Vérité*, trans. from Russian by Constantin Andronikov (Lausanne: L'Age d'Homme, 1975), pp. 248–249. Tr: translated from German text.

ground at Sophia's feet. The source of the inscription's text is Psalm 45.[2]

(Psalm 45, whose author is David, speaks of the royal bride accompanied by virgins who will be brought to the king, her lord.)

The above interpretation understands the icon as a portrayal of "Deesis" or intercession. Christ in the middle is Sophia; and Mary and John the Baptist, whose arms are upraised, are depicted in a gesture of intercession. The theme "the Bride stands to your right" apparently refers to the Church's betrothal to Christ (symbolized by Mary), or even to Mary's dignity as "Queen of Heaven."

However, identifying Christ with the female Sophia is unsatisfactory and does not correspond to the kind of Russian understanding which preserves Sophia's feminine identity and relates Her to Mary, either as someone identical to Mary, or as Mary's hypostasized earthly appearance.

An alternative understanding, in keeping with the theme of betrothal, is that the icon portrays the betrothal of Sophia who is Herself the Bride. The Biblical parallels for such an understanding are the Old Testament image of Wisdom who shares Yahweh's throne as His Beloved (Wisd. 9,4); and the New Testament image of the Holy City, New Jerusalem (Augustine's Created Sophia) who descends from heaven to become the Bride of the Lamb (Rev. 21, 2 and 9). Mary, who represents the Church—itself the Bride of Christ—parallels Sophia's espousal to the Lamb.

In such an interpretation, Sophia retains Her individual and feminine identity as God's companion as She is depicted in the Old Testament (by Solomon, who is also present in the image's depiction); and She Herself becomes an image of the Bride of the Logos.

This icon is usually interpreted Christologically. A thoroughly intelligible Sophian interpretation can also be advanced, however, even if it may seem unusual.

---

[2] Catalog of the Icon Museum in Recklinghausen, Germany, 1981, Stroganov icon, p. 141.

The icon can be understood as a mystical image of the "Hierogamy" or "Sacred Marriage" (see chapters 9 and 25) between the Logos and Sophia. The vertical line from top to bottom shows the figures to us in their pre-existential, pre-incarnational existence as Yahweh and Amon (as Logos and Sophia); and the horizontal line below shows them in their incarnational existence as Mary (Sophia become human) and Jesus Christ (the Logos become human). One holy pair, the one Hierogamy of both figures, is being depicted in two realms of existence—in the realm before their incarnation and in the realm after their incarnation.

That the figures in the vertical line are interpreted as the Logos (above) and Sophia (below) is not difficult to discern. That Mary is the left figure in the horizontal line below is clear. That the figure below and to the right, who is usually seen as John the Baptist, can be interpreted as Christ Himself is, indeed, an unusual interpretation, but, upon closer examination, a tempting one. The persons depicted to the right and also above point in the direction of this interpretation—Joachim and Anna to the right, King Solomon is above. Why are the parents of John the Baptist not shown if this is supposed to be the Baptist? Why instead of his parents Zacharias and Elizabeth are Joachim and Anna, Mary's parents and the grandparents of Jesus Christ, depicted? Why is Solomon above them, who according to the picture in the Codex Syriacus (see chapter 7) is Christ's archetype?

These remarks should suffice to make the proposed Sophian interpretation at least plausible.

The understanding that is outlined here preserves the icon's profound theological significance, the integrity of Sophia's identity, and also Her Mariological dimension that is a part of Russian Sophiology.

Stroganov's unusual icon possesses an irresistible radiance. Sophia shines in the beauty and purity of youth. There is a breathless and elevated dignity about Her as well as a loving goodness. She sits on the throne as a wise and knowing Teacher, a mighty Ruler and Victor, and as an Angelic Comforter and Guide. Sophia's ethereal form also recalls Boulgakov's characterization of Her as the Image of the Holy Spirit and Daughter of the Father.[3] The frame and inscriptions also lend a sacerdotal quality which magnifies the mystery of the icon's atmosphere and power.

THE SOPHIA CATHEDRAL IN KIEV

An extraordinary number of churches and cathedrals in Russia are dedicated to Divine Sophia, bearing eloquent witness to Russia's profound devotion of Holy Wisdom. Soloviev was especially fond of these holy places and inspired by them; and in addition to the Church in Novgorod, one of the best known is the Cathedral of Kiev.

Kiev's Cathedral presents a majestic depiction of Sophia high up in the apsis with arms upraised in a gesture of intercession. On the iconostasis shown in Plate 19 (page 127) are depictions of Mary with the Child and Christ holding a book.

The apsis depiction of Sophia is an example of Florenski's third type of Sophian icon, which depicts Her as the Mother of God. (See Plate 20, page 128.) In this depiction of "Sophia Orans" (the praying Sophia) She is ceremoniously dressed in the colors blue and gold, suggesting Her relationship to Mary. Keeping in mind the image of the Novgorod icon which depicts Sophia as the "Angel of Good Counsel"—understood as God's resolution for the plan of salvation—Her praying gesture can be understood as a prayer for the incarnation of the Logos who is the means to salvation.

Plate 19 (page 127) shows the iconostasis where the realization of salvation is portrayed. To the left is Mary with the Christ Child. Mary is depicted as "Theotokos," God's Bearer, with God's Child at Her bosom. If one accepts the premise that Mary is Sophia's human form, Sophia participates actively in the realization of salvation through Mary. At the right is Christ with a book in hand, in the act of teaching and blessing. The book can be understood to symbolize Wisdom in written form, as con-

---

[3] Sergei Boulgakov, *La Sagesse de Dieu, Resumé de Sophiologie*, trans. from Russian by Constatin Andronikov (Lausanne: L'Age d'Homme, 1983).

tained in the Law or Torah which Sophia represents in the Old Testament. In this sense the book is a symbol of Sophia-Wisdom Herself.

In this way the Cathedral's depictions can be understood to portray Divine Sophia in three different manifestations. Above in the apsis, She is presented as the divine, pre-existent Sophia, whose relationship to Mary is foreshadowed. Below, on the left of the iconostasis, She is shown as the Mother of the incarnated Logos who effects the plan of salvation. On the right of the iconostasis, She is the Wisdom of God's covenant in the Law (Old Testament) and the Good News of the new covenant through Christ (the Gospels).

Though Sophiology provides an opportunity for connecting the various images of the Sophia Cathedral in Kiev in this way, the apsis portrait of Sophia in a human form suggestive of Mary is the Cathedral's primary focus. It is a grandiose portrayal that has left an indelible mark on the psyche of the Russian people.

For more illustrations of Russian iconography relating to Mary–Sophia, see Plates 21–24, pages 129–132.

17

Sophia
According to
Teilhard de Chardin

PIERRE TEILHARD DE CHARDIN (1881–1955) was a French-man who entered the Jesuit Order at age 18 and studied physics. In 1911 he was ordained to the priesthood. He subsequently took part in scientific expeditions, was an advisor to the geological service in China, and worked for the Wenner Gren Foundation for Anthropological Research in New York. The discovery of "Sinanthropus Pekinensis" is attributed to him and his colleagues. His numerous writings were first published after his death, and since they then have attracted widespread attention (some of his main works are: *The Divine Milieu, Human Energy, The Appearance of Man* and *The Future of Man*).[1]

Teilhard de Chardin affirmed the concept of evolution and sought to integrate it into Christian theology. He thought that humanity's future evolution involved a process of socialization, whose goal was attaining an ever-increasing degree of consciousness and sense of oneness. Christ, the "Omega Point," represents the apex of this path of development. Teilhard also

---

[1] Pierre Teilhard de Chardin. *The Divine Milieu* (New York: Harper & Row, 1965); *Human Energy* (New York: Harcourt, Brace, & Co., 1947); *The Appearance of Man* (New York: Harper & Row, 1965); *The Future of Man* (New York: Harper & Row, 1965).

saw the world as a part of a unified cosmos which was formed, held together and guided by a primordial entelechy. He variously called this entelechy the "Soul of the World," the "Foundation of the World," but also the "Omega Point"; and sometimes he viewed the Soul of the World and the Omega Point in a kind of polar relationship to one another.

Teilhard de Chardin's "Hymn to the Eternal Feminine" relates his concept of entelechy to Sophia of the Old Testament and through Her to Mary of the New Testament, who clearly exists in a polar relationship to Christ. This hymn, as well as many of his essays, reveal Teilhard's poetic and mystical side. In his life he was able to synthesize religion and science, innate talent and industriousness, and the interior and exterior life into a dynamic whole.

Excerpts follow from Teilhard de Chardin's "Hymn To the Eternal Feminine" and the essay "The Soul of the World" in which he reveals Sophia's nature and creative activities. In doing so he provides modern Sophiology with a creative impulse, pointing out new paths which can lead to knowing and honoring Sophia even more.

HYMN TO THE ETERNAL FEMININE

"Ab initio creata sum . . ." (Ecclus. 24,9).

When the world was born, I came into being. Before the centuries were made, I issued from the hand of God— half–formed, yet destined to grow in beauty from age to age, the handmaid of his work . . .

God instilled me into the initial multiple as a force of condensation and concentration.

In me is seen that side of beings by which they are joined as one, in me the fragrance that makes them hasten together and leads them, freely and passionately, along their road to unity.

Through me, all things have their movement and are made to work as one.

I am the beauty running through the world, to make it associate in ordered groups: the ideal held up before the world to make it ascend.

I am the essential Feminine.

In the beginning I was no more than a mist, rising and falling: I lay hidden beneath the affinities that were as yet hardly conscious, beneath a loose and tenuous polarity . . .

I was the bond that held together the foundations of the universe . . .

I am the single radiance by which all is aroused and within which it is vibrant . . .

For the man who has found me, the door to all things stands open. I extend my being into the soul of the world—not only through the medium of that man's sensibility, but also through the physical links of my own nature—or rather, I am the magnetic force of the universal presence and the ceaseless ripple of its smile.

I open the door to the whole heart of creation: I, the Gateway of the Earth, the Initiation.

He who takes me, gives himself to me, and is himself taken by the universe . . .

I am essentially fruitful: that is to say my eyes are set on the future, on the Ideal . . .

The more, O men, you seek me in the direction of pleasure, the farther will you wander from my reality . . .

II

"Et usque ad futurum saeculum non desinam" (Ecclus. 24,9).

Christ has given me salvation and freedom . . .

In the regenerated world I am still, as I was at my birth, the summons to unity with the universe—the world's attractive power imprinted on human features . . .

My charm can still draw men, but towards the light. I can still carry them with me, but into freedom.

Henceforth my name is Virginity.

The Virgin is still a woman and mother: in that we may read the sign of the new age . . .

. . . Under the influence of Christianity, I shall combine, until creation is complete, their subtle and dangerous refinements in an ever-changing perfection which will embrace the aspirations of each new generation.

Then, so long as the world endures, there will be seen reflected in the face of Beatrix the dreams of art and science towards which each century aspires . . .

I am the unfading beauty of the times to come—the ideal Feminine.

The more, then, I become Feminine, the more immmaterial and celestial will my countenance be.

In me, the soul is at work to sublimate the body—Grace to divinize the soul.

Those who wish to continue to possess me must change as I change . . .

. . . It is God who awaits you in me!

Long before I drew you, I drew God towards me.

Long before man had measured the extent of my power, and divinized the polarity of my attraction, the Lord had conceived me, whole and entire, in his wisdom, and I had won his heart.

Without the lure of my purity, think you, would god ever have come down, as flesh, to dwell in his creation?

Only love has the power to move being.

If God, then, was able to emerge from himself, he had first to lay a pathway of desire before his feet, he had to spread before him a sweet savour of beauty.

It was then that he caused me to rise up, a luminous mist hanging over the abyss—between the earth and himself—that, in me, he might dwell among you . . .

Lying between God and the earth, as a zone of mutual attraction, I draw them both together in a passionate union.

—until the meeting takes place in me, which the generation and plentitude of Christ are consummated throughout the centuries.

I am the Church, the Bride of Christ.

I am Mary the Virgin, Mother of all human kind . . .

. . . I shall subsist, entire, with all my past, even in the raptures of contact with God—

What is more, I shall continue to disclose myself—as inexhaustible in my development as the infinite beauties of which I am always, even if unseen, the raiment, the form, and the gateway.

When you think I am no longer with you—when you forget me, the air you breath, the light with which you see—then I shall still be at hand, lost in the sun I have drawn to myself.

. . . I am the eternal Feminine.[2]

THE SOUL OF THE WORLD

Since all time, the poets—the true poets—have felt the presence of the soul of the world, in the solitude of the deserts, in nature's fruitful breath, in the fathomless swell of the human heart. Everywhere it asserted itself as a living thing, and yet nowhere could they grasp it; and their loftiest inspiration was but the distress they suffered from its elusive presence . . .

Throughout the centuries the soul of the world has constantly, from the manifold energy exerted by its magnetism, provided fuel for human enthusiasm and passion in their most intense form . . .

Even so, with the passage of time, its radiating influence seems to become progressively more distinctly rec-

---

[2] Pierre Teilhard de Chardin, *Writings in the Time of War*, Rene Hague, trans. (New York: Harper & Row, 1968, Copyright © 1965 by Éditions Bernard Grasset.), "Hymn to the Eternal Feminine," pp. 191–202. Reprinted by permission of Georges Borchardt, Inc.

ognizable, and more and more indispensable for our intellectual and emotional satisfaction. It will not be long before no structure of truth or goodness can be built up without a central position being reserved for that soul, for its influence and its universal mediation . . .

In the light of this manifold illumination (which is perhaps simply the radiance projected by its own coming) the soul of the world is gradually emerging all around us, as an absorbing and inevitable Reality. Many, no doubt, are still blind to it; but those who can see how it is growing greater have no doubt but that the day will soon come when no human ideal will be able to exist apart from it . . .

In that soul, everything works together to win the allegiance of modern man.

There is first, its quality as *Absolute*, which offers us, underlying the instability of beings and their tendency to crumble into dust, a principle of stability and unity that allows us to admire and love the beauties of the Earth, secure in the knowledge that in their attraction something solid and eternal is contained.

Its *Intimacy*, which penetrates and dissolves us, which makes its substance to be truly ours and truly within us, so that while it has its sovereignty over us it is at the same time our own work.

Its *extra-* or *supra-individuality* . . .

And, its undeniable *mystery*, rich with promises that are already, in some obscure way, fulfilled.

We must make no mistake about this: A Divinity is being born among us. A new (and age-old) star is rising in the consciousness of man, and nothing can escape its magnetic force . . .

Would it, in truth, be possible for the virtue of Christ to be exhausted? . . . for the richness of his being to be powerless, in this new age, to satisfy the hunger of mankind?

No, indeed—a thousand times no!

But if we look for an explanation, it may well be that, in Christian teaching, the *contact* between Christ and the world is not sufficiently emphasized for the needs today; and this is for lack of a theory that is bold enough openly to *make plain* the *natural medium* in which the union of both is effected . . .

On the authority of the essential principles of Revelation, we must show that Christ and the soul of the world are not two opposed realities, independent of one another, and completely distinct *in natura rerum*, but that one of those realities is the medium in which we are transformed into the other . . .

The soul of the world is an inescapable reality, *more immediate*, in one sense, than Christ . . .

. . . Christ is to . . . find support in the soul of the world and to use it as his medium of action . . .

The soul of the world, whose life is drawn from the Word infused into it, is at the same time the purchase-point required for the Incarnation. It supplies ready to hand the matter destined to form the mystical body . . .

. . . Christianity, the soul of the world and Christ are not in opposition . . .

First, there is Christ: heir of all the attributes that make the world-soul our idol, of its so intimate interiority, of its so tangible greatness, its so intoxicating mystery . . .

And then, on the other hand, there is this soul: enriched by the transcendence, the warm life, the personal beauties, of the Savior—by the exactness, too, of his teaching. We know henceforth how we should cling to it: through Christ's moral teaching, through purity, through charity and renunciation.

. . . We have both the right and the duty to give our allegiance to the soul of the world and to surrender ourselves to it. The contact we shall try to make with it is ordained for us leading to Christ . . .

In this essay I have tried to bring out the presence, between Christ and our souls, of a universal mediating reality: an intermediary which does not introduce a further gap between him and us, but removes one more division. This work will have to be tested and pursued, as every advance in the Church must be, in a quest shared by all and maintained in prayer.

Much has still to be done.

. . . We shall be asked to make it perfectly clear to what degree this existence must, in the Christian view, be considered arbitrary. There is such a thing as the soul of the world . . .[3]

A NECESSARY POINT OF CONTACT

In the essay "The Soul of the World" Teilhard de Chardin speaks about the necessary contact between Christ and the world; and he indicates that lack of this contact, or unawareness of it, leads people to turn away from Christianity with disappointment. He also says that the contact point is near at hand and is, in fact, nature and the surrounding world in which we live: It is necessary to understand that the world and nature are connected to Christ and that they link us half-intimately to Him.

To gain this necessary point of contact with Christ through nature it is important to develop the kind of intimacy to nature expressed by the phrase "Mother Nature"; and it is also important to understand that God has specifically and deliberately endowed nature with a function and purpose. Intimacy with nature along with a deeper awareness of its function and purpose is enhanced by understanding the relationship between nature and the Soul of the World and also God's Beloved—who is Sophia, and who Herself took on human form in Mary. She is the world's Soul and Mother, Yahweh's Amon (Prov. 8,32), God's Master Builder, Confidant, and Beloved, as well as the Mother and Co-Worker of Christ in the work of redemption and divinization. The cosmological and religious point of contact to God and Christ exists through Sophia, the Soul of the World. She

---

[3] Teilhard de Chardin, *Writings in the Time of War*, "The Soul of the World," pp. 182–190. Reprinted by permission of Georges Borchardt, Inc.

became a human being in Mary so that the Logos could incarnate from Her and thereby divinize the world. Nature is able to serve as the contact between Christ and humanity because of the relationship of nature's soul, the Soul of the World, to Sophia and Mary.

Sophia is nature's contact to God because She was purposefully created to be the Soul of the World. Her mediating function to God is anchored in all of the phenomena of the natural world—in the trees and flowers, the sun by day, the stars by night, and in the changing seasons. The miracle of the natural world, itself, allows us to infer the existence of the principle behind nature—Sophia, the Soul of the World created by God.

This kind of spirituality and religious understanding—which takes nature as its starting point—can be experienced and celebrated always and everywhere. It avoids the pitfalls and hindrances of an abstract and theoretical teaching, and allows human religiosity to be based on the religious significance of nature. There is a need for such a teaching today, and it is not readily found in Christianity; and yet Sophia as She is revealed in the Wisdom Books of the Old Testament, as the Soul of the World and God's Co-Worker, does provide such a teaching, a teaching which can help address the ecological distress of our times.

On the simplest level of understanding, identifying Sophia as the Soul of the World leads to recognizing that the world and nature are Her body and raiment. A deeper understanding of Her function and dignity leads to knowledge of Her role as Yahweh's Amon, God's Beloved Master Builder. And when Her relationship to Mary is understood, She leads to Christ, the incarnated Logos, and through Christ back to the Father.

Knowing Sophia can begin with the daily encounter of the natural world around us, but the revelation of Scripture helps one to know Her more profoundly, and understanding Her relationship to Mary reveals Her most completely.

There is a genuine need today for a religious relationship to nature, and understanding Sophia as nature's Soul fulfills this need. Seeing nature as Her body and raiment helps to encourage the kind of attitude that will allow us to protect and cultivate nature instead of destroying and exploiting it. Understanding nature to be ensouled, and recognizing Sophia as nature's Soul is a practical and crucial teaching for today.

Teilhard writes that the Soul of the World can lead us to Christ, but that their relationship is not sufficiently clear and emphasized. He also says that we owe the Soul of the World our allegiance. This means to commit oneself to Her recognition and devotion. We can study Her and seek to understand Her as She is revealed in the Old Testament and by the wise and devout in the Wisdom teachings of other traditions. An especially important area of investigation is Her relationship to Mary, which Teilhard himself acknowledges.[4]

TEILHARD DE CHARDIN'S LEGACY

In his essay "The Soul of the World" Teilhard de Chardin writes:

> . . . in the most complete and comprehensive, and the most authentic Christianity, the soul of the world and Christ are not in opposition. . . . The contact we shall try to make with it is ordained for leading us to Christ (pp. 187–88).

> Would it, in truth, be possible for the virtue of Christ to be exhausted? . . . for the richness of his being to be powerless, in this new age to satisfy the hunger of mankind? . . . But if we look for an explanation, it may well be that, in Christian teaching, the *contact* between Christ and the world is not sufficiently emphasized for the needs today; and this is for lack of a theory that is bold enough openly to *make plain* the *natural medium* in which the union of both is effected . . . (pp. 184–185).

> On the authority of the essential principles of Revelation, we must show that Christ and the soul of the world are not two opposed realities . . . but that one (the soul of

---

[4] Teilhard de Chardin, *Writings in the Time of War*, "Hymn To The Eternal Feminine," p. 201.

the world) of those realities is the medium in which we are transformed into the other (Christ) (pp. 184–85).

. . . We have both the right and the duty to give our allegiance to the soul of the world . . . (p. 188).

. . . This work will have to be tested and pursued, as every advance in the Church must be, in a quest shared by all and maintained in prayer. Much has still to be done (p. 189).[5]

In his "Hymn To the Eternal Feminine," which is actually a hymn to *Sophia*, Teilhard clearly acknowledges that he sees the Soul of the World in *Sophia-Mary*. We are now better able to understand what Teilhard means in saying:

We have both the right and the duty to give our allegiance to the soul of the world. . . . Much has still to be done.[6]

What is to be done? *To recognize the Soul of the World and to give our allegiance to Her, to live and work in Her sense.*

To recognize the Soul of the World means to investigate Her existence and make it manifest, understanding that this Soul of the World is a numinous, cosmic, universal, personal, primordial and entelechal being, and yet created by God, just as She is presented in the Bible of the Old Covenant as Chokmah-Sophia and by the great sages and devout of the world religions in many forms as the Noble Lady and Great Mother. In the revelation of the New Testament this Sophia *appeared and became human in Mary. Similar statements have also been expressed by Jacob Boehme (chapter 11) and Vladimir Soloviev (chapter 15), and the same thing shines forth to us from the Sophian Marian devotion in Russia through its Sophian icons and churches (chapter 16).*

---

[5] Teilhard de Chardin, *Writings in the Time of War*, "The Soul Of The World", pages as indicated. Reprinted by permission of Georges Borchardt, Inc.
[6] Teilhard de Chardin, *Writings in the Time of War*, pp. 188–189. Reprinted by permission of Georges Borchardt, Inc.

To consecrate oneself to the Soul of the World, or to live and work for Her, means to commit oneself to Her recognition and devotion and to the plans that She has for the world in our time.

Much has already happened. Teilhard's knowledge and visions have exerted a great influence on spiritual development in our time. The best pioneers of New Age thinking see in him a pioneer and protagonist of their own ideas and efforts. Most of Teilhard's writings have been published today and a profuse literature exists about him. National and international Teilhard de Chardin societies have formed which hold periodic conferences and publish regularly-appearing journals. An international committee is responsible for the welfare and publication of his work. Unfortunately, a simple and practical representation of Sophian spirituality and devotion in the sense of Teilhard de Chardin is still missing, as well as an exemplary model for realization oriented to life and nature . . . "Much has still to be done"!

18

Sophia
and Modern
Scientific Viewpoints

THE GAIA HYPOTHESIS has been developed by James Lovelock, an independent English scientist who finances his inter-
disciplinary research through profits earned from inventions
(such as his electron capture detector used in ecological research).

The Gaia Hypothesis, which derives its name from Gaia,
the Greek mythological goddess of Earth, describes Lovelock's
notion that Earth is a self-regulatory monad or unity which defends itself from destruction. Earth is shown to be a living organism in a constant process of growth, development, and
regeneration, whose tendency is toward constant improvement.
Such a point of view counteracts the perspective that sees nature
as a soulless force that can be conquered or even destroyed by
humanity.[1]

In contrast to the philosophical and poetic language of
persons like Soloviev and Teilhard de Chardin, Lovelock's Gaia
Hypothesis successfully articulates in a scientific language the
idea that Earth displays the kind of unity and self-regulating

---

[1] From a synopsis found in J. E. Lovelock, *Unsere Erde Wird Ueberleben: Gaia—
Eine Optimistische Oekologie* (Munich: Piper, 1982).

purpose that we ascribe to intelligent beings. Some quotations from Lovelock's work follow:

> The result of this more single-minded approach was the development of the hypothesis that the entire range of living matter on Earth, from whales to viruses, and from oaks to algae, could be regarded as constituting a single living entity, capable of manipulating Earth's atmosphere to suit its overall needs and endowed with faculties and powers far beyond those of its constituent parts . . .
>
> The climate and the chemical properties of Earth now and throughout its history seem always to have been optimal for life. For this to have happened by chance is as unlikely as to survive unscathed a drive blindfolded through rush-hour traffic . . .
>
> We have since defined Gaia as a complex entity involving Earth's biosphere, atmosphere, oceans, and soil; the totality constituting a feedback or cybernetic system which seeks an optimal physical and chemical environment for life on this planet. . . . If Gaia exists, the relationship between her and man, a dominant animal species in the complex living system, and the possible shifting balance of power between them, are questions of obvious importance. . . . The Gaia hypothesis . . . is an alternative to that pessimistic view which sees nature as a primitive force to be subdued and conquered. It is also an alternative to that equally depressing picture of our planet as demented spaceship, forever traveling, driver-less and purposeless, around an inner circle of the sun.
>
> If we discover sufficient evidence of planet-sized control systems using the active processes of plants and animals as component parts and with the capacity to regulate the climate, the chemical composition, and topography of Earth, we can substantiate our hypothesis and formulate a theory.[2]

---

[2] J. E. Lovelock, *Gaia: A New Look at Life on Earth* (London: Oxford University Press, 1982), pp. 9–12, 63.

The main theses that Lovelock develops in explicating his hypothesis are: that Gaia's most important quality is Her desire to optimize conditions for life on the planet; that Gaia possesses the necessary organs to support life and to optimize life conditions; and that Gaia reacts and responds to changes (such as pollution which deteriorates life conditions) according to the laws of cybernetics.

The noted scientist Fritjof Capra writes of Lovelock and his work:

> Detailed studies of the ways in which the biosphere seems to regulate the chemical composition of the air, the temperature on the surface of Earth, and many other aspects of the planetary environment have led the chemist James Lovelock . . . to suggest that these phenomena can be understood only if the planet as a whole is regarded as a single living organism . . .
>
> The planet is not only teeming with life but seems to be a living being in its own right. All the living matter on earth, together with the atmosphere, oceans, and soil, forms a complex system that has all the characteristic patterns of self-organization. It persists in a remarkable state of chemical and thermodynamic non-equilibrium and is able, through a huge variety of processes, to regulate the planetary environment so that optimal conditions for the evolution of life are maintained.

> The earth, then, is a living system; it functions not just *like* an organism but actually seems to *be* an organism—Gaia, a living planetary being. . . . These observations were made within a scientific context, but they go far beyond science. Like many other aspects of the new paradigm, they reflect a profound ecological awareness that is ultimately spiritual.[3]

---

[3] Fritjof Capra, *The Turning Point: Science, Society, and the Rising Culture* (New York: Bantam Books, 1988), pp. 283–284, 185. Capra is a professor at the University of California at Berkeley. Other important books that he has written are *The Tao of Physics, An Exploration of the Parallels between Modern Physics and Eastern Mysticism* (New York: Bantam Books, 1977), and *Belonging to the Universe: Explorations on the Frontiers of Science and Spirituality* (San Francisco: HarperSanFrancisco, 1991).

The points of view that Lovelock and Capra express, which are based on scientific research about life on Earth, reflect Teilhard de Chardin's intuitions about the "Soul of the World" and Soloviev's view of Sophia as the basis of the unity and evolution of the cosmos and humanity.

THE HOLISTIC PRINCIPLE OF ORGANIZATION AND EVOLUTION

In the early part of the 20th century Jan Smuts, a researcher, author and Boer general who was twice elected Prime Minister of South Africa, formulated the outlines of a holistic conception of life which anticipated the scientific views of persons like Lovelock and Capra. In his work *Holism and Evolution*, Smuts drew attention to nature's invisible, but powerful, principle of organization which seemed to make sense of the complex structures that scientists were discovering.

Smuts asserted that the principle which brings about wholeness is spirit. Spirit is continually evolving to higher levels and takes up matter with it, for spirit lives in matter and both work cooperatively. In describing this process of evolution Smuts attempts to reconcile Darwin's theory of evolution and Einstein's physics with his own insights. He writes:

> Wholeness . . . is a fundamental characteristic of the universe—the product of nature's drive to synthesize. Holism is self-creative, and its final structures are *more* holistic than its initial structures.[4]

The holistic structures that are thereby created are dynamic and are directed towards ever higher orders of complexity and integration, but also inwardness, for: "Evolution has an ever deepening, inward spiritual character."[5] In many respects Smuts was

---

[4] Jan Smuts, *Holism and Evolution*, (New York: Macmillan, 1926), quoted in: Marilyn Ferguson, *The Aquarian Conspiracy: Personal and Social Transformation in the 1980s* (Los Angeles: J. P. Tharcher, 1980), p. 156.

[5] Marilyn Ferguson, *The Aquarian Conspiracy*, p. 156.

the intellectual precursor to the expositions of Teilhard de Chardin himself.

De Chardin can also be cited as a scientist whose vision embraced the idea of a holistic evolution involving spirit and matter. He proposes that the entire planet and humanity will attain a higher stage of consciousness that will culminate in the perfection of a condition he calls the "Omega Point," saying that what is in store for us in the future is not just survival but "superlife."[6]

Albert Einstein is another scientist who acknowledges the harmony of an ordered universe before which he confessed a mystical reverence; and similarly the astronomer Arthur Eddington speaks of the universe's "spiritual substance," and the cyberneticist David Foster describes "an intelligent universe" whose concreteness comes from an unknowable, organized source.[7]

The English historian Peter Russel also speaks in holistic terms of the interplay between spirit and matter and also humanity and the world.[8] Humanity comprises a global brain whose brain cells are the individual human beings. Through the development of the capacity for exchanging and using information this brain becomes increasingly complex and dynamic, preparing itself for an evolutionary leap to higher consciousness. Similar to Lovelock, Russel also speaks of Earth as a self-regulating organism.

Space travel provides another example of how modern scientific efforts have given rise to a holistic worldview. Astronauts have testified to the effect of viewing the beauty of the blue globe of Earth from space. It transformed them into cosmopolitans who could not consider themselves as anything less that citizens of Earth as a whole, and they henceforth desired to work for the welfare of all of Earth.

THE PRINCIPLE OF FORMATIVE CAUSATION

The Principle of Formative Causation has been proposed by the Englishman Rupert Sheldrake. He is a biochemist who has taught at Cambridge's Clare College, has researched growth

---

[6] Marilyn Ferguson, *The Aquarian Conspiracy*, p. 51.
[7] Marilyn Ferguson, *The Aquarian Conspiracy*, p. 182.
[8] Peter Russel, *The Awakening Earth* (London: Routledge & Kegan Paul, 1982).

processes in plants, and who continues to consult for the International Crops Research Institute for Semi-Arid Tropics (ICRISAT) in Haiderabad, India as an expert in plant physiology.

Sheldrake describes the thinking which led him to formulate the hypothesis of Formative Causation as follows:

> Although a creative agency capable of giving rise to new forms and new patterns of behaviour in the course of evolution would necessarily transcend individual organisms, it need not transcend all nature. It could, for instance, be immanent within life as a whole; in this case it would correspond to what Bergson called the *elan vital*. Or it could be immanent within the planet as a whole, or the solar system, or the entire universe. There could indeed be a hierarchy of immanent creativities at all these levels . . .
>
> In fact, if such creative agencies are admitted at all, then it is difficult to avoid the conclusion that they must in some sense be conscious selves.
>
> If such a hierarchy of conscious selves exists, then those at higher levels might well express their creativity through those at lower levels. And if such a higher-level creative agency acted through human consciousness, the thoughts and actions to which it gave rise might actually be experienced as coming from an external source. This experience of *inspiration* is in fact well known.
>
> Moreover, if such "higher selves" are immanent within nature, then it is conceivable that under certain conditions human beings might become directly aware that they were embraced or included within them. And in fact the experience of an inner unity with life, or the earth, or the universe, has often been described, to the extent that it is expressible . . .
>
> This metaphysical position admits the causal efficacy of the conscious self, *and* the existence of creative agencies transcending individual organisms, but immanent within nature. . . . The universe as a whole could have a cause and a purpose only if it were itself created by a conscious agent which transcended it. Unlike the universe, this transcendent consciousness would not be developing towards

a goal; it would be its own goal. It would not be striving towards a final form; it would be complete in itself.[9]

What is novel about Sheldrake's thoughts is not the hypothesis but its modern-day scientific formulation. For the hypothesis itself was anticipated by the vision of Sophia-Wisdom expressed in the Hebrew and Alexandrian tradition of the second and third centuries B.C.E. Using a nontechnical language that is generally comprehensible it proclaims:

> She spans the world in power from end to end, and gently orders all things. . . . Who more than wisdom is the artificer of all things? (Wisd. 8,1 and 6).

Solomon, the author of these verses and the prototype of those who seek wisdom and knowledge, says that he learned:

> . . . knowledge of the structure of the world and the operation of the elements; the beginning and end of epics and their middle course; the alternating solstices and changing seasons; the cycles of the years and the constellations; the nature of living creatures and behaviour of wild beasts; the violent force of winds and human thought; the varieties of plants and the virtues of roots. I learnt it all, hidden or manifest, for I was taught by wisdom, by her whose skill made all things (Wisd. 7,17–22).

Today's scientists, astronomers, geologists, geographers, physicists, biologists, doctors, and psychologists would envy the knowledge that he speaks of which eludes the limits of the materialistic and mechanistic paradigms of the present age.

Rupert Sheldrake's hypothesis of a self-conscious and creative primordial agency, which is immanent and transcendent to the universe and guides it through other subordinate and self-conscious entities, is confirmed by Sophia-Wisdom's description:

---

[9] Rupert Sheldrake, *A New Science of Life: The Hypothesis of Causitive Formation* (Los Angeles: J. P. Tarcher, 1981), pp. 205–206.

> In wisdom there is a spirit intelligent and holy, unique in its kind yet made up of many parts, subtle, free-moving, lucid, spotless, clear, neither harmed nor harming, loving what is good, eager, unhampered, beneficent, kindly towards mortals, steadfast, unerring, untouched by care, all-powerful, all-surveying, and permeating every intelligent, pure, and most subtle spirit (Wisd. 7,22–23).

Solomon's prayer for Wisdom is still relevant today to the task of modern-day researchers:

> God . . . give me your wisdom, who sits beside your throne . . . who is familiar with your works and was present when you created the universe . . . send her forth from your holy heaven . . . bid her come down, so that she may labor at my side and I may learn what is pleasing to you. She knows and understands all things (Wisd. 9,1–11).

19

The History of the Search for the World Soul

PREVIOUS CHAPTERS HAVE discussed the relationship between Sophia and the World Soul, which seems to represent the rediscovery of an obscure and ancient idea. Yet in fact many significant thinkers throughout history spoke of the World Soul, which can be said to have been an important theme in the entire Western intellectual tradition. In the present chapter the history of this idea will be traced more closely.

As has been indicated, Greek mythology referred to Earth and the goddess of Earth as Gaia (or Ge), and the Romans also knew Her and called Her Terra (or Tulla). According to Hesiod, Gaia appeared out of the chaos. She gave birth to Uranos (the heavens) alone, married him, and then gave birth with him to the Titans.

Gaia was immeasurably wise and made Delphi Her sacred dwelling place. She spoke Her will in oracles through Her daughter Themis (which means righteousness, providence, and divine law). A python (symbolizing wisdom) guarded Gaia's Delphic Oracle and was used in communications (a patriarchal re-interpretation of the myth of Gaia later expropriated the Delphic Oracle to Apollo).

The myth of Gaia is of interest because of Gaia's role as the Mother of Earth—the creative power of Earth's life which She guides and directs (along with the help of others).

Modern scientists, such as James Lovelock, have chosen Gaia to represent their new view of the cosmos, but they are not the first to refer to such ideas whose history has been chronicled by Walter Bargatzky.

Bargatzky takes as his starting point the recent discoveries which question an inorganic model of the universe, noting that these investigations suggest that the universe is alive. He goes on to say that this idea is an old one; and though such an idea may be generally considered naive today, representatives of the "exact" sciences are the ones who are currently referring to it. He asserts (in the sense of stimulating further investigation) that the cosmos is an organic construct; and then sets out to review the history of this idea in philosophy, religion and science which focuses on the image of an ensouled universe on a macrocosmic level.[1]

FROM PLATO TO PLOTINUS

Plato was one of the first to give a form to this mythological idea:

> . . . in fashioning the universe [God] implanted reason in soul and soul in body, and so ensured that his work should be by nature highest and best. And so the most likely account must say that this world came to be in very truth, through god's providence, a living being with soul and intelligence.[2]

Aristotle subsequently built a famous model of the heavens with hollow balls which represented crystalline spheres circling

---

[1] Walter Bargatzky, *Das Universum Lebt: Die Aufsehenerregende Hypothese vom Organischen Aufbau des Weltalls* (Munich: Heyne, 1970), pp. 20, 23.
[2] Plato, *Timaeus and Critias*, Desmond Lee, trans. (London: Penguin, 1986), "Timaeus," 30, pp. 42–43.

Earth, and he considered these spheres to be living beings begotten and guided by an entelechy or soul living in them. This was a model that was still considered valid in the Middle Ages.

The teaching about a living universe blossomed fully with the Stoics, and scientific language was increasingly used to speak of this cosmos which was understood as a living creature endowed with soul and reason.

After the Stoics, the idea was taken up by the Neo-Platonists and was considered valid until the late Middle Ages. Plotinus, one of Neo-Platonism's most significant representatives, chided his Christian opponents for their scornful attitude toward the world:

> One cannot honor the invisible gods if their visible image is simultaneously held in poor esteem, or if the worst of human beings is considered immortal but the eternal soul of heaven and its bodies is denied. The order and beauty of a universe, understood as something corporeal, proves that its soul is much more pure and perfect than the human being's.[3]

FROM NICHOLAS CUSANUS
TO GIORDANO BRUNO

In the Middle Ages, well-known persons like Nicholas Cusanus championed the idea of a living universe. Cusanus was a philosopher, theologian, mathemetician, bishop, and cardinal. He preached the teaching, which was unusual to the Church, that the human being was a microcosm or a faithful mirror-image of the macrocosm which is alive. This universe is not itself God, but a reality permeated and ordered by the divine spirit. The notion that the cosmos was merely composed of accumulated dead bodies would have appeared to Cusanus as a kind of spiritual barbarism.[4]

---

[3] Bargatzky, *Das Universum Lebt* p. 29. This and subsequent quotations from the German.
[4] Bargatzky, *Das Universum Lebt*, p. 29–30.

Bargatzky continues by citing Copernicus and Kepler, whose views are of even greater interest because they were the first modern physicists:

> One might think that the idea of a living cosmos would seem strange to such thinkers, who were obviously inclined to pure mathematical proofs; whereas it is fascinating to discover that this very idea was the impetus behind their investigations. It is known how strongly Copernicus was rooted in Neo-Platonic teaching. The heavenly spheres of the ancient Greeks were still valid for him, above which was an immovable sphere to which the fixed stars were attached; and the circular motion of these spheres was still the expression of the life which filled the entire cosmos. He simply substituted the sun instead of the earth as the center of this cosmos. Why? Because the sun is the most perfect image and reflection of a living, ensouled universe.[5]

The idea of a living universe played an even greater role with Kepler. As a youth he wrote that "the world is the corporeal image of God," and it is reported that he considered psychic entities to be behind the visible world which is not composed of dead bodies.[6]

Next to Johannes Kepler and Nicolaus Copernicus there was the towering figure of Giordano Bruno—monk, poet, philosopher, and the first herald of the modern age. Everything about his astronomical ideas was revolutionary. The sun was no longer the center of the universe, but revolves with the fixed stars, which are also considered suns, around a different center. Giordano Bruno wrote:

> ... the worlds ... all move by the internal principle which is their own soul ... moving soul and moving body meet in a finite subject, that is, in each of the aforesaid stars which are worlds ... great and small animals placed in

---

[5] Bargatzky, *Das Universum Lebt*, p. 30. Tr: translation mine.
[6] Bargatzky, *Das Universum Lebt*, p. 31.

the vast space of the universe, each with a pattern of mobility, of motion and of other accidents, conditioned by its own nature.

These mobile bodies possess the principle of intrinsic motion [through] their own natures, their own souls, their own intelligence.[7]

Walter Bargatzky writes that these ideas seem to be the first indications of a living universe which contains a hierarchy of organisms. The stars themselves are only the organs of a larger organism, a comprehensive entity created by God but who is not God.[8]

FROM SCHELLING TO MODERNITY

In the 18th and 19th centuries Friedrich Schleiermacher and Friedrich Schelling pick up the thread of the idea of the World Soul. Schleiermacher understood the world as a fusion of nature and reason into an all-embracing organism. For Schelling nature is alive, the world and the universe are organic constructs, and everything is ensouled by a World Soul that joins everything into a common organism. Although Schelling's philosophy of nature is criticized for its imaginative imagery and for lacking a system, it nevertheless signifies a final and dramatic protest, albeit inadequate and in vain, against the encroachment of a mechanistic understanding of nature (Goethe was an acquaintance of Schelling and the title of his poem "The Soul of the World" with the famous line: "And every particle is alive" was inspired by Schelling).[9]

---

[7] First quotation from Giordano Bruno, *On the Infinite Universe and Worlds,* Dorothea Wiley Singer, trans. (New York: Henry Shuman, 1950), "First Dialogue," pp. 266–267. Second quotation from *The Ash Wednesday Supper,* Edward Gosselin and Lawrence S. Lerner, trans. (Toronto: University of Toronto Press, 1995), "Fifth Dialogue," p. 206.

[8] Bargatzky, *Das Universum Lebt,* p. 32.

[9] Bargatzky, *Das Universum Lebt,* p. 36.

In the 20th century the German physicist and nature philosopher Gustav Fechner proposed that Earth could be understood as a creature in the sense of the human body. Even if some of Fechner's comparisons seem exaggerated, his fundamental concepts are scientific, clearly enunciated and startlingly relevant to the present topic. In an imaginative description of Earth as seen from far away (prefiguring the reality seen by the astronauts) he speaks of Earth surrounded by the clouds and a blue atmosphere as looking "like a bride wrapping herself in a veil."[10]

After Fechner, scientific discussion about a living cosmos virtually disappears, though the notion of a World Soul resurfaces with the Russian Sophiologists and Teilhard de Chardin.

Other noteworthy names are the French authors Jean Guyau, who also considers the universe to be alive, and L. Bardonnet, who wrote a book in 1912 about understanding the universe as an organism (*L'Univers-Organisme*).[11] The English philosopher J. G. Bennett talks about the possible existence of cosmic "wholes" which are "creative," "super creative," and "autocratic," and whose existence signifies that human beings do not rank as the most elevated of living beings. Humanity is associated with the lowest "large monad" which is the biosphere of Earth. Individual human beings are parts of its physical organism and relate to it as the body cells of the human body.[12] Bargatzky concludes that:

> The living universe is a fundamental theme of Western intellectual history. It is found in all epochs from antiquity to modern times and is one of the most pressing problems ever taken up by humanity. Humans beings and all the living creatures of Earth have always been seen as a part of universal life, and this life was not just composed of spirit but also included all the material substance of the heavens and earth. The universe was alive, ensouled and

---

[10] Bargatzky, *Das Universum Lebt*, p. 39.
[11] Bargatzky, *Das Universum Lebt*, p. 40.
[12] Bargatzky, *Das Universum Lebt*, p. 41.

intelligently active, a creative unity more elevated than all higher and lower levels.[13]

He continues by saying that in contrast to this perspective, today the universe is considered dead. But this is not because the hypothesis of a living universe has been disproven; it has simply "mysteriously stolen out of our consciousness."[14]

Several reasons are postulated for this occurrence: First, modern analytical science has lost sight of the whole. Its dissection methodology fails to comprehend the essence of living things, and reliance on instrumentation and measurement restricts validity to what can be observed and proven. Metaphysics and theology have also become divorced from science. Since the dawn of rationalism, only the vocabularies of mathematics, physics and chemistry have been considered valid for knowledge about the physical world.

Another reason for losing sight of the notion of a living universe relates to the so-called "Galileo complex": There has always been uncertainty about whether such ideas were compatible with Christian dogma. This concern still exists today, and prevents many theologians and cosmologists from seriously discussing the idea.

A third reason involves the specialization of knowledge based on quantification that has become incomprehensible to lay persons. An accumulation of data has "physicalized" the cosmos, depriving it of its identity as an organism and turning it into an inorganic conglomerate.

Yet understanding the cosmos as an organism does not contradict the notion of physicality; it presupposes physicality, but looks beyond it to the possibility of fundamental organic structures and even spiritual origins.

Bargatzky mentions, for example, the pioneering work of the biologist Bertalanffy concerning the criteria for defining organisms. They must possess levels of open systems which allow for the exchange of constituent ingredients; they are able to

---

[13] Bargatzky, *Das Universum Lebt*, p. 41–42. This and subsequent quotations translated from the German.

[14] Bargatzky, *Das Universum Lebt*, p. 43.

metabolize (convert substances) and to move autonomously (they react to environmental stimuli in order to protect themselves); and they grow and develop, propagate, age and die.[15]

Bargatzky contends that such organic features can be also be found in the cosmos, galaxies, and in the entire universe. The lack of proper observational equipment and conditions, however, makes it difficult to directly verify them, and this is all the more reason to commit existing research capacities to the study of these macro-dimensions.

In a summarizing postscript Bargatzky recalls that barely 400 years have passed since Giordano Bruno spoke of the living universe as a "magnum animum" (great creature). He stresses, however, that what was especially important about the philosophical notion of a biologically alive universe was that this universe was also understood to possess a soul and spirit:

> Let us listen once again to what Plato admirably says in the dialogue *Timaeus* (92c): ". . . our account of the universe is complete. For our world has now received its full complement of living creatures, mortal and immortal; it is a visible living creature, it contains al creatures that are visible and is itself an image of the intelligible; and it has thus become a visible god, supreme in greatness and excellence, beauty and perfection, a single, uniquely created heaven."
>
> In fact a living universe, even if only the place where living galaxies are situated, would represent a spiritual phenomenon as well as a biological one. Ancient natural philosophy may have committed serious astronomical errors about the universe's configuration, but it was not wrong about the incredible spiritual implications for humanity of a living universe. This is why I say everyone has to reflect somewhat on this point regardless of the conclusion that is reached.
>
> Would it not be possible to eventually comprehend that great wonder that is behind the organic make-up of the world? We would lose our central role, but in ex-

---

[15] Bargatzky, *Das Universum Lebt*, p. 211.

change we would stand face to face with an organism in which our own existence is deeply imbedded, and which joins our life, and not just our physical life, with the endless depths of the cosmos. Such a realization would neutralize much of our fear before such a strange creature. We would recognize what was formerly self evident: that a living cosmos above all signifies life, life everywhere we look and reflect, a great unity embracing like a mother everything that lives, including us.[16]

---

[16] Bargatzky, *Das Universum Lebt*, pp. 250–252; *Timaeus* quotation: Plato, *Timaeus and Critias*, "Timaeus," 50, p. 126.

PART III

SOPHIA-WISDOM AND EASTERN TRADITIONS

20

Images of Sophia in Hinduism

SCRIPTURE TEACHES THAT Wisdom is an experience of holy souls throughout the ages (Wisd. 7,23) and also that Wisdom manifests in an infinite variety of forms (Eph. 3,10). It is no wonder then that Wisdom's traces are also found in the religious and philosophical traditions of the East. Though striking similarities are found there to the image of Wisdom that has emerged in the Judaeo-Christian tradition, differences which may seem at first unusual are also found. This, however, is advantageous to the development of the kind of understanding of Wisdom-Sophia that is truly catholic and universal.

THE "MAHA DEVI" OR GREAT GODDESS

Hinduism is a complex religion containing diverse orientations and practices extending from the sublime to the dissolute.[1] Of

---

[1] See Thomas Ohm, *Die Liebe zu Gott in den Nichtchristlichen Religionen* (Krailling vor Munchen: E. Wewel, 1950), pp. 185 ff. See also the discussion in *Kairos*, 1960, pp. 57–58; and also Swami Shivananda, *All About Hinduism* (Rishikesh: Shivanandanagar, 1961). For a general work about Hinduism see Helmuth von Glasenapp, *Der Hinduismus* (Munich: K. Wolff, 1922).

particular interest to the present study is the role in Hinduism of images relating to the feminine and maternal. The most prominent Mother Goddess figure in Hinduism is Kali, the wife of Shiva.

Kali can be mythologically understood as Shiva's Shakti, the power of the Absolute which creates, permeates, and enlivens everything. Some sects even honor Shiva's Shakti above Shiva, and She is known by many names which reflect different aspects of Her power. Kali can represent a destructive and terrifying side of Shiva's divine energy. She has been portrayed as a cruel woman or as a cruel force of nature, although in this guise She also represents catharsis and renewal.[2]

The great holy man Ramakrishna understood Kali as the Divine Mother and consecrated himself to Her. Ramakrishna had yearned for a vision of Her for a long time and had even bloodily castigated himself. But finally one day, when he was at the end of his strength, She appeared to him:

> I was overpowered with a great restlessness and a fear that it might not be my lot to realize Her in this life. . . . Life seemed not to be worth living . . . and I determined to put an end to my life. . . . when suddenly the blessed Mother revealed Herself. The buildings with their different parts, the temple, and everything else vanished from my sight, leaving no trace whatsoever, and in their stead I saw a limitless, infinite, effulgent Ocean of Bliss. . . . within me there was a steady flow of undiluted bliss, altogether new, and I felt the presence of the Divine Mother.[3]

Once when engaged in conversation about whether God could be viewed both with and without a form, he said:

> Yes, both are true. God with form is as real as God without form. Do you know what the describing of God as formless only is like? It is like a man's playing only a mo-

---

[2] Sydny Cave, *Hinduism or Christianity* (New York: Harper & Row, 1939), p. 152.
[3] Ramakrishna, *The Gospel of Sri Ramakrishna*, Swami Nikhilananda, trans. (New York: Ramakrishna-Vivekananda Center, 1958), pp. 19–20.

notone on his flute, though it has seven holes. But on the same instrument another man plays different melodies. Likewise, in how many ways the believers in a Personal God enjoy Him! They enjoy Him through many different attitudes: the serene attitude, the attitude of a servant, a friend, a mother, a husband, or a lover.[4]

God and God's power (Shakti) are not two but one divine principle, expressed by two figures which are masculine and feminine. Ramakrishna viewed all women as the manifestations of the Divine Mother, and he even saw a glimmer of Her in bad wives. He often said:

> I call to [God] as my Mother. Let Mother do whatever She likes. I shall know Her if it is Her will; but I shall be happy to remain ignorant if She wills otherwise. The young child wants only his mother. . . . All he knows is, "I have a mother; why should I worry?" . . . My attitude, too, is that of a child.[5]

He prayed to Her:

> I have taken refuge at Thy feet. I have sought protection in Thee. O Mother, I pray only that I may have pure love for Thy Lotus Feet, love that seeks no return.
>   O Mother, I throw myself on Thy mercy; I take shelter at Thy Hallowed Feet. . . . Be gracious and grant that I may have pure love for Thee, a love unsmitten by desire, untainted by any selfish ends—a love craved by the devotee for the sake of love alone.
>
> . . . .
>
> Mother, make me mad with Thy love . . .
> Make me drunk with Thy love's wine;
> O Thou who stealest Thy bhaktas' hearts,

---

[4] *The Gospel of Sri Ramakrishna*, p. 254.
[5] *The Gospel of Sri Ramakrishna*, p. 271.

Drown me deep in the sea of Thy love! . . .
Jesus, Buddha, Moses, Gauranga,
All are drunk with the wine of Thy love.
Mother, when shall I be blessed
By joining their blissful company?[6]

Ramakrishna's famous pupil Vivikananda once exclaimed:

O Mother, You walk the streets in one form and exist in
the universe in another. Above all else I greet You, O
Mother.[7]

Ramakrishna's religious orientation was very profound, but more
practical than philosophical. His simple and even childlike teachings are at the same time wise, full of love and deeply moving.

Sri Aurobindo is another important figure in Hinduism
who revered the Divine Mother.[8] Like Gandhi, he also fought for
India's independence. He later dedicated himself completely to
the spiritual life, founding an ashram in Pondicherry and beginning a prodigious activity whose influence has extended beyond
India to the entire world. In a work titled *The Mother*, Sri Aurobindo wrote the following words:

The one original transcendent Shakti, the Mother stands
above all the worlds and bears in her eternal consciousness the Supreme Divine. . . . The Supreme is manifest in
her for ever as the everlasting Sachchidananda, manifested through her in the worlds as the one and dual consciousness of Ishwara-Shakti and the dual principle of
Purusha-Prakriti, embodied by her in the Worlds and the
Planes and the Gods and their energies and figured because of her as all that is in the known worlds and in the
unknown others. All is her play with the Supreme; all is

---

[6] *The Gospel of Sri Ramakrishna*, pp. 272, 373, 435.
[7] Vivekananda, *My Master* (New York: Baker & Taylor, 1901), p. 20.
[8] Sri Aurobindo, *The Integral Yoga: Sri Aurohindo's Teaching and Method of Practice*
(Silver Lake, WI: Lotus Light, 1993). See also Otto Wolff, *Indiens Beitrag zum
Neuen Menschenbild: Ramakrishna—Gandi—Sri Aurobindo* (Hamburg, 1957).

her manifestation of the mysteries of the Eternal, the miracles of the Infinite. . . . Nothing can be here or elsewhere but what she decides and the Supreme sanctions; nothing can take shape except what she moved by the Supreme perceives and forms.[9]

He distinguishes between three levels of the Mother Shakti's activity:

> There are three ways of being of the Mother of which you can become aware. . . . Transcendent, the original supreme Shakti, she stands above the worlds and links the creation to the ever unmanifest mystery of the Supreme. Universal, the cosmic Mahashakti, she creates all these beings and contains and enters, supports and conducts all these million processes and forces. Individual, she embodies the power of these two vaster ways of her existence, makes them living and near to us and mediates between the human personality and the divine Nature.[10]

These forms of the Mother's appearance effect the transformation of the human being and the divinization of the world, but only in harmony with the human being's cooperation:

> There are two powers that alone can effect in their conjunction the great and difficult thing which is the aim of our endeavour [divinization], a fixed and unfailing aspiration that calls from below and a supreme Grace from above that answers.[11]

Only two inseparable things are necessary for traveling safely along life's road: the Divine Mother's grace and an attitude of faith, sincerity and surrender.[12] Sri Aurobindo writes:

---

[9] Sri Aurobindo, *The Mother* (Pondicherry, India: Sri Aurobindo Ashram Trust, 1972), pp. 20–21.
[10] Sri Aurobindo, *The Mother*, chap. 6, p. 20.
[11] Sri Aurobindo, *The Mother*, chap. 1, p. 1.
[12] Sri Aurobindo, *The Mother*, chap. 3, p. 9.

> If you desire this transformation, put yourself in the hands of the Mother and her Powers without cavil or resistance and let her do unhindered her work within you. Three things you must have, consciousness, plasticity, unreserved surrender.[13]

He also says:

> If you want to be a true doer of divine works, your first aim must be to be totally free from all desire and self-regarding ego. All your life must be an offering and sacrifice to the Supreme; your only object in action shall be to serve, to receive, to fulfill, to become a manifesting instrument of the divine Shakti in her works.[14]

In this service of devotion three stages are distinguished. In the first stage one is a self-confident and sometimes headstrong worker or servant; in the second the devotee becomes a flexible and accommodating instrument in the Mother's hands; and in the third stage one becomes a child of the Mother and a part of Her consciousness and strength, doing everything in, with, for, and through Her:

> The last stage of this perfection will come when you are completely identified with the Divine Mother and feel yourself to be no longer another and separate being, instrument, servant or worker but truly a child and eternal portion of her consciousness and force. Always she will be in you and you in her; it will be your constant, simple and natural experience that all your thought and seeing and action, your very breathing or moving come from her and are hers. You will know and see and feel that you are a person and power formed by her out of herself, put out from her for the play and yet always safe in her.[15]

---

[13] Sri Aurobindo, *The Mother*, chap. 6, pp. 36–37.
[14] Sri Aurobindo, *The Mother*, chap. 5, p. 15.
[15] Sri Aurobindo, *The Mother*, chap. 5, pp. 17–18.

In the above work, Sri Aurobindo portrays an eloquent, poetic and philosophical vision of the feminine and maternal side of the Divine that has profound implications for spiritual and religious life: the basis and fulfillment of religion consists in the human being's full devotion to God's Shakti and union with Her.

Though Shakti devotion to the Divinity's feminine, divine power also took on some degenerate forms (in Shivaism and Vajrayana), in its legitimate forms Shaktiism represents an attempt to relate to the Divinity in a meaningful way by worshipping the Divinity's Shakti, the "Great Mother" and the power of knowledge and love who created and preserves the cosmos.

RADHA IN KRISHNA BHAKTI

Hinduism's Bhakti devotion (especially the kind initiated by Chaitanya[16]) is another form of Hinduism that is important to the present theme. In Bhakti devotion (*Bhakti* means devotional love) Krishna and His Shakti Radha are the central figures. In an ancient *Purana* or Hindu legend Krishna says of Radha:

> I bring about creation through Her, I create Brahma and the other Devas through Her, the cosmos comes into being through Her, the world is released through Her, the world would be nothing without Her. . . . She is what burns in fire, She is the radiance of the sun, the light of the moon, the coolness in water, the power which makes grain grow. . . . She is the power of devotional love. . . . She is that one who continually devotes Herself to me in Bhakti. . . . She is the power which allows the ocean of the world of appearances (Samsara) to be traversed, She is the Holy Wisdom of Those who are (the Holy Ones), She is presence of mind, She is the art

---

[16] Chaitanya (1486–1534) was a Bengalese Brahman and a well-known prophet of the love of Krishna. At age 24 he left his wife and mother in order to devote himself to the love of Krishna (see Thomas Ohm, *Die Liebe zu Gott in den Nichtchristlichen Religionen*, p. 240).

of interpreting Sacred Scripture, She is the power of giving in those who give, She is the love of noble women to their spouses.

. . .

She is the life of everything, She is Krishna's Beloved, who is more faithful to Him than His own life, in no way less than Him. She rules over Krishna's heart. . . . She is the knowledge of the cosmos, its light and radiance and creative genius . . . She inspires human beings to write books about Krishna. . . .

When the Krishna of intimate love, the flute-playing Krishna, gazes into His own eternity, He sees before Himself Radha as His true Self. And when He "who has no inside or outside" looks outside, He sees Radha before Him. Everywhere He seeks Her, He sees Her.[17]

In the Padma Purana, Krishna reveals to a practitioner of Bhakti the inner mystery of His love for Shakti Radha (whom He nicknames *Radhika*):

In joyful lila[18] I play with Her,
Loyal to Her holy love,
Eternally. Know, that my Beloved
Radhika is the highest Divinity . . .

Those who seek refuge with us
Or with Her alone,
And serve us in the manner of Gopis,
Without a doubt they will come to me. . . .

---

[17] Walthe Eidlitz, *Die Indische Gottesliebe* (Olten: Walter, 1955), pp. 263–267. This is a sensitively written resource work on Indian spirituality.

[18] "Lila" means game, particularly in a cosmic sense as God's game and dance. Understood as a game of love, Krishna plays this game with Radha His Beloved and with all the devout "Bhaktas" (practitioners of Bhakti) and "Gopis" (shepherds symbolizing the loving souls that seek Krishna).

Therefore, take refuge zealously
At Radha's feet.
And if you find refuge with Her,
You will rule over me.

And since you took refuge
With Radha, my Beloved,
Whispering of the sacred word of the two,
Remain everlastingly in my kingdom.[19]

What is particularly interesting about these verses is that they reveal the heights to which the dignity of the Feminine and Maternal Divine is raised. Radha is of an equal status with Krishna;
She is the highest Divinity and essential to attaining Krishna's
love. In a verse from the same Purana a devotee of Shakti says:

I am Yours, O Beloved of Radhika (Krishna)
My body and spirit, my word and deeds.
Krishna's Beloved (Radha), truly I am Yours.
Both of You are my only goal.[20]

Beholding the eternal and divine union of Krishna and Radha
the devotee becomes ecstatic and only wants to be entirely devoted to them and to participate in their love. (See figure 13,
page 328.) The experience of their mutual devotion and love is
so strong that Krishna is called "Radha's Beloved" and Radha
"Krishna's Beloved."

In the above passages Radha can be understood as a symbol for the human soul who loves God, but especially the first of
the souls who love God. Bhakti devotees of the Chaitanya school
proclaim that all devotion to God comes from Radha's power.
Radha is called "Bhakti Devi," the Goddess Bhakti who represents the primordial principle of love of God. The Bhakti tradition indicates that no one succeeds in coming to God without
Her gracious nod and the strength and support that She gives to

---

[19] W. Eidlitz, *Die Indische Gottesliebe*, Padma Purana, pp. 271–272. This and subsequent quotions translated from the German. Tr.
[20] W. Eidlitz, *Die Indische Gottesliebe*, Padma Purana, p. 274.

Figure 13. Krishna and Radha. Walter Olten Verlag.

the soul. There would be no devotion to God or love of God—
even no love at all in the universe—if Radha did not exist.
Radha's nature is the substance of love, the essence of God's joyful ecstasy and power of knowledge. The Upanishads say of the
eternal God that "He has no joy in being alone." This is mythologically formulated in the following way:

> Atman was there in the beginning. He looked around and
> only saw Himself. He spoke the first words: "I am." This
> is where the name "I" comes from. He desired an addi-
> tional someone. He embraced within Himself the dual na-
> ture of woman and man, which were joined together. He
> split this nature of His into two parts, and so husband
> and wife came into being.[21]

However Radha and Krishna are also eternally one:

> They are one like the light of fire is one with the fire, like
> the scent of the rose is one with the rose.[22]

This formulation of God's love is found many times in the traditional Scriptures of India. The rhythm "bheda-abheda" (separated and unseparated, different and yet not different, divided
and never divided) which pulsates throughout all divine existence relates above all to the primordial relationship between
Krishna and Radha.[23] The Chaitanya school of Bhakti devotion
understands the divine couple Radha-Krishna as two and yet
one, the archetype of all existence and the most intimate, divine,
and primordial form at the center of all existence. The myriad
worlds are essentially a reflection of the Divine Couple's revelation. In Shiva's kingdom they are also represented by Shiva and
Parvati, and in the realm of cosmic being by Purusha and Prakriti (the primordial masculine and the primordial feminine).[24]

---

[21] Christoph Einiger, *Die Schoensten Gebete der Welt* (Munich: Suedwest Verlag,
1964), p. 390. Tr: translation mine.

[22] W. Eidlitz, *Die Indische Gottesliebe*, p. 258.

[23] W. Eidlitz, *Die Indische Gottesliebe*, p. 259.

[24] See Paul Claudel, *Oeuvres Complètes* (Paris: Gallimard, 1950), "The Legend Of

Human lovers can also be understood as a reflection of Krishna and Radha.[25] The Rasa texts state:

> Radha's love is so powerful that Her own body, the body which consists of condensed, divine ecstasy and pure knowledge, is not sufficient for Her desire to love Krishna increasingly and to make Him happy. And so out of the fullness of Her over-abundant love She takes on other forms without giving up Her own. The Gopis come into being, who are all transformations of Radha's endless power of love.[26]

The Chaitanya school of Bhakti continues to exist, impressing Westerners with its selfless devotion to God.[27]

It can be said that together with Christianity and Amida Buddhism, Bhakti devotion represents a form of religion whose central focus is love. Its sensual and erotic images, though appearing bold and provocative to Western peoples, are primarily the symbol for a profound and intimate love of God.

It is also worth noting that the texts about Radha and Krishna quoted above recall the Old Testament passages which depict Sophia as Yahweh's Amon, the Beloved who dances and plays before Him, sharing God's life, knowing God's plans and choosing from among them (Prov. 8,30; Wisd. 8,4 and 9,9).

In its own way Hinduism presents the mystery of Sophia, or the Feminine Divine. Though the perspective that it offers may in some respects seem unusual, every religion has its unique contribution to make in revealing Sophia.

Prakriti," which compares Sophia with Prakriti. "Prakriti" represents Sophia in Her role as the Soul of the World. See also Karl Pfleger, *Die Verwegenen Christozentriker* (Freiburg: Herder, 1964), p. 110.

[25] W. Eidlitz, *Die Indische Gottesliebe*, p. 260.

[26] W. Eidlitz, *Die Indische Gottesliebe*, p. 241.

[27] Thomas Ohm, *Die Liebe zu Gott in den Nichtchristlichen Religionen*, p. 241. Ohm speaks of the impression made on him and a Jesuit friend during a conversation with a Chaitanya monk who says: "Love God, and then do as you will."

21

Holy Wisdom
and Buddhism

IT IS GENERALLY KNOWN that Buddhism initially did not conceive of the dimension of the Absolute in personal terms, and that the Buddha and the original Buddhist Hinayana tradition were not well-disposed toward women and the feminine. Women were understood to represent the thirst for life which binds human beings to Samsara (the circle of rebirth) and makes salvation impossible.

Gradually, however, changes took place. In the Mahayana and Vajrayana traditions which appeared later, it was possible for the Buddha to take on the semblance of a god, and for his most distinguished qualities, such as wisdom and compassion, to become personified and be understood as having been incarnated in the Bodhisattvas. At first personifications of Buddha's qualities were thought of as masculine due to the influence of Hinayana Buddhism; but under Hinduism's influence some were later considered to be feminine. In the so-called Vajrayana (Diamond Vehicle) tradition, the cult of the Feminine Divine became particularly ritualized and was called "Prajna," which means Wisdom or profound knowledge.[1]

---

[1] Edward Conze, *Buddhist Texts through the Ages* (New York: Harper & Row, 1964), pp. 51, 185, 243.

PERFECT WISDOM
AND THE NAMES OF HOLY TARA

The following hymns are directed to the "Prajna Paramita," or Perfect Wisdom, and the Goddess Tara (who leads over from Samsara to Nirvana). They are songs in praise of Wisdom, and they echo Sophia's role as the Mistress and Mother of all creatures. (See figure 14, page 333.)

Hymn to Perfect Wisdom[2]

1. Homage to Thee, Perfect Wisdom,
   Boundless, and transcending thought!
   All Thy limbs are without blemish,
   Faultless those who Thee discern.

2. Spotless, unobstructed, silent,
   Like the vast expanse of space;
   Who in truth does really see Thee
   The Tathagata[3] perceives

4. Those, all pity, who came to Thee,
   Buddhadharmas heralding,
   They will win with ease, O Gracious!
   Majesty beyond compare.

5. Pure in heart, when once they duly
   Look upon Thee, surely then
   Their complete success is certain—
   O, Thou fruitful to behold!

---

[2] *Buddhist Scriptures*, selected and translated by Edward Conze (New York: Penguin, 1977), pp. 168–171. "Prajna" comes from *pra* (before, excellent, highest) and *jna* (knowledge or wisdom). Prajna's pronunciation (*pragnya*) reveals a common root (*gn*) with the Latin *gnoscere* (to know). *Paramita* means gone beyond or transcendental.

[3] *Thathagata* (Sanskrit) is a title of honor for the Buddha (and the Boddhisattvas) meaning: "He who has thus come," as the other Buddhas have come (Edward Conze, *Buddhist Scriptures*, p. 249).

Figure 14. Prajna Paramita. Stone Sculpture, 13th century, Java. Walter Olten Verlag.

6. To all heroes who of others
   Have the welfare close at heart,
   Thou a mother, who dost nourish,
   Givest birth, and givest love.

7. Teachers of the world, the Buddhas,
   Are Thine own compassionate sons;
   Then art Thou, O Blessed Lady,
   Grandam thus of beings all.

9. Those in need of light considering,
   The Tathagatas extol
   Thee, the Single One, as many,
   Multi-formed and many-named.[4]

17. By all Buddhas, Single Buddhas,
    By Disciples courted, too,
    Thou the one path to salvation,
    There's no other verily.

19. Who is able here to praise Thee,
    Lacking signs and featureless?
    Thou the range of speech transcending,
    Not supported anywhere.

20. In such words of current language
    Constantly we laud Thee, whom
    None of our acclaim concerneth;
    So we reach beatitude.

21. By my praise of Perfect Wisdom
    All the merit I may rear,
    Let that make the world devoted
    To this wisdom without peer.

---

[4] See Ephesians 3,10: "wisdom in its infinite variety."

The 108 Names Of Holy Tara[5]

Om. Homage to the Holy Tara!

27. "Om. You who are bright, of the beautiful eyes, Tara, joy of
    starlight, full of pity for all beings,
    Saviour of all beings, thousand-armed, thousand-eyed . . .

28. . . . Look down, look down on me,
    On all beings, and also me . . .

29. "Om, pure, quite pure, cleanser, purifier,
    . . . heart of friendliness, immaculate . . .

30. "Of great wisdom, excellent, beautifully adorned, invinci-
    ble . . .

31. ". . . Sarasvati,[6] with large eyes, who increases wisdom,
    beauty and intelligence.

32. "Om, giver of fortitude, giver of prosperity. . . . Who labour
    for the weal of all beings! Saviour and victor in battle,

37. "Protector . . . calm, dear and well-loved, lovely . . .

38. "Propitious, auspicious, gentle, knowing all created beings,
    swift as thought . . .

39. "Leader of the caravans, of the pitiful looks, who showeth
    the way to those who have lost it,
    Granter of boons, instructor, teacher, of unbounded valour
    with a woman's form,

41. ". . . Labouring only for the weal of the world, a worthy
    refuge, affectionate to your devotees,

---

[5] Edward Conze, *Buddhist Texts through the Ages* (New York: Philosophical Library, 1954), pp. 196–202.
[6] *Sarasvati* (Sanskrit) is the Goddess of Wisdom.

42. "Mistress of language, fortunate, exquisite, constant, the mother of all projects,
The assistant in all projects, a gracious defender, a nurse, a conqueror of wealth,

43. Fearless, a Gautami (Buddha daughter), the worthy daughter of the holy Lokesvara.[7]

From the same hymn the following verses speak of the effects of reciting the names of Holy Tara.

20. "(These) names . . . remove all evil, bring merit and happiness, and increase one's glory,

21. "Make for wealth and riches, increase one's health and prosperity. . . .

24. ". . . People who correctly repeat them become men of princely wealth,

25. "Free from all kinds of disease, endowed with all the virtues of sovereignty.
They avoid an untimely death, and, when deceased, go to the Happy Land.

51. "A man who, risen early in the morning, will recite them,
He will win prosperity for a long time.

The similarities between this song of praise to Wisdom and Wisdom as She is praised in the Old Testament are striking:

> From me come advice and ability; understanding and power are mine. Through me kings hold sway and governors enact just laws. . . . Those who love me I love, and those who search for me will find me. In my hands are riches and honour, boundless wealth and prosperity. . . . I follow the course of justice and keep to the path of equity.

---

[7] *Lokesvara* (Sanskrit) is the Lord of the World.

I endow with riches those who love me; I shall fill their treasuries (Prov. 8,14–21).

So all good things together came to me with her, and in her hands was wealth past counting. . . . She is an inexhaustible treasure for mortals, and those who profit by it become God's friends (Wisd. 7,11,14).

In fact, the similarity between the texts is almost perplexing. It seems unlikely that any borrowing took place. Though if this had been the case, the Buddhist Mahayana texts, which appeared later, would have been influenced by the Old Testament. Considering the philosophical differences of the two traditions, it is more likely that any apparent similarity is due to a common experience of the one, eternal Wisdom whose delight is in humanity (Prov. 7,31) and who holds sway over every nation (Ecclus. 24,6), entering age after age into human souls (Wisd. 7,27). In their yearning for Wisdom, great seekers and seers found and beheld Her, for She:

. . . shines brightly and never fades; she is readily discerned by those who love her, and by those who seek her she is found (Wisd. 6,12).

ARYA TARA—THE NOBLE TARA

Tara, the one who leads over the sea of Samsara to the otherworldly shore of Nirvana, can be understood like Prajna to be a Buddhist representation of Wisdom; and just as Paul speaks of Wisdom in a variety of forms (Eph. 3,10) so too is Tara depicted in various forms which represent different aspects of Wisdom's dignity, beauty and goodness.

A "Yantra" is a symbolic form that is meant to effect in the observer (and in the artist) a profound experience of what it represents; and this golden statue of Arya Tara, or the Noble Tara, is meant to inspire the elevated world of Wisdom's nobility, goodness, beauty, harmony and power. (See Plate 25, page 133.)

Her right hand is open and extended, symbolizing the favors She bestows, the hope that She awakens and the courage that She gives. Her left hand is raised in a teaching gesture, indicating that She imparts knowledge and insight.

She is sitting on a lotus throne which symbolizes her noble birth from an ancient and pure race. The lotus is a sign of purity and beauty, and its blossom winds around Her hips and blossoms at the side of Her head. She sits in a loose but upright Asana or yoga posture, signifying strength, composure and freedom.

Her breasts testify to Her feminine nature and signify a mother's goodness, love, tenderness, and nourishment. Her head is tilted in sympathetic humility, and yet is full of grace, dignity, and charm. Her jewels reflect Her beauty and elevated status.

This is a form which breathes stillness and control, fulfillment, and inner bliss, healing the beholder and inspiring the nobler value of the attainment of true and everlasting happiness.

SITATAPATRA TARA—
THE THOUSANDFOLD HELPER

Standing on a lotus and surrounded by a large flaming halo is the radiant white Goddess Sitatapatra (figure 15, page 339). She is one of the forms of Sitatara (the white Tara) and here She has a white parasol and a thousand heads, arms, and legs. Each of Her faces has three eyes, and each of Her thousand hands (as well as Her body) has eyes of compassion, which gaze upon all the beings of the three worlds (earth, air, and heaven). In the left hand She holds the long, golden rod of a radiant white parasol, and in the right hand the golden Dharma-chakra—the teaching wheel which symbolizes Wisdom. The rows of Her thousand heads, lying closely on top of one another, alternate in color (red, yellow, white, green, red, etc.). Her thousand feet stand on a lotus where all classes of humanity and many kinds of animals are present. All seek the protection of the Sitatapatra. She grants refuge from all manner of dangers—from thieves, enemies, and weapons, from the elements, earthquakes, and plagues, and from demons and evil spirits.

Sitatapatra represents the thousandfold, endless compassion of the white Tara who brings well-being and is always

Figure 15. Sitatapatra Tara. Tara with the white parasol. "Source of all Assistance." Thanka. Tibet, 18th century. Akademischer Verlag, Graz.

prepared to help. She is the female counterpart of Aryaval-okiteshvara, the noble and beneficent Lord of the World with eleven heads and a thousand arms who gazes downward. A legend relates that the Bodhisattva Avalokiteshvara smashed his head to pieces out of compassion and concern for those suffering in Samsara. His father Amitabha, the Jina (victorious) Buddha, formed ten heads from the pieces, set His own above it, and gave him one thousand arms so that he could provide assistance always and everywhere. The legend also says that the Sitatapatra came from a tear of the Avalokiteshvara which was shed out of compassion for the sufferings of those in the three worlds. This is the origin of the many eyes with which She compassionately gazes upon all suffering.

Above the Sitatapatra is the Jina Buddha Amitayus, the Buddha of Eternal Life, sitting on a throne in a lotus position. He holds in His hand a Kalasa bowl with the water of eternal life. At the center below is the Usnisa Vijaya, the victorious Goddess of Enlightenment (Vijaya—victor; Usnisa—enlightenment, i.e., the head protrusion resulting from enlightenment). She also carries a Kalasa bowl with the water of life and thus, like Amitayus, She also represents eternal life. She has three heads, and the gestures of Her six arms and the objects that they hold symbolize Her dignity, power, and activities. The bow and arrow signify strength in battle and victory over all foes; the bowl with the water of life symbolizes healing and the gift of eternal life; the teaching wheel symbolizes that Her teaching leads to perfection. The gestures of Her arms accentuate these meanings.

In the four corners are various red Dakinis, air spirits who are like fairies or muses. They effect good, although they sometimes appear in terrifying and shocking forms. They provide knowledge about a more elevated life and inspire human beings to heroic deeds. They also serve as initiators into the paths which lead to enlightenment and to the highest planes of Sambhogakaya and Dharmakaya and their divinities.

The four Dakinis symbolize the four streams of life bestowed by Sitatapatra together with Usnisa Vijaya and Amitayus. Sitatapatra Herself strengthens those who belong to Her for the difficulties encountered on the paths which lead to the higher life and She protects them from all danger. Amitayus and Usnisa Vi-

jaya are both carrying the vessel with the nectar-like water of life
which is an indication that they bestow this gift. Each of the four
Dakinis are initiators into their particular stream of life.

The initiation of the Dakini in the upper left corner involves initiative, persistence, and perseverance, and the bold-
ness that results in victory.

The initiation of the Dakini in the upper right corner
brings awareness of the transcendent realm and devotion to it.
She dissolves egotism, awakens higher powers and bestows
freedom, openness, ascendancy, and the capacity to transcend
taboos and conventions.

The Dakini in the lower right corner represents enlightenment and victory over the lower desires. She bestows victory,
power, dignity, and beauty.

The Dakini in the lower left corner dances with enthusiasm,
representing exultation and divine ecstasy. All of the whirlpools of
existence unite through Her into a joyful celebration of life.

Together the Dakinis hint at the fullness, intensity, and
perfection of life in Sambhogakaya and Dharmakaya that Sitatapatra Tara wants to bestow. This artistically detailed image with
seven figures full of symbolic content depicts the Buddhist belief
in the divine powers of meditation and life.

ASTAMANGALA DEVI—THE GODDESS
OF THE EIGHT FAVORABLE SIGNS

The gilded figure of Astamangala Devi, the Goddess of eight
signs promising happiness, is another example of a Yantra, rich
in content and simple in form, whose creation and contemplation is meant to effect a sublime experience.

The Goddess is sitting on a lotus flower in a meditation
position (figure 16, page 342). Her four heads are decorated with
Bodhisattva ornaments and each of Her eight hands holds a symbol of happiness. The hand of the right arm at Her chest holds a
circular banner which is the Buddhist symbol for victory. Her
other right hands (beginning with the lowest) hold the teaching
wheel with eight spokes (also called the wheel of life), a lotus
flower and an oyster. The hand of the left arm at Her abdomen

Figure 16. Astamangala-Devi. The Goddess with the Eight Signs of Happiness. Sculpture. Tibet, 18th century. Akademischer Verlag, Graz.

holds a vessel with the water of life. The left arms (beginning from the bottom) hold knots, two golden fishes, and a parasol.

The four heads signify that She watches over all directions in order to keep Her gaze on those who belong to Her. The round banner indicates that She is the world's axis and apex, the Soul, Mistress and Mother of the universe. The teaching wheel or wheel of life symbolizes Her role as the Teacher of the Dharma, the true teaching which leads to true life. The lotus flower and oyster signify that She conceals within Herself a precious jewel, the wondrously beautiful pearl which is the Buddha (recalling the mantra: "Om mani padme hum"—O, the jewel in the lotus flower, Amen!). The vessel with the water of life indicates that She is Herself the vessel which contains the waters of life and salvation. The mysterious knots indicate that She is the power which binds and unites everything together. The two fishes symbolize the love and wisdom which She extends to those who belong to Her. The parasol is an indication that She is the Mistress and Queen who protects Her own.

In keeping with the thesis that figures like the Astamangala Devi represent Sophia, it is worth considering what She reveals about Sophia, and even Mary who is Sophia's human form.

The four heads signify that Sophia watches over the entire world and is attentive to the distress of Her people always and everywhere. From all directions She graciously receives those who approach Her. The four heads can also be interpreted as indications of Her relationships to creation and the Trinity. One head is turned to creation and the others to the Trinity, signifying (according to Boulgakov's phrase) that She is the Daughter of the Father, the Icon of the Holy Spirit, and the Bride of the Son.[8]

The points of Her crowns (four crowns with five points each) and the central protrusion between them (not visible) signify the twenty-one qualities enumerated in the Book of Wisdom (7,22–24).

The symbols in the hands indicate the greatness of Her power and dignity, as well as Her love and concern for humanity. The round banner of victory recalls Mary's title as Our Lady

---

[8]Sergei Boulgakov, *La Sagesse de Dieu*, Constantin Andronikov, trans. (Lausanne: L'Age d'Homme, 1983), p. 62.

of Victory. The teaching wheel symbolizes Sophia as the Torah, or Law, and Mary Hodegitria—who leads us and accompanies us on the path. The pure and mysterious lotus flower recalls Mary's association to the "Rosa Mystica" (the mystical rose—Litany of Loreto, appendix IV). The oyster symbolizes that Mary Herself conceals the precious pearl who is Jesus Christ. The vessel with the water of life recalls Mary's association to the "Vas Spirituale," the spiritual vessel (Litany of Loreto) containing the waters and graces of salvation and perfection (She heals the sick and then mediates all graces). The mysterious knot signifies that Sophia is the greatest and most perfect Mystery of God. The ten squares of the knot signify that She is the mystery of the unity of the ten Sephirah, of the mystery of God's union with humanity and creation, and of the unity between human beings. The two golden fishes point to Her *hierogamous* union with Christ. She is the Mother of Honorable Love, and as Yahweh's Amon and the Bride of the Lamb She protects those who love one another and allows participation in the bliss of the *Hieros Gamos* or Sacred Marriage. The parasol is an indication that we can always flee to Sophia's protection and find refuge; and it also recalls Mary's role as the Madonna with the Protective Cloak.

That it is possible to make such associations from Astamangala Devi to Sophia and Mary attests to Sophia's universal significance.

SYAMA TARA—THE GREEN TARA

This statuette of the Syama, or Green Tara, combines Indian and Chinese symbology. (See figure 17, page 345). The four-cornered base depicts a turtle standing on a lotus flower. Upon the turtle's back is a four-sided pillar at the top of which is a lotus flower extending downward. The pillar (representing the Tree of Life) has two dragons winding around it. Above the second lotus flower is the figure of a majestic lion. Above the lion is a nimbus of flowers and stars, and another lotus upon which the four-handed Tara sits in a relaxed meditational position. Her upper body is decorated with jewels. Her head is youthful and is crowned by a radiant diadem.

The four-cornered base and lotus flower symbolize the world in an undifferentiated and primitive stage. The turtle

Figure 17. The Green Tara. The culmination of the synthesis of polarities. Bronze, Tibet. Akademischer Verlag, Graz.

above the base indicates the world's differentiation into heaven and earth, but they remain joined together (the turtle is a Chinese symbol for the unity between heaven and earth; its arched shell represents the heavens and the body underneath the earth).

The concept of differentiated unity extends in a different way into the statue's next level, which is made up of the two dragons and the lotus. The two polarities (yin and yang) which the dragons symbolize have now become separate. They oppose one another but also complete one another. The lotus-flower crown which is above them protects them, binds them together, and draws them upward. In conceptual terms, one can speak of thesis, antithesis, and synthesis. The four-sided pillar indicates that the quality of the synthesis of this stage remains predominately earthbound or yin, and the protective lotus flower extending downwards also adds to an overall feminine or yin quality to this stage.

The majestic lion above the dragons represents a more masculine synthesis, but his triumph is not absolute, for above him towers the Tara.

She represents a perfected synthesis. The wreaths of flowers surrounding Her are joined together by a middle wreath of stars. The Tara sits in the Lalitasana position, a restful and sovereign position atop a lotus flower. Each of the two hands behind Her body hold lotus flowers, and the two hands in front are extended in the Mudra gesture of teaching and offering. Her youthful head is crowned by a diadem with five flames.

The flowers and stars around the Tara[9] and the rest of the symbols comprising Her figure express the full content of the word "Siddhi," which means power and perfection. What She

---

[9]For more information on Tara see Stephan Beyer, *The Cult of Tara* (Berkeley: University of California Press, 1978); Edward Conze, *Buddhism: Its Essence and Development* (New York: Harper, 1959); W. Y. Evans-Wentz, *The Tibetan Book of the Dead* (London and New York: Oxford University Press, 1951); China Galland, *Longing for Darkness: Tara and the Black Madonna* (New York: Penguin, 1990); Lama Anagarika Govinda, *Foundations of Tibetan Mysticism* (York Beach, ME: Samuel Weiser, 1969); M. Pema-Dorje, *Tara: Weiblich-Goettliche Weisheitskraefte im Menschen* (Solothurn/Dusseldorf: Walter Verlag, 1991); C. Regamey, *Buddhistische Philosophie* (Bern: A Francke, 1950); Hans Wolfgang Schumann, *Buddhism: An Outline of its Teachings and Schools*, Georg Feuerstein, trans. (Wheaton, IL: Theosophical, 1974).

teaches is knowledge about the law of universal polarity; and what She offers is the power to effect the Siddhi synthesis that She embodies.

In spite of an initial philosophical perspective which did not view the Absolute in personal terms, and which was unfriendly toward femininity, the devout within Buddhism did attain a profound knowledge of Wisdom in Her feminine and maternal form, proving both the human need to truly understand Wisdom's nature and the effects of Her own irresistible and victorious activity.

22

Sophia and Mother Tao of the Tao Te Ching

THE PURSUIT OF WISDOM plays a role in all cultures and religions, and although a commonality in Wisdom teachings between cultures might be expected, the similarities between Sophia and the primordial Mother Tao of the *Tao Te Ching* are particularly striking.

The *Tao Te Ching* was composed by the great Chinese philosopher Lao Tzu (ca. 600–530 B.C.E.). Despite the fact that it contains only eighty-one verses (or chapters), it has become a classic of world literature.

An important feature of Lao Tzu's Tao is that the Tao is predominantly characterized in feminine terms. It can be said that the Tao represents the most moving and sublime expression of the feminine and maternal aspect of the Divine.

In Taoist thinking (and in all of Chinese thinking) there is a pronounced awareness of polarity.[1] The polar powers of yin and yang hold sway in all of existence, and everything exists and flourishes through their harmonious relationship to one another. This concord between yin and yang is especially important for at-

---

[1] See H. von Glasenapp, *Die Fuenf Grossen Religionen* (Dusseldorf: Diederich, 1952), "Der Chinesische Universismus," pp. 152 ff.

taining harmony with oneself, the community and the world. Both powers already exist in perfect agreement in the Tao, and thus the Tao is the prototype for all harmony in the cosmos.

UNDERSTANDING THE TAO

Lao Tzu distinguishes between two modes of the Tao's nature or existence.[2] In the first mode the Tao is absolute, unborn, and eternal being. This is the nameless Tao which does not become manifested.[3] From this mode of the Tao's nature a second mode is born which does have a relative existence—"from nothing something is born."[4]

The Tao's second mode of existence has several different aspects. As the "one" it emerges from the Tao's unborn mode, to which it is primarily related.[5] It is a living creature[6] in contrast to the absolute Tao which is without being or substance; and yet its existence is indistinct and mysterious:

> What cannot be seen is called evanescent [quiet];
> What cannot be heard is called rarefied [precious, wonder-ful]
> What cannot be touched is called minute [mysterious, subtle, fine]
> These three cannot be fathomed
> And so they are confused and [mysteriously] looked upon as one.
> Its upper part is not dazzling;
> Its lower part is not obscure.
> Dimly visible [extending itself endlessly], it cannot be named

---

[2] See Gellert Beky, *Die Welt des Tao* (Freiburg/Munich: Alber, 1972), the concept "Tao," pp. 53 ff.
[3] Lao Tzu, *Tao te Ching*, D. C. Lau, trans. (New York: Penguin, 1972), chapters 1 and 40.
[4] Lao Tzu, *Tao te Ching*, D.C. Lau, trans., chapter 40.
[5] Lao Tzu, *Tao te Ching*, D.C. Lau, trans., chapter 42.
[6] Lao Tzu, *Tao te Ching*, D.C. Lau, trans., chapter 21.

And returns to that which is without substance.
This is called the shape that has no shape,
The image that is without substance.
This is called indistinct and shadowy [entirely incomprehensible]. . . .[7]

The second aspect of the Tao which is born and has relative existence involves its designation as "the great image"[8] that carries in itself images, creatures and seeds (reminiscent of Greek philosophical concepts). They strive to become realized and their realization is essentially certain. This second aspect is related both to the unmanifested absolute and to the manifested cosmos. With its images and seeds it is the maternal "origin" or "root" of heaven and earth[9] (the Chinese character for "origin" consists of the signs for woman, fetus, and mother's mouth) and represents the universe's ideal, primordial, and maternal principle (this mode of the Tao's existence clearly corresponds to the Greek notion of the primordial Idea).

A third aspect of the Tao that is born involves a more concrete characterization of the Tao's relationship to creation, which speaks of the Tao as the "mother of the myriad creatures."[10] With this third aspect the Tao's maternalness is more vividly expressed. In one passage Lao Tzu expresses modes and aspects outlined above in concise terms:

---

[7] Lao Tzu, *Tao te Ching*, D. C. Lau, trans., chapter 14. Thomas Schipflinger uses several German translations for his composite *Tao te Ching* text, whose sense sometimes differs slightly from the English translation. Where such differences occur, Thomas Schipflinger's rendering, which is often clarifying, is noted in brackets. The German translations that he uses are: Viktor von Strauss, *Lao-Tsae's, Taao-Tae-King* (Leipzig: Verlag der "Asia Minor," 1924); Richard Wilhelm, *Laotse, Taoteking* (Stuttgart: Deutscher Buecherbund, 1972); Gunther Debon, *Lao Tse, Tao-Te-King* (Stuttgart: P. Reclam, 1978); E. Rousselle, *Lao-dse, Fuehrung und Kraft aus der Ewigkeit* (Wiesbaden: Inselverlag, 1952); E. Schwartz, *Laudse, Daodesching* (Munich: Deutsche Taschenbuch-Verlag, 1985).

[8] Lao Tzu, *Tao te Ching*, D.C. Lau, trans. chapter 35.

[9] Lao Tzu, *Tao te Ching*, D.C. Lau, trans. chapters 1 and 6; Gellert Beky, *Die Welt des Tao*, p. 99.

[10] Gellert Beky, *Die Welt des Tao*, pp. 127, 165.

> The way begets one; one [which is also the first] begets
> two; two begets three; three begets the myriad creatures.[11]

The maternalness of this aspect of the Tao is a primary theme
with Lao Tzu. Erwin Rousselle writes that this is due to the fact
that he came from a matriarchal cultural tradition.[12] Lao Tzu expresses the Tao's maternal care in the following verses:

> The myriad creatures depend on it for life yet it claims no
>   authority . . .
> It clothes and feeds the myriad creatures yet lays no claim to
>   being their master . . .
> . . . the myriad creatures turn to it [trustingly].
> The way gives them [the myriad creatures] life;
> Virtue [its power] rears them;
> Things give them shape;
> Circumstances bring them to maturity.
> Therefore the myriad creatures all revere the way and hon-
>   our virtue. . . .[13]

What is not clear is whether this Mother is meant to be interpreted as a person, yet many of Lao Tzu's expressions suggest
such a possibility.[14]

A fourth aspect of the manifested mode of the Tao involves the possibility of sharing in Tao's eternity, which is called
"returning to the foundational root of life."[15] Lao Tzu writes:

---

[11] Lao Tzu, *Tao te Ching*, D.C. Lau, trans., chapter 42.

[12] Erwin Rousselle, *Lao-dse, Fuehrung und Kraft*, p. 63.

[13] Lao Tzu, *Tao te Ching*, D.C. Lau, trans., chapters 34, 51.

[14] "The Tao is like the (primordial) ancestor of the myriad creatures" (chapter 4);
"I know not whose son (child) it is" (chapter 4); "mother of the myriad creatures" (chapter 1); "mother of the world" (chapters 25 and 52); "I . . . value
being fed by the mother" (I honor the nourishing mother) (chapter 20);
"mother of a state" (kingdom) (chapter 59); the Tao is variously described as
the beginning of heaven and earth (chapter 1), of antiquity (14) and the world
(52), and the sign for "beginning" (Shi) is "woman" along with "fetus" and
"mouth of the mother."

[15] Rudolf Backofen, *Tao-Te-King, Text und Einfuehrung* (Schweiz: Fankhauser,
1949), p. 134.

. . . The teaming creatures
All return to their separate roots.
Returning to one's roots is known as stillness. This is what
    is meant by returning to one's destiny.
Returning to one's destiny is known as the constant [this
    means: being eternal].
Knowledge of the constant is known as discernment [this
    means: being enlightened] . . .
But one should act from knowledge of the constant [those
    who know the eternal have a great and wide heart]
One's action will lead to impartiality [righteousness],
Impartiality to kingliness [rulership],
Kingliness to heaven,
Heaven to the way,
The way to perpetuity,
And to the end of one's days one will meet with no danger
    [even at the body's destruction].[16]

This idea of entering eternity relates to recognizing the Tao as
Mother and oneself as Her child:

The world has a beginning.
The mother acts as the beginning of the world.
By finding the mother,
know her children [know yourself as the child].
By knowing her children,
follow the mother.
Self submerged—no danger.

. . . .

Use the light
Return to insight,
Do not give yourself over to misfortune.
This is called "Practising Constancy."
[Whoever uses [its] light to arrive at enlightenment, loses
    nothing at the body's
destruction. This means: to enter eternity].[17]

---

[16] Lao Tzu, *Tao te Ching*, D.C. Lau, trans., chapter 16.
[17] Lao Tzu, *Tao te Ching*, Thomas Miles, trans. (New York: Avery, 1992), chapter 52.

Becoming a child in turn involves knowing the forces of yin and yang, the two polar forces which hold sway in the universe, and balancing them within oneself:

> The ten-thousand things carry yin on their backs and embrace yang in their arms.
> Made whole by natural breathing, they achieve harmony.
>
> Know the masculine.
> Keep to the feminine.
>
> . . . .
>
> Know purity [your brightness—yang].
> Keep to the mixed [preserve your darkness—yin].
>
> . . . .
>
> Know glory.
> Keep to humility.
>
> . . . .
>
> And you will return to the state of Simplicity [to being a child][18]

This fourth aspect of the Tao, according to which human beings understand the Tao as Mother and seek to become Her child and thereby share in Her eternity, can be characterized as the Tao's soteriological or salvational function. Holding fast to Mother Tao as Her child leads to enlightenment and eternal life.

HUMAN WISDOM AND TRUE WISDOM

Lao Tzu pointedly distinguishes repeatedly between human wisdom and true Wisdom, exposing the cleverness of human wisdom as pragmatic, utilitarian, and egotistical. This kind of wisdom is responsible for much misfortune.[19] True Wisdom, on the other hand, is to:

---

[18] Lao Tzu, *Tao te Ching*, Thomas Miles, trans., chapter 42, 28.
[19] Lao Tzu, *Tao te Ching*, Thomas Miles, trans., chapters 3, 18, 19, 65.

> Contemplate plainness
> Embrace simplicity
> Reduce selfishness
> Have few desires.[20]

The wise and the holy are almost identical for Lao Tzu. Selflessness, compassion, frugality, and humility are also important:

> Te gives birth, but does not possess.
> It acts, but does not become dependent.
> It leads, but does not brutalize.
> This is called "Profound Te."

> I have three treasures that I hold and protect:
>   The first is benevolence.
>   The second is restraint.
> The third is not daring to be the first in the world [humility].[21]

The sage is broad-minded and childlike in approaching others:[22]

> The sage is without a constant mind.
> The mind of the people creates his mind.

> To good people, I am good.
> To not-good people, I am also good.
> Te is good.

> Trustworthy people I trust.
> Not-trustworthy people I also trust.
> Te is trusting.

> . . . .

The sage treats [encounters] them all as his children.[23]

---

[20] Lao Tzu, *Tao te Ching*, Thomas Miles, trans., chapter 19.
[21] Lao Tzu, *Tao te Ching*, Thomas Miles, trans., chaptes 51, 67.
[22] R. Backofen, *Tao-Te-King*, pp. 116, 137.
[23] Lao Tzu, *Tao te Ching*, Thomas Miles, trans., chapter 49.

Such characteristics, and the principle of "taking no action," are the main contents of Lao Tzu's ethics of life. Yet taking no action does not signify laziness and idleness, but a peaceful and trusting inner stillness and the kind of spontaneous, conscious activity that is never forced. Relevant passages indicate:[24]

> He practices not-doing
> Consequently, noting is without order.

> . . . I understand the benefits of not-doing.
> The teaching without words
> and the benefits of not-doing
> can only rarely be found in the world.

> . . . the sage. . . .
> does not act, yet achieves results.

> Practicing Tao, you lose every day.
> You lose and you lose even more
> until you reach not-doing.
> With not-doing, nothing is not done.
> The world is constantly mastered by no-affairs.
> Engaging in affairs
> is not a sufficient method for mastering the world.[25]

This is a principle that is valid for everyone, from hermits to politicians. It reflects a kind of wisdom which is difficult for Westerners to understand, but for that reason perhaps it is all the more important. Becoming still in oneself, approaching the day's activities prayerfully while reflecting on them in the light of God's Wisdom lays the proper foundation for achieving genuine success. This is the kind of attitude which represents a "turn to true salvation" [bent over—therefore preserved"].[26]

---

[24] R. Backofen, *Tao-Te-King*, p. 86.
[25] Lao Tzu, *Tao te Ching*, Thomas Miles, trans., chapters 3, 43, 47, 48.
[26] Lao Tzu, *Tao te Ching*, Thomas Miles, trans., chapter 22.

PARALLELS BETWEEN SOPHIA AND THE TAO

Though one should be cautious about drawing parallels between Western and Eastern thought, the similarities between the Tao and Sophia are especially striking and worthy of attention.[27]

It has been indicated that up to four different aspects of the Tao which has become born and manifested can be distinguished. The first aspect is still closely related to the unborn Tao. The second is the origin or root of heaven and earth, and contains images and seeds. The third is more concretely oriented to creation and characterized in maternal terms; and the fourth involves participation in the Tao's eternity. These four aspects can be identified as: 1) the theological aspect; 2) the ideal cosmological aspect; 3) the concrete cosmological aspect; 4) the soteriological or salvational aspect. These same four aspects are also found in the Old Testament's descriptions of Sophia.

1. *Sophia's theological or God-related aspect*
In Proverbs the created Sophia is depicted as Yahweh's "darling and delight, playing in his presence continually" (Prov. 8,22, 30). The Book of Wisdom says: "She adds luster to Her noble birth, because it is given her to live with God" (Wisd. 8,3). She is also called Yahweh's Paredra, which means the one who shares the throne (Wisd. 9,4). The Book of Wisdom also says:

> Like a fine mist she rises from the power of God, a clear effluence from the glory of the Almighty. . . . She is the radiance that streams from everlasting light, the flawless mirror of the active power of God, and the image of his goodness (Wisd. 7,25–26).

Lao Tzu's statements which correspond to these Old Testament texts are: "Fullness is born from Emptiness," and "Tao gave birth

---

[27] Gellert Beky, *Die Welt des Tao*, p. 200. Beky points to the similarities between the concepts of the Tao, the "Hen" (One) of Neoplatonism and Meister Eckhart's "Godhead."

to the One"[28]; and this is "the Formless Form, and the Substance-less Shape."[29] The Chinese expression for "beget" (sheng) expresses the same inexactness as the Biblical expressions "breath" and "effluence." "Shape of the shapeless and image of the imageless" also means literally the same thing as the Biblical expressions "image" and "image of his goodness." The essence of God's goodness is that it cannot be expressed or explained. To use Lao Tzu's expression, it is without name or nameless.[30]

2. Sophia's ideal cosmological aspect

Sophia says of Herself:

> The LORD created me the first (Reschit, Arche) of his works long ago (Prov. 8,22).

> When he made earth's foundations firm . . . I was at his side each day (Prov. 8,29–30).

Genesis says: "In the beginning God created the heavens and the earth" (Gen. 1,1); and some commentators identify this beginning with Sophia, translating: "With Sophia God created the world" which corresponds to the passage: "By wisdom the LORD laid the earth's foundations" (Prov. 3,19). The Book of Wisdom also says:

> She is initiated into the knowledge that belongs to God, and chooses what his works are to be (Wisd. 8,4).

In the above passage Sophia is with God and also related to the works of creation. It is also said of Her:

> She is . . . the image of his goodness is but one . . . herself unchanging, she makes all things new (Wisd. 7,26–27).

> For wisdom moves more easily than motion itself; she is so pure she pervades and permeates all things (Wisd. 7,24).

---

[28] Lao Tzu, *Tao Te Ching*, Thomas Miles, trans., chapters 40 and 42.
[29] Lao Tzu, *Tao Te Ching*, Thomas Miles, trans., chapter 14.
[30] Lao Tzu, *Tao Te Ching*, Thomas Miles, trans., chapter 1.

On the basis of these statements, Philo and Christian commentators compared Sophia to the Greek concept of the "Idea of the ideas"(the Idea idearum) with which the *Demiourgus* constructed the cosmos.

Lao Tzu is also familiar with such conceptions. The Tao that is born is "the beginning of Heaven and Earth."[31] The "One" issues forth from the Tao as the beginning of all that follows.[32] The Tao that is born is the "Great Form"[33] and a creature or thing in which are contained images and essences.[34] This is the idea of the cosmos, and thus the Tao's ideal cosmological aspect. Lao Tzu indicates:

Ultimate and wonderful.
Existing alone without change.
Circulating cyclically without depletion.
It acts like the mother of the world.[35]

Holy Scripture makes similar statements about Sophia:

She is but one, yet . . . herself unchanging, she makes all things new (Wisd. 7,27)

Alone I made a circuit of the sky (Ecclus. 24,5).

The Tao's ability to see "clearly in all four directions"[36] is also similar to something said of Sophia: "She is so pure she pervades and permeates all things" (Wisd. 7,24).

3. *Sophia's concrete cosmological aspect*
Holy Scripture does not just describe Sophia in ideal and abstract terms but also details Her relationship to creation. She is the *Genetis* and *Technitis* of the universe. Solomon says:

---

[31] Lao Tzu, *Tao Te Ching*, Thomas Miles, trans., chapter 1.
[32] Lao Tzu, *Tao Te Ching*, Thomas Miles, trans., chapter 42.
[33] Lao Tzu, *Tao Te Ching*, Thomas Miles, trans., chapter 35.
[34] Lao Tzu, *Tao Te Ching*, Thomas Miles, trans., chapter 21.
[35] Lao Tzu, *Tao Te Ching*, Thomas Miles, trans., chapter 25.
[36] Lao Tzu, *Tao Te Ching*, Thomas Miles, trans., chapter 10.

> Everything was mine to enjoy, for all follow where wisdom leads; yet I was in ignorance that she is the source (Genetis) of them all (Wisd. 7,12).

> I learnt it all, hidden or manifest, for I was taught by wisdom, by her whose skill made all things (Wisd. 7,21).

> She spans the world in power from end to end, and gently orders all things (Wisd. 8,1).

Sophia is thus the source of the universe where She holds sway, guiding and renewing the universe ("She makes all things new"—Wisd. 7,27). Lao Tzu expresses this by calling the Tao the Mother of the myriad creatures and the Mother of the world. She gives birth to the myriad creatures and is the maternal bosom (the gate or root) of heaven, earth and the myriad creatures.

4. Sophia's soteriological or salvational aspect

The Old Testament describes Sophia's friendliness and delight with humanity (Wisd. 1,6; 7,23; Prov. 8,31). Scripture also says of Her:

> She will come out to meet him like a mother; she will receive him like a young bride. For food she will give him the bread of understanding and for drink the water of wisdom. He will lean on her and will not fall, he will rely on her and not be put to shame (Ecclus. 15,2–4).

Sophia Herself says:

> "Now, sons, listen to me. . . . Happy the one who listens to me. . . . For whoever finds me finds life and wins favour with the LORD" (Prov. 8,32,34,35).

Solomon acknowledges:

> So I determined to take her home to live with me, knowing that she would be my counsellor in prosperity and

my comfort in anxiety and grief. . . . there is immortality in kinship with wisdom (Wisd. 8,9 and 17).

Scripture also describes how the desire for Wisdom leads to mastery (over oneself), closeness to God, and immortality (Wisd. 6,18 ff.); and these same things are said of the Tao.[37]

Sophia's concern for humanity is illustrated by Her concern for the people of Israel:

> But wisdom brought her servants safely out of their troubles. . . . she gave (a good man) a vision of God's kingdom and a knowledge of holy things . . . she . . . became a covering for them by day and a blaze of stars by night (Wisd. 10,9,10,17).

Of Sophia it is also said:

> Happy is he who has found wisdom. . . . In her right hand is long life, in her left are riches and honour. Her ways are pleasant ways and her paths all lead to prosperity. She is a tree of life to those who grasp her, and those who hold fast to her are safe (Prov. 3,13, 16–18).

> Wisdom raises her sons to greatness and gives help to those who seek her. To love her is to love life. . . . He who holds fast to her will gain honour; the Lord's blessing rests on the house she enters . . . and the Lord loves those who love her (Ecclus. 4,11–14)

> Follow her track, and she will make herself known; once you have grasped her, do not let her go. In the end you will find the refreshment she offers (Ecclus. 6,27–28).

Similarly, Lao Tzu also speaks of the Tao's salvational function toward humanity:

---

[37] Lao Tzu, *Tao Te Ching*, Thomas Miles, trans., chapter 16.

> One who possesses the Mother of the state [whoever knows
> and possesses the mother of the land]
> can last a long time [eternally].
> *This means having deep roots and strong foundations,*
> *the Way of* "lasting life, good eyesight into old age."
>
> *It clothes and feeds the thousands of things*
> *but does not act the ruler.*
>
> *The world has a Source, the Mother of the world.*
> Once you get the Mother
> then you understand the children [your child-like nature].
> *Once you understand the children*
> *turn back and watch over the Mother.*
>
> . . . .
>
> till the end of your life you will not get tired [at the body's
> destruction].
>
> Tao produces them,
> Te rears them
> makes them grow, nurses them . . .
> sustains them . . .
>
> Grasp the Great image and the world will come
> it will come and not be harmed—
> a great peace and evenness.[38]

The latter statement about the Tao is particularly interesting and profound; for it indicates that when the image of the Tao (Sophia) is present and working within us, then the earth and humanity will be freed from suffering and attain peace and wholeness.

Lao Tzu reports that the Tao itself is the source of his knowledge,[39] and such a statement accords with what is said about Wisdom in the Old Testament:

---

[38] *The Tao of the Tao Te Ching*, Michael LaFarage, trans. (Albany, NY: State University of New York Press, 1992), chapters 59, 52, 51, 35.
[39] *The Tao of the Tao Te Ching*, Michael LaFarage, trans., chapter 21.

Wisdom shines brightly and never fades; she is readily discerned by those who love her, and by those who seek her she is found. She is quick to make herself known to all who desire knowledge of her . . . she herself searches far and wide for those who are worthy of her, and on their daily path she appears to them with kindly intent, meeting them half-way in their purposes (Wisd. 6,12–13,16).

Age after age she enters into holy souls, and makes them friends of God and prophets (Wisd. 7,27).

In light of the testimony given in the *Tao Te Ching* it is justified to consider Lao Tzu as someone who sought and found Sophia, and whom She met with loving and kindly intent, making him a friend and prophet of God.

Within the history of religion there is hardly another figure that bears such a remarkable resemblance to the Old Testament's Sophia as Mother Tao of the *Tao Te Ching*. Lao Tzu's conceptions and depictions of Her are profound, and most important of all is that he entrusts himself to Her and finds comfort in Her as the Mother. Describing how he seems foolish and alone amongst conceited and unrestrained people he says:

> *I am alone, different from others—*
> *treasuring the nourishing Mother.*[40]

Lao Tzu is an important witness for the relevance of perceiving the maternal aspect of the Divine, and for honoring it and living one's life out of this consciousness. His Mother Tao has much to say and give, especially today, to a Western spirituality that is predominantly masculine.

---

[40] *The Tao of the Tao Te Ching*, Michael LaFarge, trans., chapter 20.

23

Sophia and the World Religions

PRECEDING CHAPTERS HAVE attempted to explore teachings related to Sophia from outside the Judao-Christian tradition, which leads to the question of how these revelations relate to Christianity's understanding of Sophia and particularly to Her unique relationship to Mary.

In answer to this question it can be stated that what is advocated is not a kind of syncretism or blending together of different beliefs, but the spirit of perceiving and acknowledging what is of value in other religious traditions.

Much of what these traditions proclaim testifies to their profound spirituality and devotion to the Divine and the Absolute, and particularly to God's feminine and maternal dimension. Similar to the Christian point of view that the New Testament represents the fulfillment of the Hebrew tradition's Old Testament, a Christian perspective asserts that what is foreshadowed in the Eastern traditions becomes actualized in Christianity. The yearning for God's paternal and maternal embrace is fulfilled in the revelation of the Holy Trinity, whereby God the Father represents the Person of paternal love; Sophia and the Holy Spirit the Person of maternal love (see chapter 26); and the Son Jesus Christ the filial love between God and humanity. Thus the indications in the Eastern traditions about the Feminine Di-

Figure 18. Gaia—Mother Earth—Demeter. Rhein Verlag, Zurich.

vine and salvation are precursors and signposts leading to Sophia Mary and Jesus Christ who fulfill them.

But this is not cause for a feeling of superiority on the part of Christianity, for it becomes apparent that in particular Western Christian theology and spirituality is incomplete and lacking. The teachings of other cultures, especially about the Feminine Divine, can help Christians to discover new dimensions to the fullness of the Christian message, enhancing their understanding and appreciation of it.

In the West through the influence of Jewish, Greek, and Roman culture, a predominately patriarchal tradition has been inherited by Christianity which, in effect, suppressed knowledge

Figure 19. Isis with Horus. Bronze, seventh-century Egypt B.C.E.
Rhein Verlag, Zurich.

Figure 20. Mother Goddess (Celtic). Rhein Verlag, Zurich.

Figure 21. Mother Earth—Demeter. Terra cotta relief, Greece. Rhein Verlag, Zurich.

of the Feminine Divine and contributed to the present-day tension in the Churches surrounding women's issues. It is important for the Churches today to recognize the value of the feminine, and to combat obstacles to female equality and a feminine sense of self-worth. It is necessary to re-evaluate a patriarchal interpretation of Revelation and to rediscover those aspects of Scripture and tradition which positively relate to women. Genesis, for example, states that men and women were both created in the image and likeness of God; and the present work has attempted to illuminate the significance of the Wisdom tradition, as well as Sophia's relationship to Mary and the Holy Spirit (chapter 26).

It is the task of present-day Christianity to achieve the kind of catholicity, or universality, that embraces the contributions of other religious traditions about the Feminine Divine and the full significance of Sophia Mary. (See figures 20, 21, 22 on

Figure 22. Mother Earth—Diana of Ephesus. Alabaster and bronze, second century B.C.E. Rhein Verlag, Zurich.

pages 368, 369, 370, and Plate 26, page 134.) While this may seem untoward to traditional Marian devotion, the intent is a contribution to Mary's fuller appreciation and honor.

SOPHIA AND THE ADELPHIA RELIGIOSA OF HUMANITY

Understanding Sophia as the link between the world's religious traditions points to the significance of their relationship. She is the World Soul and the Mother of creation, the source of all Wisdom teachings, the inspiration behind conceptions of the Feminine Divine, and the mediating link to universal salvation through Jesus Christ. She is the Mother, and the world traditions are Her children; She binds them together into one family, the *Adelphia Religiosa* whose members have been richly bestowed with individual gifts and graces.

The relationship between the individual members of the Adelphia Religiosa should not be one of opposition, but of mutual appreciation and concern. Christianity must learn to appreciate the knowledge of the mystery of God that other religious traditions have to offer. Yet Christianity has its own task to fulfill: To communicate the Good News of God's intention for us to participate in God's inner Trinitarian life of love; to reveal the story of the Logos and Sophia Mary, telling how the Logos incarnated from Her and effected the work of redemption, the divinization of humanity, and creation, and that Christ has called everyone to become a part of the community of His mystical body through the Church. He has called everyone together to become a family in divine *hierogamous* union with Him and to celebrate with Him the Sacred Marriage.

Thus the task of Christianity is to mediate the Good News of the Christian mystery to all the members of the human family; and just as Sophia is an intercessionary mediator between God and humanity, so, too, must Christianity approach this task in an attitude of prayerful service and devotion, respecting the individuality of other family members, and accepting and integrating the gifts that each has to offer. Each family member is to be respected and the gifts and graces granted to each are to be accepted and integrated within the whole.

This is a vision of community and unity that tolerates differences and a plurality of forms. (See Plate 27, page 135.) The model is love and service, and not uniformity. The task of the Adelphia Religiosa is to embrace all the profound wisdom and powers of love manifesting in the various religions, which find their culmination and fulfillment through Sophia Mary and Jesus Christ.

It might be objected that key features of the various world religions are not compatible with one another and cannot be joined together with one another to form a whole. To this it can be rejoined that perhaps we have not yet attained to the kind of holistic thinking which can integrate seemingly disparate elements and mysteries into a comprehensive whole. It seems clear that progress, if it does come, will not result from a purely rational approach, but through intuition and the inspiration of Wisdom Herself. It is hoped that the vision of an adelphic community of religions may provide an impetus for seeking the kind of Wisdom that will allow the world religions to enter into a new relationship with one another and provide the basis for working toward peace and a better world.

PART IV

SOPHIOLOGY AND THE 21ˢᵀ CENTURY

24

Sophia
and the
New Age

THERE HAS BEEN MUCH talk in the present about the modern age coming to a close and the beginning of a New Age. Some have called it the Age of Aquarius (which succeeds the present Age of Pisces); but it could just as well be called the Age of the Spirit, to contrast it with the materialistic and mechanistic thinking of past centuries; or the Age of Wisdom, to contrast its intuitive and comprehensive knowledge with a present-day analytical knowledge of isolated bits of information.

The incipient signs of a coming New Age are apparent in many fields. In medicine there is renewed interest in natural healing; ecological concerns have become a primary focus in economics and politics; and in religion there is a pronounced interest in spirituality and overcoming science's materialistic worldview.

One noteworthy example of a new and future-oriented religious orientation is found in the documents of the Second Vatican Council of the Roman Catholic Church (1962–1965) which was convened by Pope John XXIII and concluded by Pope Paul VI. Of particular relevance are *Gaudium et Spes* (Joy and Hope) about the Church in the world today; *Unitatis Redintegratio* (The Restoration of Unity) concerning ecumenism;

and *Aetate Nostra* (Our Age) and *Dignitatis Humanae* (The Dignity of the Human Being) about the relationship of the Church to the non-Christian religions and religious freedom. *Gaudium et Spes* acknowledges the "truth, goodness, and justice" found in institutions outside the Church, both in the present and past, and indicates the Church's willingness to help such institutions.[1]

Aetate Nostra declares:

> Throughout history even to the present day, there is found among different peoples a certain awareness of a hidden power, which lies behind the course of nature and the events of human life. At times there is present even a recognition of a supreme being, or still more of a Father. This awareness and recognition results in a way of life that is imbued with a deep religious sense. The religions which are found in more advanced civilizations endeavor by way of that well-defined concept and exact language to answer these questions. Thus, in Hinduism men explore the divine mystery and express it both in the limitless riches of myth and the accurately defined insights of philosophy. They seek release from the trials of the present life by ascetic practices, profound meditation and recourse to God in confidence and love. Buddhism in its various forms testifies to the essential inadequacy of this changing world. It proposes a way of life by which [people] can, with confidence and trust, attain a state of perfect liberation and reach supreme illumination either through their own efforts or by the aid of divine help. So, too, other religions which are found throughout the world attempt in their own ways to calm the hearts of people by outlining a program of life covering doctrine, moral precepts and sacred rites.

---

[1] *Vatican Council II, The Conciliar and Post Conciliar Documents*, Austin Flannery, O. P. ed. (Northport, NY: Costello Publishing, 1975, "Gaudium et Spes," paragraph 42, pp. 942–943.

The Catholic Church rejects nothing of what is true and holy in these religions. She has a high regard for the manner of life and conduct, the precepts and doctrines which, although differing in many ways from her own teaching, nevertheless often reflect a ray of that truth which enlightens all men . . .

The Church, therefore, urges her sons to enter with prudence and charity into discussion and collaboration with members of other religions. Let Christians, while witnessing to their own faith and way of life, acknowledge, preserve and encourage the spiritual and moral truths found among non-Christians, also their social life and culture.[2]

The sentiments expressed in the above paragraphs led to the founding of a Vatican Secretariat for non-Christian religions in 1964. In a speech given on the twentieth anniversary of this Secretariat (March 3, 1984), Pope John Paul II said:

This friendly relationship between the faithful of different religions has its source in respect and love for one another . . . (the Church) wants to help all of the faithful to respect and hold in high esteem the values, traditions and convictions world of those belonging to other faiths. . . . In consequence of one's own faith, it is also possible to share, compare and enrich spiritual experiences, forms of prayer, and the ways of encountering God.[3]

Elsewhere in the same speech he continues:

It is the Secretariat's goal Christians come to know non-Christians correctly and judge them fairly, and that non-Christians correspondingly are able to come to know and evaluate the teaching and life of Christians. Christ's example should lead Christians to love and respect

---

[2] *Vatican Council II*, "Nostra Aetate," pp. 738–739.
[3] *Bulletin des Vatikanischen Sekretariats fur die Nichtchristen* (Citta Del Vaticano, 1983–1984), 56/201 ff.

everything that is good about the culture and religious striving of others. It is a matter above all of respecting what the spirit, blowing where it will, has effected in them.

The Church opens itself to dialogue in order to remain faithful to the human being . . . he or she experiences in dialogue that they do not possess the truth totally or perfectly, but that they can approach it in confidence with others together. . . . A brotherly exchange of each one's gifts leads to increasing maturity. . . . This process of exchange can even lead to the clarification, enrichment and better understanding of religious experiences and points of view. This dynamic of human encounter impels us Christians to hear and understand what those of other faiths have to impart to us so that we might utilize the gifts that God has given to them.

The Church trusts in Christ's promise that in the course of time the Spirit will guide it into the fullness of truth (John, 16,13). Thus She encounters human beings and peoples and their cultures in the consciousness that every human community possesses seeds of goodness and truth, and that God has a plan of love for every nation (Acts 17,26–27). Thus the Church wants to cooperate with everyone in the realization of this plan and so fathom all of the richness of the many forms of God's unending Wisdom. . . .

Then let us turn towards all who acknowledge God and preserve in their traditions valuable elements of religion and humaneness, and hope that an open dialogue brings all of us to take up the spirit's impulses faithfully and fulfill them with fervour. . . . With respect to the humanity of the coming third millennium, may the Church radiate an open Christianity, ready, to patiently wait, until those seeds germinate which were sown in tears but yet in faith.[4]

---

[4] *Bulletin des Vatikanischen Sekretariates*, 56/205 ff, 56/220. Tr: translation mine.

These are moving statements which are encouraging to people of good will and which represent a call to common action. One can say that they represent the beginning of the appearance of a holistic and universal perspective, which has always belonged to the Church's essence, but which can only become fully realized in the course of time. Perhaps the Age of the Holy Spirit, which was beheld by the Blessed Joachim of Fiore, St. Hildegard of Bingen, and Soloviev has begun.[5]

---

[5] Joachim of Fiore (1130–1202), a Cistercian abbott who was pronounced blessed, attributed particular importance to the "nation of the world-people" and "humanity's germative power" in the third millenium, *Patrologiae cursus completus*, J. P. Migne, ed., Series latina (Paris: 1844–1855), 488.

25

Sophia and the *Hieros Gamos*, or Sacred Marriage

THE IDEA OF HIEROGAMY or sacred union relates to the fundamental polarity inherent to all of existence and the idea of an elevated "union of opposites." Polarity and the union of opposites into a more elevated whole is an important philosophical and religious theme. Perhaps the most widely recognized symbol of polarity and the higher synthesis of opposites into a whole is the Chinese Tai Chi symbol, which depicts primordial yin and yang bounded by a circle. However, the Hebrew Star of David, and even Christianity's cross, are other examples of the fundamental significance of symbols of polarity and union.

In addition to the existence of such symbols, many religious traditions also specifically portray the *Hieros Gamos* (Greek: sacred marriage) between the masculine and feminine aspects of God, and it is Sophia-Wisdom who is portrayed as the feminine partner in this marriage. As indicated in the tradition of the Cabala, She appears as the Schekinah, the Queen of the Holy King, whose marriage archetypically signifies the holiness of procreation (chapter 9). In the Hindu tradition, the hierogamous relationship is portrayed by the love between Krishna and Radha,

Shiva and Shakti (chapter 20); and the Buddhist tradition boldly portrays the union of Buddha and Prajna (see figure 23, page 383). Though the more erotic nature of such a depiction seems foreign to Western sensibilities, the notion of the Sacred Marriage that it portrays is also found in the Old and New Testaments.

The Old Testament depicts the hierogamous love between Yahweh and Sophia. She is called *Paredra*, the one who shares His throne (Wisd. 9,4), and *Amon* or Darling and Beloved (Prov. 8,30). However, the theme of hierogamous love also extends through Sophia to the community of Israel in which Sophia appears:

> . . . he who created me decreed where I should dwell. He said, "Make your home in Jacob; enter on your heritage in Israel." . . . and thus I came to be established in Zion. He settled me in the city he loved (Ecclus. 24,8–11).

This is an indication of God's intention to share hierogamous love with humanity, which other Old Testament passages also echo.

The prophet Hosea depicts the reality of God's hierogamous relationship with His people in an exceptionally concrete way in speaking of a renewed matrimonial covenant with a wife (the people of Israel) who has been unfaithful:

> I shall betroth you to myself for ever, bestowing righteousness and justice, loyalty and love; I shall betroth you to myself, making you faithful, and you will know the LORD (Hos. 2,19–20).

According to traditional understanding, the Song of Songs represents the celebration of the love between God and Sophia, but also between God and the community of Israel and each individual soul (Song of Songs, 1,2–4; 2,4–6; 8,2–4).

The New Testament continues the theme of the hierogamous relationship between God and humanity. John calls Christ the Husband of the Bride (John, 3,29); and Paul calls matrimony a great mystery and an image of the divine archetype of Christ and the Church (every faithful individual soul):

> "This is why" (in the words of Scripture) "a man shall leave his father and mother and be united to his wife, and

Figure 23. Vajrasattva and Prajñāpāramitā: the Ādi Buddha and his Sakti. Tibetan, bronze, 18th century. Rascher Verlag, Zurich.

Figure 24. The Ancient Eleousa (the compassionate one). Ivory, Syria, sixth century. Westermann Braunschweig.

the two shall become one flesh." There is hidden here a great truth, which I take to refer to Christ and the church (Eph. 5,31–32).

Sophia-Mary mediates this hierogamous union in Her traditional role as the Mother of the Church, which the Revelation of John takes up by referring to the Holy City, New Jerusalem (Augustine's Created Sophia[1]) as the Bride of the Lamb:

> I saw the Holy City, new Jerusalem, coming down out of heaven from God, made ready like a bride adorned for her husband (Rev. 21,2).

> "Come . . . and I will show you the bride, the wife of the Lamb" (Rev. 21,9).

When Mary is understood as the Mother of the Church, and the Church as the representative of each individual member whose destiny is to join in the hierogamous union with Christ the Lamb, then traditional portrayals of Mary and Christ take on new meaning. Although they are far removed from the explicitly erotic nature of Eastern images, pictures of the Madonna and Child, Christ carrying Mary's soul to heaven, and especially Mary's Coronation in heaven (which recalls the image of Sophia sharing Yahweh's throne—Wisd. 9,4) all suggest the motif of hierogamous union. (See figure 24, page 384, and Plates 28–30, pages 136–138.)

Symbols and images of hierogamous union are common to all religions, even though the contents of the images vary. On the one hand, they portray the ineffable union of polarities in God; and on the other, the union of God with humanity. Contemplating these images can help us realize that God's grace and love alone can satisfy our yearning for love, and they can also help to stimulate our desire for this union.

---

[1] *Patrologiae cursus completus*, J. P. Migne, ed., Series Latina (Paris: 1844–1855), Augustine, *Liber Meditationum*, XIX, 40, 916.

26

Sophia and the Maternal Holy Spirit

THE NOTION THAT THE HOLY SPIRIT represents the Trinity's maternal principle may seem surprising. It is, however, a hypothesis that has its basis in Scriptural portrayals about the Holy Spirit and associations between the Holy Spirit and Sophia. In the Old Testament, Sophia is clearly depicted as a created female image of God who shares God's throne and partakes in the process of creation (Prov. 8,1; Wisd. 7,25; 9,4). In the Genesis passage which speaks of the creation of humanity God speaks, "Let us make human beings in our image, after our likeness" (Gen. 1,26). Both Theophilus of Antioch and St. Irenaenus interpret the words "Let us make" to mean God, the Logos, and Sophia; and Irenaeus directly identifies Her as the Holy Spirit.[1] Clement of Alexandria also interprets the words to mean God and Sophia "in whom He delighted as with His own spirit,"[2] although it is not clear whether Clement identifies Sophia with the Logos or with the Holy Spirit (the Russian Sophiologist Sergei Bulgakov also understood Sophia as a revelation of the Spirit and Mary,

---

[1] *Patrologiae cursus completus*, J. P. Migne, ed., Series latina (Paris, 1844-1855), Theophilus of Antioch, 6,1064C, 1077B, 1086B; Irenaeus, 7,967B; 993A; 1032B; 1038B.

[2] *Petrologiae cursus completus*, J. P. Migne, ed., Series graeca (Paris, 1844–1855), Clemens of Alexandria, *Stromata*, 8, 721B.

in whom Sophia was hypostasized, as an image of the Holy Spirit).[3]

The continuation of the above Genesis texts also hints at a female principle in God (alongside of God's masculine principle) in that humanity, who is created in God's image, is created male and female:

> God created human beings in his own image; in the image of God he created them; male and female he created them (Gen. 1,26–27).

Taken together, the above texts and interpretations suggest that there is a feminine principle in God, with which Sophia is identified in some way (as an image or archetype), and that this principle can be understood as the Holy Spirit.

Another passage about the creation says that "the spirit of God hovered over the surface of the water" (Gen. 1,2), which suggests the maternal image of a bird hatching its eggs (and recalls an image from the *Tao Te Ching* of the Tao as a protective and nourishing mother bird).[4]

One New Testament passage where the Holy Spirit is spoken of involves the baptism of Jesus (Luke 3,21–22), and compares the Holy Spirit to a dove, which became the preferred symbol for the Holy Spirit in Christian iconography. It is worth noting, however, that during those times the dove was a female symbol of matrimonial love, as portrayed in the following text:

> My beloved is knocking: "Open to me, my sister, my dearest, my dove, my perfect one" (Song Of Songs, 5,2).

It is also noteworthy that the Gospel writers used the word *Peristara* for dove, which means Ishtar's bird. Ishtar was the goddess of love and was usually portrayed as a dove. Perhaps it was not accidental and not insignificant that the Holy Spirit was associated with the dove, a female symbol of love.

---

[3] Sergei Boulgakov, *La Sagesse de Dieu, Resumé de Sophiologie*, trans. by Constantin Andronikov (Lausanne: L'Age d'Homme, 1983), pp. 65, 80.

[4] Lao Tzu, *Tao Te Ching*, D. C. Lau, trans. (New York: Penguin, 1972), chapter 10.

Language may present one barrier to accepting the idea of a female Holy Spirit because in some languages the gender of the word "spirit" is masculine (Latin: *spiritus*; German: *Geist*). In Hebrew, however, the word for spirit (*ruach*) is feminine.

Yet another New Testament passage—about Mary's conception through the Holy Spirit (Matt. 1,18–20)—can be cited to support a masculine interpretation of the Holy Spirit. To resolve this apparent difficulty, it is necessary to consider the Angel's words at the Annunciation. In answer to Mary's question about how the events announced to Her will take place, the Angel replies:

> "The Holy Spirit will come upon you, and the power of the Most High will overshadow you; for that reason the holy child to be born will be called Son of God" (Luke 1,35).

These verses, however, can be interpreted as depicting two principles—the Holy Spirit and the power of God; and one could say that the female Spirit principle maternally prepares Mary to receive the power of the Most High. In light of this explanation, and in the sense of the Creed formulation "conceived through the Holy Spirit," the Holy Spirit can be understood to have given Mary the strength and capability to receive the Son of God and become His Mother, giving over to Her the Son received by the Spirit from the Father.

In another passage which speaks about the Holy Spirit Jesus declares:

> The Spirit of the Lord is upon me, because he hath anointed me to preach the gospel to the poor; he hath sent me to heal the broken-hearted, to preach deliverance to the captives, and recovering of sight to the blind, to set at liberty them that are bruised (King James Bible, Luke, 4,18).

Jesus also promises to send the Holy Spirit, the "Comforter," who will teach and call to mind everything that He said (King James Bible, John, 14,26), and He calls the Holy Spirit the Spirit of truth who will be a guide unto all truth (John, 16,13). These activities of healing, comforting, caring for the poor and afflicted, and guiding can all be considered to reflect feminine and maternal qualities. It is also interesting to note that wind and fire, which appear during the Holy Spirit's descent at Pentecost (Acts 2,1–3), are considered the two elder daughters of the *Bagua*, the eighth trigram of the *I Ching*.

That such hints about the feminine and maternal quality of the Holy Spirit were not taken up and developed further can be attributed to the predominantly patriarchal culture of the times, although isolated voices in support of such a notion were heard. St. Cyprian, for example, called virgins consecrated to God the "most beautiful images of the Holy Spirit"; in the Didascaly of the fourth century, female deacons were called "images of the Holy Spirit who should be honored"; and St. Chrysostomus calls the Holy Eucharist the "milk from the maternal breast of the Holy Spirit."[5]

The mood and naiveté of Scholastic theology toward women is evident in the remarks of Thomas Aquinas, who asked himself whether a woman could be understood as a symbol of the Holy Spirit. He concluded that because the woman's function in the process of procreation is passive—merely providing the biological womb—she could not be taken as a symbol of the Holy Spirit, for God is *actus purus* (pure activity).[6] The influential Meister Eckhart voiced a similar sentiment, on the basis of Greek philosophy, implying the female's inferiority by indicating that what is masculine is perfect, and only what is perfect can create something masculine. The woman is an aborted man—this was the axiomatic appraisal of Greek philosophy in the Middle Ages.

Almost one hundred years ago, the Catholic theologian Matthias Scheeben performed the immortal service of interpreting the Holy Spirit as the feminine and maternal principle of the Trinity, and provided a theological basis for such a viewpoint.[7] His work, however, has unfortunately not been taken up.

---

[5] Markus Kobell, *Die Frau, das Grosse Zeichen des Heiligen Geistes?* (Harburg, privately published, 1988).

[6] Thomas Aquinas, *Summa Contra Gentiles* (Taurini: Marietti, 1927), IV, "De Generatione Verbi."

[7] Matthias Scheeben, *Dogmatik* (Freiburg: Herder, 1952), vol. II, pp. 119–120.

Figure 25. The Holy Trinity. This depiction is from the beginning of the ninth century, and is found in the Church of Urschalling, near Prien, in Bavaria. It is an interesting and seldom-encountered portrayal of the Trinity, which unmistakably presents the Holy Spirit as a woman, indicating that even in those times conceiving of the Holy Spirit as the Trinity's maternal principle was not unknown. Urschalling, Berger Chiemsee.

Today such a perspective is becoming increasingly relevant due to the justified questioning of a conception of God that is only paternal and masculine. If the Father and Son exist, it is natural to inquire about the existence of the Mother. (See figure 25, page 391.) The answer to this question may lie in reconsidering the indications given here about the possible relationship of the female and maternal to the Holy Spirit, bolstered by what has been learned about the Feminine Divine in other religious traditions and the female's role in procreation through modern science. These are questions of particular concern to women, but also to Christianity as a whole.

It can be objected that Revelation does not portray the idea of a feminine and maternal Holy Spirit in a sufficiently clear manner. It may, however, be the case that a fuller knowledge of this potential truth will only be revealed in the course of time. As Jesus said:

> "There is much more that I could say to you, but the burden would be too great for you now. However, when the Spirit of truth comes, he will guide you into all the truth . . ." (John, 16,12).

Many truths only become fully known at the appropriate time and after long debate. This was so in the case of the doctrine about the dual nature of Jesus Christ in one Divine Person, and about Mary as "Theotokos" (the Mother of God) and about Her Immaculate Conception.

Today we stand at the end of a patriarchal age and at the dawn of a new age, and recognition of the feminine and maternal identity of the Holy Spirit may represent a significant step forward. Understanding the Holy Spirit's femininity, and understanding Sophia-Mary as the Holy Spirit's most perfectly created Image, helps reveal the fundamental and essential role of the female in the Godhead, and restores the dignity of women's role in religion. These teachings may well represent the theology of the future. (See Plate 31, page 139, a Trinity icon from Russia, which includes an angel figure that is a typical representation for Sophia.)

27

The Union between Sophia and Mary

IN ADDITION TO BRINGING together numerous contributions on the subject of Sophia, it has also been a primary concern of this work to put forward the thesis that Sophia became a human being in Mary. The hypothesis of the union of Sophia with Mary raises the question of how such a union is to be theologically explained, and whether it relates, for example, to the hypostatic union of the Logos with Jesus Christ.

It can be answered that the union between Sophia and Mary is not hypostatic, for in the *Unio hypostatica* a divine uncreated nature and a human created nature are united in the divine Person of the Logos, whereby the two natures are essentially different. With Sophia and Mary, there are not two essentially different natures, but only one created nature, which appears in two different forms—a spiritual, eternal form, and an earthly, human form.

When Sophia incarnates, Her personal essence remains the same, but the existential form changes. Her spiritual form gives way to an earthly form in the temporal and spatial world. Sophia's spiritual nature is present, but it is concealed in Her incarnated and earthly form and in effect is only virtually present.

The union between the two natures of Sophia and Mary is similar to the union between the soul and body. When the soul is incarnated in the material world and bound by a human body, it is constrained by the bodily nature. This is also the case with Sophia's spiritual nature. While bound by a human nature in the material world, Her spiritual nature cannot fully manifest its inherent power. In Her humility and willingness to serve, She was prepared to take on human form and the lowliness of human existence along with Christ (Phil. 2,7–8). She was prepared to conceal Her splendor during Her time on earth and subject Herself to the conditions and limitations of human existence. She experienced every stage of human growth and development. Her knowledge, power, and splendor remained latent, though in some instances they did became manifest (in the strength of Her faith and virtue and in Her wisdom, purity, and beauty).

Thus, the union of the spiritually powerful Sophia with a human nature can be called incorporative, a union of an elevated soul with a human nature similar to the way in which the body and soul unite with the human being. Mary's body and human nature are ensouled by the elevated spiritual nature of Sophia. In this sense, Sophia is Mary's soul, and Mary is the *Sedes Sapientia* or the Seat of Wisdom (Litany of Loreto, appendix IV). Sophia incarnated in Mary's body.

The glory of Sophia-Mary's dignity and splendor only became apparent during the Assumption into heaven, when the human nature was transfigured or freed from the confines of the temporal and spatial world. Only then did She become manifest as the Queen of Heaven and Earth and the Lady of All Nations, the fulfillment of the yearning of all people for the perfected feminine and maternal nature, the *charme eternel*. (See Plate 32, page 140.) Only then did She fully manifest all the dignities and beauties of the ideal woman which were prophetically perceived and promised in Israel's Books of Wisdom, and by many other peoples. Only then did She represent the celebration of the triumph of good over evil, of beauty over ugliness, of nobility over coarseness, of unity over division, of harmony over chaos, and of life over death. She humbly emptied Herself of Her grandeur in order to become a human being, making the victory and splendor of Sophia-Mary even more radiant. In the Revelation of John, this victory is proclaimed by the woman clothed with the sun (Rev. 12,1 ff) who is victorious over the dragon.

The union between Sophia and Mary is symbolically portrayed in the many depictions of Mary with a book (representing Wisdom), and it is also expressed in liturgy by the use of texts from the Books of Wisdom on Marian feast days (see appendix II). Mary's titles in the Litany of Loreto and the Akathist Hymn (appendix IV) can also only be fully understood from the point of view of Her relationship to Sophia.

Just as the full name of the incarnated Logos is Jesus Christ, the name of the incarnated Sophia is Sophia-Mary.

In summary, the following points can be made in support of the hypothesis that Sophia became a human being in Mary:

1. The prophetic revelation about Sophia's appearance on earth (Bar. 3,37) finds its personal fulfillment in Mary (and through Mary in the Church).

2. It provides a more comprehensive and profound vision of Mary's participation in the plan of salvation. Mary works together with Christ just as Sophia was involved with creation, the world's preservation and in Israel's deliverance and guidance.

3. It provides a basis for making more intelligible the so-called hyperdulical devotion to Mary which understands Her as more elevated than the Angels and saints.

4. It integrates the three primary forms in which Mary is understood and honored: A) as the holy and archetypical Woman, Mother, and Housewife; B) as our Mother the beloved Blessed Lady, Mother of the Church, Mother of Mercy, Salvation of the Sick and Helper of Humanity; C) as Queen of Heaven and Earth (the World Soul), the Lady of All Nations, and the justified Bearer of the titles of the Litany of Loreto and the Akathist Hymn (appendix IV).

Each of these three forms focuses on a particular dimension of Mary:

- The natural and human dimension, which is particularly understood and honored by the faithful of the Evangelical and Reformed Churches;
- The supernatural and hyperdulic dimension, which is understood and honored by Catholics and the Orthodox peoples;
- The cosmic and Sophian dimension, which is understood and honored in the Russian tradition of the Eastern Church.

All of the above thoughts about the union of Sophia with Mary are intended as a stimulus toward a closer understanding of this mystery. It remains to be determined whether they help to clarify this profound mystery (which is similar to the incarnation of the Logos) or whether another explanation must be found. Progress in comprehending and formulating a mystery is always possible, and toward this end, the cooperation of theologians, philosophers, and natural scientists (especially biologists and psychologists) is desirable.

In addition, it can be said that because of the ecological crisis today it is just as important to clarify the relationship between Sophia and the world and the universe. The model of the union of body and soul also seems capable of explaining their union, although it, too, is proposed as a tentative model subject to revision. Just as the human soul animates a body composed of cells, organs, and systems that function in unison, in a similar way the world, and even the entire universe, can be considered as large systems comprising subordinate systems that are all animated by a common source—the World Soul.

The concept of the World Soul provides a basis for recognizing the unity and connectedness of all of life, which forms the Body and Garment of the World Soul, Sophia our Mother. It is hoped that such an understanding fosters humanity's sense for the maternal embrace of the universe and Earth and for the gratitude and reverence that is due them. (See Plate 32 for an artistic representation suggesting the unifying function of Sophia–Mary as the World Soul.)

Afterword

by Robert A. Powell

Father Thomas Schipflinger's book *Sophia Maria* is a compendium on Sophia, a veritable Sophia encyclopedia. It is an indispensable source of reference for anyone interested in the Divine Feminine. The material published in this work was collected and put together by Father Thomas Schipflinger during a period of more than two decades. It is his *magnum opus,* his life's work, a labor of love on the part of someone who truly reveres the Divine Feminine. Being a labor of love, its content is presented in a heartfelt way, and yet it is also scholarly. It is a work that may be read over and over again, as a source of reference on Sophia and also as a source of inspiration.

The golden thread running through this work is the relationship of Sophia to the Virgin Mary. What is unique about this book is the systematic and comprehensive account of this relationship. Father Schipflinger summarizes it in his thesis that Sophia is (was) the pre-incarnatory Mary. Yet what does this really mean? It raises many theological questions, including the central question of Russian Sophiology: What is the relationship of the Divine Sophia to the Trinity of Father, Son and Holy Spirit? This, in turn, raises the question as to whether Sophia is a created or an uncreated being?

Here I would like to put forward a perspective that, I believe, sheds remarkable light upon all these questions. It is the Sophiological perspective put forward by the Russian (anonymous) author of the work *Meditations on the Tarot: A Journey into Christian Hermeticism*.[1] The author was evidently familiar with Russian Sophiology, as the perspective he presents represents an extension of the teaching of the Russian Sophiologist, Father Pavel Florensky, frequently referred to by Father Thomas Schipflinger in this book.

In the space of this Afterword it is possible to give only a brief schematic overview of the Sophiological perspective of the anonymous author. I realize that this is a risky undertaking, but feel it is of such importance that without it the central thesis of Father Schipflinger's book cannot really be understood on a deeper level. Father Schipflinger, himself, having in the meantime become acquainted with this more recent Sophiological perspective, has encouraged me to write this Afterword and draw attention to it. As a starting point, let us consider the words of Father Pavel Florensky:

> Sophia participates in the life of the Trihypostatic Godhead; she enters into the bosom of the Trinity; and she partakes of Divine Love. But, being a *fourth* created (i.e., non-consubstantial) Person, she does not "constitute" Divine Unity, nor "is" Love, but only enters into the communion Love, and is allowed to enter into this communion by the ineffable, unfathomable, unthinkable humility of God . . .

> From the point of view of the Hypostasis of the Father, Sophia is the ideal substance, the foundation of creation, the power or force of its being. If we turn to the Hypostasis of the Word, then Sophia is the reason of creation, its meaning, truth or justice. And lastly, from the point of view of the Hypostasis of the Spirit, we find in Sophia the

---

[1] Anonymous, *Meditations on the Tarot: A Journey into Christian Hermeticism*, R. Powell, trans. (Rockport, MA: Element books, 1993).

spirituality of creation, its holiness, purity and immaculateness, i.e., its beauty.[2]

For Florensky Sophia is an exalted being, the first being of the creation, who has a special, intimate relationship with the Holy Trinity. At the beginning of the creation, according to Florensky, Sophia was brought forth from the womb of the Trinity as the Divine Plan underlying creation—analogous to an architect drawing up a plan before beginning the work of building. Sophia, as the pinnacle of creation, is able to go in and out of the Trinity, having a unique relationship with each Person of the Trinity. In her relationship with the Father, she is "the ideal substance, the foundation of creation, the power or force of its being." In relation to the Son she is "the reason of creation, its meaning, truth or justice." And in connection with the Holy Spirit, she is the spirituality of the creation, its holiness, purity and immaculateness, i.e., its beauty." These are the *three aspects of Sophia* according to Florensky.

The more recent Sophiological perspective of the anonymous author extends this to consider these three aspects more deeply. He refers to these three aspects collectively as the "Sophianic Trinity" and names them individually "Mother, Daughter and Holy Soul."[3] Further, he draws a parallel between the Sophianic Trinity and the Holy Trinity of Father, Son, and Holy Spirit (see figure on page 400). Although he does not explicitly refer to Florensky, the descriptions offered by Florensky apply very well to the Sophianic Trinity. In this case, the Mother, as the counterpart to the Father, is "the ideal substance, the foundation of creation, the power or force of its being." The Daughter, as the counterpart to the Son, is "the reason of creation, its meaning, truth or justice." And the Holy Soul, as the feminine counterpart to the Holy Spirit, is "the spirituality of the creation, its holiness, purity and immaculateness, i.e., its beauty."[4]

---

[2] *Stolp i utverzhdenie istiny* [*The Pillar and Foundation of Truth*] (Moscow, 1914), p. 349; based on the translation in Robert Slesinski, *Pavel Florensky: A Metaphysics of Love* (Crestwood, NY: St. Vladimir's Seminary Press, 1984), pp. 180–181.

[3] Anonymous, *Meditations on the Tarot*, pp. 547–552.

[4] Robert Slesinski, *Pavel Florensky: A Metaphysics of Love*, pp. 180–181.

Further, in his book, *Covenant of the Heart*, Valentin Tomberg alludes to the Mother, Daughter, and Holy Soul, and indicates their relationship to the Father, Son and Holy Spirit as follows (see also figure below):

> Creation, i.e., the world, thanks its existence to the love of the eternal Father and the love of the eternal Mother. Out of their union proceeds—"as Light from Light, God from God"—the Son and the Daughter, designated as the holy "king" and "queen," who together direct the work of creation, leading it to ever further stages of interiorization or spiritualization. However, the dimension of interiorization or spiritualization is not characterized by becoming (coming into existence) and sustaining whatever comes into existence. Rather it stands in the sign of blessing which is brought about by the spiritualizing (making holy) of the Holy Spirit, who proceeds from the Father and the Son. Corresponding to the Holy Spirit is the immanent Presence of the spiritualizing blessing—called the "Holy Soul," "the Virgin of Israel," or the "soul of the community of Israel."[5]

The anonymous author represents the interweaving of the two Trinities symbolically with the two triangles as shown in the figure below.

Father—Son—Holy Spirit   *Mother—Daughter—Holy Soul*

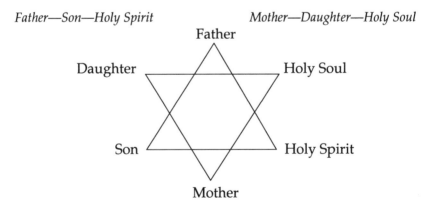

---

[5] Valentin Tomberg, *Covenant of the Heart*, J. Morgante and R. Powell, trans. (Rockport, MA: Element Books, 1993), p. 187.

These two triangles reveal schematically the interweaving of the two Trinities, the totality of which the anonymous author designates as the "bi-polar Trinity" or the "luminous Holy Trinity." In *Meditations on the Tarot: A Journey into Christian Hermeticism* he writes:

> These two triangles of the luminous Holy Trinity are revealed in the work of redemption accomplished through Jesus Christ and conceived through Mary Sophia. Jesus Christ is its agent; Mary Sophia is its luminous reaction. The two triangles reveal the luminous Holy Trinity in the work of creation accomplished by the creative Word and animated by the "yes" of Wisdom-Sophia.[6]

The Sophianic Trinity could be referred to as the "Holy Trinosophia," complementary to the Holy Trinity.[7] In support of this Sophiological perspective of the Holy Trinosophia of Mother, Daughter and Holy Soul, the anonymous author draws attention to the ancient mystery cult of Demeter (Earth Mother) and Persephone (her Daughter) celebrated at Eleusis near Athens, the city that was under the patronage of Athena (an aspect of the Holy Soul, according to the anonymous author). Through the myth of Demeter and Persephone at least two aspects of the Holy Trinosophia were evident to the Greeks. Further, the anonymous author identifies the Shekinah of Hebrew tradition as an aspect of the Holy Soul, in this instance ensouling the community of Israel. Here it is not possible to go into this in more detail. The reader is referred to *Meditations on the Tarot* for further elucidation. It suffices to say that this perspective of the Sophianic Trinity offers a basis for Sophiology comparable in scope and grandeur to the Christian theological teaching of the Holy Trinity. Yet how does this relate to Father Thomas Schipflinger's work *Sophia Mary* and its central thesis of the incarnation of Sophia in the Virgin Mary?

---

[6] Anonymous, *Meditations on the Tarot*, p. 548.
[7] Robert Powell, *Chronide of the Living Christ: The Most Holy Trinosophia* (Hudson, NY: Anthroposophic Press, 1997).

Let us consider this question against the background of the Sophianic Trinity described in *Meditations on the Tarot*. "Just as the Word became flesh in Jesus Christ, so did the Bath-Kol, the Daughter of the Voice, become flesh in Mary Sophia."[8] The implication here is that there is an analogy between the incarnation of the Second Person of the Holy Trinity—the Son (Word)—to become flesh in Jesus Christ, and the incarnation of the Daughter (Wisdom-Sophia) to take on flesh in Mary Sophia. This analogy is summarized in the figure below.

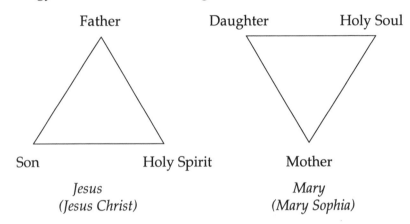

Father   Daughter   Holy Soul

Son   Holy Spirit   Mother

Jesus   *Mary*
(*Jesus Christ*)   (*Mary Sophia*)

Through the rise of Christianity the mysteries of the Divine Feminine became veiled. The mystery center of Demeter at Eleusis, and other such centers (e.g., of Artemis at Ephesus) became closed. Yet now, in the 20th century, the Divine Feminine side of existence is coming back into view again, becoming resurrected in human consciousness. The Sophiological perspective of the Mother, Daughter, and Holy Soul is one aspect of this re-emergence of the mysteries of the Eternal Feminine. Another is the relationship of Sophia to the Virgin Mary, which is the focus of attention in Father Thomas Schipflinger's book. It is thanks to him—through this book—that the mystery of the incarnation of Sophia in Mary, having remained veiled for well nigh two thousand years, is uncovered. May this work serve as a stimulus to its readers to enter into contemplation of this profound mystery into which further research needs to be done. We find only indi-

---

[8] Anonymous, *Meditations on the Tarot*, p. 549.

rect traces of this mystery in the Bible, such as the words, "Afterward did she appear on earth" *(Baruch 3:37).* Through the Sophia tradition, traced in detail by Father Thomas Schipflinger, something of this mystery is transmitted. By tracing it in this book, he has rendered a great service to all seekers of Divine Wisdom.

Robert A. Powell

Robert Powell is Founder of the Sophia Foundation of North America and author of *Chronicle of the Living Christ, The Most Holy Trinosophia,* and *Divine Sophia: Holy Wisdom.*

Appendix 1

Chronological Survey of Jewish History and the Appearance of the Wisdom Books

YEARS	BOOKS	HISTORICAL TIME
ca. 1900–1700 B.C.E.		Time of the Patriarchs Abraham, Isaac and Jacob.
ca. 1700 B.C.E.		Jacob moves with his family to Egypt.
ca. 1250 B.C.E.		Exodus from Israel under Moses, life in the wilderness, proclamation of the Ten Commandments.
ca. 1200 B.C.E.		Settlement in Canaa under Joshua.
ca. 1200–1020 B.C.E.		The time of the Judges (Samuel).
1020–931 B.C.E.		The kings Saul, David and Solomon.
from 931 B.C.E.	*Proverbs*	First collection of *Proverbs*. Division of the Kingdom (Northern Kingdom—Samaria, Southern Kingdom—Judea).

YEARS	BOOKS	HISTORICAL TIME
ca. 722 B.C.E.		Samaria conquered by Assyria (Sargon II); decline of the Northern Kingdom.
ca. 586 B.C.E.		Jerusalem conquered by Babylon (Nebuchadnezzar), decline of the Southern Kingdom.
586–538 B.C.E.		Babylonian captivity.
538 B.C.E.		Edict of Cyrus, end of Babylonian captivity.
from 538 B.C.E.		Gradual return, reconstruction, restoration.
ca. 400 B.C.E.	*Job*	Final composition of the *Book of Job* falls in the time after the Babylonian exile, written around 400.
428–348 B.C.E.		Plato.
384—322 B.C.E.		Aristotle (both Plato and Aristotle prepared the foundations of Hellenism).
ca. 330 B.C.E.	*Proverbs*	Final composition of the *Book of Proverbs*.
323 B.C.E.		Death of Alexander the Great; the Diadochi take possession of his inheritance: Ptolemy in Egypt, to whom Palestine also belongs, and Seleucus in Syria and Mesopotamia, where Hellenism quickly spreads.
ca. 260 B.C.E.	*Ecclesiastes*	Appearance of the *Book of Ecclesiastes*.
ca. 250 B.C.E.		Beginning of the translation of the Holy Scriptures from Hebrew into Greek (*Septuagint*) in Alexandria.

YEARS	BOOKS	HISTORICAL TIME
198 B.C.E.		Palestine comes under the rule of the Seleucids, who rob and oppress the Jews.
ca. 180 B.C.E.	*Ecclesiasticus*	Sirach (Sira) writes the original Hebrew text of the *Book of Ecclesiasticus*, which his nephew, Jesus Sirach, translates into Greek fifty years later (around 130).
181–145 B.C.E.		Aristobulus, Jewish and Hellenistic philosopher in Alexandria.
167 B.C.E.		Revolt of the Maccabees.
ca. 110 B.C.E.	*Wisdom*	Appearance of the *Book of Wisdom* (composed in Greek).
from 100 B.C.E.		Formation of the religious groups Essenes, Pharisees, and Sadducees.
from 64 B.C.E.		Syria becomes a Roman province; Roman influence in Palestine.
73 B.C.E.–4 C.E.		Herod I; cruel murder of relatives; Slaughter of the Innocents.
13 B.C.E.–45 C.E.		Philo of Alexandria, Jewish and Hellenistic philosopher.

Appendix II

Wisdom Book
Readings in
Marian Liturgies[1]

The primary readings are from Proverbs 8,22–35 and Ecclesiasticus 24,1–31.

In the lectionary appearing after the liturgical reforms of 1969, almost all of these readings were replaced. Only Proverbs 8,22–31 and Ecclesiasticus 24,1–4 and 8–12 continue to be listed as readings which can be chosen.

It is unfortunate that the Wisdom Book readings were eliminated and replaced by readings hardly related to the particular feast. The change took place in the 1960s when Marian devotion became deemphasized. The specific reason for the change is not clear. In effect, a custom was broken that had held sway for hundreds of years, making the relationship between Mariology and Sophia even less visible.

The Feast of the Immaculate Conception: in Vigilia: Ecclus. 24,23–31; in Festo: Prov. 8,22–35.

---

[1] From: *Missale Romanum*, XIX edition,"*Das Lectionarium zu den Festen der Allerseligsten Jungfrau*" (Regensberg: Verlag Pustet, 1936); *Das Meßbuch der heiligen Kirche*, "Das Lectionarium zu den Festen der Allerseligsten Jungfrau" (Freiburg: Herder Verlag, 1953).

The Feast of Our Lady's Appearance in Lourdes (February 11): Ecclus. 44,1–15.

The Feast of Our Lady of the Snows (Dedication of St. Mary Major) (August 5): Ecclus. 24,14–16.

The Feast of Our Lady of Mt. Carmel (July 16): Ecclus. 24,23–31.

The Feast of Mary's Assumption into Heaven (August 15). In Vigilia: Ecclus. 24,23–31. In Festo: Ecclus. 24,11–13 and 15–20.

The Feast of Mary's Birth (September 8): Prov. 8,22–35.

The Feast of the Holy Name of Mary (September 12): Ecclus. 24,23–31.

The Feast of the Holy Rosary (October 7): Prov. 8,22–24 and 32–35.

The Feast of Mary Mother of God (October 11): Ecclus. 24,23–31.

The Feast of Mary's Presentation (November 21): Ecclus. 24,14–16. On Saturdays III–V: Ecclus. 14–16.

Special Votive Masses In Mary's Honor:

The Feast of the Holy House of Loreto (December 10): Ecclus. 24,11–13 and 15–20.

The Feast of Mary's Engagement to Joseph (January 23): Prov. 8,22–35.

The Feast of Our Lady Help of Christians (May 24): Ecclus. 24,22–31.

The Feast of Our Lady Mother of Honorable Love (May 31): Ecclus. 24,22–31.

The Feast of Our Lady of Perpetual Help (June 27): Ecclus. 24,23–31.

The Feast of Our Lady Refuge of Sinners (August 13): Ecclus. 24,14–16.

The Feast of Our Lady Healer of the Sick (Saturday before the last Sunday in August): Prov. 8,22–35.

The Feast of Our Lady Mother of Divine Providence (Saturday before the third Sunday in November): Ecclus. 24,1 and 4–13.

The Feast of Our Lady Mother of the Good Shepherd (September 3): Ecclus. 24,14–16 (commune).

The Feast of the Mother of Good Counsel (April 26): Ecclus. 24,23–31.

Appendix III

Overview of Greek Philosophy before the Common Era

Greek philosophy before the common era provided the structure for Hellenistic culture and allowed it to make inroads into Western Asia and Europe. Platonic and Neo-Platonic teachings were familiar to the Greek and Roman Church Fathers and exerted a great influence on Christianity.

Hellenistic culture (along with Egyptian, Babylonian, Persian, and Indian teachings) all definitively influenced the reception of Jewish belief in Yahweh and how it was portrayed (though their influence should not be over-emphasized). The influence of Greek philosophy on the Book of Wisdom is readily apparent.

In turn the inception of Greek philosophy and its further development was influenced by Egyptian teachings.

Year	Philosopher
624–545 B.C.E.	*Thales of Milet*: Water is the primary substance of all things.
580–500 B.C.E.	*Pythagoras*: Number is the essence of things; the world is a cosmos; migration of souls.
535–465 B.C.E.	*Heraclitus*: Everything is in constant flux ('panta rhei' – everything flows); things appear in opposites; everything is guided by a World Law or Logos.
469–399 B.C.E.	*Socrates*: Induction is the means of knowledge and forming concepts; knowledge leads to morality, which is the goal of humanity; sentenced to death.
427–347 B.C.E.	*Plato*: Pupil of Socrates, influenced by Pythagoras; God is the highest idea of everything good and beautiful which is an absolute unity; the world is formed into the cosmos out of eternal matter by a World Builder, the Demiourgus (Nous, Logos) and is enlivened by a World Soul (Sophia, Idea of ideas); the soul of the human being is also an "Idea" which comes from the world beyond; in this world the soul is enclosed in a body; by means of a good life, the soul returns again into the world beyond.
384–322 B.C.E.	*Aristotle*: Pupil of Plato, tutor of Alexander the Great; we do not know by knowing the Ideas in the world beyond, but by knowing the forms contained in things through comprehension of the senses and reasoned abstraction; things consist of matter (hyle) and form (morphe); this form is also the thing's inner goal of existence (telos, thus en-tel-echia); God is not the creator but sets everything in motion.
336–264 B.C.E.	*Zeno*: Founder of Stoicism; emphasized the ethical side of philosophy; the ideal human being is wise and lives according to nature, rules the passions, endures suffering in a composed manner and experiences happiness by being virtuous; God is seen pantheistically as a kind of World Soul; all human beings are equal (cosmo-political universalism).

Year	Philosopher
341–271 B.C.E.	*Epicurus*: Founder of a sensual ethics; fulfillment of desire is the highest goal of humanity; hedonism.
360–270 B.C.E.	*Pyrrho*: Founder of methodical skepticism; human beings cannot know things.
180–150 B.C.E.	*Aristobulus*: a Jew who attempted to prove the dependence of Greek philosophy on the Bible.
13 B.C.E.–45 C.E.	*Philo of Alexandria*: attempted to create a synthesis between Hellenism and Judaism.

Appendix IV

The Litany of Loreto and the Akathist Hymn

The invocations of the Litany Of Loreto[1] (also known as the Litany Of The Blessed Virgin Mary)[2] are as follows:

Holy Mother of God
Holy Virgin of Virgins
Mother of Christ
Mother of Divine Grace
Mother Most Pure
Mother Most Chaste
Mother Inviolate
Mother Undefiled
Mother Most Amiable
    (Loveable)[3]
Mother Most Admirable
Mother of Good Counsel
Mother of Our Creator
Mother of Our Savior

Virgin Most Prudent
Virgin Most Venerable
Virgin Most Renowned
Virgin Most Powerful
Virgin Most Merciful
Virgin Most Faithful
Mirror of Justice
Seat of Wisdom
Cause of Our Joy
Spiritual Vessel
Vessel of Honor
Singular Vessel
    of Devotion
Mystical Rose

---

[1] From: Richard Klavier, O.S.C., *The Litany Of Loreto* (St. Louis/London: B. Herder, 1954).
[2] Pamela Moran, ed., *A Marian Prayer Book* (Ann Arbor: Servant Publications, 1991), p. 253.
[3] Ibid., p. 253.

Tower of David
Tower of Ivory
House of Gold
Ark of the Covenant
Gate of Heaven
Morning Star
Health of the Sick
Refuge of Sinners
Comfort of the Afflicted
Help of Christians
Queen of Angels
Queen of Patriarchs

Queen of Prophets
Queen of Apostles
Queen of Martyrs
Queen of Confessors
Queen of Virgins
Queen of All Saints
Queen Conceived without
    Original Sin
Queen Assumed into Heaven
Queen of the Most
    Holy Rosary
Queen of Peace

Among the many invocations of the Akathist Hymn[4] are the following:

It is truly worthy to bless you, the Theotokos, the ever blessed and most pure and mother of our God. More honorable than the Cherubim, and beyond compare more glorious than the Seraphim (page 7).

O animate book of Christ, sealed by the Spirit (page 8).

Virgin Bride of God . . . the palace of the only King . . . fiery throne of the Sovereign of all (page 8).

Rejoice, living table which has held the bread of life . . . never empty font of living water (page 8–9).

Rejoice, rich mountain flowing with the milk of the Spirit. Rejoice, lamp and golden jar containing the manna which sweetens the senses of the devout (page 9).

More exalted than the heavens, rejoice, you who carried the earth's foundation painlessly in your womb (page 10).

O incomprehensible depth and ineffable height . . . (page 10).

---

[4] *The Akathist Hymn and Small Compline*, N. Michael Vaporis and Evie Zachariades-Holmberg, trans. (Brookline, MA: Holy Cross Orthodox Press, 1992), p. 7. The material that follows is from the same volume.

Rejoice city of the Great King . . . O unquarried mountain and unfathomable depth (page 11).

O unconsumed bush and shining cloud that overshadows without ceasing the faithful (page 12).

Rejoice, scroll on which, O pure one, the Word was inscribed by the Father's finger (page 13).

Rejoice, Mistress of the world . . . (page 15).

Rejoice, initiate of ineffable counsel . . . (page 17).

. . . rejoice, tender love that defeats every longing . . . (page 23).

Rejoice, bringer of opposites to harmony . . . (page 23).

Rejoice, vessel of God's wisdom; rejoice, storehouse of God's providence (page 24).

. . . rejoice, bridesmaid of souls that are holy (page 25).

Rejoice, ray of the spiritual Sun; rejoice, beam of the unsetting luster;

Rejoice, lightning completely illuminating souls; rejoice, thunder that stuns the enemies (page 26).

Rejoice, tabernacle of God the Logos; rejoice, holy one, holier than the holies;

Rejoice, ark that was gilt by the Spirit; rejoice, inexhaustible treasure of life (page 27).

Rejoice, the Church's unshakable tower; rejoice, the kingdom's unassailable fortress. Rejoice, through whom trophies of victory are raised; rejoice, through whom enemies are defeated (page 27).

✦

Appendix V

The Various Dimensions of Wisdom-Sophia

[Compiled by the author and translator.]

The many contributions in this book describe Sophia in various, and in some cases, seemingly contradictory ways. Below is an attempt at summarizing some of the many ways in which She is depicted.

1. Sophia in relation to the Father aspect of God
    A) She is Yahweh's Amon or Darling (Prov. 8,30) who shares the throne (Wisd. 9,4);
    B) She is the Mother who together with the Father gives birth to the Logos (chap. 2, Philo);
    C) As the "Schekinah," She is God's partner in the *Hieros Gamos* or Sacred Marriage (chap. 9, Cabala);
    D) As *Science-Wisdom* the Mother, She is the polar partner to the Will of the Divine Nature who together with it bears the "Word of Life" (chap. 11, Boehme);
    E) Understood as a created being, She is the Father's Daughter (chap. 15, Speransky, Bulgakov).

2. Sophia in relation to the Logos/Son aspect of God
    A) She is the Logos and uncreated (chap. 4, Theodoret, Origen, John of Damascus, Epiphanius, Methodius, Sophronius, Athanasius; chap. 5, Augustine; chap. 12, Arnold; chap. 15, Florenski).

B) She is the Logos but created (chap. 4, Arius).

C) She is the Bride of the Logos (chap. 15, Speransky, Florenski, Bulgakov)

D) She is the Sister (and Bride) of the Logos (chap 15, Speransky).

3. Sophia in relation to the Holy Spirit aspect of God

A) She is the uncreated Holy Spirit (chap. 4, Theophilus of Antioch, Irenaeus; chap. 12, Arnold).

B) Understood as created She is the Image (reflection) of the Holy Spirit (chap. 15, Speransky, Florenski, Bulgakov).

4. Sophia in relation to the entire Trinity

A) She is *Ousia*, the life in common of the Trinity (chap. 15, Bulgakov).

5. Sophia as God's Dwelling

A) Understood as created, She is the City and House of God, Mother Jerusalem and Bride Zion (chap. 5, Augustine).

B) Understood as created, She is God's presence and the community of Israel (chap. 9, Cabala).

6. Sophia in relation to creation

A) She is the beginning or origin of creation who works together with God in all subsequent creation (Old Testament Wisdom Books).

B) She is the "Idea of the ideas" or "World Soul" who contains and sustains all of creation (chap. 2, Greek philosophy and Philo; chap. 9, Cabala; chap. 11, Boehme; chap. 13, Louis-Claude de Saint Martin; chap. 15, Soloviev, Speransky, Florenski; chap. 18, Teilhard de Chardin).

C) She is ideal creation (chap. 4, Augustine; chap. 13, Louis-Claude de Saint Martin; chap. 15, Soloviev, Florenski).

D) She is the beginning and entelechy or goal of creation (chap. 18, Teilhard de Chardin).

7. Sophia in relation to humanity

A) She is the Torah or Law (Ecclus. 24,23; Bar. 4,1).

B) She teaches, protects and guides humanity (Old Testament Wisdom Books; chap. 11, Boehme; chap. 12, Arnold; chap. 13, Leade, Gichtel, Louis-Claude de Saint Martin, Wirz).

C) She is the principle of perfection and wholeness in the human being (chap. 13, Leade, Wirz; chap. 15, Soloviev, Florenski; chap. 18, Teilhard de Chardin).

8. Sophia in relation to Mary and the Church
A) She is incarnated in or has a special relationship to Mary (chap. 11, Boehme; chap. 12, Arnold; chap. 13, Wirz; chap. 15, Florenski, Bulgakov; chap. 18, Teilhard de Chardin).
B) She is the Church or represents the Church through Mary (chap. 15, Florenski, Bulgakov; chap. 18, Teilhard de Chardin).

Some of the variety in the viewpoints expressed above derives from the identification of Sophia with the Logos among many of the Church Fathers (which has been described in early chapters) and Augustine's subsequent distinction between Uncreated and Created Sophia. In addition to Augustine, this distinction is visible in the thought of Boehme, Arnold, Florenski and Bulgakov.

The point of view expressed in this book is that Sophia as She is described in the Old Testament is created (as indicated by Prov. 8,22). She is the beginning of creation, the Soul of the World and creation's final goal, i.e. *Omegarcha*. She is the image of the maternal Holy Spirit, which is the feminine principle of the Holy Trinity. She incarnated in Mary and became the Mother of Jesus Christ and the Mother of the Church in order to assist the Logos with the plan of salvation for humanity and the world (just as She had assisted with the world's creation).

Appendix VI

St. Francis of Assisi's Canticle of the Creatures (Canticle to Brother Sun)

(commentary by Robert Powell)

St. Francis of Assisi's "Canticle of the Creatures" is a hymn to God and to the Divine Sophia, the Holy Wisdom of creation, manifest in the sun, moon, and stars, and in the elements of fire, air, water, and earth, and in the world of nature, the garment of Mother Earth. It embodies the love of Sophia as the Light of all creation, of which the most powerful outer symbol is the sun, followed by the bright and precious moon and stars adorning the heavens. Here St. Francis of Assisi emerges as a Sophian spirit of the first magnitude in the Christian tradition. This is now beginning to be recognized by the Franciscans themselves, who, in September 1995, held a conference at Assisi on "St. Francis and the Divine Sophia." Although St. Francis did not use the word "Sophia," his love of the Divine in nature is intrinsically Sophian. A Sophian "nature mysticism" comes to expression in the "Canticle of the Creatures," indicating that St. Francis was attuned to the Divine Wisdom weaving through the cosmos and throughout the world of nature. In St. Francis we see something of a fulfillment of the words of St. Paul:

> We know that the whole creation has been groaning in travail together until now . . . For the creation waits with eager longing for the revealing of the sons of God [through whom] . . . the cre-

ation itself will be set free from its bondage to decay and obtain the glorious liberty of the children of God (Rom. 8,19–22).

St. Francis was a "son of God" whose very presence served to liberate the creation from its bondage to decay. This freeing from bondage was the essence of events in his life, such as his sermon to the birds and his taming of the wolf. In this respect St. Francis serves as a forerunner, a radiant example of a Christian whose sphere of loving, healing, and helping activity was not limited to humanity, but extended to include also the kingdoms of nature. For it is not only humanity, but also the kingdoms of nature which await redemption. And their redemption will take place through human beings first of all becoming aware of Sophia and then integrating the practice of Sophian spirituality into their lives. Here St. Francis of Assisi's "Canticle of the Creatures" serves as wonderful material for meditation upon the great and holy task of the redemption of Mother Earth and the creation itself—a holy task which, although mentioned by St. Paul, has remained largely unfulfilled within Christianity until now. It seems likely that this hymn to God and Sophia will become increasingly more relevant now that a worldwide awakening to the Divine Sophia is underway.

Most High, all powerful, all good, Lord!
 All praise is yours, all glory, all honor
 And all blessing.

To you alone, Most High, do they belong.
 No mortal lips are worthy
 To pronounce your name.

All praise be yours, my Lord, through all that you have made,
 And first my lord Brother Sun,
 Who brings the day; and light you give to us through him.

How beautiful is he, how radiant in all his splendor!
 Of you, Most High, he bears the likeness.

All praise be yours, my Lord, through Sisters Moon and Stars,
 In the heavens you have made them,
 Bright and precious and fair.

All praise be yours, my Lord, through Brothers Wind and Air
 All fair and stormy, all the weather's moods,
 By which you cherish all that you have made.

All praise be yours, my Lord, through Sister Water,
　　So useful, lowly, precious and pure.

All praise be yours, my Lord, through Brother Fire,
　　Through whom you brighten up the night,
　　How beautiful is he, how gay! Full of power and strength.

All praise be yours, my Lord, through Sister Earth, our mother,
　　Who feeds us in her sovereignty and produces
　　Various fruit with colored flowers and herbs.

All praise be yours, my Lord, through those who grant pardon
　　For Love of you; through those who endure
　　Sickness and trial.

Happy those who endure in peace,
　　By you, Most High, they will be crowned.

All praise be yours, my Lord, through Sister Death,
　　From whose embrace no mortal can escape.

Woe to those who die in mortal sin!
　　Happy those She finds doing your will!
　　The second death can do no harm to them.

Praise and bless my Lord, and give him thanks,
　　And serve him with great humility.[1]

---

[1] Paul M. Allen & Joan deRis Allen, *Francis of Assisi's Canticle of the Creatures* (New York: Continuum, 1996), pp. 87–88

Glossary

Adelphia (Greek)—Community of brothers and sisters.

Adon (Hebrew)—The Lord of Love.

Aetate nostra (Latin)—The name of the Second Vatican Council's document about the non-Christian religions (*aetate nostra* means "in our time").

Alma Mater (Latin)—The benevolent, nourishing mother.

Alpha (Greek)—The first letter of the Greek alphabet; Omega is the last letter; Alpha and Omega thus signify the beginning and the end.

Amon (Hebrew)—Darling; Amon Yahweh signifies Yahweh's Darling, the honorary title of Chokmah Yahweh, Yahweh's Sophia-Wisdom (Prov.8,30).

Anagoga (Greek)—The feminine leader who is the guide to higher spheres.

Archegetis (Greek)—Female leader, founder.

Artemis—Greek Goddess of nature and birth; (Roman equivalent: Diana, the Goddess of fertility, Mother of the woods and mountains).

Arya (Sanskrit)—Noble: for example, Arya Tara, the Noble Tara; cf. the "Arians."

Athena—Greek Goddess of wisdom and art.

Aurora (Latin)—Dawn; Goddess of dawn (Greek, *Eos*; Sanskrit, *Ushas*).

Bagua (Chinese)—"Ba" means eight; and "gua" holy symbol. These eight holy symbols are the eight primordial powers of being and becoming which form the universe, and preserve life through their constant influence and change.

Bhakti (Sanskrit)—Love, surrender, devotion to a God, for example, Krishna.

Bodhisattva (Sanskrit)—The designation in Mahayana Buddhism for someone who is destined to become a Buddha, but who renounces the individual bliss of Nirvana in order to be reborn and work for the salvation of human beings. Bodhisattva literally means "enlightenment being" (*Bodhi* = enlightenment; *sattva* = being).

Buddha (Sanskrit)—The Awakened One. The founder of Buddhist teaching and the Buddhist community. He was born around the middle of the sixth century B.C.E. in Kapilavasthu (in today's Nepal) in a royal family of Shakya. His contemporaries later called him Gautama (his family name) the ascetic. "Buddha" is the honorary title that he received after his enlightenment, from which comes the name of his teaching and community. Another name for Buddha is Siddhartha (Sanskrit), meaning "the one who has reached the goal."

Buddhism—The teaching and community of the Buddha and his pupils and followers. In the course of time, three distinct groups have formed: Hinayana, Mahayana and Vajrayana Buddhism. Hinayana (the so-called "lesser vehicle" and Buddhism's oldest form) is the form practiced in Sri Lanka (Ceylon), Burma, Thailand, Cambodia, Laos, and Vietnam. Mahayana Buddhism (the "greater vehicle") is practiced particularly in Tibet, China, and Japan; and Vajrayana Buddhism (the "diamond vehicle") primarily in Tibet.

Cabala (Hebrew)—Jewish esoteric and mystical wisdom teaching. (Also spelled Kabbalah, Kabalah, Qabalah.)

catholic (Greek)—Combination of *kata holon*: in its entirety, general, univeral, all-encompassing; for example, the Catholic Church.

Chaitanya—Hindu holy man and mystic (1486–1534) whose special emphasis was the practice of Bhakti (love) to Krishna and Radha.

Chokmah (Hebrew)—Wisdom, Sophia; *pluralis majestatis:* Chokmot. Chokmah (Chokmot) Yahweh: Yahweh's Wisdom, who is described and revealed in the Wisdom Books of the Old Testament (especially Proverbs, Ecclesiasticus, and the Book of Wisdom).

Confusius (Kongzi, Kung Tse; 551–479 B.C.E.). Chinese wise man, moral teacher and philosopher; editor of the I Ching; his central teaching is correct behavior within society and state. He opposed the moral decay of his times with the ideal of the "noble" (Jun-zi). Confusianism, the result of his teachings, was the official state philosophy of China for centuries.

Cor (Latin)—Heart.

cosmos (Greek)—The universe, the ordered world, decoration (adj. form: cosmic).

Demeter (Greek)—Greek Mother Goddess of the earth and fertility; actual meaning: "Earth" (*de* or *ge* means earth, and *meter* means mother).

Devi (Sanskrit)—Goddess; for example Maha Devi, the Great Goddess, and a Mother Goddess like Kali and Durga.

Ecclesia (Greek)—Church; ecclesiology: church teaching;

ecclesiological—Concerning the teaching about the church.

ecumenism (Greek)—Movement which strives for unity and harmony among all Christians and all people who believe in God.

Entelechy (Greek)—An active power in the organism that is the motivating and directing force behind development and perfection; life principle, principle of development and perfection.

Eos (Greek)—Dawn, Goddess of dawn (Latin, Aurora; Sanskrit, Ushas).

Exegesis (Greek)—Interpretation and explanation of Holy Scripture.

Fiat (Latin)—"May it be or come to pass"; Mary's answer to the Angel at the Annunciation: "May it be unto me according to your word (fiat mihi)."

Gautama (Gotama, Sanskrit, and Pali)—Buddha's surname; the family Gautama lived at that time in northwestern India (today's Nepal).

Gnosis (Greek)—Knowledge; has the same root as "know," German *kennen* and *koennen*, and Sanskrit *jna* (*prajna*).

Gnostic—Adj. form of Gnosis.

Gnosticism—Religious orientation which overemphasizes subjective gnosis and tries to systematize it by means of extravagant speculation.

Gopi (Sanskrit)—Female shepherd, symbolic figure for the soul which loves and seeks Krishna.

Hellenistic—From Hellas (Greece); designation for that form of Greek culture which merged with Oriental cultures after the time of Alexander the Great. Hellenism exerted a great influence and became a world culture in the Roman and Near Eastern worlds.

hexagram (Greek)—Designation for the six columnar signs of the I Ching. They consist of two trigrams which outline the most important conditions and situations of human life. There are sixty-four in all (see *bagua*).

hierogamy (Greek)—Sacred matrimony, condition of sacred matrimony.

Hieros Gamos (Greek)—Sacred Marriage.

Hinayana—See Buddhism.

Hinduism—The religion which is still practiced today in India and several lands in Southeast Asia; Hinduism's highest gods are Brahma, Vishnu and Shiva. Its practices and teaching come from the ancient Vedas, Upanishads, and Puranas, as well as the Mahabharata Epic and the Ramayana; particular teachings: the transmigration of souls, and karma (recompense for deeds). Hinduism's worldview is pantheistic but also includes theism. Its teaching on Shakti or feminine power, which is worshipped in Shaktiism, is of particular interest. Hinduism has been stimulated and rejuvenated by its contact with Christianity.

I Ching (Chinese; other written forms: *I Ging, I King, Yi Jing*)—The Book of Changes, a classical wisdom book and oracle; composed from ancient sources during the time of King Wen (12th and 11th centuries B.C.E.) and enlarged and commented upon by Confusius (551–469 B.C.E.). The I Ching explains its 64 hexagrams, is used to provide guidance to questions, and represents a system of Chinese nature philosophy and ethics.

icon (Greek)—Sacred image, especially Greek or Russian, that mysteriously effects the presence of what is portrayed.

immanent (Latin)—Working within, existing within, resting within; antonym—transcendent.

immanence (Latin)—Restricted to being in the inner realm; antonym—transcendence.

Ishtar (Accadian)—Goddess of love, life, fertility, and battle.

Isis (Egyptian)—Egyptian Goddess of life, Mother Goddess, Mistress of the Cosmos, wife of Osiris, mother of Horus; brings blessing and fertility.

Jesus (Hebrew–Greek)—Greek transcription of the Hebrew *Jeschua* or *Jehoschua*, meaning "Yahweh is help."

Kali—Hindu Mother Goddess, Shiva's Shakti; also called the Mahadevi, the Great Goddess.

Krishna (Sanskrit, meaning "the Dark One")—Hindu God of love, incarnation of Vishnu, usually depicted as playing a flute or as Govinda, the cow shepherd; highly revered along with Radha, His lover, who symbolically represents all souls that love God.

Lady of All Nations—According to the visionary Ida Peerdeman, the title with which Mary is to be honored in the future, referred to by Mary during the apparitions that took place in Amsterdam (1945–1959). This title is extraordinarily profound and relevant today when the peoples of all nations so urgently desire peace and unity.

Lao Tsu (Chinese; *Laozi*)—Chinese wise man, philosopher and mystic who lived some time before Confusius in the fifth century B.C.E.. He was supposedly an official at the court of Zhou and afterward turned to solitude. At the wish of Yin Xi, the Guardian of the Pass, he put his teaching in book form. Taoism developed into a religion with monks, cloisters, and a community of the faithful.

Lila (Sanskrit)—Game, especially in the cosmic sense, the world creation as the game and dance of God and as a game of love; Krishna plays this game with Radha, His lover; He plays it with all His devout (Bhaktas, Gopis).

Logos (Greek)—Word, sense; the world creating principle in Greek philosophy; the masculine counterpart to Sophia; the name in Christian theology for the Son of God (John 1, 1). The Logos incarnated from Mary; the incarnated Logos is Jesus Christ; Mary is the incarnated Sophia (Wisdom).

Lokeshvara (Sanskrit; *Avalokiteshvara*)—The one who graciously turns his gaze down below, the name of one of the most honored Buddhist Bodhisattvas (Tibetan, Tscheresia).

Loreto—Italian pilgrimage location where according to legend the house of Nazareth was brought by Angels. The Loreto Litany, a series of invocations and glorifications of Mary, was named after Loreto.

Mahayana—See Buddhism.

Malkuth (Hebrew)—Kingdom; the Sephirah, which means Mother Earth; the lower part of Kether on the Sephiroth tree; often equated with the Schekinah.

Mary—The name of the Mother of Jesus. The Hebrew-Aramaic form is Miriam or Mariam. The meaning of the name is not clear. Some interpret it to mean "beautiful one" or "blessed one." As the Mother of Jesus, Mary is the Mother of the incarnated Son of God. She is also understood as incarnated Wisdom (Sophia), from whom the Logos took on flesh and incarnated. Mary is also the primordial cell of the Church and is viewed as the Mother of Humanity and the Lady of All Nations. In connection with Christ understood as the "Omega Point" (Teilhard de Chardin), Sophia Mary can be called the "Omegarcha."

Marian—Related to Mary, the Mother of God.

Mariology—Teaching about Mary and Her relationships to God, Christ, the Church, humanity, and the world.

Nirvana (Sanskrit)—Literally: extinguishing a fire or a lamp whose fuel has been used up. In Hinayana Buddhism: cessation of the cycle of rebirth; in Mahayana Buddhism: the bliss of redemption, participation in the pure, luminous, and absolute Buddhahood.

Orante (Latin)—The one who prays; a figure who is depicted praying with both arms outstretched.

Parvati (Sanskrit)—Daughter of the mountain; the wife of Shiva, daughter of Himalaya; considered mild and good in contrast to Kali or Durga.

Polypoikilos Sophia (Greek)—Wisdom in a variety of forms (Eph. 3,10).

Prajna (Sanskrit)—Wisdom, profound knowledge; a term used primarily in Buddhist philosophy and spirituality where wisdom is viewed as the highest kind of understanding (*jna* and *bodhi*) and knowledge (*vidya*). *Prajna* is also called Buddha's female complement (not Shakti as in Hinduism).

Prajna Paramita (Sanskrit)—Transcendental Wisdom (literally, "which has gone beyond").

Prakriti (Sanskrit)—Creative energy, nature, the primordial feminine; counterpart to Purusha.

Purusha (Sanskrit)—the primordial human being, the original masculine element; counterpart to Prakriti.

Omega Point "Omega" is the last letter of the Greek alphabet and symbolizes the end, perfection, and fullness; an expression coined by Teilhard de Chardin for the fullness of Christ at the end of the world through the inclusion of the entire universe.

Radha (Sanskrit)—Krishna's beloved; symbolic representation for the soul's devotional, surrendering and faithful love of Krishna (the root *radh* means surrender, satisfy, be pleasing, make joyful, fulfill).

Ruach (Hebrew)—Spirit, wind, breath, intellect, soul. Ruach Yahweh means the Spirit of God. The gender of Ruach is feminine.

Sarasvati (Sanskrit)—Hindu Goddess of Wisdom, speech, literature, art and music; Vishnu's wife.

Schekinah (Hebrew)—God's presence in the world. In the Cabala the Schekinah was personified and even hypostasized (made into a person). There are similarities between the Schekinah and the Sephiroth Chokmah (Wisdom) and Malkuth (Kingdom).

Sephirah (Hebrew; plural *Sephiroth*)—According to the Cabala, the Sephiroth are the primary dynamic powers of the manifesting Godhead; they are also the transcendent archetypes and divine ideas according to which the world is created and formed. They are the light by which the human being really knows God and creation; and the gates by which the human being enters into the mystery of God. Creation (and the human being) is a mirror image of the God who manifests and reveals Himself in the ten Sephiroth. "En Soph" is the divine, unknowable, ineradicable primordial ground, the "Deus Absconditus" or hidden God. The ten Sephiroth are: Keter (Crown); Chokmah (Wisdom); Binah (Intelligence); Chesed (Mercy); Din or Gebura (Justice or Power); Tipheret (Beauty); Netzach (Victory, Duration); Hod (Glory); Yesod (Foundation); Malkuth (Kingdom). The ten Sephiroth are polar powers but are fully and dynamically harmonious. The ones that are designated with uneven numbers are masculine (Keter, Binah, Gebura, Nezach, Yesod); and the even-numbered ones are feminine (Chokmah, Chesed, Hod, Tipheret and Malkuth), although some Cabalists hold a different opinion, viewing, for example, Chokmah (Wisdom) as a masculine Sephirah (which is difficult to understand). Pairs of the Sephirah form polar and harmonious unities (Keter and Malkuth, Chokmah and Binah, Chesed and Geburah, Hod and Netzach, Tipheret and Yesod). The tenth Sephirah Malkuth is often identified with the Schekinah.

Shakti (Sanskrit)—Kinetic aspect of the Absolute, the power that creates, fills and enlivens everything; the divine Spouse of Shiva.

Shiva (Sanskrit)—Hindu God, forms the Hindu Trinity together with Vishna and Brahma. The God of the cosmic dance and the God of time, who destroys so that something new can appear. Shiva is called the "friendly One." He also bestows life, does good deeds for humanity, and is the Lord of the animals. His wife is Parvati, the Mahashakti.

Sophia (Greek)—Wisdom, knowledge from the ground of being in its entirety. In the Bible the word Sophia is the Greek translation of the Hebrew word "Chokmah" (pl. Chokmot), meaning Wisdom. In the Wisdom Books of the Old Testament (in particular, Proverbs, Ecclesiasticus, the Book of Wisdom, Job, and Baruch) it is indicated that Wisdom was created before all creation, as the Co-Creator of the cosmos with Yahweh, as the One who shares Yahweh's throne and His Darling. According to some Sophiologists, She is the Bride of the Logos Son of God and, as such, incarnated in Mary, from whom the Logos took on flesh and incarnated as Jesus Christ.

Sophiology (Greek)—The teaching about Sophia-Wisdom.

Sponsa (Latin)—Bride, for example *Sponsa Verbi*, the Bride of the Word, the Bride of the Logos; *Sponsa Christi* means the Bride of Christ.

Sulamith (Hebrew)—The name of the bride in the Song of Songs (7,1), Solomon's beloved, the Queen of Peace, a symbol for Sophia-Mary and the soul.

syncretism (Greek)—Mixing of different religions or philosophical teachings, mostly without an inner unity or genuine synthesis.

Tao (Chinese)—The "way"; in Chinese nature philosophy it later took on the meaning of the primordial principle of being that is ultimately incomprehensible, indeterminable and unrecognizable; "Wu-ming Tao" is the unnameable Tao. With respect to the things of the world, Tao is called "You Ming Tao," the Tao that can be named. Tao is usually thought of in feminine terms, especially in the *Tao Te Ching*, as the primordial Mother of the myriad creatures and the Mother of heaven and earth. Tao manifests itself in the two primordial principles of yin and yang, the masculine and feminine ground of life. Yin and yang are held together and animated through their common origin in the Tao, i.e., through the "Chong Qi" (*Tschung Tschi*, spirit of life, breath, soul, power, actually "flowing breath, spirit of the middle") which is like the Tao and emanates from it.

Tao Te Ching (Chinese; also *Tao Te King, Dao De Ging, Dao De Jing*)—"The Book of Tao and its Power," Taoism's classic book. According to tradition, it was composed by Lao Tsu (Laozi, Laotse, Laoze) who lived in approximately the fifth century B.C.E. The *Tao*

Te Ching encompasses 81 chapters and treats the Tao's being and manner of activity.

Taoism—Chinese nature philosophy (in contrast to Confusianism) which follows the teachings of Lao Tsu and his pupils (particularly Zhuangzi).

Tara (Sanskrit)—Buddhist Prajna. Tara means the one who leads over the ocean of Samsara to the shores of Nirvana on the other side.

Tathagata (Sanskrit)—The one who has gone over, the Buddha who has entered Nirvana; also called the Buddha of Meditation.

Theologoumenon (Greek)—A theological statement resulting from the effort to clarify a particular belief but which is not considered binding as an article of faith.

Torah (Hebrew)—The cosmic order which Yahweh pours out into creation and nature and the law that is given to human beings to be observed. As the cosmic law, the Torah is identified with Chokmah (see: Baruch 4,4).

trigram (Greek)—Symbol composed of three lines or strokes; designation for the Chinese *Bagua* which are composed of three strokes and expresses the primordial ideas, the primordial grounds of being and becoming (see *Bagua*).

Upanishads (Sanskrit)—The texts and teachings of the ancient Indian philosophers (appearing between 600–200 B.C.E.); the individual soul is identified with the universal spirit (Atman).

Vajrayana (Sanskrit)—See Buddhism.

Veda(s) (Sanskrit)—Knowledge; the oldest works of Hindu literature consisting of the Rig-Veda, Sama-Veda, Yajur-Veda and the Atharva-Veda. They appeared between 1500–1000 B.C.E. and contain songs, sacrificial formulas and oaths. The Vedas are the religious and spiritual foundation for later developments in Hinduism. The Brahmanas and Upanishads (secret teaching) commented on the Vedas and enlarged upon them, and the Puranas (tales and legends) popularized them. All religious schools refer to the Vedas and Upanishads.

Viriditas (Latin)—An expression of Hildegard of Bingen which signifies the power of life in human beings and in all living creatures (Latin, *viridum* = green). Viriditas is also the power that brings germination, greening, growth and ripening; it is the fire of life in individual creatures and in the entire cosmos. In personal terms it can be understood as the spirit of life and as Sophia.

Vishnu (Sanskrit)—Hindu God; belongs to the Hindu Trinity (Trimurti) along with Brahma and Shiva. Vishnu is the God of preservation (Shiva is the God of destruction and Brahma the God of creation). Vishnu appeared on the earth as an Avatar in many incarnations. Krishna is one of His most famous incarnations. The followers of Vishnu are called Vishnuites or Vaishnavas.

Yab-Yum (Tibetan)—Father-Mother; father-mother Mudra (position). Many Buddhas and Bodhisattvas are depicted in the so-called Yab-Yum Mudra, in the most inward union which is a symbol of the *Unio Mystica*.

Yahweh (Hebrew)—Name of God which means I am the "I am," the One who is there or near.

Yang (Chinese)—The creative, paternal, masculine, active principle in Chinese nature philosophy. It is expressed and depicted in the upper portion of the Tai Chi symbol and in the four masculine *Guas* of the *Bagua*. Yang is united with yin and actively present in every creature.

Yin (Chinese)—The receptive, maternal, feminine, passive principle in Chinese nature philosophy. It is expressed and depicted by the lower portion of the Tai Chi symbol and in the four feminine *Guas* of the *Bagua*. Yin is united with yang and actively present in every creature. Yin and yang are the two primordial bases of all being and becoming, existing and working in everything. Their source is "Wu-Chi Tao," the "abyss," the ground that is above or below; they manifest in Tai Chi, the phenomenal, primordial ground from which all other creatures come.

Zion (Hebrew)—Jerusalem; actually the mountain upon which Jerusalem is built.

Bibliography

The Akathist Hymn and Small Compline. N. Michael Vaporis and Evie Zachariades-Holmberg, trans. Brookline, MA: Holy Cross Orthodox Press, 1992.

Allen, Paul M. and Joan deRis Allen. *Francis of Assisi's Canticle of the Creatures.* New York: Continuum, 1996.

Apelt, O. *Platons Works.* Leipzig, 1920.

Aquinas, Thomas. *Summa Contra Gentiles.* Taurini: Marietti, 1927.

Arnold, Gottfried. *Das Geheimnis der Goettlichen Sophia* [The Mystery of Divine Sophia]. Leipzig, 1910; facsimile with introduction by Walter Nigg, Stuttgart-Bad Cannstatt: Friedrich Frommann Verlag, 1963.

———. *Unpartheyishche Kirchen und Ketzerhistorie* [An Impartial History of the Church and Heretics]. Schoffheusen: Emanuel and Benedict Hurter, 1740–1742.

Athanasius. *Select Works and Letters.* Peabady, MA: Hendrickson, 1994.

Aurobindo, Sri. *The Integral Yoga: Sri Aurobindo's Teaching and Method of Practice.* Wilmot, WI: Lotus Light, 1993.

———. *The Mother.* Pondicherry: Sri Aurobindo Ashram Trust, 1972, 1989.

Backofen, Rudolf. *Tao-Te-King: Text un Einfuehrung.* Schweiz: Fankhauser, 1949.

Bange, W. *Eckarts Lehre vom Goettlichen und Geschoepflichen Sein*. Limburg: Pallottiner Verlag, 1937.

Bargatzky, Walter. *Das Universum Lebt—Die Aufsehenerregende Hypothese vom Organischen Aufbau des Weltalls*. Munich: Heyne, 1970.

Beky, Gellert. *Die Welt des Tao*. Freiburg/Munich, 1972.

Benz, Ernst *Die Christliche Kabbala*. Zurich: Rhein Verlag, 1958.

———. *Die Vision*. Stuttgart: E. Klett, 1969.

Bertholet, A. *Woerterbuch der Religionen*. Stuttgart: Kroener, 1976.

Beyer, Stephan. *The Cult of Tara*. Berkeley: University of California Press, 1978.

Bible. The Revised English Bible. London: Oxford University Press and Cambridge University Press, 1989.

Bibliotheka Ecclesiae Patrum et Scriptorum. Wein, 1974.

Biblishe Zeitfragen. Munster: 1919. A journal.

Biographie von J. Jacob Wirz, Ein Zeugnis der Nazarener-Gemeinde von der Entwickelung des Reiches Gottes auf Erden. Barmen, 1862.

Biser, Eugen. *Christus und Sophia: Die Neuentdeckung Jesu im Zeichen der Weisheit*. Augsburg: Katholische Academie, 1987.

Boeckler, Alfred. *Deutsche Buchmalerie in Vorgotischer Zeit*. Koenigsteim im Taunus: K. R. Langewiesche, 1976.

Boehme, Jacob. *The Claris or Key*. John Sparrow, trans. London, 1647.

———. *A Description of the Three Principles of the Divine Essence*. John Sparrow, trans. London, 1648.

———. *The First Apologie to Balthazar Tylcken*, John Sparrow, trans. London, 1662.

———. *Incarnation of Jesus Christ*. John Sparrow, trans. London, 1659.

———. *Jacob Boehme Saemtiche Schriften*. Stuttgart: Will-Erich Peukert, 1955.

———. *The Second Apologie to Balthazar Tylcker*, John Sparrow, trans. London, 1661.

———. *The Second Book Concerning the Three Principles of the Divine Essence*. John Sparrow, trans. London, 1648.

———. *The Threefold Life of Man*. John Sparrow, trans. London, 1650.

———. *The Three Principles of the Divine Essence [De Tribus Principis]*. London, 1910.

———. *The Way to Christ [Christosophia]*. John Joseph Stoudt, trans. New York & London: Harper & Brothers, 1947; New York: Paulist Press, 1978.

Boethius. *De Consolatione Philosophiae Libri Quinque*. xlviii. New York: Georg Olms/Lubrecht & Cramer, 1976.

Boff, Leonardo. *The Maternal Face of God: The Feminine and its Religious*

Expressions. Robert R. Barr and John W. Diercksmeier, trans. San Francisco: HarperSanFrancisco, 1987.

Bonaventure. *Breviloquium*. Erwin Essei, trans. St. Louis: Herder, 1947.

Bormann, Karl. *Die Ideen-und Logos lehre Philons von Alexandrian* (dissertation). Cologne, 1955.

Boulgakov, Sergei. *La Sagesse de Dieu, Resumé de Sophiologie*. Constantin Andronikov, trans. Lausanne: L'Age d'Homme, 1983.

Brehier, Emile. *Les Idées Philosophiques et Religieuses de Philon*. Paris: Vrien, 1950.

Bright, John. *Die Geschichte Israels. The History of Israel*. Louisville, KY: Westminster/John Knox, 1981.

Bruno, Giordano. *The Ash Wednesday Supper*. Edward Gosselin and Lawrence S. Lerner, trans. Toronto: University of Toronto Press, 1995.

———. *On the Infinite Universe and Worlds*. Dorothea Wiley Singer, trans. New York: Henry Shuman, 1950.

Bubnow, Nikolai and Hans Ehrenberg. *Ostliches Christentum*. Munich: E. H. Beck, 1925.

Bulgakov, Sergei. *Sophia: The Wisdom of God: An Outline of Sophiology*. Hudson, NY: Lindasfarne, 1977, 1993.

Bulletin des Vatkanischen Sekretariates fur die Nichtchristen. Citta Del Vaticano, 1983–1984.

Capra, Fritjof. *Belonging to the Universe: Explorations on the Frontiers of Science and Spirituality*. San Francisco: HarperSanFrancisco, 1991.

———. *The Tao of Physics: An Exploration of the Parallels between Modern Physics and Eastern Mysticism*. New York: Bantam, 1977.

———. *The Turning Point: Science, Society, and the Rising Culture*. New York: Bantam, 1988.

Cave, Sydny *Hinduism or Christianity*. New York: Harper & Row, 1939.

Claudel, Paul. *Oeuvres Complètes*. Paris: Gallimard, 1950.

Clemens of Alexandria. *Stromata*. John Ferguson, trans. Washington, DC: Catholic University Press, 1991.

Conze, Edward. *Buddhism: Its Essence and Development*. New York: Harper, 1959.

———. *Buddhist Scriptures*. New York: Penguin, 1977.

———. *Buddhist Texts through the Ages*. New York: Harper & Row, 1964.

Cornely, R. *Commentarius in Librum Sapientiae*. Paris: Sumptibus P. Lethielleux, 1910.

Dante. *The Divine Comedy*. Dorothy Sayers and Barbara Reynolds, trans. Baltimore: Penquin, 1962.

Debon, Gunther *Lao Tzu, Tao-Te-King.* Stuttgart: Phillip Reclam, 1978.

Denzinger. Freiburg: Herder, 1962.

Dictionaire de Théologie Catholique. Paris: Letouzeyet Ané, 1930.

Dress. W. *Die Mystik des M. Ficino.* Berlin: W. de Gruyter, 1929.

Eberharter, Andreas. *Das Buch Jesus Sirach.* Bonn: P. Hanstein, 1925.

Echter Bibel. Wurzburg: Echter Verlag, 1959.

Eidlitz, Walthe. *Die Indische Gottesliebe.* Olten: Walter, 1955.

Einiger, Christoph. *Die Schoensten Gebete der Welt.* Munich: Suedwest Verlag, 1964.

Eisenberg, Rabbi Paul. *Alle Meinen Denselben Gott, Lesungen aus dem Heiligen Buechern der Weltreligionen.* Heinz Gstrein, trans. Vienna, 1981.

Emmerich. Anna Katherine. *Leben der heiligen Jungfrau Maria.* Aschaffenburg: Paul Pattloch, 1980.

Emmerich, Anne Catherine. *The Life of the Blessed Virgin Mary.* Michael Palairet, trans. Rockford, IL: Tan Books, 1970.

Endres, Franz Carl and Annemarie Schimmel. *Das Mysterium der Zahl.* Cologne: Diederichs, 1984.

Evans-Wentz, W. Y. *The Tibetan Book of the Dead.* London and New York: Oxford University Press, 1951.

Ficino, Marsilio. *Theologia Platonica* (1559). New York; Georg Olms/Lubrecht & Cramer, 1975.

Field, G. C. *The Philosophy of Plato.* New York: Oxford University Press, 1949.

Flannery, Austin, O. P., ed. *Vatican Council II: The Conciliar and Post Conciliar Documents.* Northport, NY: Costello Publishing Co. 1975.

Florenski, P. *Die Saeule und Grundfeste der Wahrheit.* Constantin Andronikov, trans. Lausanne: L'Age d'Homme, 1975.

———. *La Colonne et le Fondement de la Vérité.* Constantin Andronikov, trans. Lausanne: L'Age d'Homme, 1978.

Franck, Adolphe. *The Kabbalah: The Religious Philosophy of the Hebrews.* New York: Carol Publishing, 1995.

Galland, China. *Longing for Darkness: Tara and the Black Madonna.* New York: Penguin, 1990.

Gebete der Menschheit herausgegeben von Alfonso M. DiNola. Cologne: Inserverlag, 1977.

Gichtel, Johann. *Theosophia Practica.* Agnes Klein, trans. into modern German. Munich: Ansata Verlag, 1979.

Gigon. Olaf. *Untersuchungen zu Heraclit.* Leipzig: Dieterich, 1935.

Glassenapp, Helmuth von. *Die Fuenf Grossen Religionen.* Dusseldorf: 1952.

————. *Der Hinduismus*. Munich: K. Wolff, 1922.

Goodenough, E. R. *An Introduction to Philo*. London: Oxford University Press, 1962.

Gottsberger, Johann. "Die Goettliche Weisheit als Persoenlichkeit im Alten Testament" in *Biblishce Zeitfragen*. Muenster, 1919.

Govinda, Anagarika. *Foundations of Tibetan Mysticism*. York Beach, ME: Samuel Weiser, 1969; London: Rider/Random House, 1969. Original in German: *Grundlagen Tibetischer Mystik*. Zurich: Scherz Verlag, 1955.

Das Grosses Lexikon der Malerei. Braunschweig: Westermann, 1982.

Haag, Herbert. *Bibel-Lexicon*. Einsiedeln: Benzinger, 1956.

Haardt, Robert *Die Gnosis: Wesen und Zeugnisse*. Salzburg: O. Mouler, 1967.

Haas, Adolf. *Teilhard de Chardin Lexikon*. Freiburg: Herder, 1971.

Hamberger, Julius. *Die Lehre des Deutschen Philosophen Jacob Boehme*. Munich: 1844; reprint: Hildesheim: Gerstenberg, 1975.

Hammerich, L. L. *Phillipians 2,6 and P. A. Florenski*. Copenhagen: Munksgaard, 1976.

Handbuch Theologischer Grundbegriffe. Munich: Heinrich Fries, 1962.

Handwoeterbuch for Theologie und Religionswissenschaft. Tübingen: Mohr, 1957.

Hegel, Georg W. *Hegel's Lectures in the History of Philosophy*. Atlantic Highlands, NJ: Humanities, 1994.

Hildegard of Bingen. *Book of Divine Works*. Robert Cunningham, trans. Santa Fe: Bear & Co., 1987.

————. *Scivias*. Mother Columba Hart and Jane Bishop, trans. New York: Paulist Press, 1990.

Hirschberger, Johann. *A Short History of Western Philosophy*. Jeremy Moiser, trans. Guilford, England: Lutterworth Press, 1976.

Hutten, Kurt. *Seher, Grubler, Enthusiasten*. Stuttgart: Quell Verlag der Evan Gessellschaft, 1966.

Internationales Kolloquium Eichstatt, 1981. *Typos, Symbol und Allegorie bei den Oestlichen Vaetern und Ihren Parallelen im Mittellalter*. Regenstatt, 1982.

Jaeger, Werner. *Aristotle: Fundamentals of the History of his Development*, Richard Robinson, trans. Oxford: Clarendon Press, 1955.

Klavier, Richard. *The Litany of Loreto*. St. Louis/London: B. Herder, 1954.

Klum, Edith. *Natur, Kunst und Liebe in der Philosophie Wladimir Solowijews: Eine Religionsgeschichtliche Untersuchung*. Munich: Otto Sagnet, 1965.

Kobell, Markus. *Die Frau, das Grosse Zichen des Heiligen Geistes*. Harburg: privately published, 1988.

Koyré, Alexandre. *La Philosophie de Jacob Boehme*. Paris: 1929, 1971; New York: B. Franklin, 1968.

La Farge, trans. *The Tao of the Tao Te Ching*. Albany: State University of New York Press, 1992.

Lang. B. *Frau Weisheit: Deutung Einer Biblishen Gestalt*. Dusseldorf: Patmos, 1975.

Langer, Mordecai Georg. *Die Erotik der Kabbala*. Prag: Josef Flesch, 1923.

Lao Tzu. *Tao Te Ching*. D. C. Lau, trans. New York: Penguin, 1972.

Lao Tzu. *Tao Te Ching*. Thomas Miles, trans. New York: Avery, 1992.

Leads, Lady Jane. *A Fountain of Gardens*. London, 1696–1701. Spiritual Diaries in four volumes.

———. *The Heavenly Cloud*. London, 1681.

———. *The Law of Paradise*. London, 1695.

———. *A Message to the Philadelphia Society*. London, 1696.

———. *A Revelation of the Everlasting Gospel Message*. London, 1697.

———. *The Revelation of Revelations*. London, 1683.

———. *The Tree of Faith*. London, 1696.

Lexikon des Geheimwissens. Freiburg, 1970.

Lexikon fur Theologie und Kirche. Freiburg: Herder, 1960.

Lilienfeld, Fairy von. "Sophia—Die Weisheit Gottes, Uber die Visionen des Wladimir Solojew als Gundlage Seine 'Sophiologia'" in *Una Sancta, Zeitschrift fur Okumenische Begegnung*. Freising: 1984.

Lost Books of the Bible. Reprint of William Hone's *The Apocryphal New Testament*, Jeremiah Jones and Archbishop Wake, trans. 1820. New York: Bell, 1979.

Lovelock, J. E. *Unsere Erde Wird Ueberleben: Gaia—Eine Optimistische Oekologie*. Munich: Piper, 1982.

Lovelock, J. E. *Gaia: A New Look at Life on Earth*. London: Oxford University Press, 1982.

Lurker. Manfred. *Woeterbuch Biblischer Bilder und Symbole*. Munich: Kosel, 1973.

Mack, Burton Lee. *Logos und Sophia, Untersuchungen zur Weisheitstheologie im Hellenistichen Judentum*. Goettingen: Vandenhoeck & Ruprecht, 1973.

Maier, Hans. *Der Mystische Spiritualismus von Valentin Weigel*. Gueterisloh: C. Bertelsman, 1926.

Das Meßbuch der heiligen Kirche. Frieburg: Herder, 1953.

Mead, G.R.S. *Pistis Sophia: A Gnostic Gospel*. Blauvelt, NY: Spiritual Science Library, 1984.

Miers, H. E. *Lexikon des Geheimwissens*. Freiburg: H. Bauer, 1970.

————. *Patrologiae Cursus Completus*. Greek Series. Paris, 1857–1866.

Migne. J. P., ed. *Patrologiae Cursus Completus*. Series latina and Series graeca. Paris: 1844–1855.

Missale Romanum, XIX edition. Regensburg: Verlag Pustet, 1936.

Montfort, Ludwig Marie Grignon von. *Das Goldene Buch der Vollkommenen Andacht zu Maria*. Fribourg: Kansius Verlag, 1918.

Moran, Pamela. *A Marian Prayer Book*. Ann Arbor: Servant Publications, 1991.

Muckermann, F. *Wladimir Solowjew*. Olten, 1945.

Mulack, Christa. *Die Weibichkeit Gottes, Matriarchale Voraussetzungen des Gottesbildes*. Stuttgart: Kreuz, 1983.

Müller, Ernst. *Der Zohar, das Heilige Buch der Kabbala*. Dusseldorf: Diederich, 1984.

Muller, Ludolf. *Das Religionsphilosophische System Vladimir Solovjevs*. Berlin: Evanglische Verlagsan statt, 1956.

Muller, Rudolf, trans. *Solowjews Leben in Briefen und Gedichten*. Munich: Rudolf Muller, 1977.

Munzer, Egbert. *Solovyev: Prophet of Russian Western Unity*. New York: Philosophical Library, 1956.

Neumann, Erich. *The Great Mother: An Analysis of the Archetype*. Ralph Manheim, trans. Bollingen Series vol. 47. Princeton: Princeton University Press, 1964.

New Oxford Annotated Bible with the Apocrypha. Revised standard version. New York and London: Oxford University Press, 1977.

Nicolas of Cusa. *De Venatione Sapientiae*. German/Latin, Paul Wilpert, trans. Hamburg: F. Meiner, 1954.

Ohm, Thomas. *Die Liebe zu Gott in den Nichtchristlichen Religionen*. Krailling vor Munchen: E. Wewel, 1950.

Origen. *On First Principles*. G. W. Butterworth, trans. No city: Peter Smith, n.d.

Origen. *The Philocalia of Origen*. New York: AMS Press, n.d.

Papus. *The Qabalah: Secret Tradition of the West*. New York: Samuel Weiser, 1977. Reprint of the 1892 French edition.

Pema-Dorje, M. *Tara: Weiblich-Goettliche Weisheitskraefte in Menschen*. Dusseldorf: Walter Verlag, 1991.

Pfleger, Karl. *Die Verwegenen Christozentriker*. Freiburg: Herder, 1964.

Philo. *Philosophical Works*. Cambridge: Harvard University Press, n.d.

————. *The Works of Philo*. C. D. Yonge, trans. Peabody, MA: Hendrickson, 1993.

Plard, Henri. *La Médiatrice Cosmique—La Vierge Sohiede Jacob Boehme: L'Universe à la Renaissance, Microcosme et Macrocosme.* Brussels: Presses Universitaires de Bruxelles, 1970.

Plato. *Timaeus and Critias.* Desmond Lee, trans. London: Penguin, 1986.

Pohlenz, M. *Stos und Stoiker: Selbstzeugnisse und Berichte.* Zurich: Artemis Verlag, 1950.

Pordage, John. *Theologia Mystica.* London, 1681.

Ramakrishna. *The Gospel of Sri Ramakrishna.* Swami Nikhilananda, trans. New York: Ramakrishna-Vivekananda Center, 1958.

Rauch, Albert and Paul Imfhof. *Tausend Jahre Marienverehrung in Russland und in Bayern.* Munich/Zurich: Schnell & Steiner, 1988. Commissioned by the Academy in Sagaorsk/Moscow and the Eastern Church Institute of Regensburg.

Realenenzyklopadie fur Protestantische Theologie und Kirche. Leipzig: Hinrichs, 1896–1913.

Regamey, Constantin. *Buddhistische Philosophie.* Bern: A. Francke, 1950.

Rousselle, E. *Lao-dse, Fuehrung und Kraft aus der Ewigkeit.* Wiesbaden: Inselverlag, 1952.

Ruhbach, Gerhard and Josef Sudbrack, *Christliche Mystik: Texte aus zwei Jahrtausenden.* Munich: C. H. Beck, 1989.

Ruppert, H. J. *Klassiker der Theologie.* Munich: H. Fries and G. Kretschmer, 1983.

Russel. Peter. *The Awakening Earth.* London: Routledge & Kegan Paul, 1982.

St. Augustine. *City of God.* Marcus Dods, trans. New York: Randon, 1994.

———. *Confessions.* E. B. Pusey, trans. New York: E. P. Dutton, 1975.

St. Irenaeus. *The Scandal of the Incarnation: Irenaeus against the Heresies.* Hans von Bolthasar, ed. John Saward, trans. San Francisco: Ignatius Press, 1990.

Scheeben, Matthias. *Dogmatik.* Freiberg: Herder, 1952.

Scheja, Georg. *The Isenheim Altarpiece.* Uppsala: Almquist & Wiksells, 1972.

Schipflinger, Father Thomas. "Die Sophia bei Jacob Boehme—Die Sophiologie Boehmes." A paper presented at the seminar "Anaturmystik und Naturwissenschaft in der Renaissance," at the University of Munich, Winter, 1985.

Schmidt, S. C. ed. *Pistis Sophia.* Berlin, 1959.

Scholem, Gershom. *The Book of Splendour (Zohar)* New York: Schoken, 1949.

———. *On the Kabbalah & Its Symbolism.* New York: Schoken, 1969.

———. *On the Mystical Shape of the Godhead: Basic Concepts in the Kabbalah.* New York: Schoken Books, 1991.

Schumann, H. W. *Buddhism: Outline of its Teachings and Schools*, Georg Feurstein, trans Wheaton, IL: Theosophical, 1994.

Schwartz, E. *Laudse Daodesching*. Munich: Deutsch Taschenbuch-Verlag, 1985.

Sefer Yetzirah [Book of Formation]. W. W. Westcott, trans. London: J. M. Watkins, 1911.

Seller, J. *Im Banne des Kreuzes, Leb ensbild der Anna Katherina Emmerich*. Wirzburg, 1940.

Serge, Hutin. "Les Disciples Anglais de Jacob Boehme," in *L"Universe à la Renaissance: Microcosme et macrosme*. Brussells: Presses Universitaires de Bruxelles, 1970.

Sheldrake, Rupert. *A New Science of Life: The Hypothesis of Causitive Formation*. Los Angeles: J. P. Tarcher, 1981.

Shivananda, Swami. *All About Hinduism*. Rishikesh: Shivanandanagar, 1961.

Smuts, J. C. *Holism & Evolution*. Westport, CT: Greenwood, 1973.

Soloviev, W. *Sophia*. Lausanne: L'Age d'Homme, 1978.

Soloviev's Collected Works. German language edition edited by Ludwig Mueller and Irmgard Wille. Munich: Erich Wewel Verlag, 1977.

Staehlin, Ernst. *Der Basler Seidenweber Johann Wirz*. Basel: Basler Stadtbuch, 1966.

———. *Der Nazarenergemeine*. Basler Stadtbuch, 1966.

Stecher, Reinhold. *Zeitschrift fur Katholische Theologie*, Innsbruck: Herder, 1953.

Steindl-Rast, David. *Gratefulness: The Heart of Prayer*. New York: Paulist Press, 1984.

Stemberger, Gunther. *2000 Jahre Christentum*. Salzburg: Andreas, 1983.

Strauss, Viktor von. *Lao-Tsae's, Taao-Tae-King*. Leipzig: Verlag der Asia Minor, 1924.

Stremooukhoff, D. *Vladimir Soloviev et Son Oeuvre Messianique*. Paris, 1935; Lausanne, 1975.

A. Strobl. "Die Weisheit Israels," in *Der Christ in Der Welt*. Aschaffenburg: Pattloch, 1967.

Suso, Heinrich (Seuse). *Little Book of Eternal Wisdom* and *Little Book of Truth*. James M. Clark, trans. New York: Harper & Row, 1953.

———. *Mystische Schriften*. Dusseldorf: 1966.

Tanquerey, A. *Grundriss der Aszetischen und Mystischen Theologie*. Paris: Tournai Société de Saint Jean l'Evangelist, Desclée and Cie, 1941.

Teilhard de Chardin, Pierre. *The Appearance of Man*. New York: Harper & Row, 1965.

————. *The Divine Milieu*. New York: Harper & Row, 1965.

————. *The Future of Man*. New York: Harper & Row, 1965.

————. *Human Energy*. New York: Harcourt, Brace, Javanovitch, 1947.

————. *Writings in the Time of War*. Rene Hague, trans. New York: Harper & Row, 1968.

Thune, Nils. *The Behmenists and Philadelphians*. Uppsala: Almquist & Wiksells, 1948.

Till, W. C. *Die Gnostischen Schriften des Papyrus Berolinensis*. Berlin: Akademie Verlag, 1975.

Truhlar. *Teilhard und Solowijew: Dichtung und Religiose Erfahrung*. Freiburg & Munich, 1966.

Vivekananda. *My Master*. New York: Baker & Taylor, 1901.

Voices of Orthodoxy. Monthly journal of the Russian Orthodox Esparchates for Middle Euorope. Berlin: 1986.

Wilhelm, Richard. *Laotse, Taoteking*. Stuttgart: Deutscher, Buecherbund, 1972.

Wirz, Johann Jacob. *Zeugnisse und Eroeffnun gen des Geistes Durch J. Jacob Wirz, Heilige Urkunden der Nazarenergemeine*. Barmen, 1863. Commissioned by W. Langewiesche.

Wodtke, Verena. *Auf den Spuren der Weisheit*. Freiburg: Herder, 1991.

Wolf, Albert Erich, trans. *The Isenheim Altarpiece*. New York: Harry N. Abrams, 1967.

Wolff, Otto. *Indiens Beitrag zum Neuen Menschenbild—Ramakrishna— Gandi—Sri Aurobindo*. Hamburg, 1957.

Zeitschrift fur Historische Theologie. Leipzig, 1865.

Zurnal Moscovskoj Patriarchii [Journal of the Moscow Patriarchs]. 1982.

Index

Thomas Schipflinger's interest in the Divine Sophia was first awakened when he came upon a Sophia icon while in Russia—this experience began a lifelong devotion to Sophia. He studied at the theological faculty in Innsbruck, was ordained as a Catholic priest by the Bishop of Innsbruck in 1947, served as a missionary in China where he studied Eastern religion and philosophy, and spent many years as a priest in Europe. Prior to moving from Austria to Germany, he was the village priest for 17 years in Eben Lake Achen, the location of the shrine of St. Notburga.